A Lancashire Gentleman

The Letters and Journals of
Richard Hodgkinson
1763–1847

To Carol and John
with love

A Lancashire Gentleman

The Letters and Journals of
Richard Hodgkinson
1763–1847

Edited

by

Florence and Kenneth Wood

ALAN SUTTON

First published in the United Kingdom in 1992 by
Alan Sutton Publishing Limited
Phoenix Mill · Far Thrupp · Stroud · Gloucestershire

First published in the United States of America in 1992 by
Alan Sutton Publishing Inc. · 83 Washington Street · Dover NH 03820

British Library Cataloguing in Publication Data

A catalogue record for this book is available from the British Library

ISBN 0-7509-0286-8

Library of Congress Cataloging in Publication Data applied for

Typeset in 10/11 Bembo.
Typesetting and origination by
Alan Sutton Publishing Limited.
Printed in Great Britain by
Butler & Tanner Ltd, Frome and London

Contents

Acknowledgements

That the 'Hodgkinson Papers' exist at all is due firstly to the meticulous filing by Richard of his own letters and journals, secondly to the same meticulous care of the papers shown by his solicitor grandson Robert Jackson and thirdly, to their gift to record offices in the early 1950s by H R Hodgkinson, FSA, a noted scholar of Roman antiquities.

We would like also to acknowledge the help given by Mr Richard Hodgkinson a descendent through the maternal line of Richard who supplied us with photographs of Richard Hodgkinson, his wife Jane and other members of the family.

The 'Hodgkinson Papers' are located in collections at the Lancashire Record Office, Preston (DDX.211) and the Manchester Central Library Archives (L15/2). We wish to express particularly our appreciation for the time, help and support given by the archivists in these two offices. Hodgkinson's letters and journals took us on an adventure the length and breadth of the country and we would like to acknowledge the help given by the following:

Archives/Record Offices: Cumbria; Cheshire; Dumfries; Hampshire; Hereford & Worcester; House of Lords; Leicestershire; Lincolnshire; Post Office; Chancery Lane, Kew; Shropshire; Wigan

Libraries: Birkenhead; Bolton; Crowland; Ewart Library, Dumfries; Edinburgh City Libraries; Glasgow City Libraries; Harris Library, Preston; Leicester Local Studies; Leigh; Portsmouth; Rochdale; Ross; Shrewsbury; Southport; Westminster City

Museums: Botanical Gardens, Southport; British Museum; Chepstow; Helen Thompson, Workington; Ironbridge Gorge; National Maritime, Greenwich; Science, Kensington; Powysland, Welshpool; Stewartry Museum, Kirkudbright; Theatre Museum (V&A)

Other: Dalmellington Conservation Trust; Chatsworth; Clerical & Medical Insurance Company; Lacon Childe School, Cleobury Mortimer; Lady Margaret College, Cambridge; Manchester Cathedral; Peterborough Cathedral; Society for the Promotion of Christian Knowledge; Westminster Abbey

National Trust: Lyme Hall, Cheshire; Woolsthrope Manor; Powis Castle; Wroughton History Group

The most interesting parts of our researches have undoubtedly come from the many people who have taken time and trouble to fill in our gaps of local knowledge, the peer of the realm including whose land we 'trespassed' on, the farmer who showed us the location of the Lyd Hole, and the young man who broke off his courting to lead us through the streets of Workington to the steps of the Helen Thompson Museum.

We are much indebted for background material in Chapter 8 to Peter Carpenter MB ChB BSc MrC Psych: *Thomas Arnold, A Provincial Psychiatrist in Georgian England* (Medical History, 1989) and *The Private Lunatic Asylums of Leicestershire* (Leicestershire Archaeological and Historical Society, vol. LXI, 1987).

Introduction

Arranging some of my papers, among others I thought these Letters between Mr Blundell and myself might be destroyed, but finding they embraced a Correspondence of more than twenty years and that they alluded to many local as well as Family Circumstances, I thought they might at some time afford some Amusement for a vacant hour to the person into whose hands they might happen to fall after my death.

Richard Hodgkinson, January 27, 1837

Richard Hodgkinson, driven by ambition to success and tragedy, aroused widely differing emotions among those whose paths he crossed. For many he was a model of virtue, industry and integrity, a man to be encouraged to take on great responsibilities, rub shoulders with his betters, mix with the lower ranks of the Established Church and join the fevered councils of extreme Protestant provincial power brokers. In his time of greatest crisis, Hodgkinson was, for others, the scheming agent of a large landowner who used his position to inflate his situation in society and to line his own pockets. Respected and admired by his wife and four children, his zealously contrived plans to further his younger son's prospects led to a tragedy from which his family never recovered.

Hodgkinson's rise from modest origins as a school usher to a position of power and influence as steward to the landed gentry might by now have been long forgotten, but for his extraordinary diligence in preserving correspondence and the journals he wrote during his long life. These parcels of documents reveal the everyday life of a resolute, self-made man during the dynamic years of the late eighteenth and early nineteenth centuries. Hodgkinson was a founder member of the bourgeoisie, but near enough to humble beginnings to have close relatives living in poverty. He became the acquaintance of peers and paupers, and from 1791 to 1836 ran the affairs of a Lancashire town for his employers with great financial skill, at considerable personal benefit to himself, and with a little charity towards the townsfolk.

To his journals and letters, Hodgkinson confided his sorrows and his successes, his vanities and his aspirations. He was also an articulate witness to events that changed the face of England more dramatically than at any time before or since. Hodgkinson was born into an England whose wealth was based on an agricultural economy; his younger years saw the rapid growth of mercantile wealth and on his travels he admired the elegant new facades of London, Bath, Bristol, Glasgow and Edinburgh, where the waxing riches of a great trading nation were flaunted by merchants and the *ancien régime* alike. The sweeping terraces and grand mansions of the wealthy contrasted increasingly with the growing urban squalor of the new industrial towns such as Manchester, barely a dozen miles from Hodgkinson's home in a still largely rural Lancashire.

Hodgkinson made three major visits to London and spent much time touring the city, admiring the sights and noting the conversations of people he met. He was present in the Houses of Parliament when James Fox lamented the slow progress of the Slave Trade Bill and when Bishops declared their opposition to Catholic emancipation. On his first visit in 1794, Hodgkinson successfully put a case against the canal mania then sweeping England and stopped the building of an important new waterway. He recorded his views on visits to London theatres, but could not be accused of falling in behind the musical fads of the day. He dismissed Mozart's *Marriage of Figaro* as 'an absurdity . . . a man . . . expresses himself in song which is ridiculous enough but to render it more ridiculous still the language is Italian which certainly not one in twenty of the whole Audience understands a single word of'.

Hodgkinson also journeyed widely throughout the English countryside and Scotland, and chronicled his opinions of the people he met, both high and low, good and iniquitous. He was an observant tourist of great curiosity and he commented tartly on local scandals and servants' gossip, noted corruption in the land, and had an eye for a pretty ankle. He respected men of manners, generally conducted his own public affairs with an uncommon degree of integrity and learned a great deal about human nature when he fell among lawyers.

Hodgkinson's prolific correspondence included an exchange of letters over many years which give an insight into the devious machinations of Blundell, an apoplectic and spendthrift priest of the Established Church, whose earthly ambitions for wealth and privilege may well have exceeded his aspirations for the hereafter. For more than forty years, Hodgkinson wrote intermittently to his nephew John, who had run away to sea and served on the lower deck in the Royal Navy in China, India and the

Atlantic during the French Wars. Other collections of letters are elegant and well-mannered exchanges with acquaintances and his employer, Lord Lilford.

Chowbent was Hodgkinson's adopted home. It was a large village within the township of Atherton, seat of the ancient Atherton family and one of six townships in the Parish of Leigh in Lancashire. Chowbent had for more than a hundred years held a reputation for vigorous nonconformity and was spiritually close to Bolton, the Geneva of the North. In Hodgkinson's early years, the village's fortunes were centred on cottage-based cotton spinning and handloom weaving, the manufacture of recently developed textile machinery, and nail- and spindle-making.

Hodgkinson arrived at Chowbent in 1784 to run the local grammar school, after two years teaching classics at a country school at Westbury in Shropshire. He impressed the local gentry not only with his ability in the classroom, but also with his skills as a land surveyor, his knowledge of farming and accountancy, and a mind quick to grasp difficult legal matters. His talents came to the fore when he was appointed steward to the Atherton family estates. Through business, marriage and friendship, Hodgkinson also became close to entrepreneurs who made large fortunes in the early industrialized cotton trade.

The fears and dramatic changes wrought by the French Wars (1793–1815), the economic depression which came in their wake and the resultant suffering of many of his fellow townsfolk clouded Hodgkinson's middle years. In his old age he viewed the unstoppable momentum of the Industrial Revolution with critical curiosity and a lack of understanding of the political and social turmoil it had created.

Hodgkinson's papers record also the pleasures and tragedies of family life in Georgian times. Blessed with four children, he derived great happiness and a degree of self-satisfaction in the early achievements of his two sons and two daughters. His daughters married well, and his elder son, David, followed in his father's footsteps in a less prominent way as a farmer and agent to a landowner. Of Hodgkinson's wife, Jane, little is known except that she was the daughter of a Scottish farmer and that she devoted her married life to raising children and running the family farm. She was twenty-seven, two years older than her husband, when they married, and it is likely that 'Mrs H' was saved from a spinster's life by Hodgkinson's matrimonial attentions.

The pride of Richard Hodgkinson's life was his younger son, Joseph, educated at Manchester Grammar School and Brasenose College, Oxford. Joseph fulfilled his father's own ambitions and entered Holy Orders and,

thanks to his father's influence, became vicar of Leigh. Joseph was also the
greatest tragedy of Richard's life. He died insane in a madhouse following
a remarkable clash of wills with his own parishioners at a chapel in Astley
township, an incident that led a virulent pamphleteer to accuse Richard of
Machiavellian plots to control the Established Church in the parish of
Leigh.

Hodgkinson allied himself to powerful Protestant reactionary forces,
and enhanced his prosperity and social status by acquiring friends and
business acquaintances among the lawyers, magistrates, cotton manufacturers, coal masters and leaders of the local militia in nearby Bolton.
Amid turbulent social unrest and demands for reform, this local gentry
controlled, sometimes ruthlessly, affairs in the fast-growing industrial
town and surrounding villages. Hodgkinson viewed the Radical politics
of the early nineteenth century as a danger to the established order and
showed little concept of them as a remedy to the ills of the time. By
1819, when demands for social justice for the working classes led to
Manchester's Peterloo Massacre, he, like others of the burgeoning middle
classes, was greatly apprehensive for his own safety as the threat of political violence and revolution pervaded the towns and villages of
Lancashire.

Hodgkinson's political opinions were reflected in the views he shared
with his social contemporaries. They had the common bond of being
vociferous and active high Tories, and in 1810 Hodgkinson joined his
friends in becoming a member of the Bolton Pitt Club. This group of
powerful men shared a deep affection for the late prime minister's distaste
for reform, Jacobins and Combinations. The intensity of their political
creed was reflected in the forty-three patriotic toasts proposed at the
Club's annual dinner in May 1820, which included 'Lord Sidmouth, the
Vigilant and Humane Guardian of our Altars and Our Homes,' and with
remarkable insensitivity, 'Mr Hulton and the Committee of Magistrates of
Manchester and the Neighbourhood who so successfully Exerted
Themselves in the Discharge of their Duty for the Preservation of the
County'. Hulton, a pillar of the Pitt Club, and his fellow magistrates were
responsible for giving the order that led to the Massacre of eleven people
at Peterloo the previous August. A further insight into Hodgkinson is
given by his social and business relationship with Col Ralph Fletcher,
scourge of the reformers and the dominant figure in the Pitt Club.
Fletcher, the head of a large family of colliery owners, leased the mining
rights for all the coal under the Atherton Estate and Hodgkinson enjoyed
the financial privileges of serving with Fletcher on the Bolton and St

Helens Turnpike Trust. Fletcher was also one of the magistrates responsible for Peterloo and was regarded by the Radicals 'as their deadly antagonist, the enemy of liberty, the violater of civil rights and the despoiler of domestic peace'. On the other hand, 'those who held that reform meant revolution, regarded Col Fletcher as one of the saviours of society'.[1] In one of his journals, Hodgkinson noted without comment that he bowed to pressure from Fletcher and grossly inflated his expenses for a visit to London on turnpike business.

Hodgkinson confirmed his conservatism when expressing his opposition to Catholic emancipation after listening to the debate on the Catholic Claims in the House of Commons in 1819. A decade later, Hulton, Fletcher and other members of the Pitt Club united under the banner of the ultra-Protestant Bolton Church and King Club. They vigorously denounced the Catholic Emancipation Act of 1829, and branded the Duke of Wellington and Sir Robert Peel as traitors for reluctantly supporting the concession painfully wrung from George IV.

Hodgkinson enjoyed a modest relationship with rich landowners such as the Lilfords, John Curwen of Cumbria and the Leghs of Cheshire. In 1844 he wrote: 'Few men in my Rank of Life have been more engaged in Public Life than I have been, or had more Acquaintance and Connections with Men of all Ranks and all Degrees from the Peer of the Realm to the Pauper in the Workhouse.' At the other extreme of the social scale, he observed the terrible effects of destitution wrought among the handloom weavers of his home town by the advance of industry, and gave occasional and modest financial help to members of his family living in reduced circumstances.

His observations of social conditions did not change his insular views from those of a loyal and prosperous Tory, but rather reinforced his opinions in support of maintaining the status quo. Apart from his work for the Turnpike Trust, Hodgkinson served his community and his own ambitions for public office as a Poor Law Commissioner under the hated 1834 Act. Apparently denied by his employer the opportunity to take up the office of a local magistrate, he satisfied his desire to dispense law and order by presiding at Atherton's court-leet for many years.

This span of history is recorded largely in Hodgkinson's own hand, and is a rare collection of documents which adds a personal dimension to an important era. Richard Hodgkinson did not record his family, social and business life with a view to being judged some two centuries later by the wider world; he wrote only of the moment in letters to friends, noted the events that shaped his life and kept personal journals of his extensive travels.

The Hodgkinson Papers fall into clearly defined sections and these are presented as separate chapters, each with an introduction that we hope will illuminate Richard Hodgkinson's vastly interesting journey through life.

Florence and Kenneth Wood, Bolton, November 1992.

Notes

1 W. Brimelow, *Political and Parliamentary History of Bolton* I (1882).

1

Atherton & Chowbent

When nineteen-year-old Richard Hodgkinson left Shropshire in 1784 to open his own school in Chowbent, he journeyed from the tranquillity of an ancient and little-changed rural England into an environment where the first stirrings of the Industrial Revolution were even then well evident. It was a change in time and space that during Hodgkinson's next sixty years would increasingly emphasize the division between town and country, industry and agriculture, landed gentry and the new and wealthy masters of industry. In just a few hours, Hodgkinson had travelled into the new England.

Chowbent was not ancient in the grand sense of having been settled by long-forgotten people and races, and when the enumerators of William of Normandy rode through the land compiling the Domesday Book, there was little to interest them in the wooded wetlands of south Lancashire. It was more than a century later in 1212, during the reign of King John, that a mention of Aderton can be found in public records.[1] The origin of the word is said to be from the Anglo-Saxon 'adre', a watercourse, and 'tun', a settlement.[2] Atherton, lying on the lower slopes of rising ground to the north, had several swiftly flowing streams tumbling southwards towards the River Mersey. These same streams in later centuries would supply power for the wheels that drove early industrial enterprises.

By 1322 the spelling appears generally to have been changed from Old English to the Norman, Atherton.[3] The Atherton family that tenanted Atherton manor was probably of Norman lineage and is variously listed in the thirteenth century as de Haderton (1246), de Adserton and de Asterton (1265), de Athirton (1293), de Atherton (1298) and, finally, in 1322, as Atherton.

The origin of Chowbent, the principal centre of population in the manor of Atherton, is rather more of a puzzle, with mentions being made

of Chollebynt and Shollebent in 1350,[4] Cholbent in 1496 and
Chowebent in about 1550.[5] It has been suggested that the name is derived
from the 'bent[6] land of Ceol', and there is a record of a de Cholle family
living in Lancashire as early as 1322.[7] What is certain is that by the six-
teenth century the family names of Chowle, Choll, Choull and Chowe
are regularly mentioned in the registers of Leigh parish. By the mid-nine-
teenth century, as the town expanded rapidly, the name Chowbent lost
favour and the title was removed from Ordnance Survey maps and
replaced by the township name of Atherton. Today the ancient name
lingers on in the collective memory and is preserved in the title of the
eighteenth century Chowbent Chapel, a Unitarian place of worship.

Religion and Strife

Religion, often of a strident nature, played an important role in the life of
the village. An early allegiance to the Protestant faith was fortified in
Chowbent during the reign of the Catholic Queen Mary (1553–1558),
when the townsfolk were greatly influenced by the preaching of the
Protestant martyr George Marsh (1515–1555) who roused towns and villages around his native Bolton.[8] Marsh, the son of a farmer, was arrested,
examined for heresy and burned at the stake at Chester in 1555. A depression in a pavingstone at Smithills Hall, Bolton, is traditionally said to be
where he stamped his foot in disgust at the injustice of his trial.

Almost a hundred years later, during the Civil War (1642–1649), the
Puritan villagers and John Atherton, the lord of the manor, identified
themselves with Parliamentarians in Bolton and Manchester in opposing
King Charles. In November 1642, 'as the people were going to church on
a sabbath morning', the troops of the Earl of Derby were reported to be
moving near to Chowbent on their way to Bolton. Soon after midday,
more than three thousand young men from the neighbourhood – farmers,
smiths, wheelwrights, weavers, and the nailmakers of Chowbent – had rallied to attack the Royalists and drive them back. 'The farmers, more bold
than cautious, outriding their foot, sustained a temporary loss on Lowton
Common, until the foot coming up killed or took prisoner about two
hundred Royalists, and plundered their village of Leigh.'[9] The euphoria of
victory was short-lived, and some weeks later, on Christmas Eve, Royalist
forces again moved on Chowbent 'and shattered the enemy', before taking Leigh by assault.[10] During the Civil War the town's first chapel was
built. A Presbyterian form of worship was followed and continued there,
but not at Leigh Parish Church, after the Restoration in 1660.

In 1715 the minister of the dissenting chapel, the Revd James Wood, supporter of the new Protestant king, George I, and the Hanoverian Succession, rallied his congregation and marched some three hundred of them to Preston. Here, Jacobites championing the pretensions to the throne of James Edward, the Stuart Old Pretender, were holding the town. On 13 November the loyal forces defeated the rebels, but Wood and his men, sent to guard a crossing over the River Ribble, apparently saw no action, and the preacher only drew his sword on one of his own men who showed signs of fear.[11] From then to the end of his long life, the minister was known as 'General' Wood. At this time the Atherton family was prominent in its support of the Stuarts. Following Wood's sally to the battlefield, he and his congregation were evicted from the town's only place of worship by 'Mad' Richard Atherton, head of the rebel cause in Lancashire.[12] Richard Atherton, dead at the age of twenty-six, turned the old place of worship into an Episcopal chapel with a living for a curate.[13] Wood, rewarded with a state gratuity or pension of £100 for his loyalty to the throne, gave some money to his followers and spent the rest on helping to build a new Chowbent Chapel (1732) which survives to this day.[14]

In the Jacobite Rebellion of 1745, the main body of the Scottish Army moved south through Wigan and Leigh. Tradition asserts that Bonnie Prince Charlie was the guest of the lord of the manor, Robert Gwillym, who had married 'Mad' Richard's daughter and whose family later took the name of Atherton. Another account says that the splendid new Atherton Hall, started by Richard Atherton and completed in 1742, was subjected by the Government to a perpetual levy as long as it should stand, in retaliation for the hospitality shown to the Young Pretender.[15]

Stirrings of Industry

In the centuries before Richard Hodgkinson arrived in Chowbent, the villagers had a reputation for nailmaking with local woodland providing a ready supply of charcoal for smelting raw iron brought from Yorkshire and Derbyshire.[16] By the mid-eighteenth century, Chowbent had begun the long and painful process of changing from a small community with thriving cottage industries to a Victorian industrial town of men, women and children toiling for long, arduous hours in coal mines, smithies and cotton factories.

The first major change in the fortunes of Chowbent came with the development of the 'flying shuttle', which by the 1760s had begun to increase the output of the handloom weavers. This created a shortage of yarn and in turn led to the invention of the 'spinning-jenny'. Arkwright's 'water frame' of the 1760s drove textile manufacture out of the home and into the factories, and brought violence to the towns and villages of Lancashire from machine wreckers whose families' livelihoods were threatened by the new technology. In 1779, Josiah Wedgwood, visiting one of his sons at a school in Bolton, wrote: 'In our way to this place, a little on this side of Chowbent, we met several hundred people in the road. I believe there might be about five hundred; and upon enquiring of one of them the occasion of their being together in so great a number, he told me they had been destroying some engines, and meant to serve them also through the country . . ... Many of the workmen having been turn'd off lately, owing to a want of demand for their goods at foreign markets, has furnish'd them with an excuse for these violent measures.' The mob at that time had 'only destroyed a small engine or two near Chowbent', but on the same day a larger group was repulsed attacking a mill at Chorley where two men were shot dead. Returning two days later, an eight-thousand-strong mob, reinforced by the Duke of Bridgwater's colliers and many others, returned and burned down the mill valued at £10,000.[17] Such was the violence that swept Lancashire in those early days of industrialization.

A contemporary description of a self-sufficient and prospering Chowbent, with a population in excess of 2,200 in 1787, comes from Dorning Rasbotham (1730–1791).[18] The antiquarian and country gentleman from nearby Farnworth wrote that the cotton trade had been established in the village at the beginning of the eighteenth century, but only for low-priced goods. 'It hath risen upon the ruins of the iron trade, which hath decreased in proportion to its rise', he noted. 'Every branch of the old fustian manufacture (in which, however, I do not wish to include muslins, the manufacture of which is trifling) is carried on here', wrote Rasbotham. 'Here is also a very considerable manufacture of nails; and several families have acquired fortunes by making spinning jennies and carding engines, which they send into Scotland, Ireland, and different parts of this Kingdom. Some of the mechanics do not keep less than 30 journeymen employed in this business.'

In 1787, according to Rasbotham, a common labourer in Chowbent earned 18d (8p) to 20d (9p) a day, and expected a cup of ale twice a day. 'A carpenter's wages are 2s [10p] a day, a bricksetter receives the same, but till this year was content with about 20d.' The hire of a man servant cost £10, but a woman could be employed for £5 to £6 per annum.

Coal had long been worked in the village, but the seams exploited were not very deep and 'did not lie more than 60 yards from the surface'. The pits 'are freed from water by pumps, and are not liable to damps.'[19] Coal sold for 2¹/₂d per hundred and was carted to the most distant parts of the township for 3¹/₂d. There was evidence of an early iron industry, said Rasbotham, judging from the cinders yet remaining, and there were quarries of building stone.

In the still largely rural landscape, farming was another important industry and land fetched from 50s (£2.50) to £6 an acre, with the rent of a small farm costing from £15 to £100 a year. To improve the land, dung was spread on the soil. Lime from Worsley and soapers' waste from Warrington also brought fertility to the heavy land. 'There is a good market at Chowbent for butcher's meat; for the consumption of which seven or eight cows, in the spring fourteen or fifteen, and from Midsummer to March about three calves, and throughout the year about a dozen sheep, were killed each week', recorded Rasbotham.

Outstanding houses in the township included Lodge Hall, an old brick building with a moat, owned by the Athertons; Atherton Hall, built by 'Mad' Richard Atherton; Owler Fold, the only freehold in the township not dependent on the Atherton family (and then, as now, generally called Alder Fold); and a ruinous old wooden house occupied by cottage tenants, which still had the remains of a moat and had been the seat of Sir Gilbert Ireland, Sheriff of Lancashire in 1649/50, whose ancestors held the office under Elizabeth I and James I.

'A Den of Lions'

Life was not merely a dreary round of toil for Chowbent villagers; they indulged a desire for spiritual, intellectual, sporting and social refreshment, activities in which the chapels of the Established Church and the Dissenters, together with local hostelries played major roles. John Wesley three times took his fiery brand of evangelical Christianity to the village. On 15 April 1774 he recorded: 'I preached at a preaching house just built at Chowbent, which was lately a den of lions; but they are all now quiet as lambs.' Two years later on 16 April 1776 he wrote: 'I preached about noon at Chowbent, once the roughest place in all the neighbourhood. But there is not the least trace of it remaining; such is the fruit of the genuine Gospel. As we were considering in the afternoon what we should do, the rain not suffering us to be abroad, one asked the vicar for the use of the church, to which he readily consented. I began reading prayers at

half-hour past five. The church was so crowded, pews, alleys, and galleries, as I believe it had not been these hundred years; and God bore witness to his Word.' His last visit was on 22 May 1781, when he preached
both in Chowbent and Bolton, 'where the people seemed to be on the
wing, just ready to take flight to heaven'.

Eminent preachers from the Unitarian faith were regular visitors to
Chowbent Chapel, and counted among the friends of the Dissenters was
Dr Joseph Priestly, clergyman and chemist who in 1774 discovered oxy-
gen.[20]

Apart from the ministrations of men of the cloth, there were also mind-
improving lectures in the village. John Kennedy, a young apprentice in
Atherton in 1784, shared the cost of a 5s subscription with Adam Murray,
a fellow apprentice, to a series of talks on mechanics and natural history
from a Mr Banks of Preston. Each boy went to alternate meetings.[21] On 5
January 1786, the choir of the Presbyterian chapel gave a concert in the
King's Head public house consisting entirely of selections from Handel's
oratorios.[22]

There are also records of merrymaking and carousing at the Bear's Paw
Inn, a meeting place for the Scottish engineers and apprentices who built
textile machinery in the village. Richard Hodgkinson described an occasion in his early days in the village when, after a day's coursing with local
landowners, a jovial evening's entertainment of food, drink and song was
held at the Bear's Paw. 'At length I was called upon for a Song. I well
knew I could not sing, but instead of making foolish Apologies I stood up
and in my best manner repeated some Poetry, which I had composed a
few weeks before. This took very well with the company', he wrote later.
Horse races were a feature of Chowbent life even into the nineteenth
century, and a poster has survived for a three-day meeting in July 1775,
which offered £50 prize money for a Gentlemen's Purse, Ladies' Purse
and a Give-and-Take. Other accounts of the sporting life mention bull
and bear baiting, and bands of strolling players who brought comedy and
melodrama to the parish.[23]

Decline of the Cottage Weavers

A plentiful supply of cotton yarn and growing demand brought prosperity
to the village's handloom weavers during the late eighteenth century.
There are records of these craftsmen walking the streets of nearby Bolton
sporting £5 notes in their top pockets to flaunt their wealth. But the
prosperous times were almost over and in 1812 the weavers of Chowbent,

reduced to poverty by Napoleon's trade blockade, sent a petition to Parliament, requesting an end to the French Wars: 'The petitioners have been for a long time labouring under a state of unexampled distress . . . whereas the price of the necessaries of life is nearly doubled since the commencement of hostilities with France, the wages of the petitioners are reduced by three fourths.'[24] The discontent and suffering of the weavers, their livelihoods increasingly threatened by the invention of Cartwright's power loom (1785), lingered on until their final demise in the 1840s. Hungry and penniless though they might have been, these descendants of independent stock were not afraid to compare their lot with those in government sinecures, 'the holders of which receive wages without performing any work'. They gave an instance, among others, of Charles George, Lord Arden, who held the offices of Register of the High Court of Admiralty and Register of the High Court of Appeals for Prizes, for which he received a net income of £12,554 a year. Since the French Wars began, vast sums had also been paid to refugees from Europe, gentry and priests, totalling £180,772 in 1801. Despite a grant of £24,226 to London silk weavers in 1801, the men of Chowbent deemed it more becoming them as Englishmen to call upon the House to cut taxes and improve trade by securing an honourable peace with Napoleon. This occurrence was still three years away, and in the event brought no relief to the weavers. The next three decades of fluctuating economic providence increased the misfortunes of the doomed handloom weavers and other working people, with riots and agitation for reform being met by the punitive legislation of the repressive ministry of Lord Liverpool. In 1816, Richard Hodgkinson wrote to his friend Blundell: 'The miserable and alarming state of this country I have not language to describe. The poor in many instances are literally starving, except when they receive a pitiful and temporary relief from the Contributions of their more fortunate neighbours . . . '. Three years later, a bare two months after the massacre of eleven people in a peaceful crowd at St Peter's Field in Manchester, and with fear and violence astir in the surrounding towns and villages, he again wrote to the rural cleric in Lincolnshire:

> The state of the country is very alarming. All sense of Morality and Religion seems totally to have forsaken the great Mass of the People. Led by appetite and passion alone they are ripe for all the horrors of a French Revolution, and Bloodshed, Rapine and Plunder form the general topic of familiar Conversation. And they are sedulous by arming themselves with offensive weapons of every denomination.

Monday is said to be the day fixed for a general Rising of the Mob. If it be so some Blood will necessarily be spilt and when civil war begins who shall say where it will end? By the blasphemous, seditious & rebellious cheap publications which daily issue from the Press, the People are persuaded that they do not occupy their proper position in society. That Property is unjustly withheld from them, that they have a right to a full share of all Property and to seize it by force is only to take their own.

That fateful Monday must have passed without incident, but in the following years the slow and terrible decline of the Chowbent poor continued.

In 1834, three more petitions demanding an inquiry into the distress of the handloom weavers in Bolton and surrounding towns were presented to Parliament. The first petition was signed by ten thousand people, the second by town officials and the third by forty-five manufacturers. Harrowing details were given to the House of Commons of the poverty and near-starvation facing the weavers and their families. John Maxwell MP said that new machinery, taxation and protectionism, together with an influx of Irish immigrants and a reduction in the armed forces, had led to an excessive supply of weavers, and that their sole subsistence (oatmeal) was subject to a duty of 100 per cent. 'If corn, woollen, cotton and silk be property, so is labour', he told an unsympathetic House. 'Let us protect British industry at its source, and aid human welfare, until we can, by reducing taxes, and placing debt more on the wealth and less on the poverty of the nation, arrive at free trade, without sacrificing the welfare of one class.' The petition was laid on the table and forgotten.

Three years before he died in 1847, Hodgkinson wrote to Mary Flavel, the daughter of his first headmaster:

We are in a wretched condition here. All the cotton, both in Spinning and Weaving is down in the factories and the poor Hand Loom Weaver cannot get half employed, and when he has work the Wages are so miserably low that with his utmost Industry he cannot earn a living. Silk weaving is now carried on to great extent in Leigh Parish, a weaver may earn from 7s to 12s a Week. A cotton Weaver not more than 5s to 8s. I am very sorry to say that the Masters are beginning to reduce the Wages of the Weavers in both Manufactures.

Slowly, painfully and inevitably the handloom weavers passed into history.

Rise of Coal

As the cottage industries declined, Chowbent's vast coal reserves began to be exploited to fuel the factories and forges of industry. In the eighteenth century the Atherton family sold leases to local entrepreneurs who worked the many seams that outcropped in the township. Early mines were shallow with access to the workings by ladders. Owing to the wretched pot-holed roads, most of the output was sold locally, unlike that of the mines at nearby Worsley and Wigan which moved large tonnages by canal and river transport. In 1776 a 99-year lease on the coal rights was given by Robert, Vernon Atherton to John Fletcher of Bolton, and Thomas Guest, a yeoman of Leigh, the heads of two families with which Richard Hodgkinson was to be intimately connected.

One of Richard Hodgkinson's tasks as steward to the Athertons, and later the Lilfords, was to supervise the operating of the collieries and ensure that his masters were paid their royalties. The miners of Chowbent were of no less an independent mind than the petitioning handloom weavers. In 1815, Col Ralph Fletcher, now running the mines, threatened the small workforce with prosecution and transportation for breach of colliery rules. Trade Union activity, not only by humble colliers but also by those in positions of authority, brought Richard Hodgkinson to state in a letter[25] in 1818: 'I fear the Combination at the colliery have such a consistency as to render it quite impossible for the Undertakers to have justice done to them without an entire new set of confidential servants. The depredations are so extensive that they could not be carried out without not only connivance, but the assistance of those whose business it is to see after our interests . . ..'

Hodgkinson never fully appreciated the potential wealth that lay beneath the surface of the Atherton estate, and in 1832 he told Lord Lilford that 'The Atherton [seams] dip one in five, that is for every five yards horizontal, the dip is one yard perpendicular. Your Lordship will perceive that thus at no very great distance the coal will lie so deep as not to pay for the raising.'[26] Hodgkinson, familiar with waterwheels being used to raise coal from the shallow mines, had failed to recognize the dramatic improvements in steam power that in other parts of Lancashire allowed water to be pumped and coal lifted from great depths. Lilford, anxious to reap some of the huge royalties being gained by fellow landowners, commissioned a report from engineer Robert Daglish. Daglish's optimistic summary resulted in Chowbent's first deep pit at Lovers Lane being opened, probably about the time of Hodgkinson's death. Coal output in the town peaked in 1913 at 669,566 tons and gradually declined until the last of the town's pits was worked out in 1966.

Atherton was for centuries famed for nailmaking, and the descendants of the nailers who made hardware for the great doors of Chester Cathedral in the thirteenth century are still today manufacturing nuts and bolts in the town. 'Often in the same smithy ploughs, scythes and pruning bills were manufactured alongside the nails,'[27] and these implements, sharpened for bloodshed, were used in the Chowbenters' martial adventures during the Civil War and Jacobite Rebellion. Hodgkinson also noted the fears of these domestic tools being used by the discontented populace at the time of the Peterloo Massacre. 'Riches are made in great number by all the smiths hereabouts', he wrote to the Revd James Blundell in 1819. 'We have one in custody now whose Deposition (with the details of a Pike made by him) we have sent to Lord Sidmouth.'

The early prosperity of the textile trade seduced some smiths from their nailers' rocks, and Aiken, in 1795,[28] said 'a great measure' had migrated a few miles to Ashton in the Willows, near St Helens.

The Athertons and Gwillyms

Henrietta Maria Atherton, who engaged Richard Hodgkinson as her steward in 1791, was not in fact an Atherton but a Gwillym. The last male in the direct line from Robert de Atherton (*c.* 1220) and a sheriff of Lancashire was 'Mad' Richard Atherton who died in 1726. His daughter, Elizabeth, married Robert Gwillym, scion of a landowning family from Langston, Herefordshire. Their son, Robert Vernon Gwillym, assumed the name and arms of Atherton, and in 1763 married Henrietta Maria Legh, the eldest daughter and co-heir of Peter Legh of Lyme, a large landowner in Cheshire. The Athertons, Leghs and Gwillyms were strong supporters of the Jacobite cause, though rarely if ever backing their convictions with force of arms.

Robert Vernon and his wife had both died by 1787 and their son and heir, Atherton Legh Atherton, died in France in 1789. This left Henrietta Maria, the eldest of three sisters, to inherit the family estates at Atherton, Bewsey (Warrington) and Herefordshire. The eligible Henrietta Maria was not without suitors, and on 31 August 1793, Richard Hill of Prescott sent a letter, enclosing a bribe, to a servant on the Atherton estate. The letter, which ended up in Hodgkinson's hands, owes more to comic opera than the disciplines of the schoolroom:

Barlow, The inclosed is with a respect to what you may do For me, as you must be well informed of my intenshens with your Sweet Lade Miss Atherton, *which I intend If It is possible to younight with har.* Therefore Axcept the inClosed Value and which I will be in Leigh in the midle of next wick, which I Could Wish to see you, If possible, when I am here. If you can forme some mode, so that I can see you, at the time, so be shure to lay a Plan, so that I can meet you in some plase or house so that I may have some considerable Convershon of Grate Momant, both for your one sake and myself, which I hope will be of greate pleashur to your sweet Mistess, Miss Atherton for Life.

Excuse hast and be shure keep this to your Self, I am with Regard to you and ever will be, Richd. Hill.

Undaunted, the love-lorn Hill later sent his picture in a Morocco case addressed directly to Miss Atherton and accompanied by the following verse:

> My Love, How sweet and how pleasant it is,
> For Lovers to you night with hands
> and hart in every gift of Love,
> My Love yours &c., &c.,
>
> Richard Hill

This note, too, fell into Hodgkinson's hands and Hill's love remained unrequited. In 1797, Henrietta Maria married Thomas Powys, who became the 2nd Lord Lilford on his father's death in 1800.[29]

In 1791, when Hodgkinson assumed his duties at Atherton Hall, the family was in serious debt, but by 1796 he had restored the family fortune by discovering a dormant Act of Parliament of 1747, which allowed Henrietta Maria to auction the Gwillym lands in Herefordshire and Monmouthshire for £18,364. In 1803 his financial skills were also used to value land in Wiltshire belonging to the Leghs and the subject of a family quarrel.

Henrietta Maria and her husband, 'an amiable and accomplished person, [who] wrote verses with ease and grace', had six sons and six daughters. Henrietta died in 1820 at the age of forty-nine after a long and painful illness. Her husband died in 1825 and they were both buried in the family church at Achurch, on the Lilford estate in Northamptonshire. Thomas Atherton Powys succeeded to the estate; the second son, Horace, was rector of Warrington before becoming Bishop of Sodor and Man; and the

youngest son, Henry Littleton Powys, served in the Army before adopting
the name Keck in order to inherit his uncle's estate.[30]

The present Baron Lilford, George Vernon Powys, is the seventh of the
line.

Notes

 1 *Lancashire Inquests and Feudal Aids*, W. Farrer (ed.) (Record Society) xlviii.liv.
 2 *Victorian History of of the County of Lancashire*,
 3 Eilert Ekwall, *Place-names of Lancashire*, (Chetham Society, 1922).
 4 *Victoria History of the County of Lancashire* (VHL, iii.437).
 5 *Ducatus Lancastrice calendarium inquisitionum post mortem*, Edw. 1, Ch.I., Record
    Commission, 1823).
 6 Bent grass is a stiff grass or sedge.
 7 *Place Names of Lancashire*.
 8 T.H. Hope, *Chowbent*, (1893).
 9 Thomas Jesland of Atherton, 'True and Full Relation of the Troubles in
    Lancashire', in George Ormerod, *Civil War Tracts of Lancashire* (Chetham
    Society, 1844).
10 'The account of Colonel John Rosworm', *Civil War Tracts of Lancashire*. In
    May 1644, Royalist forces under Prince Rupert overwhelmed the defences at
    Bolton and put the town to the sword. In October 1651 the Earl of Derby
    was taken to the town and beheaded.
11 Dorning Rasbotham, 'Notes on Chowbent' (1787), in *Bolton and District
    Historical Gleanings* (B.T. Barton, 1882).
12 This is from a lecture given by Mr H. Fishwick in Atherton, November
    1942, and reported in the *Leigh, Tyldesley and Atherton Journal*.
13 John Lunn, *Atherton, a Manorial, Social and Industrial History* (1971).
14 Rasbotham, 'Notes on Chowbent'.
15 *Atherton Parish Magazine*, bicentenary edition (1923) A.M. Fletcher; William
    Beaumond, *Annals of Warrington and Bewsey* (1873).
16 Lunn, *Atherton*.
17 Eliza Meteyard, *A Group of Englishmen* (1871).
18 Rasbotham, 'Notes on Chowbent'.
19 Firedamp is an explosive gas and Blackdamp a suffocating gas.
20 T.H. Hope, *Notes on the Athertons of Atherton* (Leigh Local History library).
21 Alexander Trotter, *East Galloway Sketches* (1901).
22 T.H. Hope, *Notes on the Athertons*.
23 Rose, *Leigh in the 18th Century*.
24 Petition of the weavers of Chowbent respecting peace (1812), Parliamentary
    debates 1st s., v23, cols 180–181.
25 Only one page of this letter, probably written to Colonel Fletcher, exists and

is in the National Coal Board records in the Lancashire Record Office.

26   Kenneth Wood, *The Coal Pits of Chowbent* (1984).
27   Lunn, *Atherton*.
28   Description of the Country 30 miles around Manchester (1795).
29   We are indebted to the work of J. Croston FSA (1891) who compiled a
      family tree of the Athertons of Atherton and Bewsey from deeds, charters
      heralds' visitations, inquisitions and Parish registers, etc.
30   William Beaumond, *Annals of Warrington and Bewsey* (1873).

2

The Hodgkinson Family & Richard's Early Years

Richard Hodgkinson's early years are well chronicled, due in part to a vanity in later life when he investigated the origins of his ancestors, entertained hopes of a family crest and tried to establish links with important families in Preston and Liverpool. His hopes of social eminence were not realized and he had to accept that his forebears were descended from farming stock at Horwich near Bolton.

Hodgkinson's father Joseph was an itinerant schoolteacher until he became headmaster of Leigh Grammar School and settled in the town in 1771. Joseph and his wife Constantia had two sons, Joseph and Richard, and two daughters, Mary and Betty. Of these children, Richard was the only one with the ability, determination and good fortune to succeed. His brother was a dyer before his death in 1791, and the sisters did not marry well. Both women lived in poverty for most of their lives with Richard, on occasion paying their rent to keep a roof over their heads. It is a sad footnote to Hodgkinson's search for social status that in the compilation of a family tree, he made no mention of Mary and Betty, or even John and Mary, the children of his brother Joseph. After they were orphaned, Hodgkinson kept in occasional contact with his niece, a factory worker, and his nephew, a sailor in King George's navy who after the French Wars settled in Gosport.

When Joseph Hodgkinson moved with his family to Leigh, Richard was already showing promise as a scholar, and in 1775 he was sent to study at Standish Grammar School near Wigan. Hodgkinson treasured all his life a collection of fifteen speeches that were delivered in Latin by pupils at the school, one of which is in his impeccable handwriting and initialled R.H. This classical education had great influence on the young pupil and is reflected in the elegant style and construction of the letters and journals written later in life. Long after he retired, and with family and friends concerned about how he filled his empty hours, Richard Hodgkinson wrote: 'I have many Resources and I have a pretty extensive Library and am fond of Reading, which I can vary now and then by whiling away an hour or two in my almost forgotten Latin and Greek.'

There was a firm bond between Richard and his father, Joseph. They showed strong similarities in their intellectual pursuits, a mutual level-headedness, self-confidence and an inclination to write jocular doggerel to their friends. Joseph wrote to his friend, the Vicar of Leigh, in 1781:

> According to Order I've furnished your Stand
> With Pens, Ink and Wafer and likewise with Sand,
> The Price, two pence halfpenny, which if you pay,
> I am, Sir, your obliged, and wish you good day.

Richard wrote to a friend in Shropshire in 1794:

> At Westbury arrived, our old friends we did greet
> Our greetings were short but good Ale made 'em sweet
> From Westbury, good Lord, how we scampered away
> Thro' thick & thro' thin & thro' mere dirt & clay
> I thrashing on Robin, as if with a Flail
> To keep within sight of your grey mare's white Tail.
> But in vain, for you c^d not have gone faster scarce
> If the Dee'l or the French had been close at your a—e.

Hodgkinson's family history was written in two parts. The first comprises notes written in 1839 about his ancestors. The second is a series of letters to a grandson about his rise in life from his years as a teacher in Shropshire to his three vain attempts to enter the church, and the opportunity he was persuaded to accept which led to a dramatic and profitable change in his circumstances.

After the death of Richard Hodgkinson in 1847, the family name soon died out. David Hodgkinson, his elder son who died in 1854, had three daughters. Joseph Hodgkinson, the younger son, died without issue. Richard Hodgkinson's daughters inspired in their children the middle class ambitions of their grandfather. Robert Jackson became a partner in a successful firm of solicitors in Rochdale; William Hodgkinson Guest was also a lawyer and Registrar to the High Court for the Manchester District;

Ellis Southern Guest became a doctor and practised in Manchester; and their brother, Robert Guest, stayed in Leigh and ran the family brewery.

The Hodgkinson Pedigree
by Richard Hodgkinson

My Father's Ancestors from a very remote period lived in Horwich not far from the foot of Rivington Hill. The Pilkingtons, whose descendants for two or three generations, have been and still are leading attorneys in Preston, spring from the same source and the same stock. One of the Pilkingtons was a candidate for the coronership of this County at the late Election, when Mr Rutter was appointed. The Hodgkinsons of Horwich were in general Farmers but it is very probable that they added sevl other callings to their farming, such as keeping a shop &c., for I find that one of these had, previous to the year 1696, lent money on mortgage on the Four Lane Ends Estates.

My Father was born at Four Lane Ends, about 1726, and he had two sisters born before him. My Grandfather married a young woman of the name of Unsworth, whose father occupied the very large Farm of Lostock Hall & the extensive Park called Lostock Park attached to it.

Mr Unsworth was holding Lostock Farm at the time of the Rebellion in 1715. The owner of Lostock was a Catholic, and much damage was done by marauders coming plundering and carrying away whatever they could lay their hands on. One day a large mob came & began to plunder as usual; she who was afterwards my grandmother and who I have been informed was at that time a fine stout spirited country Lass, observed two of their neighbours in close conversation. One of their names was Pilkington. She contrived to get near enough to hear what they said, and overheard Pilkington say to his companion 'There are two fine fat pigs in the cote which I intend thee and me to drive off by and by'. She soon made up her mind that they should not, and went boldly to the cote, knowing the pigs would soon rush into the woods which were at that time very extensive in the park and where they often fed and feasted on the acorns there. She no sooner opened the door than the pigs rushed out, and were instantly hid and safe in the wood.

My father was the eldest Son and was brought up to the farming business. He had not much school eduction; I have been told his father was averse to it, which seemed strange to me as I have always understood he was a well disposed & intelligent man. But my father was enthusiastically fond of learning, and lost no opportunity of improving himself. By perseverance and unremitting application he became an excellent English Grammarian, he was well read in History and Geography, wrote a good hand, was a good accountant, his temper was mild, his head was clear, his health sound. With these qualifications he quitted his father's house on the day of his wedding 'with all the world before him, where to choose': one may almost suppose with a determination to get out of the sight of his new mother, and out of the hearing of his father's folly.

He never attempted to stop anywhere to settle till he came to Bolton le Sands behind Lancaster. He soon got an engagement here for two months to attend a Grammar School to teach writing and accounts. It was customary at this time for writing masters to attend periodically at Grammar Schools and this custom was continued as late as when I was at Standish School myself.

A little incident occurred the first evening he got to Bolton [le Sands] which introduced him to several gentlemen of the town, some of whom were pleasant companions and some were friends at all his future visits to that place. Having secured his lodging and refreshed himself he went upon the Bowling Green where a party were at play. After watching them for some time their game was ended and they were preparing to leave: he threw a jack across the green and taking up a bowl said 'I will lay this bowl within six inches of that jack.' He did so, and taking up another bowl said 'With this I will strike the last played bowl off the green.' He did so. The Company was surprised and they politely asked him to go in and take a glass with them observing him to be a stranger and well dressed and of good address. I have often heard my father say it was always a sine qua non with him when young to dress well however low his finances.

Not having any settled Plan of his life at present . . . he got to Standish where was one of the Schools he attended and where he met with my mother. She was living with her mother, the widow of Richard Skillin. My grandmother was left in comfortable circumstances and settled herself respectably in a house of her own with her little daughter, as I have been led to suppose then about seven years old. In this situation my father found them many years after.

At what time my father began to pay attentions to my mother or how long those attentions continued before the marriage took place I do not know but she must have then been very young for he was at least eight years older than her. From the nearest calculation I can make it appear that she was born in 1733 or 1734. My grandmother never married a second time. A few years at the latter end of her life she lived in my father's

house and died there. I think when he lived at Radcliffe Bridge, but that
was before I was born.

After leaving Radcliffe Bridge my Father lived at Row Green, near
Worsley, and subsequently at High Stile near Bolton from whence he
removed to Leigh in 1771. He died 22nd Jany 1791.

My Early Life and how my
Fortunes were Transformed

[These letters were written to Robert Jackson, who in 1839 was beginning a legal career. They have been edited and matters not affecting
Hodgkinson's own life have been omitted.]

Green Bank,   24th February, 1839
I was much younger than you when I left my Father's house in Jany. 1782
to go into Shropshire among entire Strangers. I was fortunate in falling
into good hands, and Mr Flavel my Employer, treated me with a parental
kindness during the two years I resided with him.[1] As a proof that his
kindness was not a transitory feeling or founded on very limited
Principles, tho' he lived many Years after I left him and to be near ninety
years of age, he continued his Correspondence with me, young as I was,
to the end of his days, as will appear by many of his Letters now in my
possession. I consider these two years as a very valuable, if not the most
valuable, part of my Life, and very probably in them was laid the foundation of my future Character and success in Life. From that time up to the
present, my success in Life has been uniformly progressive without check
or retrograde movements. I met with frequent disappointments for a few
Years at my first setting out but from strength of Nerve and steady perseverance I surmounted them all and always with increased Means and
increased Reputation. The only regret I felt was at my very excellent
Father's disappointment at my not getting ordained to the Church. Why
he was so anxious on this Account I never could learn except he had
some Expectation that Mr Atherton would be disposed to do something
for me in that way. Mr Atherton had more than once in my hearing
promised my Father that he would provide for me.[2]

In some idle hour I may perhaps take up this Subject where I now
leave off and give you an Account of my entering in Life to get my own
Living.   Rd. Hodgkinson

15th April, 1839

In continuation of my Letter of 24th Feby. last. I made several attempts to get into the Church, some of which held out prospects of Success but before arrangements could be completed the Cup was dashed from my lips, and, I was left to experience repeated disappointment. The first attempt was one of the successes of which my Father felt rather sanguine. After I had been settled some time at Chowbent, the Rectory of Radcliffe fell to the Earl of Wilton, to which it was well known he would present Mr Foxley. Mr Foxley must reside at Radcliffe and wd necessarily want a Curate at Chowbent. I made early application to which Mr Foxley lent a willing Ear: and promised my Father to lay the application before Mr Rawstorne, the Uncle and Guardian of Miss Atherton, who was then only 16 years of age, and if it was approved by him he would gladly give me a Title. In about a Fortnight Mr Foxley called upon my Father to say that he had laid the application before Mr. Rawstorne, who after taking a few days to consider of it, had written to him to say that upon due Consideration; himself and Mr Rawstorne had come to the Conclusion that it would not be sufficiently respectful to the Inhabitants of Atherton to appoint the son of a Tenant to be the Minister at Chowbent Chapel. Thus ended Bubble the first. This Apology was singular enough but something more singular happened afterwards for in seven Years after my rejection on account of want of Courtesy to the Inhabitants of Atherton by appointing me to the Chapel, this same Mr Rawstorne actually forced me into the Agency at Atherton, placing all Miss Atherton's new and large Establishment on her coming of Age; and the Superintendence of all her Property, both in Land and Money under my sole management and control without asking for a single Testimonial of Character or a single Pound of Security.

Very shortly after the above Disappointment, the Rev Mr Barlow, Vicar of Leigh, with whom my Father and myself had long been in habits of Intimacy, was from Age and declining Health, desirous of engaging a Curate. He mentioned the Subject to my Father and to me and said he would gladly give me a Title and engage me for his Curate. I very willingly accepted the offer, and at my own request I was sent to be examined by Mr Crewdson, Head Master of the Wigan Grammar School, who in a Letter to Mr Barlow reported very favourably of my Classical and other Qualifications. Proceedings were immediately taken for procuring the necessary Papers and Testimonials to be laid before the Bishop previous to the next Ordination which was to take place in about three Months. Amidst all this Preparation poor Mr Barlow was one Morning found dead in Bed. Thus ended Bubble the second.

The next Bubble I burst myself. The Rev Mr Whitehead, Incumbent
of Westhoughton Chapel, with whom my Father had in early life been on
very Friendly Terms, became from declining Years and increasing
Infirmities, desirous of engaging a Curate. He came to my Father and
informed him that the School at Westhoughton was vacant and that it was
at my Service if I would accept of it, and as a further Inducement for me
to do so, he added that if I was disposed to take Holy Orders he would
give me a Title and make me his Curate forthwith. This I declined on
two Accounts. I did not like to settle in Westhoughton having no
favourable Opinion of it and my School being new established and very
flourishing I did think I should be making an ungrateful return to my
Friends at Chowbent and the Neighbourhood for the handsome
Treatment and the very liberal Encouragement I had received at their
hands.

After this the School was advertized and my Father suggested to me
that I ought, as an Act of Courtesy, to go on the day of the Election and
personally thank the Trustees for their very handsome Offer. I did so but
on my appearing there it was soon whispered round that I was there as a
Candidate and two persons withdrew Names from the List of Candidates
on that Account. On being made acquainted with this I desired it might
be made known that I had no intention whatever of offering myself a
Candidate. The Trustees then requested me to examine the Candidates
(four in number) which I did and Mr Ackers, whose Name I think you
must have heard as keeping a very respectable School afterwards near
Westleigh Mill, was the successful Candidate. The Trustees had a public
Dinner to which I was invited and was entertained all night and the following day (Sunday) at the House of Mr George Green, the oldest and
most respectable of the Party. Thus ended Bubble the third. A short
sequel may follow this before long in a subsequent letter. Yours very
affectionately,   Rd. Hodgkinson.

Green Bank   24th April, 1839
In continuation of my Letter of the 15th inst My School was now flourishing in a manner quite unparalleled in this Neighbourhood. I had no
Competition in Writing and Accts. nor in the application of Mensuration
to all useful and practical purposes and no one even pretended to teach
Classics. In this department I had boys who were thoroughly acquainted
with the Latin and Greek Grammars who could take half a page in
Caesar's Commentaries 30 or 40 Lines in Ovid or Virgil and 6 or 8 Verses
in the Greek Testament at a Lesson. Mr Johnson of Tildesley early took

me by the hand and engaged me in measuring and setting out all his plots of building Land and making his Leases. Mr Froggatt was also very kind to me.[3] He was at this time engaged in improving his Residence at Astley, in laying out his Gardens, Plantations and Pleasure Grounds. Of these I could give him plans finished in a Stile by no means common here, which pleased him much, and seldom a Month passed in which I did not spend one whole Saturday at least, and dine with him at Dam-house.

I enjoyed good Health and was indefatigable in my attention to Business, which was a pleasure to me. I now called all my various Talents and Requirements in requisition, letting no opportunity slip of turning them to profitable Act. I measured and mapped land, I measured Hay Stacks and Marl Pits, Roads, new, Buildings &c.,&c. I made Contracts, Leases, Bonds Wills &c., &c. I was very often engaged in References by all which Means I made Money which I did not let lie idle. I soon deposited some in Jones's Bank, but the Sum was so small, and it is now so long since (more than half a Century) that I hardly recollect how I could get into the Bank; but I have never been without a Deposit there since. It was suffered to accumulate by its own Interest, increased by such Sums as I from time to time could spare, never in any one instance drawing Money out unless to make a Purchase, or lend upon Terms to increase the Interest. This early habit of Economy, and this early Deposit, laid the Foundation of all the Property[4] I now possess, and it has been the source of much Confidence, Comfort and Support through my long Life and I have little doubt but my early habits of active Industry and Sobriety may have mainly contributed to establish my Health.

About the time I am now alluding to, Mr Rawstorne, Uncle and Guardian to Miss Atherton, then residing in Preston, came over to Chowbent and gave a Coursing day and a Dinner to the Tenants at the Bears Paw.[5] I was invited. The late Mr Hulton was there, also Mr Hilton of Pennington, Mr Taylor, Mr Froggatt, Mr Hearsley &c., &c. The Evening was spent jovially and many Songs were sung. At length I was called upon for a Song. I well knew I could not sing, but instead of making foolish Apologies I stood up and in my best manner repeated some Poetry, which I had composed a few weeks before. This took very well with the Company, and proved to be a very acceptable Substitute for a Song.

I thought no more of this till more than seven Years had elapsed and I had been some Months in the Stewardship, when walking out with Mr Rawstorne one day he alluded to it, calling it to my recollection, adding he was so struck with the Circumstance at the time, that he had at once conceived that I was a business-like young man and then being Guardian to Mr Hesketh of Rossean and wanting a Steward there sometime after that, he had it seriously in contemplation to offer me the Situation but finding by enquiries that I was doing so well for myself, was so useful to the Public and so much respected at Chowbent, that he was fearful of wishing the responsibility of disturbing me; and concluded with saying he had constantly had an eye upon me ever since.

We may hence reflect, that serious and beneficial Results may sometimes ensue from very trifling Causes. In the latter end of 1786 Mr Atherton, Miss Atherton's Brother, was about to set out on his Travels. In the first Week in November, the day before he set out, he dined with his Tenants at the Court Day at the King's Head in Chowbent.[6] I was at the Dinner. In the course of the Evening he sent for me to come to him at the upper end of the Table. He said he understood I was residing in Chowbent, a Situation he feared could neither be comfortable nor profitable. But if I would continue there till he returned, he hoped would be in about two Years, he would provide me a Situation which should afford me both Comfort and Profit. Here I was doomed to suffer another disappointment. The young man before he arrived in England on his return direction died on the 29th of March, 1789. He would have come to Age on the 4th of June following. Thus the promise both of Father and Son, which I am confident were made with great sincerity, were rendered abortive to me. This last Catastrophe left me quite isolated from the Atherton Family. But mark the singularity of what followed.

In three short Years after the death of young Atherton, without premeditation on either side, without the most remote reference to my former Connection with the Family, without the slightest Expectation on my part, or preparation to qualify me for it, I was made sole Agent, put into the Management of the whole Property, a Trust which I executed for 45 Years to the entire Satisfaction of the successive Owners, their Families and Friends. I remain your affectionate Grandfather,   Rd. Hodgkinson.

Green Bank   28th April, 1839

I had been married about four Months (being something more than 25 years old) when young Atherton died; his death annulled the last promise I had from the Family, and though I never relied upon it or upon anything else but my own Exertions, yet knowing that it was made in sincerity, I could not help feeling that I had lost something which might ultimately have brought me some advantage.

My School continued to flourish, my Industry did not relax, my

Income and consequently my annual Savings increased, so that I had a very handsome Sum to take with me when I left Chowbent in 1791. Very early in January 1791, immediately on opening the School after Christmas, having been there just 20 years, my Father died after a very few days sickness. The Trustees of Leigh School made me a unanimous Offer of it which I accepted; and opened it on the 24th of March which was just seven Years from my opening the School at Chowbent, viz 24th March 1784. I had been but very few Months, when, to my great Astonishment, I was applied to undertake the Stewardship at Atherton, a situation I never had an eye to, or a thought of in all my Life.

From his great attachment to, and confidence in, the Atherton Family, my poor Father would have been delighted at the offer, but it alarmed me. I was doing well and was satisfied with it. My reputation was established and I was daily increasing, Boarders were applying faster than I could find Room for them and I anxiously wished to be let alone. I considered that I should be thrown into more public Life and into a Society very different from what I had heretofore mixed in. My Life had so far been a secluded one compared with that now opening to me. I could not tell what effect this great change might make. My quiet and sober habits might be given up and others of a far more dangerous tendency adopted. I troubled for my Family and indeed for my own Reputation, in short, even without hesitations, I determined not to accept the Offer and I refused it three successive times. The last time was in the Gardens at Atherton after a walk of an hour with Mr Rawstorne who said when we parted, alluding to irksomeness of teaching School and the ill-paid Labours which he had urged before, 'Well, well, Mr Hodgkinson, I see you are determined and I believe it may be possible for a Scotchman to make his Pack sit easy on his back.' I went home perfectly satisfied with my determination and convinced, as I thought, that I should here no more of the Business. But by eleven o'clock the next Forenoon I was more warmly beset than ever; and I found that escape was impracticable without some sort of Compromise. I proposed that if the Trustees would let me find a person into the School for 12 months, and at the end of that time to resume it again if the Situation at Atherton did not suit me, I would make a Trial. This proposal was agreed to, Mr Blundell[7] came to the School and on the 24th of June, 1792, I entered upon my new Situation which I filled (how short sighted we Mortals are) for 45 successive Years. I have been rather prolific in this account but it formed too important an Era in my Life to be passed over slightly.

On the 24th of June, 1792, I entered upon the Business. The Steward who preceded me had only been one year in the Situation and had left Atherton before I went and gone to an Agency near Tarporley under Mr Arden, Brother to Lord Alvanley. There was no one at Atherton to give me any Instructions or Directions, or to explain to me the Books or the Plans or to go with me to show me the Property or introduce me to the Tenants. I had all this to do solus cum solo. There was one thing in my Favour. Miss Atherton was a year under Age and Mr Rawstorne, living at Atherton with his Family, was the Housekeeper, so that I had nothing to do with the domestic Establishment. This gave me an opportunity of devoting more time to the outdoor Business and this was considerably reduced by the general Knowledge I had of the Property in and about Atherton and of the Tenants there, but I had to wade in the dark through Bewsey &c.[8] where I neither knew the Property or the Occupiers. I took every opportunity of investigating this through the Summer so that by the latter end of November I was enabled to get through the first Court and Rent days with but little Inconvenience.

I was now entered upon a Career of Business which for the next four years called for the greatest Activity with the heaviest responsibility of any period during my long Service. On looking into the Accounts I found the Family was deeply encumbered with Debt. The Income was small, the Property being mostly in Life Lease and no Money could be raised by Fines, as no Leases could be granted during Miss Atherton's minority. On looking into the Papers and Writings I found an Act of Parliament which old Mr Gwillym had got about 1745 or 1746 for the Sale of all his Property in Herefordshire.[9] Under this Act he had immediately sold as much as relieved him from his then Necessities, and the Act was laid by and had so laid by for near forty years. As soon as I found this I saw my way to pay off the Incumbrances at Atherton if Mr Rawstorne and Miss Atherton would permit me. I took a favourable opportunity of mentioning it to Mr Rawstorne and he to Miss Atherton. In a few days he informed me that they both were very much pleased with the Plan and gave me full Authority to take such proceedings as I thought necessary to carry it out.[10] The Rents of the Property to be sold were something more than £500 a year. This was to be remitted to me by an old Steward there. I had some correspondence with him on my entering on the Agency and I now took the liberty of requesting him to send me a full Account of each Farm, the Tenant's Name and Rent, which he did. This was all the Foundation I had to work on in this arduous Undertaking, which took more than two years before it and all its Contingencies were quite ended. I remain very affectionately,   Rd. Hodgkinson.

Green Bank   2nd May, 1839
I now began seriously to make preparation for the Herefordshire Sales to
be as early as possible. On the 26th February, 1794, I was sent to London
to meet Mr Rawstorne and Mr Taylor to oppose the Lancaster Canal
Company and prevent them from bringing their Canal within the Gates at
Leigh and carrying it across the Avenue and in front of Plat Fold.[11]

It was in this [House of Commons] Committee where I first met the
old Lord Lilford (then Mr Powys). He was not known to any of our
party. He entered warmly into the Case, attended every day and at last
moved several Orders in Parliament to prevent, as he said, such wanton
Incroachments upon private Property. Without him we should have cut
but a poor figure in Committee.

We succeeded in the opposition, but as the Country is now in Cutting
up by Railways and Atherton has ceased to be a Family Residence, the
Owners might as well as had a Canal through their Coal Mines which
would have opened a Market for them to the North as well as to
Manchester and the South.

This was a pretty sharp breaking in for a young man just taken out of a
Country Day School and but little acquainted with public Business. I was
21 nights at the London Coffee House. On the 19th of March I left
London but instead of coming home I went direct into Herefordshire. A
Mr Young, Head Agent to the Archbishop of Canterbury, recommended
by Mr Taylor, went with me to assist in valuing. We went over all the
Property along with Mr Green, the old Agent there. Mr Young took
what he called a Valuation, and went away after the second day. His
Valuation was taken in such a hasty way, and the Amount was so unsatis-
factory, both to Mr Green and Myself, that I stayed a few days longer and
revalued the whole over again adding upwards of £2000 to his Valuation.
Rd. Hodgkinson.

Green Bank   9th May, 1839
My Letter to you brought me up to the Sale of the Estates in
Herefordshire. The Plan of the Sale, the Arrangement for it and the conducting of it was all my own. I completed my great End and Aim in this
arduous undertaking by paying off Mr Fazakerley's heavy Mortgage of
£15,500 Pounds at Mr Beardsworth's Chambers in Lincolns Inn.

I shall only trouble you with one Letter more on this Subject and in
this I shall only touch upon the more particular Circumstances that
occurred in carrying out this Business to its Final Completion in
September, 1796, by the payment of the Purchase Monies and Delivery of

the Conveyances. Where I to give you all the details I might scribble over
a whole Quire of Fools' Cap.   Rd Hodgkinson.

Green Bank   17th May, 1839
On the first Week in December, 1794, I gave Mr Fazakerley notice that
we should pay off his Mortgage at a certain time. He generally resided in
London but had a House in Prescott, where he resided a Month or two in
the Year. I went to Prescot [*sic*] to pay him half a year's interest and give
him the necessary Notice. It was dark when I got to Prescott. I sent a
Note to him by the Waiter. He sent his own Servant with an Invitation
for me to take Supper and spend the Evening with him, saying he had a
Friend or two with him from London. I went and do not remember
spending a more pleasant and cheerful Evening in my Life. In a few weeks
after this Mr Fazakerley shot himself. This was a blow upon us. He had no
family and was only a Tenant for Life. The Mortgage had been of a long
standing; Trustees had died, and it became a Question in whom the legal
Estate was vested. After some time and much Investigation it luckily
proved to be in a Mr Beardsworth of Lincolns Inn, a Gentleman to whom
I had frequently remitted Mr Fazakerley's Interest: of course had been in
correspondence with him, and we were known to each other.

Green Bank   1st June, 1839
In troubling you with the last 3 or 4 Letters I have sent you I have two
objects in view. One was to shew you practically from my own example
that a young man of but common rate Abilities, and moderate education
may pass through Life not only in Credit and Respectability, but may
acquire a Competency that shall place himself and Family in a Rank in
Society far above that he set out in. The means of acquiring these desirable Results are in the power of every young man himself and they are
neither many in number nor irksome in practice. They consist in the
undeviating exercise of Honest and Sobriety carried out by an unceasing
diligence in and attention to that worldly Calling in which he is engaged.

    My second Object was to explain my reasons for so early, and I may
almost say romantically, engaging in the Herefordshire Business. On my
coming to Atherton I soon perceived how heavily the Property was burdened with Debt and when I found the Act of Parliament I silently made
up my Mind that as soon as possible after Miss Atherton came of Age I
would not rest till I had carried out the Powers authorised by that Act and
thereby relieve her from Debts too heavy to bear. This was a Step which
neither her Grandfather who got the Act nor her Father nor any Law or

Land Agent of theirs had dared to interfere with for the last fifty years. By the former letters you will see how many difficulties I had to contend with, and lastly the happy result in the full accomplishment of all my Hopes and Anticipations. Hence you will see what beneficial Results may be produced from the Exercise of Prudence, Diligence and Perseverance in a good Cause.

    The Date of this Letter would hardly remind you that it is my Birthday. I have completed my seventy sixth year of Age which does not promise many Years on this side of the Grave.   Rd Hodgkinson

Notes

1   See The Flavel Letters, Chapter 15.
2   Robert Vernon Atherton, Henrietta Maria's father.
3   Hodgkinson's son David later became agent to Mr Froggatt.
4   Richard Hodgkinson left £10,000 when he died in 1847.
5   The Bears Paw was a public house in Church Street, Atherton, and was demolished *c.* 1970.
6   The King's Head is still the site of a public house under the same name.
7   The Revd James Blundell, a lifelong friend of Hodgkinson's and later Rector of Crowland, Lincolnshire. See the Blundell Letters, Chapter 12.
8   Bewsey, the Atherton estate at Warrington.
9   Heavy debts were a burden on the Atherton estate in the 1740s and interest charges alone came to £600 a year. The main debt was a mortage of £15,500 to Mr Fazakerley of Prescot, and other demands were made for marriage portions for the Gwillym children. To meet the debts an Act of Parliament was sought in 1742 and passed in 1747 to allow the sale of estates in Hereford, Monmouth and Gloucester owned by Robert Gwillym and his son. This Act was unearthed by Hodgkinson almost fifty years later.
10   A full account of the sale of the Herefordshire estate is contained in Hodgkinson's journals of his visits to Ross-on-Wye, Chapter 4.
11   See Richard's Visit to London of 1794, Chapter 3.

3

Canal Mania & Richard's Visit to London, 1794

A large and important piece of the complex jigsaw of the early Industrial Revolution was the development of England's network of canals. Pioneering engineers in Lancashire revolutionized transport by turning rivers into waterways for the movement by barge of vast amounts of coal. By 1742, boats on the River Douglas were taking coal from the Wigan area out through the River Ribble into the Irish Sea and on to the coastal towns of Liverpool and Lancaster. In 1757 the Sankey Brook opened the St Helens coalfield to markets in Liverpool via the River Mersey.

The resulting stimulus to trade was not lost on entrepreneurs in other parts of the county. The Duke of Bridgwater's canal to Manchester was opened in 1761. This took coal from his mines at Worsley directly into the heart of Manchester, where growing industrial and domestic markets were eager to buy from this cheap and reliable source of fuel.

In 1770, promoters of the Leeds and Liverpool Canal began the near fifty-year task of building 127 miles of canal over the Pennines to connect two more developing industrial areas. By 1796, part of the Manchester, Bolton & Bury Canal had opened markets in Manchester and beyond, for both textiles and the coal mined along the Irwell Valley.

In 1792, an Act was passed to build the Lancaster Canal from Keswick into Lancashire south of the River Ribble. A major problem for the Lancaster Canal was that there was no aqueduct over the River Ribble. Cargoes from the short south section had to be transhipped into wagons at Walton Summit and taken five miles down a tramway to Preston to join the northern section of the canal. By the last decade of the eighteenth century the principal canal system in central Lancashire had been well defined, but there was still room for enterprising companies to consolidate and improve their share of the profitable movement of goods and people. Endeavours to exploit the gaps in the system led to intense rivalry between the competing companies.

One critical gap was between the southern end of the Lancaster canal at Aspull, just north of Wigan, and the mills and factories of Manchester. A link would have given the Lancaster Canal Company a much brighter and more profitable future. Negotiations opened with the Manchester, Bolton & Bury Canal to build a connection from Aspull across Red Moss to Bolton and thence to Manchester. Another option was to build a canal between Aspull and the Bridgewater Canal through Westhoughton, Atherton and Leigh, and then on to Worsley. A line for this link was surveyed by the famous engineer John Rennie and a Bill submitted to Parliament for approval in 1794.

Thanks to the whim of Henrietta Maria Atherton, it was here that Richard Hodgkinson became first embroiled in the politics of the Canal Age. Miss Atherton, still under age, was adamant that the canal would not follow the projected line bordering her Atherton property, even though it would hardly be within view of Atherton Hall. She despatched Hodgkinson to London where he engineered a spirited attack on the Lancaster Canal proposals. The Bill was dismissed and Henrietta Maria kept her uninterrupted view through the parkland down to the gates of Leigh Parish Church.

One of the people who helped Hodgkinson defeat the Bill was Thomas Powys MP, owner of a large estate at Lilford in Northamptonshire. In 1797, Powys was ennobled as Lord Lilford, and the same year his eldest son married the eligible Miss Atherton. Before the end of the century the family had, apart from an occasional brief visit, left Atherton Hall for ever.

To relieve the tedium during the long spells when the Commons Committee was not sitting, Hodgkinson wandered the streets of London, the inquisitive provincial visitor viewing for the first time the sights of the world's greatest city. He gazed in amazement at the new bridges recently thrown across the River Thames. On a visit to the Haymarket Theatre to see a new comedy, the highlight of the evening was a surprise visit by King George III and the Queen, together with the Princess Royal and two of her sisters. 'The Queen, I thought, bore much more the marks of old age than the King', remarked the candid Lancastrian, but 'the Princesses are all fine young women'.

On his journey to London, Hodgkinson was entrusted to carry three thousand guineas for deposit in a London bank, and the unarmed but intrepid traveller ran the very real risk of being robbed by the highwaymen infesting Finchley Common. He promenaded in Hyde Park with the boulevardiers, and noted the Earl of Derby and the rather nondescript Duke of Clarence, later William IV, the Sailor King, out on their Sunday evening strolls. He admired the royal horses in the King's Mews, was offended by 'the indelicacy of a figure of Neptune' in Westminster Abbey, drank a tankard of porter in the coffee house of the Kings Bench Prison and attended an improving medical lecture on mental illness, an event that presaged a tragedy in his own life. This man of boundless energy and curiosity also visited the beasts in the Tower of London, took the coach to see the sights of Royal Windsor and finally paid his first visit to Ross-on-Wye (a town soon to be the scene of elation and despair) to view the Atherton family's Herefordshire estates. This was the first of Hodgkinson's major excursions out of Lancashire. He kept detailed accounts of every penny he spent, even down to the coppers he gave to a tea boy and the 2s 6d he paid for a pair of gloves.

Journal of a Journey to London
on Account of the Lancaster Canal
Begun 26th of February, 1794

Feby. 26
Left home about two o'Clock in the Afternoon & brought the Keeper with me to Warrington to take the Horses back. Spent a couple of hours with Mr Taylor, Mr Henry Mather & Mr John Cartwright. Went to bed about 8 o'Clock & lay till 12 at which time the Mail Coach arrived from Liverpool. Got into the Coach at half past twelve, arrived at Knutsford & changed Horses about a quarter past two, at Congleton & changed Horses & Driver about half past three, at Newcastle changed Horses at 7, at Stone in Staffordshire where we breakfasted about half past eight & changed Horses. A little short of Stone we passed by Trentham, the Seat of the Marquis of Stafford, who I was informed is a great friend of the Duke of Bridgewater's. From Stone after stopping only half an hour to Breakfast & taking fresh Horses we passed to Woolsey Bridge where we changed horses; on the right hand side of the road the Country is most beautifully variegated with fertile Hills covered with sheep & fancifully interspersed with single Trees & clumps of Trees. Several Gentlemen's seats are now seen in the Vallies, most pleasantly situated, particularly a white house a little above Woolsey Bridge the situation of which I thought the most beautiful I had ever seen & from which several young Ladies on horse-

back were coming down whom we met at the Gates. From Woolsey Bridge the next Stage is to Lichfield.

The Buildings in Lichfield are in general very good. There are three Spires on the Church much ornamented with carved Stone. Coming out of Lichfield & for several miles on the Road I was much pleased with the appearance of the Country. Thought the Land very fertile particularly the Pasture & Meadow Lands. Saw many very fine fields of Turnips. The soil for many Miles is very full of Gravel & the newly ploughed fields appear covered with Stones. From Lichfield the next Stage was to Coleshill & from thence with fresh Horses we went to Coventry where we stopped to dine. We were only allowed half an hour. The Mail stops at the King's Head. Dinner is brought in about a quarter of an hour after you get out, & before you have half dined you are ordered to the Coach.

We had only a boiled Leg of Mutton & half a Pig's face roasted for which we paid 2s a piece with a charge of sixpence for fire.

After Coventry the next place we changed horses was Dunchurch. After Dunchurch we changed horses at Daventree, Stowcester & Stone in Stratford where we arrived about nine o'Clock. In passing from Stone in Stratford to Hochley of the Hole which was the next stage I slept about one half of the way which was all the sleep I had upon the roads. From Hochley we took fresh Horses to Redburn where we only stopped to change horses & then went to Mr Wilson's (the Postmaster's house) at or near Barnett where we changed horses the last time. This is the last & most disagreeable Stage on all the road. We entered upon Barnett Heath soon after four o'Clock in the morning in passing over which & Finchley Common, I was most uncomfortable; having so frequently heard of the Robberies committed upon these Commons as I had in my care 3 thousand Guineas entrusted to me by Mr Parr of Warrington Bank to carry to Messrs Cross, Devagnes and Company, Bankers in London. However we met with no such interruption & arrived in London at the Swan Inn, Lad Lane, about quarter before six on Friday morning.

The Company I had in the Coach were perfectly agreeable & as we all came through to London we had no strange Passengers taken upon the road which made it still more so.

The Company were Mr Rollinson, Attorney of Warrington, Mr Bates, Master of the Hotel at Liverpool & a young man whose name I did not learn, but he told us he was coming to London to take possession of a Commission in the Light Horse.

In the afternoon of the 28th I saw Mr Taylor. I delivered him the Plan I brought of the Avenue at Atherton; we had some conversation about the Canal, & he was very sanguine in his expectations of our success before the Committee on Monday.

I also took a Walk down the Street in which White Hall stands; I passed through the Arches of the Horse Guards & watched a little while the soldiers exercising behind it. I then walked up the Avenue leading to the Queen's Palace, from whence I had a view of Piccadilly. The foot-walks across the Lawn between the Queen's Palace & Piccadilly I was informed were to be stopped, & the Lawn enclosed for the purpose of turning Deer upon it. I went on the backside of St James's Palace where I saw nothing remarkable & came out into Pall Mall, passed by Carlton House residence of the Prince of Wales which I thought looked very dull, & passed on again to Charing Cross from whence I had first gone to Whitehall. I also walked to Savage Gardens, Tower-hill, to enquire for Billy Greenough but could not find him.

From the Adelphi I saw the Westminster & Black Friars bridges. In the dusk of the Evening after Dinner, I walked to Black Friars bridge & found it so much larger and wider than I had conceived it to be from the Adelphi, that I was quite astonished; & upon stepping it found it to be three hundred & sixty yards over or thereabouts, exclusive of a wing at each end of 12 or 16 yards each.

After Dinner Mr Rollinson, Mr Bates & myself spent an hour together at the London Coffee House where I lodged, according to an appoint-ment made at Breakfast, we drank each a Bottle of Wine & parted. I then walked out about half an hour; returned & drank a Glass of Wine & Water among the Gentlemen in the Coffee house & never having had my Clothes off from Wednesday morning to Friday night I found myself a lit-tle fatigued & went to bed about nine o'Clock.

March lst
Got up about eight o'Clock, breakfasted & went to Mr Taylor's Lodging at Mrs Ravald's in Bedford Street, Covent Garden. It is about 20 minutes walk from the London Coffee House to Mrs Ravald's. After Mr Taylor had breakfasted we went to the place (No 37 Southampton Street) where Mr Bennett, Mr McNiven & others, surveyors &c., on the part of the Bolton & Bury extension Canal lodged. We took the Plan of the Avenue at Atherton with us. For half an hour after we came there they were very busy drawing up some reasons against the Rochdale Canal in answer to some reasons published by the opposite party for the Rochdale Canal. Mr. McNiven & another person came into the Room where I was, to examine what they had drawn up before it went to the press. I thought I perceived

a weakness in the answers which proved Mr Taylor's party was very hard pressed. When the writing was corrected Mr Bennett was ordered to take it to the Press & get it printed with all speed imaginable, as the Copies were to be distributed early on Monday Morning. I went with Mr Bennett. We passed through Covent Garden Market which was very plentifully supplied with Vegetables. We then passed Drury Lane Theatre. It is newly rebuilt & must have cost an immense sum of money. It is very lofty & the front is acceedingly handsome; but the street at the front is the most inconvenient that can possibly be conceived, not acceeding I con-ceive, more than eight yards in breadth, which must be attended with very great inconvenience & danger to, where so many Carriages constant-ly come. From Drury-lane we went on to Lincoln's Inn Fields which I admired very much; the large Grass-Plot before the Inns, has a very pleas-ing effect, amongst such numerous Streets & Piles of Buildings. From hence we crossed the Strand & went to the Temple (near Temple Bar). Here another Grass-Plot upon the Bank of the river & the situation of this place is very retired and pleasant.

In passing hence to Somerset Place we saw a Fountain before a Gentleman's door which spouted water up about 9 or 10 feet high. Somerset Place is situated upon the Banks of the Thames; it is here that all the Public offices are kept (viz): War Office, Navy Office, Tax Office &c., &c. In going to Somerset Place out of the Strand you pass under some very handsome Arches which support the Rooms where the exhibi-tions of Painters & other Artists are shewn. The Buildings in Somerset Place are amazingly extensive & though they are very lofty above ground, there are three stories below ground all round the Court. At the entrance there are two large statues one of Britannia or Liberty & the other of Neptune at her feet.

From thence we returned to Mr Bennett's Lodgings were Mr Taylor joined us very soon. We then began to talk about Miss Atherton's busi-ness & after some conversation concluded that the Plan should be engraved but as this would be attended with very considerable expense I thought it proper to advise with Mr Rawstorne about it & accordingly set out to Mrs Heber's to see if he was arrived. In going thither I passed down the Strand to Charing Cross, through Pall Mall, St Jas.'s Street, & Piccadilly. Here I lost my Road & got into Berkeley Square & Grosvenor Square both which are very beautiful Places, having Green Plots (encom-passed with iron Palisades) in the middle with walks round them. When I came to Mrs Heber's Mr Rawstorne was not arrived. It was now about 2 o'Clock. As they expected him very soon, I was invited to stop till he

came which was in abt half an hour. He informed me he had been
detained two hours by the Carriage breaking down but had received no
hurt. He hesitated about having the Plan engraved but said he would go
& see Mr Stanley & desire me to stop till he returned. He came back in
about half an hour. Mr Stanley was not at home; but he accidentally met
with Mr Blackburn who gave him great encouragement about our business. He then said the Plan should be engraved. Mr Bennett had recommended Mr Baker at No 32 High Street, Islington. Mr Bennett was
obliged to go to the Printer's & could not go with me. It was half after
four & I had not dined. I went to my Lodgings, ordered a little roasted
Veal which was ready in about half an hour. I eat [*sic*] it as speedily as possible & drank a Pint of Porter & set off at half after five to go beyond
Islington Turnpike which is above 2 miles from the London Coffee
House. I could not get a Coach as I was uncertain of the distance & was
therefore obliged to walk. With some little difficulty I found the place but
Mr Baker was not within so I lost my labour. I went to my Bed Chamber
about 10 o'Clock & sat up writing till the Clock at St Paul's struck 12.

March 2nd

Mr Rawstorne desired I would come to his Lodgings by nine o'Clock. I
got there just as he was coming down Stairs. We came to breakfast with
Mr Taylor & there found our business would not be brought forward on
Monday. It was still the opinion, that the Plan should be engraved & Mr
Taylor & myself thought it advisable to reduce it to a smaller scale. When
Mr T & Mr R & I parted, it was agreed I should meet them on Monday
at 1 o'Clock at the Rochdale Committee Room. While the Porter was
gone with a Note from Mr Bennett to an acquaintance of his for a
Pentographer I assisted Mr B & others in writing Letters from Bamford
Esquire to attend the Rochdale Committee the day following. No
Pentographer could be got by which disappointment I was much embar-
rassed. Mr B thought we might get one in the evening & I was obliged to
drop all intentions of doing anything at the Plan before the night. Mr
Bennett having to go to Mr Yates's, Queen's Square, I walked with him.
We passed through Covent Garden into Long Acre, the upper part of
Drury Lane into Holborn. From hence we went through several small
streets to Bedford Square at the upper end of which stands the Duke of
Bedford's House. It is a large handsome looking house but I was informed
he means to pull it down for the sake of laying open some fields of his
behind for the purpose of building on. Queen's Square is not far distance; &
in our return we crossed Bloomsbury Square on our road to Holborn, the

squares are much alike & vary in little else but size consisting of a grass plot with gravel walks round encompassed with handsome iron rails surrounded by large, handsome houses with a spacious Coach-road entirely round.

About three o'Clock we returned to Mr Bennett's lodging & got a little bread & butter & set off to Hyde Park to see the Company there. And indeed the concourse of Gentlemen & Ladies on foot, on Horseback & in Carriages is truly astonishing. Was a person out of the Country to be taken (immediately upon coming to Town) into Hyde Park at four o'Clock on the Sunday Evening, he would think all the Inhabitants of London were collected to that one place. The number of Carriages is truly astonishing; for the whole length of Hyde Park which, in one view, I conceive cannot be less than a Mile from 3 to 5 o'Clock you may see Carriages two fold continually passing. In Hyde Park, there is one road for the Carriages, one for the Horses & one for foot people. Many of the Nobility walk out on foot. I met the Earl of Derby returning. I also saw the Duke of Clarence who was on foot. He is of the middle size, rather broadset & has nothing striking in his appearance.

In Piccadilly we passed Lord Grenville's house, which is a handsome looking white Building & pleasantly situated; as also the Duke of Queensbury's which is a large but very plain Building. At the farther end of Hyde Park you come to Kensington, the Seat of the Princess Royal. We went through the first door we came to in to the Pleasure Ground. Kensington, with the Pleasure Grounds I thought by far the most beautiful place I had seen about London. We walked up to the House which I think cannot be much less than three quarters of a Mile from the place we entered. The house is not very elegant in its appearance but it is very extensive; And its situation amidst such fine open Ground, variegated with Trees planted in Rows & Clumps, & the neat gravel walks all around with seats along the roadsides & under the trees for the accommodation of spectators make it quite charming. Of the Gardens we saw nothing except the Greenhouse. This is a pretty piece of Building but I saw nothing uncommon among the Plants. From Hyde Park Corner we returned through St. Jas.'s Park by Buckingham house (or the Queen's Palace) by St. James's Palace & Marlborough house which is a very handsome Building very near St. Jas.'s Palace. From the bottom of the Park we came by Charing Cross & returned to our Lodgings very much fatigued.

March 3rd
As I could get no Pentograph yesterday I bought a new one this morning & by eight o'Clock sat about reducing the Plan. I delivered it to the

engraver about 12. At one o'Clock I went down to the Rochdale Canal
Committee room. I found Mr Taylor's party, as I suspected very much
overpowered by the Duke of Bridgewater's. Colonel Egerton was the
principal speaker on the Duke's side & Colonel Stanley on the opposition
party. Mr Wilberforce was there also, he is a very little man rather mean
in his appearance. Mr Blackburn was Chairman. About three o'Clock the
Committee adjourned until nine o'Clock in the morning. I returned to
Mr Bennett to his Lodgings. In our road we went into the King's Mews.
A Groom shewed us into one Stable where there were 8 very fine black
horses. All stallions with long Tails one of them was better than seventeen
hands high. In this Stable were also 8 dark bay geldings with set Tails, four
of which the King drives himself in his Phaeton. In another stable were 8
cream coloured horses with long tails only used to draw the King in state.
One of these was seventeen hands high.

As I was returning to the House of Commons I met with Mr Taylor,
who desired me to see Mr Rawstorne & inform him that Colonel
Egerton had procured that a private Committee should be chosen to consider Miss Atherton's Petition, which Committee would sit whenever Mr
R thought proper; but that Colonel Egerton desired it might be post-
poned a day or two till the Rochdale Bill was gone through. To this Mr
Rawstorne was agreeable.

In my return from Mr R I went to the Play at Haymarket. I had not
been sat down many minutes before the King & Queen entered & also
the Princess Royal & two of her Sisters. The musicians played 'God Save
the King', the Company clapped hands for some time & then called for
the Song. In a few minutes the Curtain was drawn up & all the Players
came forward & sang the Song which was encored. The Queen I thought
bore much more the marks of old age than the King. The Princesses are
all fine young women.[1]

The Play was a New Comedy called the Box Lobby Challenge. It is
humerous piece, but some passages are rather too loose. I was much
entertained with it. I did not stay to see the Entertainment.[2] There is a
great air of neatness in the Theatre but it is a very small one.

March 4
Set out soon after eight o'Clock to Islington to see how the Engraver
went on with the Plan; found it in great forwardness. In my return I came
passed St Bartholomew's Hospital; an Hospital for sick and lame poor.
The Buildings are spacious, consisting of four uniform Edifices enclosing a
Square of about a hundred yards each way. I also passed by the Blue Coat

Hospital, where I was told above 1,000 boys are fed & educated. The old Bailey was also in my way. This is an immense piece of Building being as I conjecture about 160 yards in the front. About 10 I breakfasted & wrote a Letter to Mr Slow.

As I expected the Rochdale Committee would meet by 12 o'Clock. I set out to the House of Commons but took a road I had never been before. I went over Bl-Friars Bridge & took the south side of the River to Westminster Bridge. Westminster Bridge is a noble piece of Architecture it consists of 17 Arches & is, I conjecture, a quarter of a mile over. I stepped 400 paces upon it exclusive of the 2 wings.

Upon coming to the Committee Room I found they did not meet till one o'Clock. I went into Westminster Abbey, where I found amusement enough for a whole day. This Building with its Contents is the greatest curiosity I had met with. The Building itself is astonishing whether you consider its antiquity, height, extent, or mode of construction. And the monuments furnish an endless fund of entertainment to the Artist, the Poet, Historian, Biographer & the Scholar. The first I saw was a quarter length behind the door where I entered with an inscription of 'Orare, Ben Johnson'. The next is raised to Butler, with these lines at the bottom 'Ne cui, vivo deerant fere ommia, Deessteti iam mortuo tumulus, Hoc tandem posito marmore curavit, Joannes Barbrous London insis 1721.' Near to the above are the monuments of Milton, Philips, Dryden & Cowley. In the next division are the monuments of Shakespeare, Thompson, Rowe, Gay, Goldsmith & Handel. Handel is a full length with a Scroll in his hand inscribed with the Music & Words of 'I know that my Redeemer liveth'. In this division Johnson, Garrick & Henderson are interred, but no monuments yet erected to their memories. There are monuments likewise to R. Busby, Doctor South, Sir Clowdisley Shovel, Sir Isaac Newton & many more impossible for me to recollect. But there is none more delicate neat or expressive than the little monument erected by his present Majesty to the memory of Major Andre who was taken as a Spy by the Americans & executed in 1780. It consists of two groups of figures one I conceive representing his being taken & the other the Flag of Truce sent by the British to treat for his ransom. But some rude hand has already mutilated this beautiful piece of Sculpture, having struck off the head & hand on one of the principal Figures.

In one Division at the East end of the Church are two very large monuments adjoining. One sacred to the memory of the late Earl of Chatham, a full length in the attitude of speaking; the other to the memory of Captain William Bayne, Captain William Blair & Captain Lord Robert

Manners all of them mortally wounded fighting under Admiral Rodney
on the famous 12th of April. These are two fine pieces of Sculpture & display the powers of the Artist. But I cannot help conceiving there is an
indelicacy in the figure of Neptune in both of them; his being represented
by the figure of a man naked large as life, & nearly lying on his back. And
the indelicacy is still more striking, as in both of them Liberty is represented by a very fine woman.

From the Abbey I went in to the Committee Room; nothing particular
occurred there. After the Committee broke up Mr Taylor desired Mr
Blackburn to get me up into the Gallery of the house of Commons which
he did very politely. It being the last day appointed for receiving private
Petitions very little business was done besides. I saw Mr Pitt, Mr Fox, Mr
Sheridan Mr Anstruther, Mr Manwaring &c.

5th March
Breakfasted with Mr Taylor & corrected some clauses intended to be
inserted in the Lancaster Canal Bill. About 10 o'Clock Mr Rawstorne's
servant & I took a walk. We went over Black Friars Bridge & passed the
Obelisk to the Kings Bench Prison. We went in & drank a Tankard of
Porter in the Coffee House. The Prisoners are very numerous but in general shabby in their appearance. There were several women & some of
them genteely dressed among them. From hence we went to the Tower,
but could not be admitted to see the Armoury & were told it had not
been shewn for near two years. We were shewn, however, the wild
Beasts for which we paid nine pence each. They are a curiosity. The first
is a very large lioness, the next the old Lion with the spaniel dog, which
has lived in intimacy with him for 8 Years. The Lioness had Cubs about
20 months ago, a female & a male, which we saw & two very large beasts
they are already. There are two large Tygers, one very tame, the other
fierce, spotted very beautifully; there is also a black Tyger, which is not
near so large as the others. There is a Lynx too, which cannot be tamed
by any means whatever. There are several smaller Beasts of which I cannot recollect their names. The last we saw was a Wolf; its colour is brown
& its size that of a large Bull-dog.

In my road to the Committee Room I called upon John Hurst who
formerly lived in Leigh. He promised to come to my Lodgings on the
morrow evening at 8 o'Clock. Nothing particular occurred in the
Committee Room. After the Committee I went into the House of
Commons & heard Mr Wilberforce speak very spiritedly in favour of the
Leeds & Liverpool Canal Deviation.

6th March

Went to Islington to see if the copper plate was finished; found it done & got a proof Sheet. Ordered 200 copies. Returned to the Coffee House, breakfasted & went to meet Mr Rawstorne at Mr Taylor's. Mr Taylor took down Mr Rawstorne's examination & mine. Went to the Committee in the afternoon, the whole of which was spent in debates upon the Clause respecting the Barrier Lock at Manchester; nothing certain was concluded upon, & the Committee broke up in great confusion. Mr Stanley said he could not bring Miss Atherton's business on before Monday. Called upon Mr Havan (solicitor for the Lancaster Canal) to inform him when the business would come on. He said he was very sorry for the misunderstanding which had taken place, that he was very uneasy about it & that it had given him a great deal of concern. He said he could not account for it, how the mistake was, but he would not say that Miss A. might not understand him. However, to do away all suspicions that he might be supposed to have mislead Miss A. wilfully he meant to move the House (if she declared she was mistaken) to have her assent erazed & if her dissent with that of all her tenants inserted instead. From 7 to 8 o'Clock I spent with Mr Richard Cartwright, son of D. Cartwright of Cawsey Bridges who is a Surgeon in Middlesex Hospital. About 8 o'Clock John Hurst formerly of Leigh came to spend the evening with me.

I cannot help mentioning a circumstance related in the Newspaper of today, hardly creditable; but a Clergyman who came in to the Coffee House said he was present at the transaction. A Couple were in marrying at a Church in the Town; when the Clergyman came to the Passage where the husband engages to nourish his wife in sickness & in health, the intended Bridegroom said very archly & 'What shall I do with her if she be lame or lazy?' The Question so unexpected raised a general laugh & the Reverend Divine stubbornly refused to proceed any further.

7th March

Went to Mr Rawstorne before Breakfast. Colonel Egerton came in just after I arrived. Had some conversation with Mr R & promised to come again in the morning. I went to Islington for a few Plans took them to the Committee Room & distributed them. Returned to my Lodgings & dined. Wrote to Mr Slow. Spent the evening with Mrs Bennett.

8th March

Went to Mr R in the forenoon. From Grosvenor Square I went to

Islington & had a very pleasant walk being chiefly through the fields. I crossed Holborn passed through Bedford Square, by the front of the Foundling Hospital to Bagniggie Wells. This a Tea drinking house with very pleasant Gardens; I went passed the New River-head by Sadlers Wells & came to the High-road a little before the Turnpike. I went to Mr R's again in the evening. He had been with the Master of the Rolls who promised him his warmest support but highly disclaimed against any Compromise. Assisted Jack Ravald in folding up Cases of Plans & Cards till after 10 o'Clock & then returned to my Lodgings.

9th March
Breakfasted at my own Lodgings. Went to St. Paul's Church in the Forenoon. It is a most amazing Structure; & a most noble monument of the architectural abilities of Sir Christopher Wren. The Dome in the Centre surpasses anything of the sort I ever saw. It's size & construction are its only merits; it is very unfavourable to the due performance of religious ceremony, which is gone through in one corner of the Church only; & the rest is filled with gazing spectators who ramble about & pay no attention to the service.

10th March
Went to Mr R by 9 o'Clock. He informed me that the Duke of B. had sent for him, & Colonel Egerton would call upon him at 11 o'Clock to go with him. He did so, Mr R went; but the Duke was in the most violent passion; & did nothing but rail against Mr Taylor. Mr R. took his Hat & walked out.

    The Committee met upon our Business in the Afternoon; Master William Rawstorne went through his Examination very well; Mr Rawstorne was very much pressed in his Examination on account of having held out some inducements to the Lancaster Canal Company, last year, to bring the Canal by Leigh. Committee adjourned. Came to my Lodgings, dined & wrote to Mrs Hodgkinson.

11th March
Breakfasted at my Lodgings. Did not see Mr R till he came to the Committee. Mr R & myself entreated Mr T not to call upon my evidence as I could prove nothing but that Atherton Hall, was Miss Atherton's place of residence, that the Canal passed through the Avenue, or suchlike circumstances which all the Committee admitted before. We urged the loss of time &c., but he would not be persuaded & by his stu-

pidity had well nigh brought both me & himself into a very unpleasant situation. I really believed Mr —— a very improper person to conduct such a business; & had Miss A's affairs no better advocates than him, I persuaded it would have cut a very poor figure in the Committee. Colonel Egerton at the Close of the Evening proposed a compromise of the affair. Here Mr Mason declared he had sent a special Messenger to Leigh to use all the means he could to purchase the places in Lease lying about the Gates. At last the Committee adjourned to Thursday the 13th.

12th March

As we had nothing to do in the Committee nothing particular occurred. Peter Marsh came to the spend the Evening with one.

13th March

Went to Mrs Heber's where I stayed till 12 o'Clock. Then walked down to the Committee. Only four members appeared in the Opposition, the principal speaker of whom was Colonel Crawthorne, he is a most noisy fellow & talks such nonsense that I wonder Gentlemen will listen to him. Mr Mason informed the Committee that he had witnesses coming from Leigh with a Petition in favour of the Canal but could not positively say when they wd arrive. The Committee adjourned till tomorrow.

14th March

Went to view the Monument near London Bridge which was erected in commemoration of the Great Fire which burnt down the City in the Year ——. At one o'Clock went to the Committee, our business was gone through & a motion by Mr Powys⋆ that the Committee should make their report to the House on Monday was carried unanimously. Spent the evening at my Lodgings with Mr Peter Marsh & Mr Thomas Johnson.

15th March

Wrote to Mrs H. At 8 o'Clock Mr Thomas Johnson called upon me & took me to the Lectures at Dr Fordyce's. The subjects were discourses upon two kinds of delirium; in the first of which, after the death of the Patient, the vessels of the brain are found to be much distended with

---

⋆ Created Baron Lilford of Lilford in 1797, and on the 5th Dec. 1797 his son was married to the Miss Atherton on whose acct. the Committee was held.

blood; in the second the brain of the patient appears nothing different from that of a person who dies of any other disorder. The symptoms of the disorder in both cases are similar only in the first they are permanent, in the second transitory. The symptoms in both are strongest during the night, in the latter case the patient is in a great measure sensible during the day. The symptoms are dullness in the Eyes, flushing in the face, & a quick succession of ideas without any arrangement; in the first case the eyes are often bloodshot. Sometimes the delirium ceases for 6, 8, or 10 days entirely, but this is so far from being a favourable symptom that the Doctor never knew a patient recover who experienced it.

In the morning I took a place in the Stage-Coach to Windsor to set out at one o'Clock. Fare six shillings. I met with a very pleasant Companion in the Coach a Mrs Else, who was going to meet her husband at Windsor who had been travelling upwards of 2 months. She said he was at the Star & Garter, where she advised me to stop at as being the most reasonable house in Windsor. I did so. Mr & Mrs Else went amongst their Customers. I took a Walk out & rambled as far as Eton College & which is scarcely half a Mile out of Windsor. It being near dark I could see little of the College except its size. The Bridge over the Thames here is only a wooden one; the River is about 40 yards wide.

I spent the beginning of the Evening in a Company of Townspeople whose principal conversation was a contested election which was just over at Windsor. There are only 300 voters here & the contest cost each of the parties £3,000. The latter part of the Evening I spent with Mr & Mrs Else; Mr Else had lately met with Mr Maxwell of Bolton, an acquaintance of mine, at Buxton; this accident brought on conversation which made the Evening pass very agreeably.

16th March
After breakfast Mr Gurley (the landlord) who is a very polite man went with me to shew me the Castle. We first walked round the outside. From the terrace there is a most beautiful view sufficient to compensate for the trouble of coming from London to see. The wall on this side which rises scarcely a yard above the terrace walk, is, I conjecture, not less than 50 feet above the Land below. On this side lies the little Park, a charming piece of Land, & laid down almost as smooth as a Bowling Green. A view of Eton College lies just before you at the distance of about a quarter of a mile, & the fine River Thames, at your feet, winding between the Towns of Windsor & Eton, & losing itself at a distance among the beautiful fields which it enriches.

We then went into the Castle & were conducted through a great variety of handsome Rooms with painted Ceilings & very full of historical & other pictures. We went into the King's Bedchamber, the Queen's Bedchamber, the King's private Chapel, the room where the Knights of the order of the Garter are installed, the Ballroom which is hung round with Arms, Armour, Drums &c., in a very picturesque manner; we were shewn also a little closet, wherein is deposited the Banner which the Duke of Marlborough is obliged to deliver every year by 12 o'Clock on the second of August on pain of forfeiting Blenheim house & £5,000 a year.

After we had been shewn through the Palace, we went into the Chapel in the Castle Yard (where Service was in performing) which is one of the neatest places I ever saw. The Chancel window is one of the most compleat pieces of colouring in Glass that can possibly be conceived. It is a representation of the ascension of our Saviour. The figures are as fine, the Colours as soft, & the clouds as natural, as I have ever saw in oil painting. The window may be about 10 feet by 10 and is arched; it is but lately put up & stands a complete memorial of the revival of the art of staining Glass.

At the other end of the Chapel is a large window, full of antient Glass. In this the Colours are very bright and striking, but the figures are ill shaped, scarcely intelligible, & have no appearance of a painting. There is a large & sweet organ in the Chapel.

As the Coach was to set out at 2 o'Clock & the morning rather wet, I had not time to go anywhere else — & indeed there is little to be seen here, except the Castle unless a person has opportunity of going into the Parks which I believe would furnish ample entertainment for several days, particularly to such as are fond of Agriculture & Cattle, as the King himself is & to which he devotes much of his time, which makes him much attached to Windsor. I left Windsor at 12 o'Clock & arrived in London about 6.

17th March
Breakfasted at my own Lodgings. Walked out, & saw passing by, the Funeral of Judge Gould. The Hearse was drawn by 6 Horses & four mourning Coaches followed, each drawn by 6 Horses. The Hearse was ornamented with Escutcheons & all the Horses were covered with velvet cloths ornamented with Escutcheons. Went down to the Parliament house about 3 o'Clock & was much disappointed to find our Business did not come on any farther than reporting the Evidence. Debates on the Third Reading of the Slave Trade Bill. Lord Sheffield made a motion for postponing it to Friday (four days). In his Speech he made very free with

Mr Wilberforce calling the whole of the Bill a senseless proceeding. Mr Fox spoke against the delay. There would be delay enough he doubted in the house of Lords. Members should consider the Bill was going to a house of slow proceeding. Much has been said about the framing of a new Calendar in a neighbouring country but the house of Lords, he said, had long used a new Calendar with respect to Business; that a Year in the house of Lords with respect to the slave trade last year had been 4 days of 4 hours each.

As I was walking upon the Terrace at the Adelphi I saw a Carriage come up & stop at a door near the Terrace. Observing several persons standing opposite the Carriage & inquiring the cause I was informed that the Turkish Ambassador was about to get into it. Curiosity prompted me as well as the rest & I waited till he came out. He is a middle sized man of a sallow colour with a black beard several inches long. He had a Turban on his head, the Crown of which was a dark colour & the Band white. The sleeves of his under Garment buttoned close round his wrists. It was made of light blue silk & trimmed with Gold Lace. His outward Garment was a large flesh coloured silk Cloak, hanging down to his feet. His attendants were dressed much in the same way but they had a very dirty appearance such as arises from a want of change of Clothes. They had no beards except what grew on their upper lips.

18th March

Mr Rawstorne, his two sons & servant, left London this morning. I was to take a place in the Mail Coach & follow them. But Mr Young, who was to value Miss Atherton's Estates in Herefordshire, changed his mind from going thither in a few weeks & purposed being there next Sunday, so instead of taking a place in the Mail Coach to Lancashire I took a place in the Post Coach to Hereford.

19th March

Left London at about 12 o'Clock & arrived about 9 where we supped. Travelled all night & about 6 in the morning breakfasted at a place called the Broadway.

20th March

Arrived at Worcester about 11 o'Clock & came into Ledbury to Dinner. The Road between Worcester & Hereford is very bad & hilly. Came to Hereford about 6 o'Clock in the evening. The Town was very full of company, it being the Assizes.

21st March
I could find no conveyance to get from Hereford to Ross. I therefore was under the necessity of either hiring a Chaise or two horses & a man to bring them. Being informed the roads were bad I preferred the latter, & had a very pleasant ride to Wilton Castle, which was abt half a mile short of Ross where I arrived at 2 o'Clock in the evening. I found Mr Green at home, he is a pleasant intelligent man about 56 or 60 years of age. His daughter Miss Green, who keeps his house is a person who has had an exceeding good education, she is handsome & gentile in her figure & her manner is very pleasing.

Wilton Castle has a very romantic appearance & is pleasantly situated upon the Banks of the River Wye, within 20 yards of the water; the Walls of the Castle (enclosing a space of Ground; not much less than a statute acre) are in a great measure entire, except on the west side, where Mr Green's house is now built. The house is a small neat Building white on the outside, which has a very pleasant appearance amongst the strong ragged walls almost overgrown with Ivy.

22nd March
After Breakfast I walked alone as far as Dadney Farm about two miles off. It is rented by Mr Jones who farms at least 500 Acres; I found his Bailiff or Foreman ploughing of whom I learned many interesting particulars concerning the price of Grains, workmen's wages &c.,&c.

23rd March
Being Sunday I went to Ross Church. After service I walked into the Chancel where a most beautiful monument is erected to the 'Man of Ross' so celebrated by Mr Pope. He died in the year 1724 aged 88 as appears by the stone over his Grave in the Chancel; but there is no date whatever upon the monument which has only been erected about 10 years & the whole of the inscription is 'This monument was erected to the memory of Mr John Kyrle commonly called the Man of Ross.'

There is at Ross a blue Coat School for 30 boys & 20 girls, founded only 2 Years ago by a man who had been brought up at a Charity School at Ross which had long been broke up. He acquired a large fortune in London & left £200 a year for the founding of this School. The Children live with their Parents & have their Schooling & Clothes given them.

24th March
Mr Green, Mr Young & I went over Langstone Farm & several small

ones adjoining. Langstone is about five Miles from Ross & the Road is the worst I ever travelled. The house is pleasantly situated & the Grass plots, steps, gates & palisades being in pretty good repair make it still to retain the appearance of a Gentleman's seat, though it had been in the hands of Tenants about 50 years. The house wants some repair. Went over the rents of the Farms except that in Monmouthshire. We had a very long day's work & were eight miles from Ross when we finished.

26th March

Went to view the Estate in Monmouthshire which lies 16 miles from Ross. The views from the Road as you go to Monmouth are exceedingly picturesque. On the left hand side there are a range of hills from Ross to Monmouth (10 miles) chiefly covered with wood; but some few of them are so rocky & barren as to be quite bare. Every two or three Miles the navigable River Wye approaches quite up to the Road; running round the Hills, sometimes between two so near together in such a manner as not only to please but surprize you. Monmouth is but a small Town & the Buildings in it, in general, but very indifferent. There is a tolerable Market Hall, in the Front of which, was set up last year, a statue of Henry V, who, (the inscription says) was born at Monmouth 9th of August, 1387.

27th March

I spent the day at Mr Green's, except a part of the afternoon, when I took a ride to a small place about 5 miles off belonging to Miss Atherton which we have not seen before.

28th March

I left Wilton Castle soon after 6 in the morning; a place which I trust I shall long remember with gratitude for the polite & kind attention I received there. I took horses from Ross to Ledbury. Arrived at Ledbury about 9 o'Clock; got into the Coach about 10 & arrived at Worcester (where I dined) at 2. I left Worcester at 4, to go for Birmingham where I arrived at 9. The City of Worcester is by far the most pleasant place I passed through either going to or returning from London. The Streets are wide & the Buildings very good. At Birmingham I had no time to take a view of the Town, as it was dark when I entered, & the Manchester Coach was ready to set out. I left Birmingham about half after 9, travelled all night, & breakfasted next morning at Talk o'th hill & arrived at Manchester about half after two in the Evening; in about an hour I left Manchester & came to Plat-Fold about seven at Night.

Accounts for the Journey to London

1794	£	s	d
Mar 4 Rec'd cash from Mssrs Croft & Co's Bank	52.	10.	0
Mar 18 Rec'd from Do	7.	10.	
Took cash of Miss Atherton's	6.	6.	4
Do of my own	3.	18.	0
1794 Feb 26th			
Paid Turnpikes to Warr. 2 hors.			7
Pd for Liquors at Warr		2.	1
Chambermaid at Do.			6
Pd for Horses/Hay/Corn		1.	8
27th			
Gave the Coachman who left us at Congleton		1.	0
Gave the Guard do.			6
Breakfast & waiter at Stone in Stafford		1.	2
Coachman & Guard at Coleshill		2.	0
Dinner at Coventry		2.	8
Gave the Coachman & Guard at Stone in Stratford		2.	0
Expended at do.		1.	0
28th			
Gave the Coachman, Guard at London		2.	0
Paid for Breakfast at the Swan		1.	2
Gave the Boot Cleaner			2
Paid for a Glass of Wine & Water & a sheet of paper			7
Teaboy callg at Coach			1
For a Coach to the Bank at Pall Mall		2.	6
Pd at London Coffee House for a bason of Soup			
& a glass of Brandy & Water		1.	0
Paid at do. for Dinner, a Mutton Stake		2.	3
For Wine after Dinner in Co. with Mr Rollinson & Mr. Bates		2.	0
Pd for Wine & Water			6
Mar 1st			
For Breakfast at the London Coffee House		1.	0
Paid for Dinner at do.		2.	0
Paid at do. for Bread, Butter & Cheese for Supper			3
For 2 Glasses of Wine & Water		1.	0
Paid for a penknife		1.	6
2nd			
Paid for Dinner at do.		2.	0

Pd for a Glass of Rum & Water	6
Paid for do. near Hyde Park	3

3rd

Pd for a Pentagraph	5. 5. 0
Pd for a Box of Colours	10. 6
Pd for Breakfast	1. 0
Pd for a pair of Gloves	2. 6
Gave 2 Grooms at the King's Mews for shewing me thro the stables/C.H.	2. 0
Paid at the Haymarket Playhouse C.H.	2. 0
Supper & Liquor	1. 6

4th

Breakfast	1. 0
Supper & Liquor	2. 0

5th

Pd to T Payne Bookseller	9. 6. 6
Pd to see the Wild Beasts in the Tower C.H.	1. 0
Pd for a pair of Shoes	6. 0
Dinner & Liquor	3. 6

6th

Breakfast	1. 0
Pd for an oval picture frame	2. 0
Pd for a Muff for Mrs H.	
Supper & Liquor	1.10

7th

Pd Mr Dawson's Bill	1. 7. 6
Pd Mr Davies Bill	24. 14. 0
Pd for Dinner & Liquor	2. 3
Spent with Mr Bennett	1. 0
Supper & Liquor	1. 3

8th

Pd for Breakfast	1. 0
Do. for Supper & Liquor	2. 0
Paid for a Coach to Grosvenor S	2. 6

9th

Pd for Breakfast	1. 0
Pd for Dinner & Liquor	2. 3

10th

Breakfast	1. 0
Dinner & Liquor	2. 6

A Coach to Ludgate Hill	2. 0
To the Play	2. 0
11th	
Breakfast	1. 0
Dinner & Liquor	2. 3
Wine & Water	1. 0
Pd for Washing	2. 0
12th	
Breakfast	1. 0
Supper	1. 0
Liquor	1. 3
13th	
Breakfast	1. 0
Dinner & Liquor	2. 6
Wine & Water	6
14th	
Breakfast	1. 0
Pd Mr Baker, Engraver	5. 12. 0
Pd for a Map of London	3. 0
Do. of the Roads in England	7. 6
Dinner & Liquor	2. 6
15th	
Breakfast	1. 0
Coach fare to Windsor	6. 0
Gave the Coachman	1. 0
16th	
Gave the Boot Cleaner	3
Exp at Windsor	7. 10
Fare to London	6. 0
Gave the Coachman	6
Gave a Sevt. at Windsor for Shewing the Castle	1. 6
Negus[3]	6
17th	
Breakfast	1. 0
Shaving box, 2 Raz; & Strap	2. 6
Soap	6
Supper & Liquor	2. 3
18th	
Breakfast	1. 0

Dinner & Liquor	2. 0
Negus	1. 0
Mending Boots	1. 0
Washing	2. 0
Porter	2. 0
Lodging	1. 8. 6
Boots 3/- Chamberm. 2/6	5. 6
Waiter	3. 0
Indian Rubber	1. 0
19th	
Fare to Hereford	2. 0. 0
Dinner & Waiter at High Wickham	2. 4
Coachman & Guard	1. 4
Supper at Oxford	2. 3
20th	
Breakfast at Broadway	1. 0
Guards	6
Negus & Br. & Butter at Worcester	9
Dinner at Ledbury	2. 0
Coachman at Worcester	1. 0
Do. at Hereford	1. 0
Supper at Do.	1. 6
21st	
Breakfast & Liquor at do.	1. 6
Waiter & Chambermaid	1. 0
2 Horses to Ross	7. 0
Servt. Man	2. 6
Hay, Corn & Ale	1. 6
24th	
Gave the Servant at Langstone	2. 0
25th	
Pd a Bill at Ross for Mr Young & myself	1.18. 9
Servants	3. 0
26th	
Washing	1. 0
Horse hire & expense to the Est. in Monmouthshire	
16 miles from Ross	6. 6
27th	
Gave Mr Green's Servants	5. 0
2 Horses & a boy to Ledbury	7. 6

Hay & Corn at do.	1. 0
Breakfast at do.	1
Fare to Worcester	5. 0
Dinner at do.	2. 2
Fare to Birmingham	9. 6
Tea at Bromsgrove	1. 0
Fare to Manchester	1. 1. 0
28th	
Coachman at Newcastle	1. 0
Breakfast at Talk o'th Hill	1. 0
Coachman at Manchester	1. 0
Dinner at do.	1. 9

Total   £64.18. 0

Notes

1   The King was fifty-six years old in 1794, and the Queen, Charlotte Sophia, was fifty. The Princess Royal, Charlotte, had five sisters alive at this time.
2   The 'Box Lobby Challenge' was a comedy written by Richard Cumberland and first performed at Drury Lane on 22 February 1794.
3   Negus was sweetened and spiced port and hot lemon.

4

The Hereford Estates & Richard's Tribulations

The second great challenge to Richard Hodgkinson's maturing skills as an estate manager came only a few months after his success in thwarting the plans of the Lancaster Canal Company. These adventures began in July 1794, and were the result of investigations he began to find a way for Henrietta Maria Atherton to pay off huge debts of £15,500 which had burdened the family for fifty years. Trawling through old documents Hodgkinson discovered that Henrietta's grandfather, 'old Mr Gwillym', had also been no stranger to debt, and in 1745 had acquired an Act of Parliament that enabled him to raise funds by selling his Herefordshire estate. Not all of that estate had been disposed of and Hodgkinson advised Henrietta to revive the old Act and sell off the remaining lands.

The sale fetched £20,145, enough to pay off the mortgage and to leave Miss Atherton a handsome bonus. Hodgkinson's elation at his success quickly turned to dismay, as laggardly and devious country lawyers delayed completion and led the tyro agent on four long journeys to London and Herefordshire to try in vain to speed final settlements. This adventure began in July 1794, but it was the end of September 1796 before all the purchasers of the farmland settled their accounts.

Human nature changes little, and among the prosaic and more ingenious excuses put to Hodgkinson for the procrastination were: a solicitor has put the wrong name on a deed; the solicitor is out of town (repeatedly); the money/drafts/deeds are in the post; the bank has insufficient money; it is the wrong type of credit note; it is too near Christmas; and one particularly prevaricating solicitor claimed to have been delayed by the tide.

Hodgkinson was also treated badly by Mr Harvey, the lawyer he chose to represent the Atherton family interests and whose early promise as 'a man of honour and a Gentleman' was subject to a second opinion. Harvey did not take kindly to the Lancashire intruder doing the job he felt was his by right, and his double-dealing more than once caused Hodgkinson considerable trouble.

During this frustrating time, Hodgkinson alleviated the tedium and anxieties of the long delays and used his idle hours to refresh his intellect by making a grand tour of the Wye valley and the new Georgian developments at Bristol and Bath, 'where the most common streets are superior . . . to anything in London'. A visit to the family home of the Gwillyms moved him to a write a soliloquy on the inevitability of life and death, and the peccadilloes and immoral behaviour of a country parson, in whom 'divinity is most shamefully disgraced', brought a diatribe of indignation from Hodgkinson's pen. He also recorded details of his visits to London and the dangers of travelling by coach in the harshest winter in living memory.

On his first journey to Herefordshire Hodgkinson travelled through Shropshire and visited an old friend as well as his elderly former headmaster, a father figure for whom he felt great affection. In a long night ride he tarried in the ghostly ruins of an old abbey, before being astounded by the dramatic wonder of the glowing furnaces of the Darby family iron enterprise at Coalbrookdale, 'a scene which I would gladly ride 20 miles to have another view of'.

His second and third attempts to conclude the Herefordshire business, in January 1795, were continually thwarted and made little progress. In his determined final visit to London and Ross in August 1796, Hodgkinson was away from home for more than five weeks but finally reached a settlement, although not without last-minute procrastination from the legal profession. But all ended well, and, with the heavy mortgages on the Atherton estates paid off, Henrietta Maria Atherton entered into her marriage with Thomas Powys in 1797, with rich holdings unburdened by debt.

The many and varied threads in the affair of the Herefordshire estates are quite complicated and it is to the great credit of Hodgkinson, lacking any legal training, that in the end he was triumphant. On his last visit to Herefordshire, Hodgkinson was away from home for five weeks and three days and he travelled 'near a thousand miles, and had experienced more anxiety and unease of mind and contended with and surmounted more difficulties than I had ever met with in my life before'.

Below is a list of who was who in the Herefordshire saga:

Individuals Involved in the Sale
of the Herefordshire Estates

Lot	Purchaser	Solicitor	Auctioned	Amount Paid
1	Rev Thomas Jones	Mr Harvey	£8053	£7216
2	Mr William Morgan	Mr Phillips	£1495	£1349
3	Mr Enoch Evans	Mr Phillips	£1000	£907
4	Mr John Lewis	Bourne & Williams	£1355	£1223
5	Mr John Evans	Mr Woodhouse	£90	£82
6	Mr George Mynde	Mr Harvey	£1935	£1745
7	Mr Walter Hill	Mr Eccles	£1395	£1397
8	Rev John Jones	Mr Lechmere	£1550	£1397
9	Mr John Hall	Mr Harvey	£180	£163
10	Mr W Tovey	Mr Phillips	£855	£776
11	Mr John Watkins	Bourne & Williams	£420	–
12	Mr George Mynde	Mr Harvey	part of lot 6	–
13	Mr Thos Bennett	Mr Harvey	£735	£667
14	Mr Wm. Wiseman	Mr Stokes	£955	–

Lilford Cash Book: DDL i ACB/8
September 1796

Mr Young the Auctioner received £569 2s 4d less £42 stamp duty, poundage, & expenses

Mr Harvey, solicitor at Ross believed he should have had charge of selling off the Hereford estates and not Richard Hodgkinson

Others: Mr Green, Miss Atherton's agent, lived at Wilton Castle
Mr Cope, caretaker at Langston House, died in 1795
Mr Fazackerley, holder of the Atherton mortgages of £15,000
Mr Beadsworth & Mr More, solicitors for Mr Fazackerley
Mr Curteis, Mr Fazackerley's banker, receiver of the mortgage money
Miss Clarke, already the owner of the Walford estates
Lord Foley, holder of the deeds of Lot 14

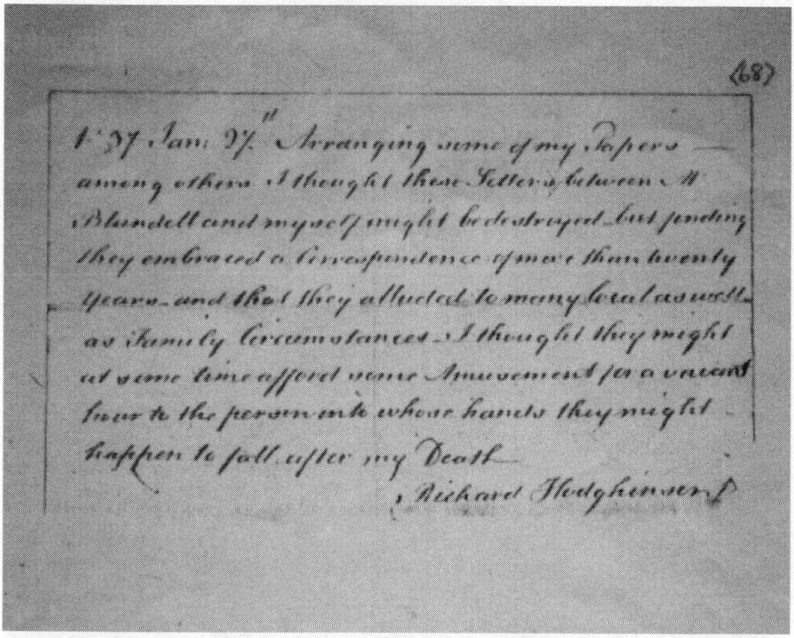

(68)

1837 Jan: 27th Arranging some of my Papers —
among others I thought these Letters between Mr
Blundell and myself might be destroyed but finding
they embraced a Correspondence of more than twenty
years — and that they alluded to many local as well
as Family Circumstances — I thought they might
at some time afford some Amusement for a vacant
hour to the person into whose hands they might
happen to fall after my Death

Richard Hodgkinson

Plate 1 Richard Hodgkinson's note about the Blundell letters, saying that he was going to throw them away but that he thought they might give someone an hour's amusement after his death (Lancashire Record Office, DDX 211/4)

Plate 2   Richard Hodgkinson, a self-made and ambitious Georgian gentleman (by permission of Richard Hodgkinson)

Plate 3   Jane Hodgkinson, 'an affectionate, willing and efficient Help-mate' (by permission of Richard Hodgkinson)

Plate 4   The Atherton family arms

Plate 5   Chowbent chapel. Built in 1721, it was the place of worship of Mary Hodgkinson and the Scottish craftsmen who settled in the village in the mid-eighteenth century

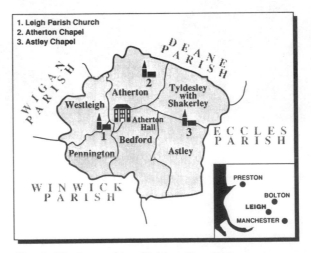

Plate 6   The six townships of Leigh parish, *c.* 1800

Chowbent Races, 1775.

To be RUN for, in the PARKS, near *Chowbent*,

On *Wednesday* the 26th of *July*, the *Gentlemen's Purse*, Value 50l.

BY any Horse, Mare, or Gelding, that never won above the Value of 40l. at any one Time, Matches excepted. Five Year olds to carry 8ft. 5lb. six Year-olds 9ft. and Aged 9ft. 6lb. A Winner of one Prize, in the present Year, to carry 3lb. extraordinary, the Best of three Four-mile Heats.———Entrance 5s. The Stakes to go to the second Best.

On *Thursday* the 27th will be Run for, the *Ladies Purse*, Value 50l.

BY any Horse, Mare, or Gelding, that never won above the Value of 30l. at any one Time, Matches excepted.———Entrance 4s. The Stakes to go to the second Best, three Four-mile Heats.

On *Friday* the 28th will be Run for, the *Town's Subscription*, Value 50l. *Give* and *Take*.

BY any Horse, Mare, or Gelding, that never won above the Value of 40l. at any one Time, Matches excepted. Fourteen Hands, Aged, to carry 8ft. 7lb. higher or lower in Proportion, allowing 7lb. for every Year under seven. A Winner of one Prize, in the present Year, to carry 3lb. extraordinary, the Best of three Four-mile Heats. To be subject to the King's Plate Articles, and to such other Articles as will be then and there produced.

To enter and measure at Mr. RICHARD ALDRED's BARN, two Days before Running, and to start each Day precisely at Three o'Clock. Three reputed Running Horses to start each Day or no Race, unless agreed to by the Stewards.

N. B. No Person will be permitted to erect any Booth, or Stall, or to sell any Kind of Liquors or Victuals, but who shall be Subscribers to the said Races.

☞ ORDINARIES and ASSEMBLIES as usual.

Plate 7 Lancashire sporting life – a poster for Chowbent Races in 1775 (Wigan Heritage Services)

Plate 8 Robert Gwillym and family at Atherton New Hall, c. 1746, painted by Arthur Devis. The hall was completed in 1742, and Richard Hodgkinson organized its demolition in 1825 (Yale Centre for British Art, Paul Mellon collection)

homas 2nd Lord Lilford

Plate 9 Thomas, 2nd Lord Lilford, 'an amiable and accomplished person, who wrote verses with ease and grace', by William Pickersgill. He married Henrietta Maria Atherton in 1797 and fathered their six sons and six daughters (Christies)

Plates 10 & 11   Henrietta Maria Lilford was forty-nine when she died in 1820 after a lingering illness, and her husband survived her by only five years. These are their memorials in the Lilford family church at Achurch, Northamptonshire

Plate 12   Richard Hodgkinson moved to Greenbank, this country home on the outskirts of Chowbent, in 1828, two years after his son Joseph died in an asylum. Both Richard and his wife died here

Plate 13 Robert Jackson, a favourite nephew, for whom Richard Hodkinson wrote an auto-biographical account of his life. Jackson was responsible for the safekeeping of the Hodgkinson Papers after his uncle's death (Picture: Richard Hodgkinson)

Plate 14 The Hodgkinson family grave at Leigh parish church. Buried here are Richard Hodgkinson, his wife Jane and his sons, David and Joseph

Nec magis expressi vultus per ahenea signa,
Quàm per vatis opus mores animæque virorum
Clarorum apparent.

———————————————

Omnes mihi singulari quadam et eximia
laude digni videntur, qui honestis artibus et
disciplinis dant operam; sed ii praecipue, qui
studia, moresque hominum celebrare suscipiunt.
Sculpturae suus certè debetur honos, per hanc
aeque ac coloribus artem pingendo vultus et
externa forma bene exprimuntur; dum
Musa non minus exactè mores hominum
ostendit, et egregias animi virtutes. Ut tabella
bene picta nostros oblectat oculos, sic carmina
bene composita dulcem auribus reddunt
sonum, et inter legendum mores animumque
tam planè videmus, quam si spectemus
alicujus effigiem ab Apelle depictam.

Plate 15   The earliest surviving papers in the Hodgkinson collection were written when Richard Hodgkinson was a young scholar at Standish Grammar School near Wigan. This is a Latin example in which Richard expounds on the superiority of the written word over art and sculpture (LRO DDX 211/11)

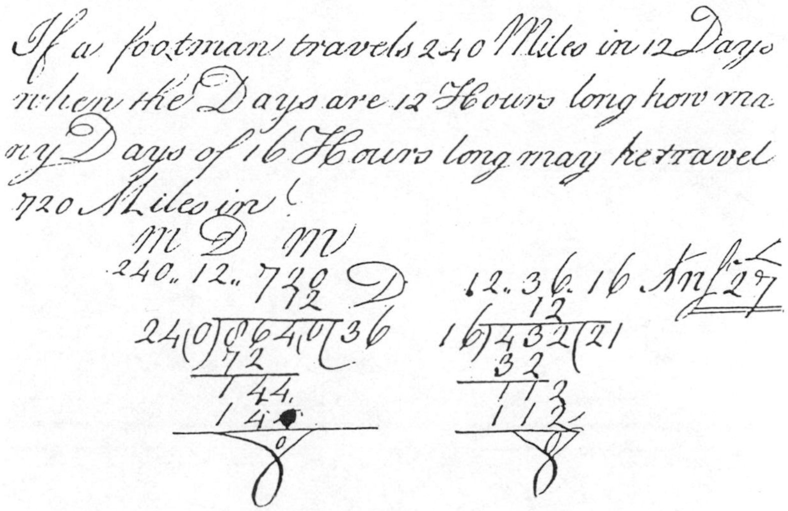

If a footman travels 240 Miles in 12 Days when the Days are 12 Hours long how many Days of 16 Hours long may he travel 720 Miles in?

M   D   M
240 .. 12 .. 720   D   12 . 36 . 16   Ans 27

24(0)(640(36   16)432(21
        72   32
      144   112
      144   112
        0   0

Plate 16   Two examples of Richard's school work from an arithmetic notebook (LRO DDX 211/19)

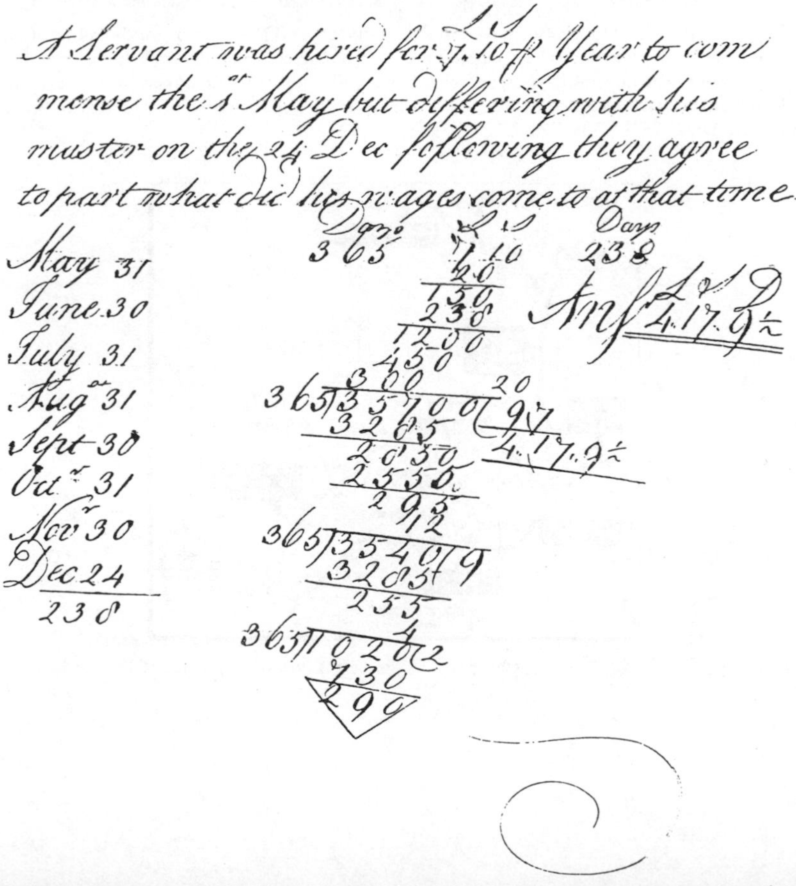

A Servant was hired for £7.10 p Year to commence the 1st May but differing with his master on the 24 Dec following they agree to part what did his wages come to at that time.

Days   £ s   Days
365   7.10   238   Ans £4.17.9¼

May 31   20
June 30   150
July 31   230
Aug 31   365)35700(97   20
Sept 30   3285   97
Oct 31   2050   4.17.9¼
Nov 30   2550
Dec 24   295
  238
              365)35409(
                 3285
                  255
                    4
              365)10202(
                  730
                  299

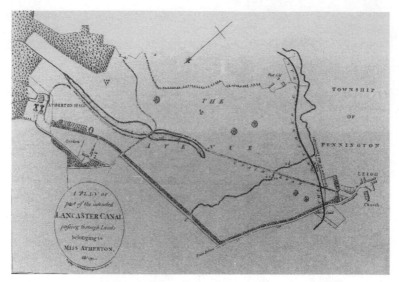

Plate17   Richard Hodgkinson journeyed to London in 1794 to stop the building of an important canal extension which would have crossed the Atherton estate. While a committee of MPs was hearing the case, Richard hurriedly engaged Mr Baker, an engraver in Islington, to make two hundred copies of this plan to support the appeal (drawn by Lord Lilford, DDLi 24/13 Box 274)

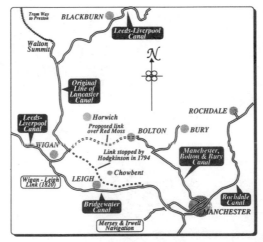

Plate 18   The height of canal mania – part of the Lancashire canal system, 1820

Plate 19   Atherton hall, the home in a rural setting of Henrietta Maria Atherton and her sisters, Elizabeth and Hestor (Manchester City Libraries, Local History Unit)

Plate 20 'I cannot help conceiving there is an indelicacy in the figure of Neptune', wrote Richard Hodgkinson after viewing a memorial in Westminster Abbey to Captains William Bayne, William Blair and Lord Robert Manners, who died for their country serving with Admiral Rodney at the battle of Dominic in April 1782 (by courtesy of the Dean and Chapter of Westminster)

Plate 21 'From the terrace there is a most beautiful view sufficient to compensate for the trouble of coming from London to see': Richard Hodgkinson's visit to Windsor Castle on 16 March 1794. He was shown round the castle, including St George's Chapel, by the landlord of the Star and Garter (Windsor Castle Royal Library, copyright Her Majesty the Queen)

Plate 22   St Chad's church, Shrewsbury, built in 1792. 'The church is a most beautiful piece of Architecture and is built of stone almost white.': Richard Hodgkinson

Mr White, Lord Foley's solicitor
Mr James Taylor and Mr John Gorst, Miss Atherton's solicitors
Mr Davies, Taylor and Gorst's London solicitor

Monday 1794 July 25th
Left Atherton about 9 o'Clock in the morning on my journey into
Herefordshire for the purpose of selling Miss Atherton's Estates in that
county. I took a horse as far as London Bridge (alias Stockton Quay)
about 2 miles beyond Warrington where I met the Boat & came up to
Preston Brook, where I got into the Chester Coach about 4 o'Clock &
arrived at Chester about 7. A Mr Fawkes, surveyor to the Duke of
Bridgewater was in the Boat; he had a horse waiting for him at Preston
Brook, on which he accompanied the Coach to Chester. The Coach
stopped at the White Lion where I took a place for Shrewsbury in the
Coach which set out in the morning (Tuesday) at 8 o'Clock. Mr Fawkes
& I went & slept at the Hop-pole. The Coach left Chester about 8
o'Clock & arrived at Wrexham at 10, where it stopped an hour. There
we stopped at the Eagles where I met with Mr Thos Sidebottom formerly
a pupil of mine at Westbury. He has married a Lady of three hundred a
Year Fortune & resides in the neighbourhood of Wrexham. We stopped
an hour at Wrexham & then went on to Ellesmere where we arrived
about one o'Clock. Here we dined at the Royal Oak (Mrs Prices) stayed
till 3 o'Clock. We arrived at the Lion Inn Shrewsbury abt 6 without anything material occurring upon the road. I drank Tea & supped with a Mr
—— [no name inserted] of Liverpool who came with me in the coach
from Chester & whose company was very agreeable. After Tea I walked
out. I went first to the Quarry & of course past the new Church which is
just erected in the stead of St Chads which a few Years ago was destroyed
by the Steeple falling down upon the body of the Church. The Church is
a most beautiful piece of Architecture & is built of stone almost white.
The western entrance is very handsome thro' a Portico supported by 4
large Cylindrical Pillars & leads under the Steeple which is a Dome also
supported by cylindrical Pillars. The Body of the Church is a perfect
Circle of near 30 Yards Diameter as I conjecture. I did not see the inside.
No spouts are to be seen on the outside to convey the water down from
the top. But at the East end I observed the mouths of two spouts upon the
surface of the ground which were conveyed within the walls & it happening to rain at the time I was there I could hear the water falling down, &
see it discharge at the aforesaid mouths. The whole of the Building taken

together has a most handsome light & picturesque appearance so much so, that I fully acquiesced in the sentiments of the Bishop who consecrated it. 'I admire, says he, the beauty & the neatness of the Building, but it wants the solemnity necessary in a place of worship, I almost conceive I am entering a Theatre.'

The Quarry is the pride of Shrewsbury. The walk upon the Bank of the River, & the Trees on each side of the walk are in themselves extremely beautiful but the situation is so low, that in no one position scarcely can you see 100 Yards from you. The two principal, & indeed only objects worth notice, which you can see here, are the new Church (which I have before described) situated on the upper part of the Quarry, & the House of Industry, which is a fine piece of Building, situated upon King's-land on the opposite side of the River.

There is a new Bridge in building just above the Quarry in the room of the Welch Bridge, which is to be taken down, it is to consist of 5 Arches, 4 of which are already turned. It is built of white stone, such as the new Church is built of & will when finished, if we may judge from its present appearance be a good & handsome piece of Architecture, & a great ornament to this part of the Town. But when this Bridge is finished still farther improvements are intended to be made, several old Buildings are to be taken down, a new Street on the Welch side, is to be brought up to the Bridge & continued past the new Church. This when executed will be a capital improvement to the Town of Shrewsbury, & if the Buildings in the new Street on the Quarry side, (one of which consisting of 4 dwellings is already erected) may boast a situation equal to any Houses in any Town in the Kingdom.

The best houses in Shrewsbury are situated upon or near the Walls all of which you have the best view of by walking round the Town upon the Bank of the River.

The river nearly encompassing the Town, forms a peninsula on which the Town is built, the Isthmus, lying between the new Gaol & the Welch Bridge, over which Isthmus the Road leads to Ellesmere. From the Quarry I followed the Riverside down to the new Bridge, over which lies the London Road. I had often seen & admired this Bridge many years ago, while I lived at Westbury, & then thoᵗ & still think it the handsomest I ever say. But from the lowness of its situation, much of its beauty is lost, & tho' in my opinion far superior to Worcester Bridge, it neither strikes the eye, nor excites admiration so much.

From the Bridge I went on along the side of the River to the new Gaol. The Plan of this Gaol was settled under Mr Howard, whose labours for the improvement of Prisons are well known. The situation is excellent, & the Building capital; but if we were to judge of the morals of the Salopians from the size of their Prison we sh^d not judge very favourably, for it is universally allowed to be too large by one half. The Gaol Yard adjoins to the Old Castle, which has been lately repaired by its owner Lord Pulteney, at a considerable expense. I scarcely know any Town, so small as Shrewsbury, which can boast so many good public Buildings.

The new Church, the House of Industry, two handsome Bridges over the Severn, the new Gaol & the Shire Hall, all of which have been erected within these very few Years conspire to make the Town of Shrewsbury respectable.

The public Schools are upon a very extensive establishment, four or five Masters being very amply provided for. When I lived at Westbury the credit of these Schools was not very great, owing to the neglect of the Masters; how they are managed at present I had not an opportunity of enquiring; but under proper regulations, there cannot be a doubt, but they would be, neither the last nor the least of what Shrewsbury has to boast.

30th
On the Wednesday morning after Breakfast I left Shrewsbury on a Hackhorse to go Pontesbury (about 7 miles off) to see my respected friend Mr Jandrell, who was my fellow Usher at Westbury 11 Years ago & whom I had never seen since Christmas Day 1783. In my way to Pontesbury I called at Cruck-meole to see Mr & Mrs Warter, whose son Mr John Warter, who is now Minister at Ledbury in Shropshire, was under my care at Westbury. I was received with a very hearty welcome, & the satisfaction & pleasure expressed by the whole family, was such as I naturally expected from people who had always behaved to me with the utmost respect, & civility, & I may add friendship. I want words to express the ardour of affection with which Mrs Warter received me; she took leave of me with the most earnest prayers for my health & welfare & her last words were a benediction.

I arrived at Pontesbury about 11 o'Clock & sent for Mr Jandrell to the Public House. I felt my spirits a little flattered when the Messenger was gone, at the idea of seeing so soon & to him so unexpectedly, a friend whom I valued so much, & whom I had not seen for so many years. Mr Jandrell knew me immediately, & the meeting was such as true friendship & valuable esteem will ever dictate. He ordered my horse to his own Stable, & I went with him home, where I experienced a most hearty welcome from Mrs Jandrell. Mrs Jandrell & I had once seen each other when she was very young & I believe before Mr Jandrell had seen her. We were however in fact, strangers, to each other except from my Letters to Mr Jandrell & his Letters to me. Mrs Jandrell fully answered my expectations of her; she is a little neat woman & exceedingly active, her economy & management in the family are remarkable & her affection & love for Mr Jandrell are by no means the least of the good qualities I observed in her. Mr Jandrell has at present only two Children both boys. The eldest is about 7 years of age & about 10 days before I arrived had the misfortune to break his thigh, I am very sorry to add it is apprehended, that he will be rather shorter on that side than on the other.

In the Evening of the same day about 4 o'Clock, we set out on Horseback to Westbury about 4 miles distant where we had lived together two years as assistants to Mr Flavel. Mr Flavel removed about 8 Years ago from Westbury to Cleobury Mortimer; & I was much affected to see the School which in Mr Flavel's time was famous thro' Shropshire & all the neighbouring Counties, now in so short a time entirely neglected & forgotten. My good old Friends, Mr & Mrs Newcombe were very glad to see me. We repeated over the frequent entertainments & pleasant Evenings Mr Jandrell & I had spent in their house where we were always welcome and Mrs Newcombe paid us the compliment to say we were the only two assistants, that Mr Flavel had, who added any respectability to his School.

We called upon all the rest of our acquaintances, by whom we were cheerfully received & after spending a very agreeable evening, returned to Pontesbury about 11 o'Clock.

31st

The following day Mr Jandrell took me to see a very singular character, a Mr Richard Heighway. He is a native of Pontesbury but has resided in London several Years. Some time ago he came into the Country, with an intention to settle here. He fixed upon a situation, almost as romantic as imagination can conceive & has built a new house upon it. A little above his house is a most beautiful waterfall, issuing out of a large wood, which covers a high Hill behind his house. In the front of his house is a very high & barren mountain, the upper part of which is very steep & rocky; the lower part is a gentle descent which reaches Mr Heighway's house. Here he has inclosed a considerable quantity of land (as far as the steepness of the mountain will permit) which is now in an improving state of cultivation & produces very good Corn. His Garden which lies at the Front of the house is extensive & laid out with great taste; the walks, the water, & the Plantations are beautiful but every thing here is in its infancy, in a few years this promises to be a very sweet place. The Garden has no cultivation, but from Mr Heighway's own hand. He digs, plants, sows & prunes & when he is tired with this, he goes into the house & amuses himself with Portrait Painting in which he is a very Capital artist. Mr Heighway's appearance promises nothing of Genius. He was at work in this Garden when we arrived there. Mr Jandrell introduced me as wishing to see some of his Paintings & immediately he laid down his spade & took us into his painting Room, where I found some very capital performances. There were portraits of several of Mr Jandrell's boarders which were very striking likenesses & finished in a very masterly manner. I was informed he sends a Painting or two annually to the exhibition in London.

From Mr Heighway's we returned to Dinner. After Dinner I proposed returning to Shrewsbury & taking a place in the Coach for Worcester the following morning. But Mr Jandrell was very pressing for me to stop another day to which at last I consented on a proposal of Mr Jandrell to send home immediately the horse I brought from Shrewsbury & himself to accompany me to Norton the following Evening (Friday August 1st).

Tho' Norton is 25 miles from Pontesbury, we did not set out till half after 6 o'Clock in the Evening. A great deal of rain had fallen in the forenoon & the weather was very unpromising when we set out. We had not gone three miles when it began to rain & having no upper Coat with me intending to travel chiefly in the Coach I had every reason to expect a very uncomfortable ride. However after riding a few miles, the Evening cleared up & became very pleasant. About 4 miles short of the Iron Bridge we called at a Farm-house where Mr Jandrell was acquainted. The family was gone to bed, but a young man came down & furnished us with some good refreshment (viz: Bread & Cheese & 3 Jugs of Ale). About 10 o'Clock we proceeded on our Journey & Mr Jandrell, wishing to take the nearest way, turned into a Road leading by Bilder's Abbey[1] up to a Gentleman's (Mr Williamson's) Seat by which we might have saved near a mile. But after passing through one field, we found the Gate by the Abbey locked. We rode round the end of the Abbey & in to it on the other side, hoping to find a passage thro' some of the Arches beyond the Gate, but in vain. As we were riding round the inside of the Walls, I do not remember when I experienced so awful & dismal a scene. All was silence, except the Owl; which made the trampling of our horses seem prodigious. And the little light of the Moon but a few days old, admitted thro' the holes for the windows, & shining upon the quivering leaves of the Ivy, which grew in prodigious quantities upon the Walls, added to the gloom & horror of the place. Tho' disappointed of our intentions I was not displeased at our visit to the Abbey.

Reflections upon the Abbey engaged my attention till I arrived at Coalbrook Dale, where new objects presented themselves.

The Iron Bridge, particularly engaged my attention. I got off my horse & walked over it. The iron rails (as battlements on each side) are upwards of five feet high & very strong. I stepped the length of them to be about 55 Yards. At each end of the Bridge, there is a wing of stone, (included in the 55 Yards) of ab^t. seven Yards each. Just below the Bridge was a view, which struck me particularly & which I stopped my horse to admire. There are here several furnaces for smelting Iron which are perpetually on Fire. On the opposite side of the River extending a long way is a very high Bank or rather Hill, chiefly covered with wood, and interspersed with numerous Cottages & other Buildings. It was now near midnight, the Moon was set, & the Furnaces flaming prodigiously. The light was so great as to render objects distinctly visible at the distance of a quarter of a mile; & shining upon the opposite Bank & also upon the River, opened a view grand beyond description. I stopped, I gazed & admired, I rode on & stopped again, till Mr Jandrell, fearful I sh^d. keep him out all night, hurried me from a scene which I w^d gladly ride 20 miles to have another view of. We arrived at Norton as the Clock struck twelve.

We lodged at Mrs Pearce's (Mr Jandrell's Mother) from whom I experienced a very kind reception & liberal entertainment.

Aug 2nd

On the Saturday forenoon we took a ride to Bridgnorth distant ab^t 5 Miles; we dined with a young man, a Mr Lloyd, a Clock maker who fortunately for me happened to dine at Mr Jandrell's the day I came there. He provided me two horses & a man to take me to Cleobury the following day. From Bridgnorth we returned about 5 o'Clock in the Evening, & supped with W^m. Thomason of Stockton, formerly a Pupil at Westbury. On Sunday morning after Breakfast I took leave of Mr Jandrell, who sent a man & horse with me to Bridgnorth, where I arrived about 11 o'Clock, drank 2 bottles of Cyder with Mr Lloyd & then took the Post-horses for Cleobury, which is 13 miles off.

Aug 3rd

Cleo Mortimer is the place where Mr Flavel now resides, the Gentleman in whose School I was classical assistant at Westbury, which place he left about 10 years ago. It was in the Year 1782 & 1783 that I lived at Westbury.

I arrived at Mr Flavel's about 2 o'Clock where I was a very unexpected & a very welcome Guest. During my residence in Lancashire Mr Flavel has three times applied to me to procure him assistants & I have always succeeded. These little services, added to the attachment he formed for me during my residence with him, have placed me high in his esteem, as appears from different Letters of his now in my possession which I have received from him during an absence of 10 Years.

In Mr Flavel's family I found a serious alteration. When I left him he had 6 Children, now he has only three. His eldest son is 20 Years of age & a very hopeful youth; he has been 12 months at Cambridge, in Clare-hall, & happened to be at home on the long vacation when I called. His second son Richard, he buried last November, aged 18. He was apprenticed in London to Mr Davies, Mrs Flavel's Brother, a Jeweller & Silversmith. His third Child, a daughter, he buried a short time before his son Richard, aged about 16. His third son, William, who was a fine boy about 3 Years old when I left Westbury, he buried at 10 Years of age. All of them died of consumptive disorders. He has a fine girl of about 12 Years of age & a boy of about 10. But the burial of three Children all of the same disorder, has been so severe a stroke upon Mrs Flavel, that she is quite dispirited & seems apprehensive of living to bury the other three.

Mr Flavel's situation at Cleobury is very eligible. The House & School together is one of the most complete Buildings for the purpose I ever saw. Situated upon an eminence it commands a view of the whole Town; the Gardens at each end of the House are extensive & pleasant & the House itself is large & convenient. Mr Flavel has the House, School, Out-buildings, Gardens, Yards & one Piece of Land all free of Rent, Keep, Taxes or Repairs with a salary of £40 per Year for teaching Writing & Acc[ts] to Children of Cleobury. There is also a separate School Room of £25 a year for another Master to teach the Children to read only. Mr Flavel, since he came to Cleobury has altered his Plan of taking Boarders. At Westbury he took in all that came, at present he wishes to confine himself to about 23 & the more so, as his son now after 12 months residence at Cambridge seems inclined to give up all ideas of the School & to push his fortune on at Cambridge & in this his father leaves him perfectly to his own choice. I intended to leave Cleobury immediately after Breakfast on the Monday morning, but Mr Flavel would not hear of it & begged I would stop another day at least. This I could not do with any satisfaction; at last he consented I should go after dinner. At dinner they

urged me very much to return thro' Cleobury & stop a day or two more
with them; & at length, they seemed so very anxious, that I could not
resist promising I would do so if I found I could do it with any degree of
convenience & propriety.

Hereford is 33 miles from Cleobury, so far at least I intended to travel
that Evening. Time passed on agreeably & imperceptibly & it was 2
o'Clock before I could get Mr Flavel to order the horse. I was to have his
Horse to Tenbury (8 miles off) & his Servant to fetch it back. The Horse
was ready, Mr Flavel came with me to the Door; he then ordered the
Horse to be led thro' the Town & he would walk with me a little way; he
seemed anxious to say something or other, but still hesitated, I perceived
it, but knew not how to relieve him. At length when we were quite out
of the Town & he could not walk any farther with me without delaying
me much, he stopped, & took me by the hand, 'Mr Hodgkinson, says he,
this visit from you, is as agreeable to me as it was unexpected, & adds one
more to the numerous obligations I already lie under to you. The obligation will still be increased by your returning this way, but the contingencies of business may not leave it in your power; therefore it is very probable this is the last time I may ever see you, & I cannot let you go without
assuring you how much I regard & esteem you. You were a very young
man at the time you lived with me, but your steadiness in & attention to
my business, & your regularity of conduct in the house & school caused
both me & Mrs Flavel to have such an affection for you, as an absence of
upwards of ten years has not in the least obliterated. And of all the
Assistants I have had in my School, there is not one except yourself whom
I look back to with a desire of having any connection with. I am now
near 60 Years of age, my family is reduced from 6 to 3 Children, my
eldest son, I am pretty well assured never intends now to have any thing
to do with the School; my Children are amply provided for, I want an
assistant & companion to make the decline of life comfortable, & I wish it
was as much in your power to accept an offer from me, as it is both in my
power & inclination to make that offer an eligible one.' I could bear no
longer, the old Gentleman's goodness overcame me, I shook his hand, bid
him farewell & hurried away as fast as I could.

Aug 4th
I arrived at Tenbury a little after 4 o'Clock. The road from Cleobury to
Tenbury is the worst Turnpike I ever travelled; I was informed it was for-
merly only a bye road, but had lately been made into a Turnpike.
Turnpike now it certainly is, of which I had convincing proof, for I

passed three Toll-Gates, at 2 of which I paid before I got half way to Tenbury. In some places, the road was so bad, that I got over into the Fields & in other places the road leads thro' the middle of Corn Fields, for half a mile together without any fence on either side.

I was directed to put up at the Swan in Tenbury which is a very good house. I ordered a Chaise to take me to Leominster which is 12 miles. The Road was very good & I got there about 6 o'Clock. After Tea at the Unicorn, understanding that the road to Hereford was very hilly & the night coming on, I thought I could go quicker on horseback than in a Chaise. I ordered a couple of Post horses & a Servant with which I set out for Hereford (13 miles off), at a quarter past 7. I got in about 9. I put up at the New Inn where I met with very good attendance & a good Bed. I ordered 2 Post-horses to be ready at 6 o'Clock in the morning & myself to be called at half after 5. The Chambermaid & Ostler were both very punctual. I left Hereford a little before 6 & had a very pleasant ride to Ross (14 miles) where I arrived in time for Breakfast on Tuesday morning.

Aug 5th

I found Mr Green & Miss Green both very well. Before we had finished Breakfast, a young man of the name of Harvey, an Attorney in Ross, called upon Mr Green, by appointment, to go with him over the Langstone Estates. Mr Green did not return till after Dinner. As the time of the Sale approached I found myself proportionally anxious about the issue. I saw, or thought I saw, numerous obstacles in the way; Mr Green & Mr Young (who was to sell the Estates) were not upon good terms; it was Mr Green's Interest that the Estate sh^d not be sold, because then his agency w^d be discontinued; we were about to sell the Estate in the Country where the purchasers are too apt to enter into combinations ag^t the seller. The times were unfavourable to selling Land in general, owing to the scarcity of money & the deadness of trade. These & numerous other inconveniences presented themselves & I was really very uneasy. Upon the return of Mr Green I was a little relieved. I found he was acting upon the most honorable principles, that he meant & expected that the Estate sh^d be sold; & he said he did not doubt but there w^d be purchasers for every Lot.

Aug 7th

On the Wednesday morning two Quakers took Mr Green to Langstones. Every person who called made me have better hopes. In the absence of

Mr Green I stepped up to Ross & called upon Mr Harvey; he was, in some degree, positive that we sh^d not only sell all the Lots but that we sh^d sell them well.

Ab^t 5 o'Clock in the afternoon Mr Young arrived. He came to Mr Green's & we spent 2 hours at least in comparing our sev^l papers & adopting the Plan we meant to pursue at the Sale. We put down upon a piece of Paper the lowest sum we meant to take for each lot, Timber included. The sum total amounted to £16,500. This paper was to be entrusted to some person who was to be appointed to buy in for Miss Atherton at those sev^l sums provided no person sh^d bid more. Who this confidential person was to be, we c^d not easily determine. Mr Green tho^t we fixed the valuation of each Lot very low. I tho^t so too; but our fixing them at that did not prevent people bidding more, & as our intention was to sell if possible it w^d have been folly to fix the buying in prices too high. Mr Young tho^t Mr Harvey w^d be a very proper person. This I c^d not come into for two reasons, first because Mr Harvey had told me that he was to bid for several lots for his clients, & second that as Mr Harvey had also told me he sh^d have no objection to purchase all the Estates together I tho^t if we did not succeed at the Sale, he w^d be a proper person to offer the whole lot to by private Contract; & then his being acquainted with our lowest values w^d be much against us. Mr Green s^d it was unnecessary to fix upon any person to buy in, he was very sure that every Lot w^d go for beyond our value, & that he himself w^d engage to give our value for every Lot. Here I asked Mr Green if he w^d engage that he & his friends would bid up as high as that value & take care that no Lot went below it. He said he might do that very safely & w^d do it. Then, says I, a very material point is gained in favour of the Sale. Mr Young may now assure the Company that the estate will be sold without reserve & that no buyer in was engaged on the part of the owner. This assertion I was very certain would give confidence to the company, & from what I had heard of the disposition of the People, I did not doubt its good effect. With this resolution we left Wilton Castle.

Aug 8th

At one o'Clock on Thursday we opened the Sale. And I never saw, on such an occasion so numerous & so respectable a Company. Mr Young opened the business by assuring them that our determination was to sell every Lot, & that no person was authorised to bid a single shilling for the owner. (It is to be observed that Mr Green was to be the real purchaser of every Lot he sh^d buy at our value).

Tis wonderful what effect this declaration had upon the Company. The Sale began at one o'Clock, it consisted of 14 Lots, & yet it was over at three o'Clock, & the Estate sold for £20,145. And when the last Lot was knocked down, the Company in general declared aloud, that they never saw a Sale conducted upon so open & liberal a Plan. And that in return for the complaisances paid by us to the Company, & for the candour & generosity of our declaration, they were glad we had succeeded so well. The good effect of our Plan was visible thro' the whole day. The Sale was gone thro' without any interruption; not a rude or uncivil expression was used by any of the company; the deposits of 10 per cent were paid upon every Lot without any hesitation; we had a very genteel Company to dine with us, and, in short, we experienced the treatment of Gentlemen rather than that of Surveyors & Auctioneers.

I cannot conclude the acc^t of the Sale without mentioning Mr Harvey with all possible respect. During my stay at Ross & thro' the whole of the Business, his behaviour was so much that of a man of business, a man of honour & a Gentleman, that I shall be very happy, if ever it shall be in my power to convince him how much I feel the obligation.

The Contracts were signed, the deposit money paid, & the Rec^t given, before 7 o'Clock. This put it in my power to leave Ross on the Friday morning, which I had not expected to do before Saturday or Sunday. Mr Young was going for Bristol in the morning, (Friday) on his way to Ireland; & finding I had a day or two to spare, offered me a Seat in the Chaise with him to Bristol, as he understood I had never been there. I immediately closed with the offer. I had been for a few days before the Sale a good deal fatigued both in body & mind, & I tho^t it w^d be an agreeable relaxation. I felt myself perfectly in humour for it, I was so pleased at the success of the sale; & I conceived myself perfectly disengaged from business, as I sh^d only be expected at Atherton on the Tuesday following, which I sh^d be able to accomplish, after going down to Bristol. We left Ross at eleven o'Clock & arrived at Gloucester (16 miles) a little before 2. We stopped here till ab^t 3, dined & took a Chaise for Newport (16 miles), at Newport we only changed Horses, & proceeded immediately for Bristol (at the White Lion, 18 miles) where we arrived between 7 & 8 o'Clock. We had a very pleasant journey; the good success of our business had left us in perfect good humour; we met with no accident or disappointment to interrupt it, & we enjoyed it to the full. Immediately on our arrival Mr Young ordered Supper, a plate of Turtle & Lobster, & some Veal Cutletts. We then went to secure our places in the Coaches for the following day.

I took a place in the Mail Coach for Birmingham, which was to set out at 7 o'Clock the following Evening; & Mr Young took his place for Milford Haven. I also took a place in a Coach to Bath to set out at 10 o'Clock next morning. We then sat down in the Coffee Room & amused ourselves with reading the Newspapers till supper was ready. I shall take the trouble of transcribing the Bill delivered to us for Supper

White Lion, Bristol		
Turtle	8s	6d
Veal Cutlett	2.	0
Lobster	2.	0
Potatoes		6
Bread & Cheese		6
Beer		6
Punch	2.	6
	16.	6

We left nothing of the above particulars, except ab^t half of the Veal Cutlett, so that the Quantity of each c^d not be very great.

I got up bet: 5 & 6 o'Clock next morning to see as much of Bristol as I possibly c^d. before I went off for Bath, for the Bath Coach only returned to Bristol at the very time the Birmingham Mail w^d be ready to set out. Bristol is an extensive City, & was improving very fast, till the present war put a stop to it. It is amuzing how many new Buildings there are in Bristol just covered in; & which have been in that state for upwards of 12 months without a single stroke of work being done at them since.

Bristol is a considerable way inland, & what Vessels come thither are obliged to come in & go out with the Tide, up the River Avon which runs thro' Bristol. The Docks are by no means capacious, but the Quays are very wide & commodious. Over the River Froom which falls into the Avon at Bristol, there is a Draw Bridge which leads to Clifton & the Hot-wells, & also to the Road to Wales. It is over this Bridge that one must go to the New Buildings before ment^d which are built upon the high lying grounds which overlook Bristol on this side. The situation of these Buildings is exceedingly beautiful; but in all probability very few of them will be inhabited by their original owners if things do not take a very sudden & unexpected turn. A great number of large Vessels were lying between the Draw-bridge & the mouth of the Froom, which forms a Dock for them. They Float when the Tide is in & aground when it is out.

There is a large handsome Bridge of 5 Arches over the Avon in the road
to Bath; there are Flags & Chains on each side for the safety of foot people. The Exchange is a large Building, similar in Plan to the Exchange in
London; the Streets in general are flagged & paved in the same manner
they are in London. There are several Glasshouses in Bristol. The Market
is very well supplied with Butcher's meat of excellent quality. The white-
ness of the Veal I could not help admiring, being uniformly so in every
Calf I saw. The Calves were all large, non weighing less, as I conjectured,
than 40lb per quar. The price of Flesh meat, both here & at Bath was the
same as in the Country.

Bristol is exceedingly well supplied with Vegetables. Tis astonishing to
see the quantities of all kinds of Garden-stuff produced in the Market;
there was also great abundance of Fruit of all sorts.

I had not an opportunity of seeing so much of Bristol as I cd wish.
From what I did see I was impressed with a very favourable idea of it.
And it has in my opinion every requisite for, & every appearance of a
place of very extensive & spirited Business.

Aug 10th
At 10 o'Clock I set out for Bath, where I arrived at 12, after a very agreeable ride. I was informed Dinner wd be ready at 2. I immediately set out
upon my Circuit. I was perfectly amazed at everything I saw. It is impossible to give an idea of Bath to a person who never saw it. The most common Streets are superior to anything I ever saw in London. The Houses
are all built of Free-stone which gives them a most grand appearance, particularly those lately erected, which is the case with the greatest part of
Bath, it having been above doubled in size within the last seven Years.
But here as at Bristol the war has put a stop to all Building. But there are
more men at work here than in Bristol, at finishing the Buildings already
erected, but most of them I believe are employed by Lord Pulteney, who
is building a Street which is supposed will be superior to any in the
known World. It is now I conceive not much less than a quarter of a mile
long & upwards of 20 Yds broad. All the houses are built of Free-stone,
they are all uniform & of the same height being 4 stories high besides the
Kitchens & Garretts. To get to these Buildings you pass over a Bridge
built over the Avon by Lord Pulteney whose Daur is Marchioness of
Bath. This Bridge is built in such a manner as not to be perceptible to a
stranger; it is exactly level with the Street, there are no Battlements but
Houses uniform with the rest, prevent you from seeing the River when
you are actually passing over it.

Noble as Pulteney Street may appear, the Royal Crescent in my idea has much more of Grandeur in it. Pulteney Street lies low. The Royal Crescent is an eminence, which commands a view of all the lower Town. But there is a new Crescent just finished which is elevated as high above the Royal Crescent, as the R. Crescent is above the rest of the Town. But why do I single out any particular Buildings? If I must particularize all that is worth of notice, I might write a Volume. Lansdown Crescent, the Queen's Square, St James's Square, the Circus, the North & South Parade, the new Pump Room, Marlborough Buildings & Laura Place, w^d all claim a preeminence. But they so far beggar all description that I must content myself with barely mentioning them. Vauxhall Gardens are not yet complete but they are in great forwardness. They are situated about a Mile from the middle of the Town upon the Banks of the Avon. I went to them thro' Pulteney Street & followed the River till I came to the Gardens. At the Gardens is a Ferry Boat, you ring a Bell & a man comes & takes you over directly. He demands six pence, for which he gives you a ticket & this ticket is a license for you to go to any part of the Gardens you please; & when you wish to return you deliver your Ticket at the Barr of the Coffee-house which is built in the Gardens & receive six penny worth of any kind of Liquor you choose. Here are handsome Colonades for drinking Tea in, a Bowling Green, Grass & Gravel Walks, Plantations, a Fishpond, a Wilderness laid out in a very curious manner. Seats upon the Banks of the River &c., &c. In short nothing is wanting to make these Gardens agreeable to the numerous Nobility & Gentry who visit Bath. There is also a large Music Room in the Gardens, but it is not yet finished. I was so taken up here that I forgot both the time of the day & the distance I was from my Inn, where when I arrived, the Coach had already been waiting for me near half an hour. I sprung in immediately & was soon carried out of the sight of the most beautiful place I ever saw.

I had delayed the Coach so long that I found it necessary to give the Driver a shilling to drive us at an extraordinary rate; & even with these exertions I was but just in time; five minutes w^d have lost me the Coach at Bristol. I left Bristol at 7 o'Clock on the Saturday Evening (Aug^st 9th) & passing thro' Newport, Gloucester, Tewksbury, & Bromsgrove, arrived at Birmingham at 9 o'Clock Sunday Morning. I was very much disappointed to find no Coach going for Manchester before 8 o'Clock at night. However I passed the day as well as I could, & amused myself with taking a view of the Town. The Stagnation of Trade, has put a stop to all improvements in Birmingham, as well as other places. I cannot say whether this place or Manchester may be larger, but I conceive that the Streets in general are wide & more commodious than in Manchester. There are several Canals (viz: the Shardlow, the Warwick & the Worcester). The Shardlow Navigation has a communication with the Staffordshire & thereby with Manchester. By the appearance of the newness of the Buildings, Birmingham must have increased immensely within a few Years last past.

I left Birmingham at 8 o'Clock on Sunday, passed thro' Wolverhampton, Stafford, Newcastle, & Wilmslow & arrived at Manchester by 11 o'Clock on the Monday morning; I got a Post-horse as soon as possible & got to Plat-fold without having met with any bad accident or suffered the least inconvenience.

Copy of a Letter Sent to Mr Jandrell on my Arrival Home

> Safe at home, thank my Stars, after travelling thro'
> Half the Kingdom in zigzag to get to see you.
> I've a mind a poetical Letter to send,
> To describe my long route, & amuse my old Friends,
> But my Muse, an odd Jade, now neglected so long
> Will not hear my her Prayers, or inspire my Song,
> Let me beg, let me pray, let me curse, let me swear,
> It signifies nothing she turns a deaf ear.
> But lend or lend not her poetical fire,
> I'll write I'm determined for you can inspire
> How I jog'd on my horse, how I sail'd in the boat
> How I rode in the Coach or how trudg'd it on foot,
> Till I came to Pontesbury tis needless to tell,
> Besides t'would my Letter too needlessly swell,
> At Pontesbury arrived, (Uh! that is the place
> That had fill'd my ideas for months, weeks & days),
> You see I next want to get to your Wife
> This may appear strange but tis true, on my life,
> And when seen I admired her & say what you will
> Be you pleased or displeased I'll admire her still
> But to you or your Wife to say much tis no matter
> For say what I will you will say I but flatter.
>
> To Westbury then we must post it away
> I mounted on Robin & you upon Grey.

We gallop'd, We cantered, We trotted & walk'd
As we variously rode we variously talk'd
Of a thousand old Frolicks the road to beguile
Which now, but to think of, can make me to smile.

At Westbury arrived, our old friends we did greet
Our greetings were short but good Ale made 'em sweet
From Westbury, good Lord, how we scampered away
Thro' thick & thro' thin & thro' mere dirt & clay
I thrashing on Robin, as if with a Flail
To keep within sight of your grey mare's white Tail.
But in vain, for you c^d not have gone faster scarce
If the De'el or the French had been close at your a—e.
From Westbury to Bromley's from Bromley's we come
To Pressot's from whence at midnight we get home.
But my Muse grows so tir'd & so short grows my time
I must finish in prose what I started in rhyme.
But just let me tell you before that I end
Whether prosing or rhyming I still am your Friend.

Hodgkinson's Second Journey to Pursue the Business of the Herefordshire Estates

1795 Jany. 25th
Left Atherton ab^t one o'Clock in a Post Chaise in Company with Mr
Richd Eccles & arrived at Manchester at 4. We drank Tea with
Mr Brettargh (a Nephew of Mr Eccles) & afterwards spent an hour with
Mr James Gordon, who is a joint Executor with me under the Will of Mr
David Cannon. We supped at the Lower Swan (Mr Dixon's) & got into
the Stage Coach for Birmingham ab^t half after nine. The following are the
Stages from Manchester to Gloucester viz

Name of the Places	Distances each	Time when we arrive at
to Wilmslow	13 Miles	12 o'Clock
Congleton	13 Do.	2 o'Clock 26th Jan
Newcastle	13 Do.	4 o'Clock
Stone	9 Do.	half past 7

Stafford	7 Do.	9 o'Clock
Four Ashes	10	11 o'Clock
Birmingham thro		
Wolverh.	20	2 o'Clock
Bromsgrove	13	7 o'Clock
Worcester	13	10 o'Clock
Tewkesbury	15	12 o'Clock
Gloucester	11	Morng 2 o'Clock
	137	

At Birmingham we took two places in the Bristol Mail which was to set out at 5 o'Clock. We had only time to dine before we got into the Coach. After travelling abt 9 miles a Gentleman, passing the Coach on Horseback called out to the Coachman to stop, for one of the fore-wheels was nearly off. The cry alarmed the passengers & we insisted on being let out. We found the axle-tree had given way; & a messenger was sent forward to Bromsgrove to prepare two Chaises against we came up to carry us on to Worcester. The Wheel was dangerous, & I wanted to walk to Bromsgrove, which was abt 2 miles off. The Coachman insisted that he cd drive us safe & that by walking we shd not get time enough for the Chaises. The rest of the Passengers being willing I acquiesced & we did get safe to Bromsgrove witht further accident. From thence we were carried in Chaises very expeditiously to Worcester where we got Supper. The Evening was very cold and uncomfortable raining & freezing at the same time. We arrived at the Bell Inn in Gloucester at a quarter past two in the morning. After waiting abt half an hour we were shewn to a very good Bed which we found acceedingly comfortable after the fatigues of our Journey. We lay till 9 o'Clock & getting up I ordered a Chaise to be got ready, while we breakfasted, to take us to Ross where we arrived at the Swan Inn abt one o'Clock.

After dinner we went down to Wilton Castle to Mr Green's whom we found in good health, as also Miss Green who was quite recovered from a late severe sickness.

Having sevl. questions to ask from Miss Clarke's Law Agent, we found upon enquiry of Mr Green that Mr Phillips of Monmouth was the person. As he was Solicitor for 3 Lots in the present Sale, & two other Solicitors also lived at Monmouth we determined to go thither the following day.

28th
Left Ross abt 9 o'Clock in the morning in a Post Chaise & arrived at

Monmouth a little before 11. We put up at the King's Head, where we
met with very good entertainment. We waited upon each of the persons
we wanted to see & very luckily found them all at home. Particulars
which occurred with each Solicitor will be mentioned hereafter. We had
completed our Business at ab^t 5 o'Clock & in half an hour afterwards left
Monmouth. The Evening was very fine & clear & the new Moon made
the River and Hills very beautiful. We got out of the Chaise at Wilton &
went to the Castle where we drank tea with Mr Green.

29th

Thursday being the Market-day at Ross we stayed in the house all day
supposing that we might be called upon by some of the Purchasers or
Solicitors. Mr Thos Phillips of Monmouth had also promised to come
over, & go with me to Miss Clarke's of the Hill whose Father purchased
the Walford Estates from Mr Gwillym in the year 1750, to search for the
Marriage Settlement of Mr Gwillym with Miss Atherton bearing the date
the 19th and 20th Oct. 1738, but he disappointed me.

In the evening I went for Mr Jones, the Banker, & Mr Harvey to take
supper with us, they came & we spent a very agreeable evening.

30th

On the Friday morning we went to Langstone after Breakfast, Mr Jones
accompanied us with his Gun; but we saw no game. The morning being
frosty, we had a very pleasant walk over the fields. We called upon old Mr
Cope whom we found but in an indifferent state of Health. We made
ourselves acquainted with several particulars, which we had come about,
at Langstone; From thence we went to the Trecella Farm to inquire ab^t a
Field called 'the Meadow at Garden Bridge' which was not to be found in
Mr Smith's Plans; the reason of which omission will be explained hereafter in my remarks about Lot 2nd. It is a field lying up to the back part of
the house, & extends along the lane side as far as the bridge below the
Church. From Trecella we went by Whitfield and called upon Parson
Jones, the Purchaser of Langstone.

Divinity is most shamefully disgraced in Mr Jones. His appearance is
that of a Drover or Butcher. His wife who is now living was a Mrs
Edwards, a Widow, with who he & his Brother boarded. In consequence
of an Agreement bet. Mr Jones & her Servant Maid she was kept in a state
of intoxication for sev^l days, in which condition he married her, & it is
reported in the Village where they then lived that when she came to herself she did not know which of the Brothers she had married. She has an

annuity of £200 a year which drops when she dies. The servant above ment. continued to live with them after they were married. In consequence of a connection between Mr Jones & her, she was sent four times into Wales to lie in. He has also a Daur. a fine Girl abt 14 years of age whom I saw at his house, which he had by a Sister of the Servant's. Not long ago he advertised for Boarders in the News Paper in consequence of which advertisement four boys came soon after to reside with him, & are now in his house which are all well known to be the fruits of the connection between him and his Servant.

We returned, after a very pleasant walk to Wilton Castle where we were engaged to dine. Miss Green had provided us a very handsome Dinner, & we spent an exceedingly agreeable evening. Immediately after Tea we came to our Lodgings & sat up till 11 o'Clock examining and arranging our papers.

31st Saturday

Mr Green came to our Lodging in the Morning, dined with us, & stopped most of the day. We had engaged him to come up to assist us in fixing & ascertaining the description of the Premises mentioned in the several Lots, & to inform us of the Boundary Lands adjoing each Estate. With respect to ascertaining the particulars Mr Green could not materially assist us, the names of the owners of the adjoining Land he principally knew. Mr Green left us about 3 o'Clock and we spent the remainder of the Evening as usual, in fruitless attempts to make the Abstracts & the particulars agree.

Feby. 1st Sunday

Wrote to Mr Rawstorne. Also wrote a Letter to Mr Phillips of Monmouth which I sent by special Messenger. I desired him as I wished much to see Miss Clarke's purchase Deeds of the Walford's Estate to send a clerk over, if he could not conveniently come himself the following day. He wrote for ansr. that he shd certainly be at Miss Clarke's the following day & wd call upon me.

Went to Church, & heard a very good Sermon, upon the following Words, 'Let me die the death of the righteous & let my last end be like his.'

Today we dined & drank Tea with Mr Jones the Banker, who entertained us very handsomely. Mr Jones is an intelligent, smart, spirited man. His conversation upon Agriculture, Trade & Politics is sensible & solid, & his behaviour is highly pleasing & agreeable. He is Brother to the Mr

Jones who rents the Dadney Farm. Mr Jones, after Tea, took us to the
News Room, where all Strangers are permitted to go. We found very little Company there.

Feb 2nd Monday morning.
I left Ross between 6 & 7 o'Clock, & walked to Langstone. I breakfasted
with Mr Evans, and after breakfast called upon Mr Cope to inquire if he
knew whether there were any Box or Drawers in the house containg
papers & Writings. He took me up stairs & opened a Drawer in a Chest of
Drawers which he said belonged to the Atherton Family, in which I
found a quantity of old Parchments & Papers, few of them bearing date
later than the year 1700, & most of them relating to the Walford Estate
which were sold so long ago as the year 1750. I brought a few old Leases
&c. back with me to Ross. From Langstone I went with Mr Evans over
the Public-house Farm & there discovered an error in the Plan which will
be mentioned hereafter in my remarks upon that Lot. We then went up
to Mr Walter Green at Hebrage ab^t 2 miles farther to enquire if he had
any Writings relating to the Estate in his posession; & found he had none
except one Act of Parliament which he gave me. I here was much divert-
ed at seeing a dog turn the Spit, a thing which I had never before seen. I
stopped ab^t half an hour, & we returned to Langstone, where I just sat
down, while I called over to Mr Evans, the Premises contained in the first
Lot, and then I came on to Wilton Castle where I arrived ab^t 3 o'Clock,
after walking near 14 miles. It was very bad travelling, the roads being a
complete Sheet of Ice, particularly the foot-paths in the Fields which
made it dangerous walking, as the Road I went was very much up and
down hill.

   After arranging our Papers a little & making our Memorandums, we
spent the Evening & supped with Mr Harvey, & returned to our Inn ab^t
10 o'Clock. Mr Harvey had been to see his Uncle Mr Mynd the
Purchaser of the Dadney Farm who he said sent his compliments to us
saying that he expected to pay his money when bo^t. the Estate, alluding to
our having hinted that it w^d be most agreeable to us to have the money
paid in London.

Feby 3rd Tuesday
Breakfasted at our Inn. After Breakfast went down to Mr Harvey's office &
delivered him a Copy of the Court-Roll of Chief Rents payable to the owner
of Langstone Estate amounting to £1 17s 3d annually, being the exact sum
collected by Mr Green. He himself exam^d the Copy along with me.

After returning from Mr Harvey & coming to our Inn ab^t 11 o'Clock a Servant from Mrs Clarke's of the Hill near Ross, the owner of the Walford Estate bro^t a Letter from Mr Phillips, atty, of which the following is a copy,

'Sir, I believe you know that Mrs Clarke is not to be seen at an early hour which prevented my coming on to you last night. Mrs Clarke says that the Deed* is in her possession which you enquire after and that Miss Gwillym had Copy of it some time ago. I am Sir, Yr Hble Servant, Thos Phillips.'

At Dinner I could not help observing to Mr Eccles that I tho^t Mr Harvey had acted very much upon the reserve with respect to the Business we had come about, every time we had been in his Company. Mr Eccles was of the same opinion. We had determined to leave Ross the following day & I began to consider that it w^d be worth while to make a Friend of Mr Harvey. In short I found it necessary to give him a Fee. I went down to him immediately and ment. the Letter I had rec^d from Phillips adding that as we had so many Deeds to get copied perhaps we sh^d find it advisable to apply to Mr Phillips to furnish us with Copies of the Deed of Settlement at Miss Clarke's, & I understood he was a little dilatory in business. I sh^d be much obliged to Mr Harvey if he w^d push him on & as I could not desire him to have any trouble on Miss Atherton's Acc^t without being paid I desired his acceptance of five Guineas, & added that perhaps we sh^d be under the necessity of troubling him further in the Business. He said that he did not see how we c^d well finish the business without employg some Attorney in the neighbourhood & that he w^d assist us in anything we wanted done. And that if we would drop him a line authorising him to apply to Mr Phillips for one Copy of the Deed he w^d take care that the rest of the Copies wanted sh^d be ready in time. I also found from his conversation that he had some expectation of being engaged in the business & hence I conjecture his reserve originated upon finding a Clerk sent out of Lancashire.

After returning from Mr Harvey's I went down to Mr Green's to take an Acc^t of Rent & Arrears of Rent due from the sev^l Tenants; after which I rec^d from him £200 in Bills & Cash on Acc^t of Rents. I stopped to drink Tea at the Castle & returned to Ross ab^t 7 o'Clock. We supped at our Inn. After Supper I settled the Bill of our Expences at the Inn & ordered a Chaise to be ready at 8 o'Clock in the morning to take us to Gloucester.

*The deed he alludes to is the deed of settlement of 19 and 20 Oct 1738 upon the marriage of Rt. Gwillym the younger with Elis. Atherton & delivered to Mr Clarke in the year 1750 with his Title Deeds of the Walford Estates.

Feby 4th Wednesday.

Left Ross ab^t half past eight & arrived at the Bell in Gloucester at 11. I purposed pass^g thro' Tewksbury to Worcester but Mr Heath recommended us to go thro' Upton as being much the better road. We took his advice & ordering a Chaise came on immediately. We arrived at Upton (16 miles from Gloucester) ab^t 2 o'Clock & ordering a Chaise there we came on directly to Worcester where we arrived a little before 4.

We drove to the Hop-Pole where we dined & waited till the Bath Coach arrived at 6 o'Clock in which we came on to Birmingham were we arrived ab^t half after 11. The Coach came on but very slowly owing to the depth of Snow upon the Road. We were set down at the Castle Inn where I expected a Coach w^d set off at 4 o'Clock in the morning, but was very much disappointed to find that that Coach had stopped running & that we c^d not leave Birmingham before 10 o'Clock the follow^g night.

5th Thursday.

After Breakfast we took a walk around the greatest part of the Town. Returned to Dinner. After Dinner we took another Walk & spent the rem^r of the Evening in writing these memorandums.

At 10 o'Clock we got into the Coach for Manchester. The Frost this Night, I think, was the sharpest I ever remember. We passed thro' the same Towns we had done in going to Birmingham the week before, & arrived at Manchester ab^t half past 3 o'Clock the following day. I ordered Dinner immediately & a Chaise to be ready as soon as Dinner was over. We left Manch^r ab^t 5 o'Clock & got safe home ab^t 7.

Expenses of Richard Hodgkinson

1795. Jany 24th – Set out from Home to Herefordshire

	£	s	d
1795 Jany 25th took cash of Miss Atherton's	14.	15.	6
Feb 3rd Rec^d of Mr Green – Bills	190.	10.	0
do. Cash	9.	10.	0
Expences	27.	1.	6
Brought home	187.	14.	0
Jany 24th			
Chaise hire to Man	1.	2.	6
Post boy		2.	6
Turnpikes		1.	0

Fare to Birmingham (self & Mr Eccles)	2. 2.	0
Supper & Liquor	3.	0
Waiter		6

26th

Coachman at Newcastle	2.	0
Expences at Do.		9
Do. at the Swan Inn, Stafford	2.	4
Coachman at Birmingham	2.	6
Dinner at Do.	5.	0
Fare in the Mail to Gloucester (52 miles)	2. 2.	0
Expences at Bromsgrove		3
Supper Liquor & Waiter at Worcester	4.	0
Coachman at Tewksbury	2.	0
Do. & Guard at Gloucester	3.	0

27th

Breakfast at do.	2.	4
Chambermaid	1.	0
Chaise to Ross	16.	0
Turnpikes	1.	9
Post boy	2.	6
Papers	1.	0

28th

Turnpikes to Monmouth	1.	6
Expences at Monmouth	7.	6
Post boy	2.	6

31st

Washing	1.	6

Feby 1st

Messenger to Monmouth	3.	6

3rd

Fee to Mr Harvey	5. 5.	0
Premium to Mr Jones for a Bill	1.	6

4th

Bill at the Swan Inn, Ross	5. 4.	6
Turnpikes from Ross	1.	9
Postboy from Ross	2.	6
Expences at Gloucester	1.	6
Chaise from Do. to Upton	16.	0
Turnpikes do.	1.	6
Postboy	2.	6

Expences at Upton	2.	0
Chaise from Do. to Worcester	10.	0
Turnpikes	1.	0
Post boy	2.	0
Coach-fare from Worcester to Birmingham	18.	0
Expences at Worcester	5.	0

5th Feb

Coach fare from Birmingham to Manchester	2.	2.	0
Bill at Birmingham		14.	2
Chambermaid		1.	0
Waiter		1.	0

6th

Breakfast at Newcastle	2.	0
Coachman at do.	2.	0
Expences at Wilmslow	1.	0
Coachman at Manchester	2.	0
Dinner at Manchester & Ale	3.	8
Chaise to Leigh	17.	6
Turnpikes	1.	6
Postboy	2.	6

Took cash of my own	4.	5.	6
Expended		13.	6

1795 Jany 27th

1lb of Hair powder	1.	0
Pot of pomatum		6

Feby.

Pd. for a stand for dry toast	10.	6
do. for a ladle for brown sugar	1.	6
Total	13.	6

Distances from	**Miles**
Manchester to Wilmslow	13
Wilmslow to Congleton	13
Congleton to Newcastle	13
Newcastle to Stone	9
Stone to Stafford	7

Stafford to Four Ashes	10
Four Ashes to Birmingham	
thro' Wolverhampton	20
Birmingham to Bromsgrove	13
Bromsgrove to Worcester	13
Worcester to Tewkesbury	15
Tewkesbury to Glocester	11
	——
	137

Hodgkinson's Third Visit to Ross and his Tour of the Sights of the Wye Valley

Memorandum of a Journey from Atherton to Ross in Herefordshire with an acc^t of an excursion to Chepstow & a description of Persfield in Monmouthshire,   by Rd. Hodgkinson.

August 20th, 1795

Left Atherton about 4 o'Clock on a journey into Herefordshire to prevail upon some of the Purchasers of Miss Atherton's Estates there to get on with their Conveyances, who seem to be unwilling to complete their Purchases. I supped at Manchester & got into the Birmingham coach at 10 o'Clock, passed thro' Wilmslow & Congleton & got to Newcastle ab^t 6 in the morning. We dined at Wolverhampton & arrived at Birmingham a little after 5. The Bristol Mail had been gone about half an hour, & a return Chaise standing at the Inn ready to set out for Bromsgrove which is 12 miles from Birmingham. I engaged it & arrived at Bromsgrove a little before 9. From 6 o'Clock this Morning to 4 in the Evening, there was very much Rain. The Harvest is very backward. I do not remember to have seen a whole Field of Corn cut between Newcastle & Bromsgrove. The Corn in general looks very well.

22nd

I got up a little after 5 o'Clock to see if I could get a place to Worcester in the Coach from Birmingham to Bristol. It came up ab^t 6. I found room in it & arrived at Worcester at 8. The Harvest, between Bromsgrove &

Worcester was generally begun & 3 Fields, & only 3 I think, I saw cleared of the Corn. This day being Saturday a Coach from London to Hereford was to pass thro' Worcester, & I was told w^d come in ab^t 10 o'Clock & leave at 12. I breakfasted at Worcester with a Gentleman who was in the Coach when I got in at Bromsgrove, who told me during Breakfast, that the day before he had been in Company with an American Captain who was just come from Brest, who informed him that he had seen 18 Vessels laden with Corn, 15 of which belonged to Liverpool, come into Brest-water & deliver their cargoes to the French, for which they were paid in French Crowns & then departed. I left Worcester in the London & Hereford Mail ab^t half after 12 & arrived at Ledbury ab^t 4 where I dined & then took a Chaise to Ross which is 13 miles off & got to Wilton Castle about 7.

The day was very fine & I was much delighted to find all the way a very plentiful Harvest generally begun & in the Neighbourhood of Ross a few fields were cleared.

23rd
Being Sunday Mr Green and I went to Church both Morning and Evening. After service I wrote a letter to my Wife and another to Mr John Gorst. I called at Mr Harvey's but was informed he was gone to London & that he is expected at home on the Morrow.

August 24th
Mr Green, being so kind as to lend me his Horse, I set out at ab^t 11 o'Clock & went to Langston to spend the day amongst the Reapers. I found Mr Evans very forward with his Harvest, having housed about one half of both his Wheat and Barley. His reaping is done by Welchmen who annually come up for that purpose. He finds them Victuals & Drink and gives them 14s per Cover for Reaping, 3 of which Covers make two Statute Acres.

Mr Evans informs me that the greatest part of his Purchase-money is already paid into the Hands of his Solicitor, Mr Phillips, & that he has desired him to lose no time in completing the Purchase as soon as Miss Atherton is ready. I went all thro' the House and found it very much out of repair. The Hall is entirely uninhabited, old Mr Cope who lived in it being dead since I was last there.

Mr Cope's Executors had made a Sale of his Household Furniture a few weeks before. And the House was stripped of every thing, except here & there a piece of old lumber not worth carrying away & particularly a pair of Bedsteads with Head & Tester (but no hangings) which bore the marks of ancient Grandure & State, but now were covered with Cob-

webs & Dust. This Bed, I was informed, was for the sole purpose of laying out the Corpses of such of the Family as died, when Langstone was
the residence of the Gwillym Family. This idea, I confess gave a gloomy
cast to my reflections, & I c^d not help thinking that if Miss Atherton was
with me, it w^d furnish her with a good moral Lesson.

A few years ago this gloomy deserted place was the residence of gaiety
and splendor. The ornaments upon the dusty walls & tops of the Rooms,
with the heavy Cornishes, shew that taste and fashion once resided here.
The spacious Hall & Parlour tell us that many a joyous Feast has here been
held. That many a Bottle, & many a Cask of native Cyder, has here have
been quaffed, while, doubtless, Wit & Humour passed around. The jolly
Farmer, here, no doubt, has many a time well drench'd his skin, & pleased
that his Esqr has deigned to make him drunk, gone reeling home, &
envied not the Courtier of his Prince's smile.

The stately Palisades & lofty Iron Gates are now grown over with rust,
& the Garden Wall is mouldering to the Ground. Here, dismal as it now
appears, was the residence of a worthy Family, honoured & respected by
all who knew them, the boast of their Friends, and the pride of
Langstone. Miss Atherton might reflect that from this Family she descended by no distant line, this house having been the Seat of her Grandfather
even after he was married, she might see to what herself must come, that
she like her Ancestor must ere long sink into the Grave & by degrees into
Oblivion too. And that her House, which now seems to bid defiance to
time, will like this become deserted and only be admired for its massy
ruins, & gloomy appearance.

The Clock, upon the top of the Dove-house, here, struck five. Its
sound thro' the empty Hall seemed like the knell of some departing Spirit.
I stopt, and tho't it bid to remember that time, not to be recalled, is continually passing on, & not to forget, in reflecting for Miss Atherton, to
reflect for myself.

I returned to Wilton about 7 o'Clock after having spent a day as agreeably as any I ever passed in Herefordshire. The day was warm & pleasant,
but not much sunshine.

25th
After Breakfast I went up to Ross to inquire for Mr Harvey, & was sorry
to find him not returned, as I was anxious to see him before I went to
Monmouth. I then called upon Mr Jones the Grocer & accompanied
him to his farm ab^t half a mile off. We there spent the forenoon among
his Reapers. Upon our return to Ross he took me up into the Town Hall

which he has filled with Sheeps' Wool in which he deals very largely. He informs me that the Wool of Herefordshire Sheep is as fine as any in the Kingdom. The prices at present are from 24 shillings to 28 shillings per Stone of 12 $^1/_2$ lbs. It is sorted into 5 or 6 kinds of different qualities, the best of which bears a high price. He shewed me one Lot which he expects to sell for £36 per Pack of 12 score. Mr Jones is likewise concerned for the Gloucester Bank & he informed me there were lodged in their Bank ab^t £6,000 on Mr Jones's Account & ab^t £1,100 on Mr Myndes' acct tow^{ds} their purchase money for Miss Atherton's estates.

In the evening I walked as far as the Hill, the seat of Miss Clarke. In my return I called at Mr Harvey's who I found was not yet returned.

26th

I spent chiefly in walking about the diff Farms in the neighbourhood to observe the Reapers & the Harvest. In the afternoon I went to Mr Jones' the Grocer's, Farm; I returned with him to drink Tea at his house. In the Street we met with Mr Harvey who was just arrived & in search of me. I was much disappointed to find that Mr Harvey had no later Acc^{ts} respecting his Drafts passing before Miss Atherton than I had before I left home. He has be 10 days from London having been at Southampton, Portsmouth & Spithead upon a visit to his Brother who is in the Navy.

27th

About 10 o'Clock this morning I set out from Wilton upon Horse-back to go to Monmouth to wait upon the different Solicitors there. After a most agreeable ride, the morning being very fine, I arrived at Monmouth ab^t 12 o'Clock. I found that all the persons that I wanted to see were out of Town & w^d not return before night.

Having dined at Monmouth about 3 o'Clock, I set out for Chepstow which is ab^t 15 miles hence, & like Monmouth is situated upon the Wye. As the road is generally upon the ascent till you come within ab^t 5 miles of Chepstow there are no very striking views direct before you except the very large & extensive Woods belonging to the Duke of Beaufort which you pass close to in descending to Chepstow, a stone Wall inclosing the Woods for a long way adjoining the Turnpike road. After you have ascended the Hill from Monmouth, which is done in travelling two miles, the road for sev^l Miles is carried upon the summit of the highest ground in the neighbourhood, & on either hand is a most delightful Valley; that on the left is narrow & bounded by barren Hills at no great distance beyond which runs the Wye, but that on the right is amazingly extensive, & cultivated as far as the eye can discern, except here & there a large Mountain which rises out of this Valley, & by its' height and steepness seems to be beyond the art of improvement. The Hills which bound the view on this side are at such a distance as not to be discernable what state they are in. After we ascend the Hill, beyond the Duke of Beaufort's Woods, the Descent to Chepstow is almost without interruption. The River Severn & its' shore on the Gloucestershire side are full in view all the way you descend. I arrived at Chepstow ab^t 7 o'Clock, I put up at the George Inn but I understand the Beaufort Arms is the best Inn.

I walked out immediately upon my arrival, & pursuing my walk down the first street I got into the Church Yard, crossing the Church Yard between two beautiful Rows of Trees planted diagonally across the Church Yard, I was led into a narrow Passage which brought me to the Quay. The first object I perceived was a large new Vessel in building, nearly finished. She was bored for 20 Guns. Coming down to the Bank of the River I perceived I was very near the Bridge, which crosses the Wye into Gloucestershire. I passed over the Gates which excluded the Water from the Dock where the Vessel is in building, & in a few minutes came to the Bridge.

The Bridge is built of wood & covered with Planks, like swivel Bridges over Canals. In the middle of the River is a very large stone Pier, on one side of which is a small house, which has the appearance of hav^g formerly been a Toll-house which I understand it was some years ago. From this Centre Pier to the Gloucester Shore the Bridge is supported by the County of Gloucester, & from the same Pier to the Monmouth Shore it is supported by the County of Monmouth. On the Monmouth side, the Piers are built of Stone, but all the rest is wood, on the Gloucester side it is entirely of wood & supported by Wood. On each shore there is a projection of stone extending into the River ab^t 20 Yards. The Centre Pier is about 9 Yards over & this is paved. From the Pavem^t on each side to the Stone Projection is ab^t 60 Yards. So that the whole length of the Bridge is ab^t 169 Yards (viz:)

	Yds
Stone Projection on Monmouth side	20
Do – on Gloucester side	20
Planked on the Monmouth side	60
Do on the Gloucester side	60
Centre Pier	9
	169

I had been told that this Bridge is 70 Feet above the surface of the Water & that the Tide rises here 40 Feet. The current of Water descending was strong & muddy & deep Banks of mud appeared on each side, left wet from the reflux of the Tide. I was astonished to find that I c^d not calculate the surface of the water in its then state to be above 30 Feet or 35 Feet at most below the Bridge & to conceive it to sink 40 Feet lower still was impossible. In going from the Bridge down again upon the Quays I observed a Piece of Timber fixed upright against the wall, at the mouth of the Dock before mentioned, numbered with feet to ascertain the height of the Tide, & from bottom to top it had only 19 Feet marked upon it. This confirmed me in my opinion that my calculation at the Bridge was sufficiently high. In walking along the River-side however I asked sev^l persons respecting the height of the Bridge & the rising of the Tide who invariably said that the Bridge is 70 Feet high and the Tide rises 40 Feet. It is however, to me, an unaccountable thing, for if the water ever sinks 40 or 30 feet below what I saw it I am very much deceived, & still it is very surprising that everyone I asked the question of sh^d give the same ans^r unless we may suppose that this particular height of the Bridge & rising of the Tide has been given out for some length of time & is now taken for granted without examination & indeed it gives some colour to this supposition, when we consider that everyone's ans^r was exactly the same.

I intended to walk down to the conflux of the Wye with the Severn. But ab^t half a mile below the Town the River seems to have washed its way thro' the vast Rocks, which hang over it on the left hand side as I came down, & by these means the Rocks are here on the right. The foot of these Rocks is washed by the River, so that I c^d proceed no further this way. It now drawing dark, I returned to my Inn to Supper.

28th

I arose early in the morning. I ordered my horse to be saddled to go as far as the old Passage over the Severn at Beachley to Aust on the opposite Shore. I passed over the wooden Bridge which neither I nor my horse was very fond of. I reached Beachley ab^t 7 o'Clock hav^g put up my horse, I went into the House, and ordering a Glass of Wine and Water & a Biscuit I was shewn into a very handsome Parlour, whose large bow-window seems to hang over the water & commands a fine view of the opposite Country, & a vast tract of the River, with its high red Cliff on the opposite Shore. The water is, as I am told, about 3 miles over here. After enjoying this scene ab^t a quarter of an hour I walked down the Beach to the conflux of the Wye with the Severn. This scene is very striking & the more so when we recollect, that these two Rivers rise out of the same Hill (viz:) Plimlimmon in Montgomeryshire & within a quarter of a Mile of each other. From this point, are seen, Vessels riding in King-road & besides many nearer objects, the beauty of the view is increased by distant prospects of stupendous Hills on the Welch Coast. I was sorry my engagem^t w^d not permit me to stay longer here. If you except the grand view of the Water, the ride from Beachley to Chepstow is more agreeable than from Chepstow to Beachley.

Chepstow is situated on a sweet declivity, but rather steep. Most of the way from Beachley you have a full view of it & from the nature of the ground on which it stands, every house in it may be seen at once, one rising above another & as all the Houses are white & covered with red tile, it gives the whole a beautiful & picturesque appearance. At the bottom of the Town & near the Bridge stands the famous old Castle. The new House at Persfield stands directly in view & being situated upon an eminence is seldom lost sight of.

About 10 o'Clock I returned to the Inn, I breakfasted & then walked down to the Castle which is boldly placed upon a huge Rock washed by the Wye; the whole looks of lasting solidity, & is made beautifully picturesque by the numberless evergreens that hang ab^t its Walls, & the same Ivy which entwines the Rock, entwines the Walls. Its Area is said to occupy five Acres of Ground. It consists of three Courts: the second is converted into a Kitchen Garden, the uppermost is entirely neglected & over-run with Weeds, the lowest lies open & serves as a Court to that part of the Castle which is inhabited.

The Chapel, which stands at the upper part of the second Court is very large, I conceive not less than 100 feet long, & was once very much ornamental, it was three stories high as appears from the holes for the Floor-Beams. In the wall which faces you upon coming out of the Chapel there are sev^l. large holes in which I suppose the Guns were fixed and from whence you look down upon the River, washing the foot of the Rock, upon the extremity of which this Wall is built, & from whence likewise you have a beautiful prospect of the Bridge on the right hand, & of the Park & House at Persfield on the left. One of the large Towers in the lower Court upon the left hand as you enter is in tolerable repair, in which after ascending 18 steps I was shewn into the Room where Henry Marten, one of the Judges who sat to condemn Charles 1st was afterw^{ds} confined 27 Years & then died there. After ascending 56 steps more, I came upon the leads from whence I had an extensive & fine view. I was then taken to the other side of the Court, where I was shewn what was formerly the Kitchen, the Butler's Pantry &c., &c., & amongst the rest of the Cellar, which is a lofty room, arched & having a Door opening to the River, which is at least 40 feet below, from whence Casks might be drawn up out of the Boats & taken in here.

The Castle belongs to the Duke of Beaufort but it has been many years under a lease of lives, & an old woman, upwards of 80, who I saw as I passed thro' the habitable part of it, is the last, she was born here, where she still resides in comfortable apartments & makes a good subsistence by the fruits of the Garden Peaches &c., which are plentiful on these warm Walls when other places fail & I sh^d suppose the gifts she receives from people who come to view the Castle must considerably increase her income.

Returning from the Castle I lost no time in mounting my Horse and proceeding to Persfield.

Persfield was the paternal estate of Mr Valentine Morris, to whom it is much indebted for its' present decoration, but from a liberality too great for his circumstances, he was doom'd to make atonement by a long confinem^t in the Kings' Bench. It was then sold to a Mr Smith, who after being in possession of it ab^t 9 Years was obliged to assign it over for the Benefit of his Creditors owing to an imprudent connection in the Banking line with a man in Chepstow. It is now in the possession of a Colonel Wood who purchased it ab^t 12 months ago from Mr Smith's Assignees.

The walks are now open for Strangers only 2 days in the week & lucky for me Friday was one. I rode to St. Arvans, a small Village at the farthest corner of the Park from Chepstow where I left my horse. I walked up the foot path thro' the Park to the house which is more than half a mile. The old House is taken down & a new one is in building, the shell of which is only completed. I here met with the Gardener & we began our perambulation. We first stopped at the large Beach-tree, which commands a landscape too beautiful for pencil to paint. Immediately under your feet is a vast rock, totally covered with a shrubby underwood, the foot of which is washed by the Wye. Beneath is a Valley consisting of a complete Farm, but at such a depth that every object is diminished & appears in miniature. It is a peninsula almost surrounded by the River & what makes the whole picture perfect is its' being entirely surrounded by vast rocks & precipices, covered with thick wood down to the very waters edge. Pursuing the walk we arrived at a Bench, which commands a most delicious view; on the left you look down upon the valley with the River winding many hundred feet 500 (I am told) beneath, the whole surrounded by the vast amphitheatre of wooded rocks; & to the right full upon the Town of Chepstow; beyond it the Severn's windings & a prodigious prospect bounding the whole. We next came to the Grotto, a point of view exquisitely beautiful; it is a small cave in the Rock stuck with stones of various kinds.

From hence we returned to the Beach Tree already men[t]. & proceeding thro' a winding walk cut out of the Rock we came to an extremely romantic Cave, hollowed out of the Rock, at the mouth of which some swivel guns were formerly placed, but are at present removed. Advancing thro' the Cave, by a passage cut thro' the Rock, a little further we meet with an[r]. Bench inclosed with iron Rails, called the Lovers' Leap, on the point of the Rock which is nearly pendent over the River, & may be truly called a situation full of the terrible sublime. You look immediately down upon a vast hollow of Wood, all surrounded by woody precipices, & tow[ds]. the right is seen the winding River. Having taken a final view of the scenery from this tremendous Precipice, I was conducted to the corner of the adjacent Field, where formerly stood the Temple, commanding a most glorious prospect in an opposite direction; the conflux of the Wye & Severn & the Bristol Channel opening into the main Sea.

I here presented my Guide with a present of half a Crown & dismissed him.

About a mile beyond these Walks is a very romantic Cliff, called the Wind-Cliff which I was determined to Climbe. The ascent on the back of the Hill is not steep, carriages easily ascend, one with 3 Ladies in came up while I was there.

The Wind-Cliff is an eminence above the rest & commanding the whole in one view. The Wye runs at the foot of the Hill; the Peninsula lies just below; the deep bosom of the semicircular hanging Wood is full in sight; over part of it the great Rock appears; all its base & all its accompaniments are seen; the Country immediately beyond is full of lovely Hillocks; & the higher Grounds of Somerset & Gloucester rise in the Horizon. The Severn, seems as it really is above Chepstow, three or four miles wide, & below the Town it spreads almost to a Sea. This comprehends almost all the Scenes at Persfield.

It was now two o'Clock, & I was under an engagem[t] to be at Monmouth at 5. I was therefore obliged reluctantly to leave this rich prospect after but a short enjoym[t] of it.

I could not help remarking from this place, as I did from every view at Persfield, what a prodigious Improvm[t] it w[d] be to all the Scenes there, if the River was not within the reach of the Tide. But here the Tide rises to a vast height, & the water is excessive muddy; & at low Water, a large deep muddy Bank appears on each side, which has a very disagreeable aspect. And this renders the unexampled scenes at Persfield, liable to the same humiliating reflection as all other sublunary things are, that they are not perfect.

I arrived at Monmouth ab^t 5 o'Clock, & without delay waited upon Messrs Bourn & Williams. Mr Williams s^d their Df^t had been 9 weeks before Mr Gwillym their Counsel in London & tho' they had repeatedly written for it they had only rec^d it a few days ago. He s^d Mr Gwillym had made some objections to the Title, but as the other Purchasers took to their Purchases they w^d accept the Title likewise. He further added that he had heard some alterations were to be made in the Draft, but as he did not know what they were he sh^d leave them to be done by Mr Atherton. Their purchase money they c^d pay by a Draft at sight in London any day on receiving instructions for that purpose. And the Draft of their Conveyance sh^d be sent to Mr Davies on Monday next.

I then waited upon Mr Stokes, Solicitor, of the 14th Lot. Mr Stokes alleges that the Titles of the other Purchasers may be very good & yet his Client's Title may at the same time be very objectionable, as the Est. is not in Mortgage, like the rest & therefore his Client cannot be secured by the rec^t of the Mortgagees. That the Fee is in Lord Foley, & that Mr Atherton in a conversation he had with him made it plainly appear that Lord Foley c^d not at present sign. However, he said, if his Draft (which he insisted upon my bringing with me) c^d be any way altered so as to be approved by Mr Atherton, he w^d accept of it, & the Conveyance sh^d be engrossed in five days after he rec^d the Draft back & that the Purchase money c^d likewise be p^d. at any time.

Mr Phillips not being yet returned I was obliged to stop again all night.

Aug 29th
At nine o'Clock I met with him. He told me he meant to go hand in hand with Mr Harvey & Mr Hill & whenever they completed he w^d do the same & that he intended no affront to Messrs Taylor & Gorst in not writing to them, thinking that it was understood, that whatever was communicated to Mr Hill or Mr Harvey was the same as communicated to himself, as was the case.

He said likewise that a few days ago he had seen Mr Lechmere to whom he had promised his Draft, & upon asking him whether he tho^t my going to Hereford to wait upon Mr Lechmere w^d be of any use he ans^d by no means for Mr Lechmere ^{wd} be ready at the same time as himself. 'But,' added he, 'I understand some of the Purchasers do not mean to complete immediately. Mr Hill whom I saw last week, told me that as the second half year was now broke into, he sh^d not think of completing his Purchase until after Christmas, and by that time all the Solicitors might be ready at once to tender the Deeds for signing & the money for their Purchase which he tho^t w^d be most convenient for Miss Atherton, as part of the money without the whole c^d be of little service & thus the division of the Rents w^d be avoided.'

I ans^d I had heard of no such intention before & that we had no suspicion of any such thing. But, I said, I intended to wait upon Mr Hill either that Evening or the following morning but I had not yet seen him, as I conceived I had little or nothing to say to him knowing that his Draft was already before Mr Atherton & having no suspicion but that he w^d immediately complete. Mr Phillips assured me that he had no other intention all along, than to follow the Steps of Mr Harvey & Mr Hill & that when ever they were ready he sh^d be so too.

I returned to the Inn to prepare for my departure, but being determined to know Mr Phillips' mind as fully as possible I went to him a second time & told him that as we were very anxious to raise the sum of £15,500 to pay Mr Fazakerley off which might be done by him & Mr Harvey with the deposits already received, I therefore asked him whether (if Mr Harvey wd now come forward, which I had no reason to suspect to the contrary) he wd come forward with him; even tho' Mr Hill sh^d persist in his late resolution & Miss Atherton sh^d choose to submit to it. He ans^d that two of his Clients, Evans & Tovey were completely ready but how Morgan was he c^d not say but as it was Market Day at Monmouth he expected to see him there & w^d either send me a line to Ross in the morning or otherwise w^d write to Mr Gorst the following week. I rec^d no letter from him.

On my arrival at Ross I immediately waited upon Mr Harvey & acquainted him with what I had heard from Mr Phillips. He seemed to know nothing ab^t it but s^d if we c^d get the Drafts approved by Mr Atherton he tho^t he c^d bring Mr Phillips forwards.

Aug 30th
Mr Harvey & I waited upon Mr Hill the day following. I asked Mr Hill, as Mr Gorst had desired me to do, whether he sh^d invest upon having a Copy of the Act of Parliam^t in the matter directed by Mr Butler. He ans^d certainly he sh^d, first because as Mr Butler had been consulted he tho^t it

only right to adhere to what he proposed, and secondly that some time or other the Purchasers might be called upon to produce their Papers, & then they sh^d be under the necessity of procuring such a Copy at their own expence which w^d be a very hard case. Upon my suggesting to him that we were apprehensive it w^d cost little less than a hundred pounds he said, that if Mr Butler & Mr Atherton c^d agree that any other way w^d be safe, he would acquiesce.

He then began, as Mr Phillips had done, by saying he supposed some of the Purchasers w^d not think of completing their Purchases before next Candlemas, & he himself for one sh^d not. The business had been so strangely delayed & the Year was now so far advanced that he did not think it proper or necessary. Besides, said he, if the Business was to be expedited as much as possible, it c^d by no means be finally completd in less than 5 or 6 weeks, which w^d bring it almost to Christmas.

Upon leaving Mr Hill, I asked Mr Harvey what he tho^t was best to be done as the matter had taken a very unexpected turn. He ans^d it w^d not suit his Clients very well who had their money ready, & that it w^d be best for us to get the Drafts thro' Mr Atherton's Hands as fast as possible & he tho^t something might then be done.

I took my leave of Mr Harvey, saying he sh^d hear from Mr Gorst in the course of the ensuing week.

Aug 31st

I left Wilton Castle a little after six in the morning upon Mr Green's Horse & arrived at Ledbury ab^t 9, expecting to get a place in the London & Hereford Mail to Worcester. At 10 the Coach came up but was full inside & out. Observing a young man equally disappointed as myself, I proposed to him to join at a Chaise to Worcester. He accepted the proposal & we came to Worcester ab^t one o'Clock. Happening both to be travelling the same way rather than wait 3 hours for the arrival of the Bath & Bristol Coaches, & perhaps find them full as we had done that at Ledbury, we agreed to travel on in the same way to Birmingham, by which means I got in time enough to secure a place to Manchester in the Coach which set out the same night at 10 o'Clock which chance I sh^d have lost by waiting for the Stage Coaches at Worcester, they coming into Birmingham an hour after the Manchester Coach sets out.

I left Birmingham at 10 o'Clock at Night, & passing thro' Litchfield, Leek, Macclesfield & Stockport, arrived at Manchester ab^t half after 5 o'Clock the following day.

I called at Mr Fullerton's where I drank Tea. I left Manchester ab^t half after 6 o'Clock on foot & came to Plat–Fold about 10.

Richard Hodgkinson's expenses

	£	s	d
1795 Aug 20th			
Cash of my own	6.	0.	0
Cash of Miss Atherton's	10.	0.	0
Turnpike to Manchester	0.	0.	5
Exp. of Horses & Servant to do.	0.	2.	6
Supper		1.	6
Coach fare to Birmingham	1.	5.	0
21st			
Coachman at Newcastle		1.	0
Dinner at Wolverhampton & liquor		2.	6
Coachman at Birmingham		1.	0
Paid for a case of Instruments		7.	6
Exp. At Birmingham all night		3.	6
22nd			
Coach fare to Worcester		9.	0
Coachman at do.		1.	0
Breakfast at do.		1.	0
Coach Fare to Ledbury		6.	0
Dinner & Liquor at do.		2.	0
Chaise to Ross		13.	0
Turnpikes & Postboy		4.	0
27th, 28th & 29th			
Expences at Monmouth self & Horse 3 days		17.	4
Exp wth diff Solicitors there		6.	3
31st			
Gave Mr Green's servant		5.	0
Paid for washing		1.	0
Gave a man for fetching Mr Green's Horse from Ledbury		2.	6
Exp. of Horse & man at do.		1.	3
Breakfast at do.		1.	0
Expended in travell^g in a Chaise to Ledbury to Birmingham 42 miles	1.	6.	0
Expences at Birmingham		3.	0
Coach Fare to Manchester	1.	5.	0

Sept lst

Expences at Cheadle	1. 6
Coachman at do.	1. 0
Dinner & Liquor at Macclesfield	3. 0
Coachman at Manchester	1. 0
	8. 15. 9
Deduct for a Case of Instruments	7. 6
Expence of the Journey	8. 8. 3

On my own Acc^t

1795 Aug 22nd

Bot at Worcester a walking stick	0. 0. 6
Sonatas for the Flute	4. 0
Duetto for do.	3. 0
Pair of Silk Stockings	13. 0
The Duenna	6
Armstrong's Art of Preservg Health	6
Pleasures of Imagination	1. 0
	£1. 2. 6

The Conclusion of the Affair
of the Herefordshire Estates

Memorandum of a Journey from Atherton to London, from London to Ross in Herefordshire &c., from Ross to London, & from London to Ross a second time, to receive the Purchase money of Miss Atherton's Estates & discharge Mr Fazakerley's Mortgage,

by Rd. Hodgkinson.

1796 Aug. 18th

Left Atherton ab^t 2 o'Clock on a Journey to London to settle if possible the sale of Miss Atherton's Herefordshire Estates. Came to Warrington ab^t six. Sent off by the Birmingham Coach from the Red Lion a Box containing the original Deeds &c., of the said Estate to be delivered to the Purchasers. The Box was directed for Mr John Green, Ross, to be left at the Bell Inn, Gloucester, till called for. Wrote at the same time to the Master of the Bell Inn to take care of the said Box & also to Mr Green to inform him of the Box being sent & to desire him to send for it as soon as possible.

I got into the Coach about half past 12 o'Clock & arrived in London without any thing material occurring at 5 o'Clock on Saturday morning the 20th.

20th
After breakfast I waited upon Mr Davis, N⁰. 8 Carey Street, who is Agent for Messʳˢ. Taylor & Gorst, to enquire whether he knew if the Lord Foleys were in Town. He said their Agent, Mr White was in Town & lodged at Gray's Inn Coffee house & he sent his Clerk immediately to him. He broᵗ. word back that the Foleys left London on Monday last & wᵈ. not be in Town till Parliament met, but that Mr White said he wᵈ. call upon Mr Davis after Breakfast & consult with him upon some Plan to get the Deeds down to them to be executed.

I then went out to call upon Mr Young respecting the deposit money in his hands, but he refused to part with it till the Purchases were completed & the whole money paid. He was setting out into Ireland that Evening & he left directions with his Clerk to pay the money provided I succeeded in completing the Purchases before he returned.

I went again to Mr Davis to enquire if Mr White had been found, he had not. I stayed till 2 o'Clock & he did not come. I then proposed to go to Dinner & at Mr Davis' request agreed to come again at 5 o'Clock. He still had never been & Mr Davis & I went to his Lodgings where we were told he was gone into the Country & wᵈ. not return before Monday.

21st
On the Sunday morning, being very fatigued, I did not leave my bed till near 10 o'Clock. I breakfasted & went to divine Service at St Andrew's Church, Holbourn.

After service I called in Cow Lane, Smithfield, upon Mr Booth, Miss Topham's Cousin, with a letter from her. I appointed him to come & spend the Evening with me on Monday at my Lodgings. I then called at Mr Butler's to have seen Peter Marsh but unluckily found he was gone out to spend the day.

The disappointmᵗ. of not meeting with Mr White on Saturday, & the consequent uncertainty of the success of my journey, considerably depressed my Spirits, & caused me to spend the day without much satisfaction. After divine Service I walked into Hyde-park & from thence thro' St. Jaˢ. Park & over Westminster Bridge towards Lambeth, but having been at all those places before & at a time when they were more crowded with Company, I did not find myself much entertained. I returned to my Lodgings & went to Bed early.

22nd

I got up ab^t. 7 o'Clock & went into Smithfield Market. I tho^t. the prices asked for the Cattle were very high. From my own judgm^t. & what I overheard of the purchasers calculating the weight of different Beasts, I supposed six pence per pound was asked for the whole carcase.

After Breakfast I went to Mr Davis to enquire if he had seen or heard any thing of Mr White. He sent his Clerk to enquire, who bro^t. word that Mr White was returned to Town but that he was gone out & no one c^d. tell how soon he w^d. return. Upon hearing this I determined to go to Grays' Inn Coffee house myself and wait till he did come in. I ordered a pint of Wine & desired the waiter to let me know when Mr White came in. After waiting ab^t. an hour he came in & I introduced myself to him, informing him of my business.

He lamented that the Deeds had not come sooner while the Foleys were in Town, but promised to assist me in getting them executed as soon as possible. He appointed me to call upon him the following night at 9 o'Clock & he c^d. then inform me what w^d. be best to be done.

I then called at Mr Davis' to inform him what had passed & in his office I wrote to my wife, Miss Atherton & Mr Gorst.

Leaving Mr Davis I went to Dr. Cartwright's at N°. 15 Percy Street, Rathbone Place, to dinner. Having drunk a few glasses of wine after dinner I returned to fulfil my engagement with Mr Booth. It was just 7 o'Clock when I got into the Coffee-house, & in ab^t. 20 minutes he came in. We immediately agreed to go to Vauxhall where it was what is called an extra night in honour of the Duke of Clarence's birth day.

The appearance of the Gardens was brilliant beyond description & the Company was very numerous. The Music & Songs were lively and cheerful but the chief amusem^t. consisted in walking thro' the long extended Colonnades in various directions, which are lighted and ornamented in a beautiful & picturesque manner by globular lamps of various colours.

In one part of the Gardens was Apollo's grand triumphal Carr. This was a large machine in imitation of a Chariot drawn by two Horses of astonishing magnitude. In the Chariot were seated the Duke of York's Band in uniform, who played several fine Marches & Airs. The four wheels of the Carr were hung round with an astonishing number of variegated globular lamps, & turned round all the time the Music played. The Carr & Horses together I imagine were upwards of 20 Yards long.

Being quite fatigued with walking & having at least 2 miles to walk to my lodgings, we left the Gardens ab^t. 12 o'Clock, which is an earlier hour than any of the Company think of retiring & even before it was all arrived, for we met sev^l. Carriages full of Company only entering as we came away.

23rd
I called upon Mr Davis who went with me to Mr Beardsworth Chambers, where we were informed that he was gone out of Town & w^d. return in ab^t. 10 days. I then called upon Peter Marsh who promised to call upon me at 6 o'Clock when we agreed to go to Hughes at the Royal Circus to see the entertainments of Horsemanship, Rope-dancing &c. The Horsemanship here is equal if not superior to Astleys, but in every other respect I think Astleys excels.

At 9 o'Clock I waited upon Mr White according to Appointment & he informed me that he w^d go down with me into Oxfordshire on Thursday & invited me to breakfast with him the next morning.

24th
At 10 o'Clock I waited upon Mr White to breakfast according to appointment. We agreed to take a Post Chaise at 7 o'Clock on Thursday Morning & so proceed to Mr Andrew Foley's & from thence to Oxford. From Oxford I go into Herefordshire & Mr White proposed to return for about a week to Town, & then to drop me a line to meet him at Stoke in Herefordshire for Mr Edwd. Foley's Signature. After Breakfast we went down to Mr Davis' office to get his Clerk to indorse the Attestations & affix the Seals for the Foleys.

Called upon Miss Atherton's Taylor, Mr Emmot of Leicester Square, & got him to take measure of me for a suit of Clothes. I then went in to Kensington (which I found much further than I expected) to pay Mr Whible, the Tallow Chandler's Bill.

In the afternoon I called upon Mr Booth to ask him if he w^d. go with me to the Play. He said he was previously engaged. I went alone to the little Theatre in the Hay-market, which is the only one open during the Summer & was very well entertained.

25th
At seven in the morning I went to Gray's Inn Coffee-house & found the

Chaise & Mr White both ready. We set out immediately & arrived at Uxbridge a little after 9 where we breakfasted. We got to Hasley, the seat of Mr Andrew Foley, which lies 2 miles out of the Road ab^t. 8 miles from Oxford, at 3 o'Clock. We found Mr Foley at home & he executed all the Deeds before Dinner.

We dined & drank Tea there, after which Mr Foley took us round his Farm, which he is very fond of. He then took us to his Stables & shewed us all his Hunters which he ordered the Groom to bring out one by one. He behaved uncommonly politely during all the time we stayed. We left ab^t. half past 7 & got to Oxford at 9 o'Clock.

Having ordered Supper we went into the Coach office where Mr White took a place to return to Town the next day & I was informed that the Gloucester heavy Coach from London w^d be in Oxford in ab^t. an hour. I got a place in it to Gloucester, & left Oxford at 11 o'Clock.

Of all the travelling in a Coach I ever experienced, that of this night was the most disagreeable. There were 4 women in the Coach, one of whom was an outside Passenger, but had been taken in at the beginning of the night on acc^t. of a Child she had upon her lap. The other three were, as I found out before we parted, Servants to a Family who were going to spend a fortnight at Cheltnam. The silly conversation & affected consequence of these 3 females was intolerable, & the insults & abuse they poured upon the poor woman with the Child w^d be almost incredible c^d I relate them.

We had not travelled more than three hours when stopping at a Toll-gate, one of the outside Passengers called out that one Wheel was broke. I immediately got out & found one of the fellys[2] of a hind wheel broke quite off, & both the Timber & the Iron lost. The Coachman said by driving slow he c^d take us safe to the next Town, Burford, ab^t. 4 miles off. I & 4 outside passengers determined to walk all the way, the rest sat still. After going ab^t. half a mile the danger became so great that I prevailed upon the whole company to leave the Coach, & let the man drive on & get it repaired as soon as possible. It was ab^t. 2 o'Clock when the company all got out of the Coach & had near 4 miles to walk. The morning however was very fine & we got to Burford ab^t. 3 o'Clock.

Upon our arrival the Coachman told us that the Wheel c^d not be repaired before 8 o'Clock. Upon which I determined to go to bed. Ab^t. half past 7 the Coach was ready. We arrived at Cheltnam ab^t 12 o'Clock where we stopped half an hour. Cheltnam was very full of Company.

Ab^t. 2 o'Clock we came to Gloucester. I went to the Bell Inn, got Dinner & ordered a Chaise to Ross. I was very glad to find that the Box I had sent from Warrington had been sent to Ross the day before.

I got to Ross at half past five, drank Tea with Mr Jones the Grocer & then went down to Wilton Castle where I found Mr & Mrs Green very well, who gave me a hearty welcome.

27th

After Breakfast I went up to Ross & calling in at Mr Jones' I met with Mr Harvey & we immediately agreed to take a Chaise & go to Monmouth, as I wanted to give the Solicitor there notice of my arrival, & particularly to see Mr Stokes who had not sent up his conveyance; & to press him to send it off immediately that Mr White might get it before he left Town, as in that case he had promised to call upon Mr Andrew Foley for his signature as he came down.

Mr Williams we met with who promised to come to Ross on Wednesday or Thursday following & complete his business. Mr Phillips was gone into Devonshire & was not expected for ten days. Mr Stokes was from home & w^d not return till the following morning. I saw the Conveyance which the Clerk said sh^d. be sent off to London by the Coach on Monday.

28th

Being Sunday I went to Church in the morning, dined & drank Tea with Mr Jones. Mrs Jones is dead since I was last here & yet it is reported that Mr Jones & Miss Green are ab^t. to make a match of it.

29th

Mr Harvey & I took a ride to Mr Mynde's of the Ash, the purchaser of the 6th & 12th Lots, to have some conversation ab^t the proportioning of the Rents some part of which since March, 1795, when the purchases where to have been completed; the purchasers lay a claim to. I thought Mr Harvey as well as Mr Mynde talked very unreasonably. But nothing was finally concluded upon. We then went on to Foy, ab^t 2 miles further to see Mr Jones, the purchaser of the 8th Lot. He said he left the whole of his business to Mr Leckmere, of Hereford, his Solicitor, to whom he desired me to write, requesting he wd come over to Ross to settle the Business. I wrote to him as soon as we returned.

I dined with Mr Harvey at 3 o'Clock & returned to the Castle to Tea.

30th
I stopped at the Castle all day, apprehending some of the Purchasers might call upon me.

31st
After dinner the Hereford Post brot me a Parcel out of Lancashire containing a Deed for Miss Clarke to execute, which Deed I delivered to Mr Harvey the following day for him to get it executed by Miss Clarke when she executed the deeds of the purchaser of the 1st Lot which contain a similar covenant.

The Post likewise brot me a Letter from Mr Leckmere saying he would call upon me at Ross on Friday morning & desired me to let Mr Jones know to meet him. The Evening being pleasant I walked up the River side to Foy to acquaint Mr Jones with Mr Leckmere's intention. Mr Jones behaved very politely, fetched me some fruit & invited me to stop Tea. I accepted the invitation & spent a couple of hours very agreeably. When I came away he took me thro' his Garden & Farm & accompanied me a mile or more thro' the Meadows. He asked me if I ever knew a Mr Wareing of Lancashire, a very tall & thin man & who died of consumption some time ago. He said he had formerly served his Church for him at Foy & at the same time was one of the Masters at Hereford School. I found he alluded to my old School-fellow James Wareing of Standish. It was quite dark before I got to the Castle.

1st Sept.
This being Market-day at Ross I expected to meet with several of the Purchasers & was not disappointed. Mr Tovey, Mr Morgan, Mr Bennett, & Mr Evans all waited upon me. They expressed great dissatisfaction at the Business being so long unsettled and made heavy complaints of the loss they had sustained by having their money lying by them so long. How I settled the matter with them will be seen in the Accts.

I dined with Mr Harvey. After Dinner 2 Mr Simmons of Pingethly, near Ross, came in & stayed all afternoon. They are related to Misses Atherton by marriage of one of the Gwillyms of Langstone to a Miss Jane Simmons of Pingethly, by which Marriage the pedigree of the Atherton family to the Title of the present Estates now sold here, sets out.

There are 5 or 6 Brothers. The eldest is a Captain in the Herefordshire Militia. The rest are all at home without employment except fox-hunting & shooting. They are all very wild young men, & are supposed to be running thro' their fortunes very fast. They have a Mother living, their Father has been dead some Years.

2nd

I went up to the Swan Inn to meet Mr Jones of Foy & his Solicitor, Mr Leckmere. Mr Leckmere pointed out some Copies which were wanting & which I promised to send. Mr Jones required Interest for his deposit money at 5 per cent which I granted, he allowing the Rent up to the 2nd August. I dined with Mr Harvey and immediately after dinner Jones, the Purchaser of Langstone came. But he is such a Beast & such a Brute that I can give no account of what passed between us, only that his demands were so unreasonable that we cd not agree.

3rd

After Breakfast I went to Mr Harvey's & found Mr Jones there again. He talked more reasonably than he had done the proceeding Evening & upon his urging & making it appear that considerable sums of his money had been taken up at 5 per cent I found it necessary to agree with him upon such terms as appear in the book of Accts. tho' I must confess I thot them a little unreasonable, but the money must be had soon & if he had object-ed to paying it, the loss would soon have been considerable, & the other Purchasers would have been alarmed.

After I had done with him, which was abt 12 o'Clock, I set out on horseback to Monmouth, to take Mr Lewis's deeds for Lot 4th to Mr Williams to let him see what parties had executed, as he had neglected to come to Ross as he promised.

When I came to Monmouth I found he had been from home three days & was not returned. I then called at Mr Lewis's & was told he was not yet retd. from Bristol fair.

I informed Mrs Lewis who I was & what was my business. She said they had long been expecting me, but they had been informed that my coming had been prevented by a suit in Chancery being set up agnst Miss Atherton by one of the Gwillyms of Little Birch. I told her no such thing had happened. She seemed very apprehensive of having trouble abt the Estate & said they had better be without it than be brot. into a Law-suit thro' it. I then went to the Beaufort Arms & dined. After Dinner I went to Mr Stokes who recd me with great politeness and promised to pay his money as soon as his Deeds retd. but was not willing to do it before. I stayed till near 6 o'Clock when I went again to inquire for Mr Williams and found him just arrived. He said he would come to the Inn to me in a few minutes, when he had changed his boots & got clean shoes & stockings on. He did not come however till near 7 o'Clock. I shewed him the Deed, told him how we were situated, & desired he w^d be so kind as [*sic*] furnish me in some way or other with his Client's money. He first promised me to empower his Agent in London to pay for it; he then said Mr Lewis perhaps might wish to pay for it at Ross, which if he did, they would come over to Ross on Monday. But he protested that I might depend upon having the money one way or other.

It was nearly dark when I left Monmouth & had 10 miles to ride to Ross thro' a very hilly Country. The night was very dark & I was sometimes so confused that I could hardly recollect the Roads, at many places I cd not see the Road before me & was obliged to trust to the horse to find the way himself. I had got little more than half way when it began to rain, & I then wished I had stayed at Monmouth. However I got safe to the Castle about half past nine.

4th
Went to Church morning & evening & spent the rest of the day at the Castle.

5th
Went to Ross to Mr Jones's bank, & settled Mr Tovey's Acc^t. I then went up to Mr Harvey's where I met Mr Bennett, purchaser of Lot 13th. I had seen him on Thursday when he talked very reasonably & fairly. I saw him in the Bank this morning likewise before he went to Mr Harvey's, when he seemed willing to agree to my proposal of giving me two Guineas & accepting of the last half year's Rents in lieu of the loss of Int. in having the money laid by him. When I came up to Mr Harvey's I found Mr Harvey had been talking to him in a manner very unfavourably to us, & he began to talk of Int. of his deposit money, & quit possession of the Premises occupied by Mrs Gwillym, which, he said, she w^d not give up till she was ejected, and wished me to engage that she should be ejected if necessary at Miss A's expense.

Mr Harvey drew a memorandum in writing to the above purport & was very solicitous for me to sign it, this however I refused to do. But upon Mr Bennett's saying that if I would only promise that he should have quit possession he would excuse my signing the Paper, which I accordingly did promise; & indeed I thot the request reasonable in the part of Mr Bennett, as this Mrs Gwillym & her family are the persons who have been reported to have set up the suit in Chancery. But I c^d not help observing that in this instance, as in many others, Mr Harvey shewed himself no friend to Miss Atherton & her cause & I am very certain that without him I c^d have made much better terms with all the parties. I was obliged to give up the two Guineas which Mr Bennett had partly agreed to pay before he saw Mr Harvey.

6th

Mr Harvey & I set ab^t 9 o'Clock to go to Stoke to get Mr Edwd Foley's signature to the Deeds. We found Mr White had come there the day before. We were very soon introduced into the Library to Mr Foley, who executed the Deeds immediately, & then very politely invited us to stop all night wh^ch we c^d not do. I am informed he is accounted the most polite & well bred man in the Kingdom. Stoke is a most beautiful place, situated near the Turnpike road from Ledbury to Hereford. The Park is very extensive, said to be eight miles round, & is well wooded. After Dinner we returned & a Servant was sent with us upwards of three miles thro' the Park to open the Gates & direct us the next & best road.

We came after ab^t an hour's ride to a place called Woolhope, where Mr Morgan (Rector of Ross) is the Vicar. This Mr Morgan is the gentleman who in one of my former memorandum Books I men^td to have fought a Duel & lost one eye. He is an acquaintance of Mr Harvey's. We stopped with him two hours or more during which time the Bottle went briskly round. He knows many Gentlemen in Lancashire, particularly Lord Grey, Mr Foxley, Colonel Legh, Mr Lowe of Chowbent &c. We got to Ross at 9 o'Clock.

7th

Mr Morgan purchaser of the 2nd Lot, came to the Castle early in the morning. As we walked up to Ross to go to the Bank, he said he was afraid the Deed was made in his Father's name, which was Willm instead of his which was George. That his Father had some time ago sold him the Est. and his money must pay for it. Upon examination it was as he said & Mr Phillips had made it in the father's name, notwithstanding he had been instructed to the contrary. This was a sad stroke upon me, for without his money, I had not enough to pay Mr Fazakerley's Mortgage & Mr Harvey & I were to set out for London that morning. Mr Phillips was not at home, nor ever had been since I came into the Country.

The Father was come to Ross with the Son, we therefore recommended that Mr Harvey sh^d immediately draw up a short Lease & Release from
the Father to the son which the Father agreed to execute; it was to be
ready by 2 o'Clock. Upon this the young man went with me to the Bank
& gave Mr Jones an order to pay me the money. How I settled the Rents
with him, will be seen in the Acc^ts.

For Mr Tovey's & Mr Morgan's money Mr Jones gave me a Draft at a
month which I accepted, imagining I c^d either get them discounted in
London or prevail upon Mr Curteis (who was to have the money I was to
pay) to receive them, especially as I expected to have Dfts at sight for ten
thousand pounds at Gloucester.

Mr Harvey rec^d the two Mr Jones' money, Mr Mynde's & Mr
Bennett's. These sums I never saw, he was to pay them to me only upon
the execution of the Deeds & he bro^t a Letter from Mr Jones of Ross to
Mr Turner, the Banker in Gloucester to furnish him with a Letter of
credit to that am^t upon the Bankers in London; but how was I astonished
when I found that he got a Letter of credit only for Mr Mynde's & Mr
Bennett's money & had got two Dfts for Mr Jones' money amounting to
upwards £8000 made payable to me at 10 days sight. Upon my enquiring
the reason of this affair which I foresaw w^d detain us the ten days in
London he ans^d that Mr Turner said they had not had sufficient notice
from Mr Jones of Ross that the sum w^d so soon wanted, & the sum was
too large to order it to be paid at sight in London. He said that Mr Turner
w^d write to the Bankers desiring them to disc^t the Bills at sight if possible.
I was confounded; the Dfts being made payable to me were in fact rec^ts to
the Purchasers, & at the same time thro' me entirely upon the credit of
the Bank to the am^t of £10,000. I had also written to Mr Beardsworth
appointing the day I sh^d be with him. Delay was dangerous for he was ab^t
leave Town. I therefore tho^t it best to take the Drafts & go on trusting to
the hope of having the Bills discounted at sight. We left Glocester ab^t 3
o'Clock & went to Cheltnam before we dined. At almost 7 o'Clock we
left Cheltnam to go to Burford, a stage of 16 miles, we got there bet. 9 &
10, and having supped retired to bed, but not to rest.

8th
We got up ab^t 5 o'Clock, & taking a Chaise we came on to Oxford
where we only changed horses, & then travelled a stage of 12 miles bef.
Breakfast.

We were anxious to get into London time enough to have the Bills
accepted but in this we failed it being 5 o'Clock before we got in. After

having dined I went to Mr Beardsworth's Chamber when I met with Mr More his Partner, who said the Reconveyance of the Lancashire Estates was ready & as Mr Beardsworth had signed it there was no occasion for him to [*sic*] the completing of the business as he c^d receive the money and deliver me the reconveyance. But I said Mr Beardsworth's signature was wanted to all the Deeds & his Rec^ts to them, to the sum of £15,000. At this he was quite astonished, said he was not acquainted with any such thing, & that no Dfts. to that purport had been laid before them & that if it was so he must peruse all the Dfts. which he c^d not promise to do in less than a fortnight.

I desired him to go with me to Mr Davis & enquire further into the matter & where the neglect was. Mr Davis was very ill in bed & we c^d only see the Clerk who confused instead of elucidating the business. In this situation we were obliged to retire for the night.

9th

I lost no time to present my Bills in the morning at Sir Jas Esdailes' Bank for acceptance. They were immediately accepted, but I c^d not get a promise to have them discounted.

If ever I felt an unhappy moment in my life it was this. The Deeds refused to be executed & the Bills to be discounted; I to be detained in London a fortnight at great expence. The Purchasers who had entrusted me with their money dissatisfied & alarmed & nothing but disappointm^t to write to my friends in the Country. In this state of mind I passed all that day & the following night. I went to Mr More in the forenoon & he advised to send for all the Dfts. up out of the Country for his inspection.

10th

Perfectly dissatisfied I waited upon him again the following morning (Saturday) & take [*sic*] him Mr Stokes Deed which was just come up out of Lancashire, very luckily the Dft was with it, which I desired him to cast his eye over saying I believed they were all upon the same Plan, & that they had all been settled by Miss Atherton. Looking at the foot of the Dft for Mr Atherton's signature he saw that Mr Atherton had settled it on the part of Mr Beardsworth as well as Miss Atherton.

This cleared up the affair & accounted for the Dfts not being laid before Mr More. Mr Beardsworth & Mr More waited upon Mr Atherton & Mr Davis, & being satisfied Mr B. said he w^d. dispence with the perusal of them & execute as soon as I bro^t. the money.

Here it was I felt the great inconvenience of havg Notes instead of
Cash. But for this the business might have been settled. I wrote to the
Glocester Bankers & desired they w^d actuate me by sending Cash to
enable Esdailes' to take up the Notes. Nothing c^d be done & I was obliged to give up all hopes of leaving London till the Notes became due. This
extreme disappointment & delay where, when I left Ross, I expected
none, had such an effect upon me that I c^d neither eat or sleep. In this
anxiety I continued till Tuesday morning.

11th
Being Sunday Peter Hawk called upon me after Breakfast & we went to
service in the old Jewry Chapel in hopes of hearing the famous Dr. Rees,
but were disappointed. After service we had a very pleasant walk thro'
Finsbury Square to Bedlam, thro' Moore Fields & up the new City Road
almost to Islington; we then crossed over to the left & were soon at
Ludgate Hill. After Dinner we went to Mr Kenyon's in Thames Street,
where we drank Tea & returned ab^t 9 o'Clock.

12th
On Monday I made no advance at all in my business. I wrote Letters to
Mr Green, Mr Jones, Messrs Taylor & Gorst & to Mr Cannon & Mr
Rawstorne.

13th
During Breakfast Mr Curteis called for the first time. I stated to him in
what manner I was situated, & when the Bills w^d be due. He immediately
said he tho^t he c^d bring the matter ab^t so that we c^d finish it in 3 or 4 days.
He said he saw no objection to his takg the Bills upon my indorsm^t. & w^d
walk with me to the Bank. Being satisfied there, we went to Mr
Beardsworth's Chambers, & there he gave directions to Mr More to get
his Mortgage Deeds ready by Friday & he w^d accept my Bills & Cash in
the manner I proposed.
    This Evening at 6 o'Clock Mr Harvey set out in a Coach to
Canterbury to see his Brother who is in the Army & purposed to return
on Thursday.

14th
Mr Curteis called upon me at Breakfast & we then walked to Mr
Beardsworth's Chambers to see that everything was getting in forward-
ness. He paid me the Compt. to say, as we went along, that I had arranged

my affairs like a man of business. In the Evening I went to Covent Garden Theatre with Mr Boothe.

15th

Mr Curteis called as I was at Breakfast. He took me with him in a Coach to Mr Beardsworth's Chambers. We found everything going on well. I then went for Mr Davis' Clerk & we ex^d. over the old Deeds which Mr Beardsworth was to deliver up & I found them right. The Clerk told me he understood that Mr More was gone to Mr Davis (at his Country seat at Hammersmith) to speak to him ab^t. the paym^t. of the Bill due to them for what they had done in the business. Mr Curteis called upon me in the Evening & said Mr More had desired him to mention to me that they sh^d expect their Bill to be paid bef. they delivered up any Papers. He said it was always a matter of course in paying off Mortgages & had taken the liberty of mentioning it to me, that I might be prepared for it in the morning & that it might not retard our settling the business. Mr Harvey ret^d to dinner & bro^t his Brother with him.

16th

At eleven o'Clock we went to Mr Beardsworth's Chambers to pay the money and rec. the Title Deeds. We found Mr Curteis & his Father there getting their own Mortgage forward & were just ready to execute it as we went in. Mr Beardsworth had executed most of our Deeds the day before & finished the whole immediately. Mr Curteis accepted the Dfts. upon my indorsing them; & the Bal^{ce}. was paid in Bank Notes.

As soon as I ent^d the Room Mr More presented me with their Bill for what they had done in the business amount^g. to the amazing sum of a hundred pounds. Demonstrance was vain, I was given to understand I must either pay the Bill or the business must stop. After all was finished I carried the Writings &c., to Mr Davis where a new Box was ready to pack them up in to send them into the Country.

17th

In the morning I took Mr Hill's Conveyance & delivered it to Mr Davis' Clerk to be given up to Mr Hill when he paid the purchase money which he purposed to do the 29th. Inst. Ab^t one o'Clock Mr Harvey & I left London in a Post Chaise & came thro' Hounslow, Slough & Benson to Oxford where we arrived at the King's arms abt 9 o'Clock.

18th

After Breakfast being desirous to see some of the Colleges, the Waiter got a person to go with us. He took us to All-souls, Christ Church & the New College. We did not see any of the Libraries except at All-souls. We saw little but the Chapels & the Halls. It being the long vacation, no Gentlemen were left & Oxford had a dull appearance.

Ab^t 12 o'Clock we left Oxford, & passing thro' Burford, North-leach & Cheltnam came to Glocester ab^t. 8 o'Clock. It being then dark & a long stage of 16 miles to Ross we concluded to stop all night.

19th

At 7 in the morning we left Glocester & got to Ross ab^t 10. I breakfasted with Mr Harvey & then went to the Castle where I dined. Ab^t. 3 o'Clock I went to Ross & ordered a Chaise to take me to Monmouth, intended to stop 2 or 3 days there to try to settle the business with the parties there who had not yet completed. Amos Jones went with me. We got to Monmouth ab^t 5 o'Clock. In a short time I met with all the parties who fixed to come to Ross & settle the Business on Thursday next. Having now nothing to stay for I ret. the same Evening.

20th

Finding myself this morning for the first time since I left home perfectly disengaged & without any appointm^t with any one, I determined to spend the day quietly at the Castle. Till Dinner I amused myself with drawing out & balancing my Acc^{ts}. up to the present day & was not a little pleased to find them exactly right. In the Evening Miss Green had company to Tea, a pleasant party.

21st

Spent all day at the Castle.

22nd

This being the day on which I was to expect the Monmouth Gentlemen to settle their business, I spent the forenoon bet. hope & fear, having been so often disappointed by them before. At noon my fears were realised; having not seen or heard a single message from any one of them. In returning from Ross to the Castle I met Mr Stokes' Clerk who informed me that Mr Stokes was taken very ill the preceding Evening & c^d not come, but desired I w^d leave his Client's Deeds with Mr Green & he w^d pay the money to him. The apology was too palpable not to be seen thro', even tho' I had not been informed that this is Mr Stokes usual mode of evasion. I doubted much when I saw him on Monday that his money was not ready, tho' I am credibly informed that he is making his Client pay Int. for it ever since Mar. 1st 1795, when the Sales were first to have been completed, at which time he pretends he borrowed it for him.

After Dinner I sent to Mr Evans, Mr Phillip's Client, to Monmouth, to see why Mr Phillips did not come according to his promise & get the money from him if possible. All afternoon I waited for Mr Lewis, but he not coming I was returning to the Castle ab^t 8 o'Clock completely disappointed & mortified. I had not got more than half way when a person overtook me on horseback, & accosted me. I did not (it being dusk) immediately recognise him, but soon discovered it to be Mr Lewis. My temper was too much ruffled not to complain of the treatment I had experienced, but he apologised by saying that he had been at Bristol the day before & in returning that morning had come to the Passage too late for the Tide & was obliged to wait for its return. I know not how far this apology w^d have satisfied me, had not he bro^t me into perfect good humour by informing me that he had bro^t his money with him, & w^d pay it me if I w^d go back to Ross with him. I returned to Mr Jones' Bank (where we were to settle the acc^t) while Mr Lewis put up his Horse. At Mr Jones' I found Mr Bourne (Mr Lewis' Solicitor) who said he had just called at the Swan, & being told there that he or his partner Mr Williams had been expected during the day to come & settle this business, which he knew nothing of having been a week from home, he had stepped down to see how far he might be of use in it. Just then Mr Evans returned from Monmouth & told us he had bro^t. his money from Mr Phillips. It was then agreed that Mr Bourne sh^d examine Evans' Conveyance as well as Mr Lewis' & as the night was far advanced & he much fatigued he begged it might be deferred till 7 in the morning when he w^d attend & examine the Deeds while I rec^d the money. The latter part of the Evening made amends for the anxiety of the preceding part of the day & I ret^d to the Castle very well satisfied.

23rd

I failed not to attend at the Bank at 7 o'Clock & for once found the parties as punctual as myself. Mr Bourne gave me no trouble with respect to the Conveyances or Copies. We had finished the whole business ab 10 o'Clock. A Chaise being ready at the door, Mr Jones & I got into it & were driven to Ledbury in ab^t an hour & a half, which is 13 miles. Taking another Chaise at Ledbury we arrived at Worcester ab^t 3 just in time to dine before the Bristol Coach came up, in which I got a place to Birmingham where we arrived abt 9, from whence at 10 a Coach set off for Manchester where I got safe to abt 7 o'Clock the following night. It being dark & I having a thousand pounds in my Bags, I thott it prudent to stop all night. I got into the Chaise at 6 o'Clock in the morning & was set down safe at Atherton abt 9, after an absence of five weeks & three days, during which time I had travelled near a thousand miles, & had experienced more anxiety & unease of mind & contended with & surmounted more difficulties than I had ever met with in my life before.

Notes

1   This was Buildwas Abbey.
2   A part or the whole rim of a wheel to which the spokes are attached.

5

The Scots in Chowbent: Richard's Grand Tour, 1800

Inventions by four Lancashire men led to the technological revolution in cotton spinning and weaving which opened the flood gates for the Industrial Revolution of later decades. In Hodgkinson's lifetime the rigours of the factory system, urban squalor and the mighty engines and machines of new-born industry, changed for ever the face of England.

Kay's 'flying shuttle' (1733), James Hargreaves' 'spinning-jenny' (1764), Richard Arkwright's 'water frame' (1769) and Samuel Crompton's 'mule' (1779) brought mixed fortunes to Chowbent: prosperity to the craftsmen who set up a thriving trade building these new machines and selling them throughout the country, and hard times for the cottage-based textile industry.

These dramatic changes in the textile industry coincided with the arrival in Chowbent in the 1760s of brothers William and David Cannon (or Cannan) from the Scottish lowlands of Galloway. Like many other Scots of that time they were forced to seek their fortunes far from the hills of the Glenkens and away from the impoverished family farm in the parish of Kells. But 'thanks to the laudable desire for education in the Scotch of all ranks',[1] the brothers were literate and William had learned the trade of carpenter. Why the brothers chose to pursue a living in Chowbent is not known, but their decision could well have had its origins in both the cattle trade and the religious backgrounds of Galloway and Chowbent. There had long been links between Galloway and Newton-le-Willows some eight miles from Chowbent where Scottish drovers had taken their cattle to market. The Cannons, brought up in an area possessed with the anti-Popery of the Covenanters, would also have felt at home with the Dissenters of Chowbent, whose forebears had gone to battle against the Royalists in the Civil War and against the Jacobites in 1715. William Cannon embraced the cause of Unitarianism and his family worshipped and were buried at Chowbent Chapel.

With brother David in business as a prosperous provision merchant, William Cannon set himself up as a clock and textile machine maker. His business thrived and soon he had many journeymen travelling the country installing his machines. Neither did he forget his native Galloway, and before 1770 two or three young Scots had travelled to Chowbent to become bound apprentices. In the next few years more ambitious farm boys made the journey, and four of them were to make a contribution to the rapid expansion of the cotton industry out of all proportion to their small, exclusive number. In 1780, Adam Murray travelled to England to become an apprentice with William Cannon. He was followed in 1781 by nineteen-year-old James M'Connel, a nephew of Cannon. Murray's brother, George, went next, and in February 1784, fourteen-year-old John Kennedy followed, and later recalled the journey he made on pony during one of the harshest winters in memory. He marvelled at the few streetlights of Dumfries and was astonished to see his first four-wheeled waggon drawn by four horses. On his arrival in Atherton, all of Cannon's Scottish workmen repaired to the Bear's Paw Inn to hear news of their native country. 'But such a Sunday I never saw before, for everybody in the place seemed to come to the alehouse as soon as dinner was over, and such carousing and drinking was quite unknown in our native glen', he wrote.[2]

James M'Connel, later to be Kennedy's partner, contemplated on at least one occasion abandoning his apprenticeship and running away. 'Before he had been long at Chowbent, it was his duty one day to carry a clock across his shoulders to a place seven miles distant, where it was to be put up. The cord, or other part of the apparatus, shift it as he would, hurt his shoulder so badly that he was sorely tempted to throw his burden on the ground and to run away then and for ever from clock, clock making and machine-making. But he withstood the temptation.'[3] These four young apprentices acquired great wealth in the cotton trade and remained friends all their lives. In later generations these early cotton entrepreneurs of the Murrays, M'Connels, Kennedys and the Gregs of Styal Mill in Cheshire, together with the renowned Manchester-based engineer, Sir William Fairbairn, all became connected by marriage and were mutually helpful to each other.[4]

A few years before these Scots were apprenticed to William Cannon, Samuel Crompton is said to have used a Chowbent machine shop to solve a problem while designing his Mule.[5] It is likely the spindle-making shop in question was William Cannon's, for he employed upwards of thirty apprentices at one time making spindles, jennies and looms. William Cannon was also one of the few spindle manufacturers who had the conscience to pay Crompton 10s 6d for the 'sight of the Mule'. Despite the glowing eulogies of Gilbert French, Samuel Crompton's biographer, Crompton had neither the skills nor the tools to construct his mule to completion, unaided. There was also a lifelong friendship between Crompton and John Kennedy, the latter a vigorous supporter of the campaign to win a substantial Government award for the inventor of the spinning mule, who made so many men rich and left himself penniless. Both John Kennedy and James Murray wrote letters of introduction to the Glasgow and Paisley textile cotton firms to enable Crompton to gather statistics to support his claim to Parliament.

In the midst of all this change in the textile industry, nineteen-year-old Richard Hodgkinson arrived in Chowbent to open a grammar school in March 1784. In such a prominent post in so small a community he quickly became well known and made early acquaintance with the young Scottish apprentices. Despite his aspirations to take the cloth in the Established Church, Hodgkinson courted the niece of William Cannon, then an active member of the dissenting Unitarian Chapel. Probably much to the relief of the twenty-seven-year-old spinster, Hodgkinson, two years her junior, asked for her hand. Richard and the rosy-cheeked Jane,[6] 'inclined to stoutness', were married in 1788 and formed a union between two vigorous and ambitious families.

Their apprenticeships completed, the Murrays, Kennedy and M'Connell left Chowbent to make great fortunes in Manchester. The Murray brothers went into partnership, as did M'Connel and Kennedy. The latter pair, according to Samuel Smiles, owned the largest spinning concern in the Kingdom by 1817. Another apprentice of Cannon's was John Hodgkinson, the nephew of Richard Hodgkinson, who ran away to sea in 1796.[7]

Hodgkinson remained friends with the Scottish mill owners for the rest of his life. As late as 1826, Jane Hodgkinson, when asked to allow an autopsy on the body of her demented son, Joseph, gained solace from the knowledge that a son of one of the Murray brothers had also 'had his head opened' after an early death.

By 1800 Richard Hodgkinson was prospering. He had money in a bank, rented a large farm from Lord Lilford, and was a respected and envied man of the parish. In the spring of that year he decided to make a private visit to Scotland to pay his respects to his wife's parents and examine the possibility of buying the famed Galloway cattle for his farm. On 31 May he climbed on board the stagecoach to Carlisle on the first stage of a twenty-day journey, during which he toured Galloway and visited the towns of Ayr, Glasgow, Stirling and Edinburgh. As was his custom he kept a detailed account of his travels, noting the people he met, the gossip he heard, the customs he observed and the countryside through which he passed.

Always shrewd and objective his observations are leavened with the gossip of the day, sharp political criticism, bemusement with certain Scottish customs and admiration for the growing towns of Glasgow and Edinburgh.

Memorandums of a Journey
into Scotland, June 1800

May 31st

I left home abt 8 o'Clock in the Evening & went to the 4 lane-ends in Hulton to sleep, having previously engaged a place in the Mail Coach to Carlisle.

June 1st

Left the lane-ends abt 5 o'Clock in the morning & arrived at Preston to breakfast abt 8. Paid fifteen pence for Breakfast. Arrived at Lancaster abt 12 o'Clock where we only changed horses & proceeded to Kendal where we arrived abt 3 o'Clock. After passing Preston not more than 2 Miles it was astonishing to see the impoverished state of the land, & slovenly mode of cultivation. This was the more surprising, as a Gentleman from Preston, who was then in the Coach said that Land adjoining to the Town was let as high as from fifteen to twenty pounds, plowing seven yards and a half to the perch & that he himself paid ten Guineas per Acre for a pasture Field & that he had for two years been looking out for a small Meadow to rent, but could not meet with any, so many people wanted and such high prices were given.

Some compensation was made for this dreary prospect when I arrived in the neighbourhood of Lancaster, the rising Grounds there being covered with a rich and beautiful verdure. From Lancaster to Burton, & from Burton to Kendal, there are vast tracts of waste or Common Land. About

Kendal as abt Lancaster, the Land appears rich and in high state of cultivation. The Country is beautifully wavey, consisting of alternate Hill &
Dale, as you proceed from Kendal to Penrith, & many of the Hills are
covered with delightful hanging Woods of Brush Underwood, which at
this time of the year added much to the variety and richness of the Scene.
The uncultivated and Common Grounds continue or rather increase here
& are far more extensive than the cultivated Grounds but the latter gain
much by the contrast and add much to the pleasure and gratification of
the traveller.

After having travelled a few miles from Kendal you pass by a line of
Buildings consisting of 36 Dwellings, 3 or 4 of which have never been
covered in, and none of them have ever been finished or inhabited. They
were erected by Lord Lonsdale whose hand seems to blast everything it
touches. A little farther on, & upon the road-side you come to a Village,
likewise built by Lord Lonsdale, the entrance into which is like the
entrance in to a Castle with Towers & circular Wing-walls. This too is
tumbling into ruins for want of Inhabitants. Part of it is occupied by a set
of Carpet Manufacturers brought thither by his Lordship, but whose productions I am informed are never brought to Market, but are all used or
kept at Lowther-hall which stands some distance behind this village but
cannot be seen to the Road.

The Road from Preston hitherto had been exceedingly good but here
it began to grow worse and continued so to Carlisle where I arrived abt
11 o'Clock, supped & went to bed immediately.

June 2

After Breakfast I waited upon a Mr William Wood, a Cotton Spinner
and Manufacturer to whom Mr James McConnel had given me a Letter.
After sitting with him a few Minutes he happened to mention a Fair for
black Cattle which was holding this day at Rossley abt 9 Miles from
Carlisle. As I could not get on from Carlisle before the following day, I
determined to return to the Inn and hire a horse to go to the Fair. After
several fruitless enquiries by the Ostler at different places for a horse, the
Master of the Coffee-house where I lodged, a Mr Hardisty, was so
obliging as to let me have a mare which he kept for his own riding. I
mounted abt half past 11 o'Clock & after a very pleasant ride arrived
upon the hill abt one o'Clock. The site was quite a novel one to me, &
the day being fine & the Roads & Hill quite dry, it was extremely
pleasant and entertaining. On one part Horses were shewn for sale.
There were a great number but the vilest set I ever saw together. In

another part calving Cows were shewn and amongst them were several Cart Loads of Calves of from 3 days to 3 weeks old, belonging to the Cows to be sold. In another quarter the Irish Cattle were shewn & in another the Scotch. There might be from four to five thousand head of Cattle upon the Hill besides the Horses. Great numbers of Booths were erected where every accommodation of eating and drinking might be had. I was told the shew of Cattle was fully as great as at other times. The prices something lower than they had been of late but still very high. I returned to Carlisle abt 4 o'Clock in the Evening after spending a day very much to my own gratification & which left me nothing to regret for being detained at Carlisle a day longer than I expected.

Soon after I returned I went to drink Tea with Mr William Wood. After Tea we walked round the Walls which formerly included the whole of the Town but I conjectured there are now as many Buildings without as within them. The Walls are in general very ruinous & must now be a complete nuisance to the Town's people. There is only a parapet wall on one side. In some places the parapet is thrown down, in other places it is in tolerable repair, but the whole is so completely neglected that I am informed it is no uncommon practice for a person who lives near the Walls when he wants a few Stones to get a part of the parapet thrown down by boys or other ways & convey the stones away in the night time.

From the North East corner there is a view of the Race-Ground which like the River-dee at Chester lies under the walls and upon the Banks of the River and has very much the appearance of the River-dee. Indeed all the Vallies which are seen to the North and North-east of the Walls are very beautiful. In going along the North Wall you pass a large house lying within the Walls which belongs to Lord Lonsdale & like the rest is uninhabited. This I understand he pays a visit to at every election as he constantly opposes the present Members & here he creates new freemen as he wants them which has given this house the name of Mushroom-hall.[8] A little further, but by-passing over a very decayed part of the Wall, you come to the Castle. This is kept in tolerable order. Here is a Garrison constantly kept, at least nominally so. A Governor with six hundred pounds a year, with all the subordinate officers of a Garrison. But the offices are now mere sinecures. There are a few Cannon mounted which are fired off upon particular occasions, & I was informed that there is an armoury in the Castle containing abt ten thousand stand of Arms. Four old invalids constitute the Garrison at present.

From hence there is a beautiful view of the Bridges which cross the Rivers in going out of the Scotch & Irish Gates. There are no less than three Rivers contiguous to Carlisle, the waters of which are clear and limpid beyond description which must be one cause of the preference given to Carlisle printed Cottons, great quantities of which are printed here. At some distance from the Castle stands the County Gaol, a disgrace to the County as to Carlisle. One side of it stands to the public street & they have lately been obliged to block up the lower Windows to prevent the Prisoners conversing with passengers in the Street. The Felons are all crowded together & the whole prison is so ruinous and weak as to require a constant guard of Soldiers.

Here we finished our perambulation & it being nearly dark we went to the Inn when I kept Mr Wood to supper. I promised to breakfast with him in the morning.

June 3rd

At 9 o'Clock I breakfasted with Mr Wood. He then proposed, as we had the Evening before gone the Circuit of the Town, to walk with me thro the Center. It was a pleasant well-built Town and the Inhabitant seem dressy & fashionable. The Shops were neat and handsomely ornamented. After amusing ourselves abt an hour he led me to the subscription News Room which is accommodated with News papers, Maps &c.,&c., in a very genteel stile. He entered my name in a book for such purpose, as stranger introduced by him, which one of the Rules of the Coffee Room requires of every Member. He here asked me when I proposed being in Glasgow, & being answered the middle of the next week, he said he hoped to see me there, as he was going to Glasgow on Sunday next with an intention of stopping a whole week. Having given me direction where to find him in Glasgow he left me abt 12 o'Clock.

After perusing the Newspapers I thought I could not spend the remaining half hour before dinner better than in viewing the Cathedral. I easily found the man who keeps the Keys, and the usual fee of one shilling soon unlocked the Doors. As you approach the Cathedral you cannot help being struck with the ruinous appearance of a large stone Building which belongs to the Cathedral but which stands abt 10 or 15 yards from it. Some of the Windows are entirely out, nothing being left but the large iron bars, some of them have part of the glass remaining in them & others are built up of stone or bricks. But I think not one whole glass window remains in the Building. But how was I astonished when my guide informed me that in one part of it were kept the writings and records and in another part a Library. The Cathedral however was clean and in decent repair, much more so than I found myself inclined to expect. The Choir is but small and it is kept neat and has a venerable look. There are a Dean and Chapter here viz: a Dean and four Prebends not one of whom reside at Carlisle. There are likewise a Lecturer and four Minor Canons. There are no Monuments in the Cathedral worth notice. The present bishop is the Honorable Doctor Vernon, brother of Lord Vernon.

The Duke of Devonshire has very considerable Estates adjoining to Carlisle. These Estates formerly belonged to the Duke of Portland, until the memorable year of 1768 (memorable for the dissipation and corruption of the Electors of Members of Parliament, and for the folly of the elected) in which he expended in elections in the County of Cumberland, it is said, upwards of one hundred thousand pounds. This reduced him to the necessity of selling his property abt Carlisle, which the Duke of Devonshire purchased, who is now I am informed, frittering it away by selling off Lots of ten or twelve thousand pounds at a time.

About two o'Clock I sat down to dinner at the Inn. There was a very agreeable party. About half after three I got into the Coach for Dumfries. The other Passengers were a very agreeable young man who had lodged with me at Carlisle, a Mr Campbell of Castle Douglas, an eminent Drover, & a young woman who had lived in the service of Sir James Graham, of Netherby, near Carlisle. She was very communicative concerning Sir James's family. She informed us that the whole of Longtown, the next town to Carlisle, which we passed through, was the sole property of Sir James. That he was a Member of Parliament for Rippon in Yorkshire, which he represented through the interest of a Lady. That he had married Lady Catherine, the eldest daughter of the Earl of Galloway whose portion was only a thousand pounds which he had generously given back to her next youngest sister. She likewise acquainted us with many little anecdotes of himself and Family, too telling to repeat here, but such as the inferior domestics of such a family are always too forward in repeating to a Stranger. After this loquacious lady had exhausted all her eloquence I fell into conversation with Mr Campbell. He said he was returning from the County of Norfolk where he had been selling 300 head of Cattle. That he went into Norfolk with Cattle three or four times a year, but never shewed them for Sale before he came there. From him I learned some useful information respecting the enquiries I intended to make in Scotland. He kindly gave me an invitation to call upon him if I came near Castle Douglas.

At Gretna Green, or rather at a Village called Spring Field, we changed Horses and drank Tea. We were abt to get into the Coach again but who should come into the house but the old Blacksmith who performs the ceremony for all the matrimonial fugitives from England. Curiosity prompted me to go into the house again, & contrive by treating him to have a little talk with him, but the old sloven, for which he is completely, was so intoxicated, as to forbid all attempts at conversation. We left Spring Field soon after six o'Clock but did not arrive at Dumfries before eleven.

From abt 4 or 5 miles north of Carlisle to Dumfries, the road is the most complete I have ever travelled. The Land is chiefly wild and uncultivated, some parts moorish, in others extensive tracts of peat Moss which the Inhabitants were cutting, amongst the labourers at it there were at least three women to one man. Along the road side north of Spring Field a very considerable tract of the country has been lately inclosed. And though it seems very unproductive at present, it may probably in a few years experience extensive improvement as Lime-stone has been discovered in the neighbourhood. Two large Kilns have been erected near the Road-side, and were on fire as we passed. There is but little depth of Soil here and when a field is ploughed the whole surface is apparently (and almost in fact) covered with Stones. The largest of them are gathered off and are used in making Fences which almost universally here consist of stone-walls. I apprehend it will be with great difficulty and expense that this Land can be brought into a tolerable state of Cultivation. And as the Stones constantly rise, if the Surface be broken, I should conceive, that if it could be well laid down for grazing it would be the most profitable to keep it for that purpose, as the labour would be much the least in that state.

At Dumfries I slept at the George.

June 4th

I breakfasted with Mr Campbell and several of the Yeomanry Cavalry who were come to Dumfries to be reviewed, it being the King's Birthday. There is a company of Yeomanry Cavalry at Dumfries, and also a numerous Corps of Volunteer Infantry consisting, as I was informed, of two hundred men. These, as well as all the regulars in the Town, which consisted of a Company of Light-horse and abt four hundred of the regular Militia,[9] were all drawn out upon what is called the Sands in honour of his Majesty's birth-day. The day being fine, the men and horses looked exceedingly well. They went through a few evolutions & fired three rounds. It being Market-day Dumfries was very much crowded. In three different places of the Town an effigy was hung upon a Gallows, piled round with combustible materials, which were to be set fire to in the course of the day. The boys of the Town were running after all passengers begging a Baubee to burn Tom Paine, tho the Effigy was meant to represent a Mr Stott who lived abt two Miles out of Dumfries & who, upon a proclamation of the Magistrates desiring the Farmers and others who had Meal in their possession, to bring it to Market, had alleged that he had none. But being suspected as a forestaller,[10] the populace were determined to examine his house. He admitted them without hesitation and they found not more than fifty stone of Meal. But he refused to let them into the Barn. However they broke open the Doors and upon examination found a large quantity of both Meal and Flour hidden among the Hay, a very great proportion of which was rendered useless by over keeping.

Having hired a horse to New Galloway and a man to fetch it back, I left Dumfries abt one o'Clock. After travelling abt 2 miles on the road leading to Castle Douglas I turned to the right into a new Road which is to be made from Dumfries to Port Patrick. This new Road is so laid out, as to be carried almost upon a level through a very hilly Country and is at present, as far as it is finished, one of the most complete roads I ever travelled. For several miles here the road is through a mountainous and barren country capable of sustaining but few Cattle and but few are to be seen upon it. Here and there, but very rarely you pass through a cultivated Farm, the Lands of which lie open to the Road and a person called a herd is obliged to watch the Cattle to keep them from straying or trespassing upon the Corn-land. I travelled upon this new Road abt two miles beyond a river called the Water of Orr where I left the public road and was taken by bye Roads, some times very rough, to a village called Cross Michael or Cross Michael Kirk. For a considerable distance on the south of this Village the Country is covered with, indeed almost universally, consists of Hillocks or rising Grounds, perhaps a mile in circumference at the base, smooth in surface and cultivated to the summit. These have a pretty appearance and form a pleasing Contrast to the rough barren and craggy Mountains which encompass them.

At Cross Michael, having travelled 18 miles from Dumfries, I stopped abt an hour to refresh myself and horse. From Hence to Newgalloway is abt eight miles. The road is very good and lies upon the Banks of the River Ken all the way to New Galloway. It is a very pleasant ride, the Valley consisting chiefly of tolerably good Meadow Land, the River runs in the middle and the rocky barren hills rise to an enormous height on each side. At no great distance from Cross Michael Kirk the river forms a very extensive Lake, called here Loch, which continues nearly a mile in breadth up to New-galloway. On the Banks of this Loch, on the North west corner of it & abt half a mile from Newgalloway, stands a Gentleman's seat called Kenmore Castle, formerly the Seat of William,

Lord Kenmore who was beheaded for taking part with the Rebels in 1715 and now is inhabited by his grandson, Mr Gordon, who usually goes by the name of Kenmore abt Newgalloway. From the Road the House stands full in view on the North, West and South sides, it is surrounded with Woods and a few plantations rise beautifully on the West side, a considerable height into a large and craggy mountain which bounds it on that side. The River here is called the Ken and to get into Newgalloway you pass a handsome stone-bridge of five Arches which adds very much to the beauty of the Landscape. About 7 o'Clock I arrived at the Kenmore Arms in Newgalloway, which is abt 8 miles from Cross Michael Kirk. Being yet upwards of four miles from my Father in law's, I thought it too late to go there that night. I therefore sent a Messenger with a Note to him saying that being entirely unknown both to himself and family, I thought it more prudent not to come into his house so late but I would be with him to breakfast by 9 o'Clock in the morning. The Messenger brought me word that a Horse would be sent for me by 7 o'Clock. After having despatched the messenger I felt my spirits low and flat. Tired with a long journey knowing no one and unknown to all, removed at a great distance from my Family, and in the morning to be introduced to the person who gave being to one who constitutes the principal happiness of my Life, alike a stranger to himself and all his family, I could not but feel an unusual flatness of Spirits. In this temper of mine I walked out and took the road towards Kenmore.

I was soon within the Woods, the gloom of which agreeing with my present temper of mind put me perfectly in humour for contemplating the fate of the unfortunate family of Kenmore Castle. I could easily fancy to myself the unbounded influence of and universal respect paid to the ancient Lairds of Scotland as well as to the Barons of England as also the extensive hospitality and festive scenes of mirth and jollity which must have surrounded such a house as Kenmore and I had too plainly before my eyes the gloom and desertion which long have followed and here eternally must follow, one unfortunate action of a single individual. I almost began to doubt the justice of that power which Governments assume of inflicting punishment on any but the actual criminal. And though it may be right that the ruling power may be by a summary and severe punishment crush its rebellious subjects, and render them incapable of further resistance, yet when we consider that the Government itself may be a usurpation and that resistance to it may be a justice we owe to our Maker and our fellow Subjects as well as ourselves, a wise and considerate man will hesitate before he subscribes to a sentence which not only inflicts death upon the criminal but entails poverty and disgrace upon all his posterity.

In the midst of these reflections I met a woman of whom I made several inquiries. She informed me that she lived in the family when she married. That the present possessor is abt 50 years of age, that he has a wife but no Child, that he lives quite retired, is a very sober and regular liver and is much beloved in the neighbourhood. The little amusement he takes, except looking after his Farm, is fishing & shooting and this but very sparingly. At present and during the last Summer he has taken much delight in training a Company of Volunteers, amounting to 60, which he has raised in the neighbourhood and which have received Clothes & Arms from the Government & are now receiving pay. His grandfather, Lord William Kenmore, was beheaded in favouring the cause of the Stuarts in 1715 and his Estates confiscated, but they were restored to his Widow upon her supplicating them from the King on bare and bended Knees, to bring up a numerous family. During my stay in the Country I was informed that the present Mr Gordon entirely ruined his affairs and spent his Estate in the year 1768 (of notorious election memory) in a contested election with Mr Spalding for Newgalloway in which he was elected but lost his seat on being convicted of Bribery. After this he fought in a duel with Mr Spalding in which after receiving Mr Spalding's fire without injury, he shot Mr Spalding through the body, who though he was not killed upon the spot never recovered and died after lingering several years. This with his ruined circumstances drove him into France where he resided to the death of Mr Spalding and on his return brought with him his present Lady who is said to be an Englishwoman. His mother, who had several Estates, in her own right near Durham sold them & cleared off the Mortgages as far as her circumstances would afford & after having entailed the Estate, gave it back to her son whose present income is supposed to be abt £1200 per annum. Mr Spalding's brother who is a great East India merchant is now the Representative for Newgalloway, Wigton, Glenluce and Whitehorn, which send one member to Parliament amongst them.

Mr Spalding's Estate, which adjoins Newgalloway, at his death, was so involved in debt as not to be worth a shilling to his brother, who was the next Heir, but having acquired great wealth in trade, he wished not to part with the family Estate. He therefore paid off all the debts which amounted to the full value of the property. So much for contested elections.

June 5th

A Horse was sent for me by 8 o'Clock and at 9 I arrived at Little Barskeoch abt 4 miles from Newgalloway, the Farm which my Father in law holds. My reception was such as I had reason to expect, kind and affectionate and as Mr Cannon and I had corresponded occasionally for many years, we had only to see each other to become thoroughly acquainted. In the afternoon Mr Sloan of Knowshean, my wife's Uncle, came to spend the Evening with us and brought with him a Mr Newall of Strangfasket; the farmers here are always called by the name of the Farm they occupy. We spent a very agreeable evening and Mr Newall invited us to Dinner the following day.

June 6th

Mr David Kennedy of Knocknaling, brother to John Kennedy of Manchester, and who had been at Atherton abt 4 years ago, came to Breakfast with us at Mr Cannon's. About 11 o'Clock Mr & Mrs Cannon & their daughter, with Mr Kennedy & myself, set out to Strangfasket where we met with a very hearty welcome from Mr & Mrs Newall & their Son, who sometimes attends Newton Fair with black Cattle & who promised to take a bed with me the next time he comes there. After we had been seated a few minutes a most beautiful, gentile and well bred lass came into the Room, she might be abt nineteen years of age, dressed in a fashionable Stile with her hair plaited and fastened with a Comb on the crown of her head, and tied round with a green silk handkerchief. She had a neat pair of slender Slippers on but what appeared to me very singular, she had no Stockings on. I know not how I was peculiarly prepossessed in favour of this young lady. Another girl abt twelve years of age was introduced, dressed partly in the same manner & without Stockings. I supposed them to be Sisters of the young Mr Newall who appears to be 25 years of age. We had the usual dinner here, Scotch-broth, Salt-beef and a pudding with the addition of a joint of Veal. Mr Newall is here called a Laird & is proprietor of his own Farm which is accommodated with the best buildings of any house I was introduced to in Galloway. Mr Newall's brother was formerly Laird of the greatest quantity of land of any Gentleman in the neighbourhood, his Estates stretching between the rivers called the water of Ken and the Water of Dee. He mostly spent the whole of this property in supporting Kenmore in his contest for Newgalloway in 1768. These Estates were purchased by a Mr Forbus,[11] the present proprietor, formerly a Copper Merchant and who acquired his immense property by his Contract for coppering Ships in the American

War. He is said to have netted his Income last year at forty thousand pounds per annum. This the Commissioners refused; he then gave in sixty thousand per annum; this the Commissioners said they should accept for one year but still they thought it too low. What must the Nation have suffered from the depredation of such a fellow as this.

After dinner the conversation was various and among other things the ingratitude of Clergymen to their Patrons was mentioned. Young Newall asserted that he did not know an instance where the Patron had not been insulted by the Clergyman whom he had beneficed. And as a proof that such was the general opinion he related an anecdote of the Earl of Galloway. He & Kenmore dined one day in Company with a Clergyman to whom Kenmore had given a very good Living. In the course of the Evening he greatly insulted both the Earl and Kenmore. The Earl relating the circumstance a short time after to his friends added, that he did not wonder at Kenmore being insulted because he had given the man a Living. But, damn the fellow, says the Earl, why should he insult me I cannot conceive for I never did him a kind turn in my life.

Another subject of conversation was what at present forms the topic of the whole neighbourhood. A Mr McAdam, a Young Gentleman of £20,000 a year income, has just taken into his house as a Companion, a Miss Walker, the daughter of a respectable neighbouring Farmer. He has had connections with other young women, none of whom has been pregnant by him, and it is believed that if he can have a child by this young woman that he will marry her. One of the company observed that it was Stipulated in the Contract between them that he should marry her if she should be pregnant. But young Newall said there was no truth in the report. He had been informed of their meeting and connection from Mr McAdam himself. He met with her at a Wedding in the Country. He took a fancy to the girl and before they parted made her some proposals to which she seemed not averse. In a day or two he sent a Servant and Horse to fetch her. She refused to go with the Servant but followed on foot to a Mill close by his Gate & sent him word she was there waiting for him. This, said young Newall, is the only part of the transaction either singular or wonderful; that a young woman bred up in a retired part of the Country and under the eye of respectable parents, could so soon lay aside her native modesty as to go alone to the house of such a Gentleman and meet him upon such terms at such short an acquaintance. He met her and took her home. He proposed to settle fifty pounds a year upon her if they should part. She answered she did not know what she should do with it for she had not spent five pounds a year for some years passed. He was so pleased with her disinterestedness that he made the settlement for sixty Guineas a year & this is the only Contract between them. A transaction of this sort in a Country like this surprised me a great deal.[12]

But I was much more surprised, when we left the house, at being informed of the conduct of the Mother of that beautiful girl I mentioned before & whom I took all along to be Mr Newall's Daughter. Her Mother was the Daughter of Mr Newall brought up in this sequestered part of the Country under the eye of her parents, except a short time which she spent at Boarding School in Dumfries. At a very early age she formed a connection with an Officer in the Army and had actually left her father's house & got to the place appointed for their meeting to elope with him. The woman of the Cottage where she came to went & acquainted her Mother what she was abt who came & carried her home again before the Gentleman arrived. Some time after this a Gentleman of the name of Rawlinson, in gentile practice in the law at Kirkcudbright, paid his addresses to her and married her. She lived in repute with him while she bore him four Children, the eldest of whom is the girl I have before described and the youngest a boy abt ten years of age. About eight years ago her husband, Mr Rawlinson, died and in a very short time after that she (without making any provision for her Children or seeing them settled in any way) left the Country in company with a gentleman who carried her to London where the only account that has been heard of her is that the Gentleman has discarded her and it is now supposed she is upon the Town. The eldest & second daughters live with Mr Newall, the youngest is with Mr Rawlinson's mother and the boy Kenmore is educating who has no Children of his own. At 5 o'Clock we left Mr Newall's and went abt two miles over the Hills to drink Tea at Knockshean with Mr and Mrs Sloan, the brother of my Wife's Mother.

June 7th
My Father in law and I went to Breakfast with his brother James at the Shields, a very large Farm where their father lived and where they were all brought up. We tarried here till 12 o'Clock, and then crossed the Country abt four miles to Knocknaling to dine with Mr David Kennedy, oldest brother to J. Kennedy of Manchester, who farms his own Estate worth abt a hundred pounds a year. It is a pleasant romantic situation lying between the Ken and a Rivulet (here called a Burn) which falls into the Ken at the south east corner of the Estate. It is sheltered by a high Hill in the North nearly at the foot of which stands the house. On the East is a Wood several acres in extent and on the West and southward from the

house to the Rivulet is some well cultivated Land. We spent a very agreeable afternoon.

June 8th

At 11 o'Clock we got on horseback to go to the Kirk which is called the Kells Kirk & stands close to Newgalloway which is within the parish of Kells. Mr Sloan with his two Daughters accompanied us. The youngest, took an opportunity to inform me by the desire of her Mother, that the sum of forty pounds belonging to my Wife's own Sister, which had been ever since the death of her Mother's Father by whom it was left her as a legacy, in the hands of her Uncle, Mr Sloan, had been lately called out of his hands and placed in the hands of her two eldest half brothers Jas. and Wm. Cannon, who had jointly taken a very large Farm called Berlie, abt 5 miles North East of Newgalloway. She said that as my Wife's Sister is not likely to be married & that at some future time I might have a interest in this money, they thought it a necessary piece of information to give me. Near the Kirk stands a Hut which they call a Public-house where we crouded our horses loose into a small Outbuilding. We must have something to drink. Six of us, Men and Women, went in and soon drank all the Beer he had which consisted of 2 Bottles only. It was the most miserable Hut I think I ever saw either here or anywhere else. It was all open from top to bottom and from end to side, no floor, no partition, except what was made by a bed set crossways, which it is the fashion here to board up on three sides. The fire lay upon the Hearth without chimney and the Smoke, after spreading all over the house, escaped through a hole in the middle of the Roof.

The Service at the Kirk consisted of extempore prayers, and 2 Sermons, one following the other, a Prayer and a Psalm only intervening. After service a collection is made for the Poor every Sunday & this is the only poor rate they pay. After this was done a young man was called upon by name and standing up in the Seat he was publicly reproved by the Minister for Fornication. After service I was introduced to Mr Gillespie the Minister. I could not dine with him though he pressed me much. When I came to the Public-house not less than 15 of our friends and others had stowed themselves into this hovel and were eating Bread & Cheese and drinking Whiskey. We spent six shillings which just amounted to half a year's Rent of the Inn.

Here I was met by Jas. Cannon, my Wife's eldest half brother with whom I was to go and sleep at his Farm. He and his second brother, William, both unmarried, farm Berlie jointly and their eldest Sister Mary keeps their house. After dinner we walked out upon the Farm. Their Rent is £170 a year and they suppose the circumference of their Farm may not be less that seven miles. The number of acres they do not know.

June 9th
We breakfasted early and at seven o'Clock James and I set out on horse-back for an excursion which was to take up 2 days. After travelling abt 6 miles across the Country over craggy rocks and barren mountains we came to Cross Michael Kirk, which I had passed in my way to Newgalloway. The road from hence to Castlewort, or Castle Douglas as it is now called, is extremely good & runs in the Valley all the way lying at no great distance from the River, of course this was the richest and by far the most improved part of the Country I had seen. Near Cross Michael Kirk the River Ken falls into another River called Dee where they jointly take the name of Dee until they are discharged into the Sea at Kircudbright. A little below the junction of these Rivers the New Road from Dumfries to Port Patrick (14 miles of which I rode over in coming from Dumfries to Cross Michael) is to cross. Three Arches for the new Bridge are already thrown over the river but the Battlements are not yet completed. The Cattle here are superior in size to those kept among the Mountains and bear an advanced price of from twenty to thirty shillings per head. Just above the new Bridge stands a large handsome house belonging to one Captain Lowrie, the Grounds are neatly ornamented with Plantations, and the new Bridge will be a great addition to the Scene. We arrived at Castle Douglas, 8 miles from Cross Michael, abt 10 o'Clock. Here we refreshed ourselves and horses and took a walk through the Town. There is nothing particularly worth attention here, except a Lake of considerable extent adjoining to the Town in the South-side. Here is a good Inn and the Houses in general assume a neatness unknown in the Country places. From hence we rode 9 miles to Kircudbright. The roads were not so good as we had in the morning & frequently lay over the tops of steep hills, the inconvenience of which was fully compensated for by the variety of views which it presented to us. From the top of the Hill before you descend into Kirkcudbright, you have a fine view of the Town and the surrounding hills beautifully variegated and enriched by numerous and extensive Plantations belonging to Lord Selkirk, whose Seat is upon St Mary's Isle, abt 2 miles south of Kirkcudbright. Over the Town you have a view too of a vast tract of the Irish Sea. About a mile before you enter the Town you pass a very large Nursery for raising Trees

of all descriptions. It is kept in very neat order & is well stocked. It belongs to Lord Selkirk. There is little in the Town worth noticing.

Ships of light burden only can come hither. The mouth of the River is of difficult Navigation. There is but little accommodation for Shipping either with respect to Harbour Quay or Warehousing. A great trade, I understand, was carried on here a few years ago but how or why it was lost I did not learn. It is however a neat & pleasant place. The vicinity of Lord Selkirk's house & his extensive Plantations & Improvements, the advantage arising from its Navigation & of the establishing of a Bank in it, give it the preference over most places in the South of Scotland. Having soon taken a survey of the Town we found ourselves at leisure to pursue our walk to St. Mary Isle. We had but little hopes of reaching the house supposing it to be too far distant. But led on by curiosity from walk to walk we at last found ourselves in the back yard of the house which is so completely encompassed with Wood as not to be seen at a distance from any part of the Island. Just as I was speaking to a Servant woman in the yard, a genteel man came out of the door to whom I addressed myself, told him I was an Englishman that curiosity had led me from the Town to view the Island & hoped no offence. He immediately invited us into the House, insisted upon us resting ourselves a little, and taking a Draught of Porter. We staid long enough to drink two Bottles. He informed us that his Lordship was on his way to London where he would stop abt 2 months. This is the house which Paul Jones & his Crew plundered of all the Plate in the American War,13 being disappointed with meeting of Lord Selkirk at home whom they proposed to make prisoner. Upon asking our kind host whether the report is true that the Plate was afterwards restored, he said it was very true. That the Knives and Forks were now lying upon the Table. That the Plate had been purchased from the Crew by Paul Jones and by him restored to the Family, it was considerably bruised but not an Article missing. After resting a little he gave us directions which way to pursue our walk so as to see the whole of the Island to the best advantage. The road we took is the outermost and takes the whole circumference of the Island. The Island is covered with wood, in my opinion there is a great deal too much Timber upon it. The House is not to be seen except you are at it, and the Gardens which are large and in high condition, are not perceived till you come to them. Even the walk we pursued is quite covered, except here and there a break intervenes to open to view the Sea. Tho' called an Island it is only a Peninsula, joined to the main Land by an Isthmus, which is two or three hundred yards broad when the Tide is at the highest.

At 3 o'Clock we returned to dinner. About 5 we mounted our horses to pursue our journey to the Gatehouse ten miles westward from Kircudbright, and where reside two Cousins of my Wife's, Daughters of Mr Jas. Green, one married to a Mr McAdam farmer of Disdow & the other to a Mr Heron farmer of the Hill-head. The Ferry-boat at Kircudbright carried us and our horses over the River at the end of the Town which shortened our journey near 4 miles. This ride is very romantic. The road we took being rather a bye road, we had often very steep hills to rise and descend. On the North-side are bleak and barren mountains, on the South the Lands are cultivated almost to the Waters' edge which is at no great distance; and here are two or three Gentleman's Seats which are always well planted round, and beyond these is a full and extensive view of the Irish Sea which is only bounded southward by the Isle of man. We arrived at the Gatehouse at 7 o'Clock where we soon met with Mr McAdam who insisted upon us sleeping at his house. The Town is but small, yet being a new Town as it were, having been built not very many years, it has an appearance of neatness and I may say elegance which I have not seen in Scotland before. It stands upon the Banks of the River Fleet over which there is a good Bridge at the South-west end of the Town to which Vessels of considerable burden can come and unload Coals and Limestone &c. From the Bridge eastward you have a fine view of the elegant mansion called Keighley[14] late the residence of Mr Murray, who died abt a year ago and whose eldest Daughter, abt 15 years old, was buried this day. He parted from his wife (who is still living) many years ago and has had three Children, 2 of whom, a son & Daughter, are yet living, by another woman, who has resided with him as his wife and yet resides in Keighley-house. For several years before his death he consulted the most eminent Lawyers, both in England and Scotland, to assist him in settling his Estates upon these Children, which I understand he has at last succeeded in, at vast expense; and abt 2 months ago his Parks and several hundred Acres of land which he had held in his own Hands were lett by auction for a term of eleven years until the boy comes of age. There are several spinning Factories for Cotton Twist in the Gatehouse. At 9 o'Clock we went home with Mr McAdam. His house is a mile out of Town and Mr Heron's is the next house to it. We had determined to sleep with him & breakfast with Mr Heron.

June 10th
We rose at 5 in the morning to take a ride into Keighley Parks to look at sixty very fine Bullocks which Mr McAdam had there. He took these

Parks at the Sale (or Roup)[15] as it is called here at the rate of forty shillings & ten pence per scotch Acre, 4 of which make 5 English Statute Acres. This is here thought a most extravagant price. It is the best grassland I had been upon in Scotland, but there is much rough land in it, some rocky, some swampy and some covered with Gorse and Brush-wood. At the Southside of these Parks rises a very strong spring of most excellent water. I conceive it discharges more than 20 Gallons in a minute. We returned to Mr Heron's to breakfast abt 9 o'Clock whither Mrs McAdam had gone before to acquaint them of our coming. I was kindly received and handsomely entertained at both the houses. Mrs McAdam has 7 Children, one of which a girl of abt 3 years of age is suspected will be dumb. Mrs Heron has just recovered from her confinement of the third child. About 50 yards westwards of Mr Heron's house is a prospect which may vie with most in the Kingdom. The house is called the Hill-head and stands abt middle way from the foot to the summit of a very high hill rising gradually from the Town Northward. On the West and very near the Town rises a Mountain vast and craggy. Between this and the Hill you stand upon, is a small but rich & beautiful Valley, in the Centre of which stands the Gate-house. Elevated as you are above the Town, every house is seen distinctly & the houses being all white, it gives the scene a very picturesque appearance. Casting your eye a little farther you see the Masts & Rigging of the Vessels below the Bridge. Southward you have a full view of Keighley House with all its Woods and over those appears the Sea as far as the eye can carry. The Mountains on the Isle of man were seen here more clearly than yesterday. From Cross Michael Kirk to Castle Douglas, thence to Kircudbright & thence to the Gate-house & abt it, the land is not only better of itself but is in a higher state of cultivation than any abt Newgalloway. This no doubt is owing to the facility of getting Lime at Kircudbright and the Gate-house which is brought in the Stone from England and burned there. Whereas the Newgalloway Farmers have to fetch it from the same places though twice the distance from them or more, being not less 20 miles from Lime. This they fetch in Carts drawn by one horse & it is astonishing to me how a single horse can drag even an empty Cart over their mountains.

We left our Friends at 11 o'Clock & were conducted by Mr McAdam through his Farm & put into away over the Mountains which would shorten our Journey near three miles. This road led us through the most barren tract of Country, of equal extent I had ever seen. For near six miles we travelled over Hill after Hill without seeing a House or a cultivated piece of Ground. No Cattle were to be seen except a few Sheep and what to me was a very novel sight, a flock of abt 30 Goats with as nearly as many kids. After having passed what may be called these horrible defiles we came to the Public Road from Newgalloway to Newtown Stewart now called Newtown Douglas. This is the worst Public Road I travelled in all of Scotland. Soon after we fell into this Road we came to and for abt 2 miles rode along the side of the most beautiful Lake I had yet seen. It is called I think the Woodhall Loch. On the opposite side and a little up the Hill stood a Gentleman's Seat called Wood-hall, finely situated with a Southern aspect, sheltered on the North by a high Hill and on the North East by a fine hanging Wood down to the Waters' edge. It seemed strange that abt these Houses improvements are not extended, at 300 Yards distance all is wild & rough as the Mountain overhangs them. After travelling a few miles forward we came within sight of the road we travelled the morning before in going to Castle Douglas and very soon came to the South-end of the Loch of Ken, but on the opposite Bank to what I had been before. Here the ride is romantic indeed, the length of the whole Lake which I conceive may be abt three miles. The Lake close on one side and on the other as close; as steep and lofty hill more rough & craggy than any I had seen, in some places the bare Rock appeared perpendicular for many Yards, in other places stood large stones of several tons in weight alone as if unsupported and ready to fall upon you. At the North-end of the Lake you had a constant view of Kenmore Castle and part of the Woods, except when the Rock in sundry places boldly projected into the Lake and hid them. Out of these large single stones the Bridge for the new Road over the Dee, before mentioned, is built. They have found out a method of cleaving them with Wedges and when no very strong seams are in the stone, it will cleave very clear. I saw several pieces lying, which were large enough for Chimney Pieces, as clear as if they had been wrought out of Free-stone.[16] It is of a rough granite appearance and resists all the efforts of the Chisel. It is cloven here, and put into a Boat & carried down the Lake to the Bridge.

At a Farm called Bonfett situated at the Head of the Lake we were to dine with a Mr Grearson who married Barbary Sloan, Daughter of Jas. Sloan an own Cousin of my Wife's. We came hither a little after 2 o'Clock and I was received and entertained with a greater degree of cordiality and respect, if possible, than at any place I had yet been at. Mrs Grearson is just on foot again after lying in of her third Child. They are now in mourning for their two first, both of whom they have lately lost by inoculation of the Small-pox. I am informed that both Mr and Mrs Grearson are afflicted in the extreme but the circumstance was never

mentioned by them to me. After a very agreeable afternoon we left them
abt 8 o'Clock.

We called upon Mr Jas. Cannon at the Shields as we passed by. He came
to the Door to us without his Shoes. We would not dismount, so he said
he would walk with us a little way & without going in for his shoes, he
walked above a mile with us in his stockings only. We got to Barsceough a
little before ten.

June 12th [Journal wrongly dated]
This being the last day I proposed to stop in Galloway I promised Mr
Cannon to spend it wholly with him. At 2 o'Clock Mr Jas. Cannon of the
Shields and Mr William Sloan came to dine with us. Nothing material
occurred, except that my Wife's half brother James informed me concerning the money which had been called out of Mr Sloan's hands. The reason he gave was, that Mr Sloan's circumstances were well known to be on
the decline & that the money was thought not to be safe. He said he had
thirty pounds of Agnes's money and his brother William had twenty
pounds.

The description of the Northern part of the shire of Galloway which I
have this journey principally been concerned with will not take up much
time or many words. The more fertile parts I have already described in
my account of the journey on the 9th. The farmhouses which are generally situated in the Vallies, or with a Southern aspect or upon the Banks of
Burns (little Rivulets) are usually surrounded with some little land in a
tolerable state of cultivation and not infrequently with some little wood
abt them. Except these and the Lands below Newgalloway upon the
Banks of the Ken and the Dee with the Lands in the neighbourhood of
Castle Douglas, Kircudbright and the Gate-house, the rest of the Country
from a little above Cross Michael directly westwards to the Shire of Ayr
and from the Gate-house North-eastward to Berlie in the Parish of
Balmaclelan each line being abt twenty miles; all this tract I say of the
North of the Shire of Galloway with very few exceptions is one continued range of Hill on Montain piled. Mountains, barren, craggy, rough and
rocky to the surface, and often above the surface. Abounding in Heath
(here called Hether) with a few weak and feeble stalks of Fern intermixed.
The grass, to a stranger, appears scarcely visible but the Sheep, no doubt,
having such extensive range, find sufficient and nutritive food. Amongst
these mountains are found considerable tracts of Peat Moss, which constitutes the general fuel of this country. The surface of the Ground is so covered with stones as that enow may be found upon any piece of Land to

enclose it, especially if it can be plowed. Stone Walls here called Dykes, are the only Fences. And they are here raised, and the Stones for them collected together at all prices for 20s to 30s per rood of 6½ Yards. The highest is seldom above 5½ Feet, nor the lowest less than 4 Feet. The Hay here is all made of Rye Grass & Clover. Nor do I remember to have seen in all Scotland Hay-grass of any other description, except the Water Meadows on the Banks of the Rivers. When the Land which is capable of being plowed is turned over the surface is wholly covered with Stones, some so large that they must be carried off even though not wanted for Dykes. Sometimes the Rock or the surface of a massy stone is laid bare for Yards together by the Plow. Lime is the principal manure here used, but which in the sparing manner they must use it on account of the badness of their bye Roads & the great distance they have to fetch it seems to me incapable of affording any effectual improvement. Marl I am persuaded would be the best manure for this Land to give it a retentive quality. But this is scarcely, it at all, to be found here. Clay is frequently found in some places among the Hills and I recommended my brother in law to try this upon a small patch. Before I left the Country I was informed that Mr Spalding, the Member, had just written to his Agent to set 40 Cart Loads of Clay upon half an Acre of his Land immediately. He is beginning to divide his Estates into smaller Farms which I am persuaded will be the means of improving it. Much remains to be done here, that is practicable; but much, after all must ever remain undone. Nature forbids any very extensive improvement.

With respect to the Plan I had proposed of purchasing Cattle here for stocking my own farm in future & annually, I am yet doubtful abt. I find both the Farms and Farmers very different from what I had expected. I had conceived that the business of the Farmer here was wholly to breed Stock. That their principal attention was turned to this one object and that their sales consisted only of what themselves had bred and that they sold their Cattle off once or twice a year as they became old enough. But I was very much mistaken. They breed not half enow to stock their own Farms (except Sheep) and they must as we do to the Highlands for the Rest. The Country is well situated for bringing the Highland Black Cattle in to rest and freshen awhile and then for conveying them through Dumfries and Carlisle into England. Besides the Fairs held amongst them there is a very large fair at Dumbarton abt 16 miles from Glasgow where seldom less than forty thousand head of Highland Black Cattle are exposed to Sale. This Fair happened to be on the very day I came into Scotland. Many of the Galloway Farmers were gone to it. Young Mr

Newall was there and he and his next neighbour bought eight score. I suppose not less than 500 were brought into the neighbourhood where I was. This makes all the Farmers here into Jobbers. They are constantly buying and selling even amongst each other. And their Farms being so large that (as they express it) a score or two off or on make no difference. They are perpetually buying in and selling off Cattle of all ages and in all states and conditions, at all times of the Year whenever an opportunity offers. This is the Land of Drovers. If a man gets a little money to spare, he commences Drover. They are continually sending Cattle into England by which means they become personally and thoroughly informed of the state of our markets and Stock of Cattle in the Country.

With regard to Sheep the case is somewhat different. These they breed wholly among themselves and never buy any except a few from one another. What they have to sell are usually fetched away into England by Englishmen in the Month of March to be fatted. These are sold at three years old. Some Farmers keep their Wethers or part of them through the Summer to Lammas[17] which is supposed to be as long as they can improve upon this poor land. They are then sold off to go to better pastures where a few weeks makes them fit for the Butcher. The prices of these last are from 14s to 16s apiece and I think twenty-one counted for a Score.

The expence of driving Black Cattle to Atherton is supposed to be from seven to ten shillings per head. One man will drive from 20 to 30. Two men will bring any quantity of Sheep from one hundred to two hundred.

1800 June 12th
I left my Father-in-law's house abt 9 o'Clock in the morning on horseback accompanied by my wife's half brother Samuel. We took the Road over the Hill which leads to Mr David Kennedy's at Knocknalling before mentioned & passing below the house abt half a mile we followed the Riverside a considerable way. The bed of the River (Ken) may here properly enough be called the Giants' Causeway. It is entirely upon the Rock Fragments of which stand thick & close together, frequently 2 or 3 feet high which must make a flood here have a very grand & awful appearance. After quitting the River-side we clambered over Mountain after Mountain. The Road very unaccountably, always leading directly over their summits till we arrived within abt a Mile of Cas-fern.[18] This I conceive was the highest elevation I was upon in all my journey. In looking back over the Road we had travelled it was easily discernible that we

had been perpetually ascending & could overlook all the Hills which abt New-galloway seemed to have no rivals.

The descent from hence to Cas-fern, abt a Mile, is the steepest I had ever travelled. We deemed it prudent to dismount & lead our horses. Here I expected to meet a Daughter of Mr Wm Sloan's whom I had never yet seen. When I was at Knockshean having expressed a wish to see her, her Mother said she would send a message to desire her to meet me here. She was waiting for me & this mutual wish of seeing each other arose from her being the most favourite Companion to my Wife, of all her Cousins. She is the most smart lively & pleasant woman I had seen in the neighbourhood but she is unfortunately married to a man of the name of Wallace, who not only neglects her but his family too, which consists of 4 Children leaving them frequently for Months together to be supported by his brother who happily has both the means and inclination to do it. Though we were perfect strangers to each other, I spent 2 very happy hours in her company & left her at last with great reluctance.

I was going to Ayr where I intended to sleep that night. Samuel did not know the Road any farther but luckily while we stopped here a Mr Grearson (who married an aunt of my Wife's & whom I had seen at his own house 3 days before) happened to call to refresh himself & horse. He was going to see his son who lives upon a large Farm within five Miles of Ayr. The Meeting was fortunate & agreeable. It added a Companion to the party with the additional satisfaction of his being acquainted with the Road.

We left Cass-fern abt 12 o'Clock & went as far as Damellenton (a corruption of Dame Ellen's Town of which Dame Ellen there are some legendary stories in the Neighbourhood). In this ride we passed near the Seat of Mr McAdam of whom mention is made on the 6th June in this Journal. In this wild & romantic Country where there are no hedges or hedge-row Timber, the Gentlemen's Seats which are universally surrounded with Plantations have always in my eye a very pleasing effect. Such is Mr McAdam's Seat. But the country here and still as you approach the Shire of Ayr, begins to lose a good deal of its rugged & barren appearance, & assume a more pleasing and fertile look. When we arrived at the Inn the Landlord had scarcely time to put up our horses. The Drum was beating the Volunteers to Arms & he could not be absent at the Roll-call. Damellenton is the most contemptible Town, Village (or whatever you choose to call it) I ever saw & yet they muster there from 40 to 50 stout active Volunteers. This is the case at every little Village you pass situated in Mountains & Wilds where one should conceive that if an

Enemy did unwarily come thither, his greatest exertions would be to get away again as speedily as possible. With some considerable assistance of our own we got our Horses taken care of & then went into the House to take care of ourselves. But there was neither Beef Mutton or Veal in the house, no Fish, no Cheese; I began to tremble. At last it came out that the good woman had got Ham & Eggs. These would do for a very good reason, & give here her due she was expeditious enough in cooking them. But there was no Ale, no Porter, & we were obliged to be satisfied with the universal Scotch Beverage, Whiskey. One would be astonished, when one reflects how so few houses as are in Damellenton could be so inconveniently jumbled together. Though there is a fine plain adjoining yet it is situated upon the side of a Hill of steep descent. At the upper end of the Town you turn at right Angles into a Street which admits of only one carriage at a time & yet there is rather a spacious opening before the principal Inn. No pavement at all in it but a rough gravel which is very much torn up by the rapid descent of the Rains down so steep a pitch. The Gentlemen in Scotland, almost universally very much to their credit, and the improvement of the Country spend much time and pains in altering and amending or in laying out entirely new Roads. Among these is Mr McAdam, though but a young man who has by his influence & the weight of his purse gained almost dictatorial authority abt the Roads in this neighbourhood. By one bold effort he has made an entire new Road which does not come within 200 Yards of the Town by which you escape not only the danger & difficulty of going through the Town but the Road is kept upon a much better level. About half a mile west of the Town, there is extensive Moss deep & rotten, or rank Moss as it [is] called in Lancashire. Over this Moss Mr McAdam was determined to carry the new Road & actually has carried it contrary to the advice & expectation of every other person concerned, as it was deemed totally impracticable. Though he was resolved to carry his own Plan into execution, he generously paid all extra expence & expended no less a sum than four hundred pounds of his own money. It has been completed in 3 or 4 Years & is now an exceedingly good road, but I am informed it still sinks a little every year & requires to be frequently raised with gravel of which there is a great abundance in the River not 500 Yards distance. At no great distance from the Town you come very near to the Lake called Dom-loch, seven miles long & a mile broad. Upon a small Island in this Loch, Dame Ellen built a Castle part of which is still standing & is seen from the Road. There were a massy pair of Iron Gates at the Castle & but a very few years ago the Proprietor wished to remove them by taking advantage of a hard

Frost & sliding them over the Ice but they had not proceeded half way to the shore with the first Gate but the ice gave way & the Gate went to the bottom where it still remains. The River Ayr runs through this Loch by which means it is always well stocked with Salmon & Trout of superior quality. The features of the Country here become softer & less harsh. It is mountainous still but the Hills are not craggy nor covered with Heath. They produce a fine abundant pasture to their very Summits & furnish a very ample bite of Grass for the Cattle which are here more numerous than upon the rugged barren mountains of Galloway. The Hills here descend with a fine but rather steep declivity for a mile or more to the River with a Southern aspect. And I conceive that if Plantations of 40 or 50 Yards broad and at three or four hundred Yards distant from each other were run up the Hills directly north & south they would not only add very much to the beauty of the Country but would likewise suffi-ciently inclose it & furnish complete shelter for the Cattle of which they stand very much in need from the East & West winds.

Here I saw both Coal & Limestone raised & not more than three hun-dred yards asunder and I was told what to me appears very singular, that not only here but from hence as far as Glasgow & all this part of Scotland, that wherever Coal is found they are certain Lime-stone is not far off & vice versa where there is Limestone, Coal is sure to be found.

The Land and Country gradually improve as you approach to Ayr. The Hills sink into the gentle declivities and the face of the Country assumes a fine open wavy appearance and when you come within a Mile of the Town you find yourself surrounded with numberless Acres of Land in a high state of Garden Culture.

It was a fine Evening abt 6 o'Clock when I entered Ayr. The Garden Grounds were almost covered with men & women to whom I suppose small portions had been allotted for raising Potatoes & other Vegetables.

Ayr is a pretty, lively, smart Town part of it consists of old Buildings & part of new & modern Edifices. The Streets are commodiously wide & opposite the King's Arms Inn where I lodged there is a fine opening for the Market. Here is a very good & extensive Quay, but the entrance of the River is dangerous & Vessels of more than three hundred Tons bur-then cannot come up to Ayr. The bed of the River at low-water is very narrow indeed. Below the Quay & upon the Beach have been lately erected very extensive Barracks. The Southern Wall is 265 Yards long & this length with an Area of 70 Yards wide forms a space sufficient I should conceive to exercise 2,000 soldiers. I saw 500 drawn up & exercised in it by the Duke of Buccleugh their Colonel (a Militia Regiment) & they

seemed to occupy but a very small portion of it. The Buildings are all of
Stone & are very extensive. On the West Side & with a handsome Front
to the Area stands a very good Building for the accommodation of the
Officers. Here the Duke of Buccleugh messes with his Officers with
whom he spends the whole Summer without any of his Family or any
retinue of Servants. He seems a smart active man, of the common or middle size, & I am told he is a very strict disciplinarian. His son Lord
Dalkeith is Colonel of the Dumfriesshire Militia.

Near the Barracks a new and extensive Pile of Buildings has been erected for the accommodation of Professors in various branches of Literature
& for the Students. The foundation is similar to those of Edinburgh &
Glasgow. Lord Cassel's I think is the Lord of the Manor here. His Seat is
but a few miles distance.   Ayr is not a large Town. The Public Buildings
are but few so that before dark we had fully satisfied our curiosity. I had
taken a place in the Mail Coach to Glasgow which was to set out at 8
o'Clock in the morning. We had ridden 34 miles from my Father in law's
to Ayr & had pretty much fatigued ourselves with walking abt the Town.
We supped early & went to bed.

June 13th
I arose abt 6 o'Clock & looking through my window into the Market
Place I was struck with a sight pretty & novel, it was the Butter-women. I
suppose no less than 30 women, principally young, were standing together all without Hats or Bonnetts & many without Caps, most of them slip-
shod & many not shod at all. Tho' the Scotch women are not remarkable
for cleanliness in their houses yet they always appear light airy & neat
when in public. This group of females was to me peculiarly picturesque &
pleasing. Everyone had a light fancy plaid, some blue & white, some
green & white & others red & white, which answered the double purpose
of covering their Shoulders or their Heads as occasion or the weather
required. When over their Shoulders, it was large enough to cover the
Baskets suspended on their arms. After I was dressed & at leisure, I could
not resist the temptation of going down among the Caledonian Lasses
where I stopped till the Coach was ready.

At 8 o'Clock I got into the Coach & left Ayr. The Land abt Ayr is of
the best quality & in the highest state of cultivation of any I had seen in
Scotland. I was particularly pleased at the high state of cultivation of a
large Estate not far from Ayr belonging to a Dr. Fullerton of Rosamind.
The Road leads through the Estate, the northern part of which is very
beautiful. A regular systematic plan has been pursued in laying down the

land for Grass, & every advantage has been taken of its fine sloping aspect to the Sun. There was a Field of Rye-Grass (the common Grass for Hay in Scotland) nearly ready to cut, of at least 60 statute Acres, & in such a perfect & uniform state of cultivation as not to be perceptible, that any one part of that large Field, not even a single Butt, was richer or poorer than another. I would ride my horse 20 miles on purpose to see such another Field. Dr. Fullerton has made Plantations upon this Estate exactly in the manner I hinted at in page ———. The effect is exactly what I supposed it would be & I am surprised the practice is not universal.

From hence there is a view of a Rock northward of Ayr projecting far into the Sea where it was once proposed to have made a Harbour, instead of the one which has since been made at New-port Glasgow, Port Irwin still more Northward likewise may be seen from hence. Vessels of 250 tons burden may be admitted there. From the appearance of the Country I conceived it very practicable to bring a Canal from Port Irwin 8 or 10 Miles into the Country among the Coals of which there are great abundance all the way from Ayr to Glasgow. I mentioned my idea to a fellow traveller who said the making of a Canal in the line I pointed out was even now in contemplation. A few miles north of the Road you may see a tract of the Country called Dunlope famous for producing Cheese of an excellent quality, equal I was told to the Cheshire.[19] The first Village we passed after leaving Ayr was Kelcase where Robt. de Bruce founded a Charity for the relief of persons afflicted with the King's Evil.[20] The fund is now applied to the relief of the Poor & is under the management of the Family of the Est. at Cragge. Between Ayr & Kilmarnock, abt 13 miles, there are not less than 5 or 6 villages populous and engaged in various manufactures. One of them, I think Rickerton, has been almost entirely destroyed by fire a few weeks before I passed through it. Many of the Buildings were already repaired & most of the others had workmen at them. This I was told was the third time this Village had suffered materially from Fire & yet, strange to say, the people still continue to cover their houses with Thatch (except a very few indeed) tho Slate may be had Coast-ways at a reasonable rate. A large Village called Netherton-holme, nearly adjoins to & may almost be called part of Kilmarnock where we breakfasted. From Kilmarnock to Glasgow abt 14½ Miles I do not recollect anything worth particularising; but I cannot quit Ayrshire without observing it is a beautiful and rich county bounding in Lime-stone, Coal & Free-stone, not one of which three useful & necessary Articles is to be found in Galloway. Ayrshire is farmed & deservedly so for its breed of Milch Cows. They are but small, not weighing when fat I should suppose more than 130lb per Quar., but the quantity of Milk they produce is astonishing. I was told that 4 scotch pints, each of which is two English Quarts, is reckoned but a moderate quantity for one of these little Animals to give twice a day & that 5 & 6 Scotch pints is very often the produce at one time. They have a very handsome & useful breed of Draught Horses, stout & well made abt 14¹/₆ hands high; they seemed extremely active & to travel very quick in the one-horse Carts which are the only Carts used here & they were without exception the handsomest Horses & in the best condition of any I saw in all my journey.

I arrived at Glasgow at 2 o'Clock. As we passed over the Bridge I was surprised at the sight of at least 300 women all busily employed in a large piece of Grass-land upon the Banks of the River. At first I could not imagine what they were abt, but upon a nearer approach to them I discovered that they were spreading new washed Linen upon the Grass to dry and air. I found upon enquiry that all the Families in Glasgow send their Servants & Domestics to wash their Linen at Public Wash-houses where they are accommodated with hot & cold Water, Tubs &c., & Ground to lay their Clothes on at a certain fixed price. Upon the Piece of Ground where these women are is one of these Public Wash-houses belonging to the Corporation & which I was assured clears £700 per Year. There is seldom any Custom generally followed in any place or Country, however absurd, ridiculous or inconvenient it may appear to a Stranger, but upon full investigation will be found to have originated in reason and propriety. This is exactly the Case with Public Wash-houses in Glasgow. Few houses here are solely inhabited by one Family. The general Custom is for one Family to occupy only the Rooms of one Floor & thus 5 or 6 Families (for the Houses are amazingly lofty) live under the same Roof, each accommodated by one general stone-stair Case, winding from bottom to top. An Englishman will easily conceive how ill adapted this is for cleanliness, no back conveniences, no Yards or Gardens. Public wash-houses are therefore resorted to, not only for convenience, but from necessity & are attended with this very great advantage that the Clothes may be exposed upon a fine piece of Grass-lands to the free and open air, which from the construction of the Houses is impossible to be done at home. This description applies likewise to Edinburgh, where the houses are seldom less than eight Stories high. It is not, to be sure, a very delicate or very decent sight, to see a sturdy Scotch-wench bare foot & bare legged tucked up to the Waist, splashing & trampling in a tub full of dirty Clothes.

The Coach drove to the King's Arms Inn. Dinner was upon the Table. Immediately after Dinner I went to Mr Handyside's where Mr Wood of

Carlisle said he should lodge. He was gone off in the Mail Coach abt an hour before. Mr Handyside however was so polite as to say he would accompany me through the Town. He led me thro the Northern part of the Town which is situated upon rising Ground on the summit of which stands the High Church which in England would be called the Cathedral. This is the most complete piece of Gothic Architecture in the Kingdom. It was founded as early as the Year 1123. It is a most beautiful as well as a most majestic Building & on the Outside is in complete repair but in the inside, like all the large Churches in Scotland which I saw, has a cold and comfortless appearance, is much neglected not only with regard to white washing & cleaning, in general but also with respect to repairs. It is lighted by 157 windows & is supported by 147 Pillars high & low. From this elevated situation a most extensive & beautiful prospect is presented. The whole Town is overlooked, particularly the new part of it down to the Banks of the Clyde. Eastward the whole Vale of the Clyde rich & populous. Westward the large manufacturing Town of Paisley with the intervening Country which is very beautiful, also the Castle of Mearns & Cruickstone noted for the residence of the unfortunate Mary Stuart and the noble fortress of Dumbarton. To the north the Campsie Hills at the distance of ten miles & to the South those of Cathkin, in distant five miles, close the Landscape.

From the High Church we continued our walk through the most ancient part of the Town which stands upon the summit of the ridge of Ground which runs here East and West & thus descended down High-street into the Center of the Town. In the High-street stands the College or University. The front is abt 110 Yards, three stories high, built of polished Ashler stone. The main Gate is in the Center & is well ornamented with rustic work. At a considerable way north & south of this Gate are two others, each of which leads into an Area surrounded with Buildings, the residence of the Professors. The Street is but narrow here and the whole has a gloomy appearance. The finest appendage to the Buildings of the University is the Garden which slopes gently eastward to a Rivulet called the Molendinar Burn. Within this Area are included seven Acres of ground always kept in Grass, except the Borders which are planted with shrubbery.

At the bottom of High-Street stands the Toll-booth or Prison. Adjoining to this stands the famous Tontine Coffee Room & Hotel. The Coffee Room is 72 feet in length & of proportional breadth and is universally allowed to be the most elegant in Britain and most probably in Europe. At this point four principal Streets meet & the great concourse of people here assembled & the perpetual passing & repassing resembles the Strand in London far more than anything I have seen either in Bristol, Bath, Birmingham, Manchester or Edinburgh. Near here is Mr Robert Kennedy's Warehouse. Having a Letter of recommendation to him from his Brother John in Manchester, Mr Handyside introduced me to him & he invited me to Tea & to spend the Evening with him. Mr Handyside left us. In going to Mr Kennedy's House which stands on the Southside of the River over the New Bridge, we passed through the main Street viz: Iron-gate & Argyle Street, which is superior to any thing I have ever seen except Bath. Having spent a very pleasant hour at Mr Kennedy's he accompanied me in my perambulation of the Southern part of the Town. After traversing a few Streets in which nothing particular appeared we arrived at the Green. This is one of the finest ornaments & useful appendages I know to any Town. It belongs, not properly to the Corporation but to the City. It extends upwards of three quarters of a Mile upon the Banks of the Clyde. Near the entrance is the public Wash-house before mentioned. About half-way up is a small but neat Building for the accommodation & recovery of persons apparently drowned & that the eastern extremity are beautiful Serpentine walks. Besides the money arising from the Wash-houses a great number of fine Cattle are grazed upon the Green, the proprietor of each paying 40s for five months grazing. The usual Stock is abt 130. This must be a very great accommodation to so populous a Town. Leaving this Serpentine walks we entered the Village of Coulton, which now adjoins the Town. The Buildings here are chiefly of Brick covered with Tile, the materials for making of which abounding in the neighbourhood. These Buildings are principally inhabited by Weavers. Ascending still Northward we came to the Barracks. These are new & extensive but do not, I think, comprehend so large an Area as those at Ayr. Descending from hence thro the Street called Gallow-gate we arrived at the Toll-Booth & Hotel before mentioned. It being now growing dark I took Mr Kennedy to sup with me & after spending a pleasant hour retired to Bed.

June 14th
In consequence of the advice of Mr Kennedy not to omit the opportunity of seeing Stirling Castle, I was hurried from Glasgow a day sooner than I intended. A Coach being to set out from Glasgow to Stirling this afternoon at 4 o'Clock I took a place in it. Having determined to see Paisley which is situated 8 miles westward from Glasgow & being obliged to attend to the Coach at 4 o'Clock in the afternoon, I arose very early to

have an opportunity of walking up to the Canal before I went to Paisley. The Bason of the Canal is I think little less than a Mile from the Center of the Town and is upon the summit of the rising Ground which lies North of the Town & must be upwards of a hundred feet above the level of the Clyde. This is a branch from the great Canal which by uniting the Firths of Forth & Clyde, joins the Eastern & Western Seas. This Canal is one of those vast undertakings which always indicate the wealth & commerce of a nation. It is 35 miles in length, 16 of which is on the summit of the Country 156 feet above the level of the Sea. Its depth is eight feet & the width 56 feet on the Surface & 28 on the bottom. There are 20 Locks into the Eastern & 19 into the Western Seas. I regret that I had not an opportunity of going to see the great Aqueduct Bridge, which carries this Canal over the deep Valley & River of Kelvin, it is supposed to be the largest Fabric of the kind in the world. I cannot leave Glasgow without observing that it is one of the most beautiful and well built Towns I ever saw. The Inhabitants have acted wisely in leaving the Old Town and choosing fresh Ground for their Improvements which has given them an opportunity of laying out large wide & commodious Streets & Squares. The grandeur of the Town is much indebted to the abundance of free-stone of an excellent quality which adjoins to it & the Inhabitants to have spared no expence in setting it out to the best advantage. The Houses which seem to have been first built in the new part of the Town are over-loaded with ornament which gives to many of them a dull and gloomy appearance, but those now erecting & of a modern date are more plain & neat. It is well adapted for Trade and Commerce being abundantly supplied with Coals & having a navigable River & a Canal both communicating with the Western Ocean. To these advantages it certainly owes all its prosperity. Advantages which have been embraced & the spirit for Commerce & for Improvements displayed by the Citizens of Glasgow does them very great Credit. As I could have an opportunity of returning from Paisley in a Coach at 12 o'Clock but could not leave Glasgow in any Coach before 10 I determined to walk thither, therefore having viewed the Canal & Bason I left Glasgow at 7 o'Clock.

The Road is exceedingly spacious & fine & there is a gravel walk for foot passengers all the way from 5 to 6 feet wide. The Country between Glasgow & Paisley is well inclosed with Quick-thorn Hedges, and as may well be supposed, adjoining two such large Towns is in a high state of cultivation. There are great numbers of Gentlemen's Seats at different distances from the Road on both sides all the way which gives a grandeur to the neighbourhood scarcely to be described. The passing & repassing of people and Carriages of every description upon this Road is immense. I could not help being surprised at meeting so many smart & fashionably dressed women without Shoes & Stockings. In so populous a neighbourhood, where so many Strangers came & where the lower class of people can acquire great wages by their labour, I expected to have found that custom almost wholly laid aside. I arrived at Paisley at abt 9 o'Clock & went immediately to the Inn where the Coach would come to in which I meant to return to Glasgow. Having breakfasted I began my perambulation. Paisley is situated upon the Banks of the River Cart which is navigable from the Clyde for Vessels drawing seven feet water, so that an easy communication is open by water from Paisley not only with Glasgow, Greenock & Port Glasgow, and the West of England but also through the great Canal with Leith, London & the Continent of Europe.

The old Abbey is a fine Gothic piece of Building, but at present is only a small part of what it formerly was. I imagine the part now standing is nothing more than the Chancel. The great north Window is of beautiful workmanship indeed; the whole outside has been profusely ornamented, than which scarce anything lighter or richer can be imagined. There are several other Churches in Paisley but time would not permit me to visit them. The Town-house, which contains the Prison, Court-hall &c., is a fine Edifice with a Spire & Clock & stands in the Center of the Town. There are a great many handsome Houses in Paisley, but they are frequently surrounded by old Buildings, and have nothing like the uniformity of Glasgow. I was upon the whole disappointed with the appearance of Paisley, for I had been told before I left England that it was the handsomest Town I should see in Scotland. The Manufactures are carried on to a great extent, consisting chiefly of light Goods such as Muslins, sewing Thread, Silk Gause &c. The Country abt is beautiful & picturesque both from nature & art. Northward, the barren Mountains of the Highlands appear over Dumbarton. The three hours I spent at Paisley were fully employed in traversing the Town & examining it as far as circumstances would permit. It is a large Town containing at least 23,000 Inhabitants & is well accommodated with 3 Stone Bridges over the River. At 12 o'Clock I got into the Coach to return to Glasgow after having spent the forenoon very much to my satisfaction. In the Coach conversing with the passengers concerning Coal & Fuel, a Gentleman said there is a seam of Coal abt six miles west of Paisley & sixty fathom thick.

After returning to Glasgow I had only time to dine & rest me a little before the Coach was ready to set out for Stirling, which is abt 30 Miles distant. One of the Passengers was an elderly, fat, plain dressed man. As soon as we got into the Coach he began to inform us what trouble he had been at in sending round the whole Town for a Chaise but without success, that he had very seldom ridden in a public Stage Coach, that he was anxious to have got off earlier as he should have dined at Sir William Graham's where he was going to spend a few days. I suspect he wished to impose himself upon us as some man of consequence & be a very troublesome Companion. However he became very conversible & agreeable. We entered fully into the subject of farming both in England & Scotland. He knew Mr Newall of Stringfascet with whom I had dined a few days ago. For the sake of keeping up the chat, I informed him of the conversation that had passed there abt Mr McAdam (mentioned before in these memorandums) as being to me a very singular case. He said he had dined with Mr McAdam several times since the occurrence had happened, and that the young woman always sat at the Table, that he was very sorry for her & lamented her situation very much. After travelling abt 12 miles he said he must leave us at the next Stage as Sir William's house was a few miles off the public Road, & that he should take a Chaise at the next Inn. When we came to the Inn, I being next the Door got out first & going into the house I observed the waiter hurrying his Master to the Coach saying, Sir William was in! Sir William was in! My curiosity was excited & I asked the Waiter who informed me that my fellow traveller was Sir William Cunningham of Ayrshire.[21] I modestly ordered my bottle of Porter into another Room but he soon sent for me and insisted upon my staying with him as long as I did stay and pressed me much to partake of a Beef-stake with him. Before we parted he informed me that Mr McAdam was his eldest Sister's son & in case Mr McAdam should die without lawful issue, that all his Estates would descend to his (Sir William's) eldest son, who was an officer in Ireland where he had been 5 Years and during all the troubles there. When I returned into the Coach I recollected that Sir William seemed anxious to put an end to the conversation abt the young woman when I first mentioned it & I could not help reflecting how cautious we should be of the Subjects we introduce before Strangers.

As it now began to grow dusk and I had only a young woman for my fellow traveller as ignorant of the Country as myself, nothing particular occurred during the rest of the Journey. We arrived at Stirling abt 11 o'Clock. I observed that the whole of the Country we had passed thro' was more of a Corn Country than any I had passed through before. It will not be improper to mention here a circumstance respecting Corn which struck me particularly. It was in the middle of June, the Corn which is chiefly Oats or Barley was abt 6 inches high & not yet in the ear and I do

not recollect seeing a Corn Field in all of Scotland (and particularly
adjoining to large Towns where the land was highly manured) which was
not almost covered, and in many cases wholly covered with a yellow
Flower so that a blade of Corn could not be seen. I saw no attempt to
weed this Flower out anywhere & I conceived it would entirely choke
the Corn & prevent its growth. I mentioned the subject & my surprise to
every person I had an opportunity that was likely to give me any information & among the rest to Sir William Cunningham. The answer I got was
always the same. That the Flower was called Mustard, that it was a weed
by no means disliked by the Farmers, that it was now in its full bloom, but
in abt a month none of it would be seen, that it would drop down to the
Ground, would leave the Corn entirely disencumbered and would rather
serve to enrich than impoverish the Land.[22]

Upon my arrival at Stirling I found that a Coach would set out for
Edinburgh on Monday morning at 8 o'Clock. This was convenient for
me, as it would leave me the whole of Sunday to myself and as the hurry
of travelling had thrown me much in arrears with my memorandums, I
determined to embrace this opportunity for fetching them up. Having
supped I retired to bed at midnight.

June 15th
I arose at 7 o'Clock & having a Room to myself I sat down to write until
it was time to go to Church. The Landlord sent a boy with me to shew
me a seat. The boy when we got into the Church seeming uncertain
where to place me, a Gentleman passing by took me by the arm, & led
me into a handsome lined Seat near the Pulpit. I have before observed
that collections are made weekly for the Poor. In large Towns & where
the Congregations are numerous a collection in the Church would be
troublesome, a person therefore is seated in the Porch with a large Copper
Dish before him into which the contribution is thrown. The service is
conducted in a manner very similar to our own, only the Prayers are
given extempore, & here the Clergyman preached without Notes. There
were several Christenings. The Children are presented to the Clergyman
when he is abt to Baptize them, by the father. The Congregation was
numerous and all very smartly dressed in the English Fashion. The Ladies
seem very partial to Veils, I remember seeing a young woman in the
Street here, with a deep Veil, without Shoes & Stockings & an Umbrella
in her hand.

After service I went out of the Church Yard thro' a door which led me
into a Plantation growing upon a very steep Bank & through which a

gravel walk leads on to the South-side of the Castle. Here I found an
object well worth my while in coming to see. The Castle & the Rock on
this side and indeed all round, form the truly grand sublime. The Hill
upon which the Castle stands, is here for a considerable way so steep that
Cattle cannot stand to graze upon it. From the bottom to the place where
the Rock rises perpendicular is, I think, not less that a hundred Yards, the
walk is made abt half way from the bottom. If you look downward you
have a view of a fine rich Valley not very extensive here, as it is bounded
by Hills at no great distance. If you look upwards to the Castle, I have
never seen anything so awful and so grand. About 50 Yards above the
Rock rises perpendicularly as if it were a wall to a height not less than a
hundred feet, from the top of this is continued the Castle wall with
Towers and other Buildings to an amazing height that to look at it almost
makes one tremble. As you advance Westward and till you come to the
Western extremity of the Hill you are constantly seeing more & more of
the most beautiful Valley I ever saw. When you come to go along the
north western side of the Hill, the Rock is not so compact & firm as
under the Castle. The violence I suppose of the western Storms has
washed away the thin covering of Soil which was formerly upon it and
also the soft parts of the Stone, and has left it in a state which is grand and
awful beyond conception. In some places appear as if large Columns
raised by art, and composed of vast stones standing upon the end. Some of
these Columns are perpendicular & some slanting at a Angle of 15 or 20
degrees. Farther on, the Rock is still more irregular, the soft parts having
been washed away, or mouldered, so as to leave pieces of Rock of all sizes
from one Ton to 50 seemingly wholly detached from the Mountain and
to be only supported by other Stones as if accidentally propping them up.
In some places you may thrust your hand between them, in some your
arm, & in some your whole body. Walking among these, looking up, and
seeing them as it were tottering over your head, a stranger cannot help
feeling a momentary alarm. At the Northwestern extremity you rise a
high piece of Ground covered with Grass from the summit of which the
prospect is the most enchanting that imagination can conceive.
Northward & immediately under you is the beautiful Bridge over the
Forth. The River both above & below the Bridge, winds abt in the most
fantastic manner. Its meanderings are beautiful beyond description, sometimes sweeping quite across the Valley, then returning again & almost
coming in contact with the point it set out from. One while it encom-
passes a piece of Ground in the form of a Horse-shoe, another in the form
of a Semicircle, thus visiting and enriching every part of the Valley in a

most delightful but indescribable manner. Some idea may be formed of the extent of its windings from this circumstance, that by water the distance is not less than 24 miles to a Village which by land is only seven miles from Stirling. Westward is a fine rich Valley which on this day was beautifully ornamented by Corn Fields covered with the yellow Flower before mentioned and at the distance of abt two miles were several Acres of bleaching Ground which amidst the green Meadows added to the variety of the Landscape. At the upper end of this Valley and at no very great distance are several black and craggy mountains which continue to rise one above another as far as the eye can perceive. Northward is a mountain whose rocky Base extends to the River and whose sides are beautifully enriched with Brush wood. Eastward is a fine level open tract of Country which extends all the way Edinburgh and I am informed that the Castle of Edinburgh may be seen from hence. In this direction and abt half a mile distant stand the lofty remains of an old Abbey where I was told some of the Scottish kings are buried. This has a picturesque appearance standing upon a semicircular piece of Ground amid the most intricate windings of the River.

After Dinner and after Tea I visited again this charming spot, each time taking a different Rout thro' the Town but found nothing worth particular notice. The Town stands upon a steep hill rising from East to West and on the highest extremity of which stands the Castle. Before you reach the Gates there is a fine open, containing at least two statute Acres, from hence the whole Town is overlooked and the whole of the plain towards Edinburgh. There have been very lately several new Buildings erected within the Walls & it is now used as a Barracks for 1000 men. The West York Militia were lying in it when I was there. I cannot leave this place without paying to it this just tribute, that I never saw a place in all my life which gratified and delighted me so much as Stirling Castle and its Environs. The Town is large & the neighbourhood populous. The Inn I was at is the Golden Lion kept by Mr Wingate. It is very extensive and is the cleanest & best managed of any Inn I was at in Scotland. I could not help being surprised at the great number of Horses & Chaises kept here. Upon enquiry I was informed that Stirling is, at it were, the key to the Highlands and that the posting is very considerable.

June 16th
About 8 o'Clock in the morning I got into the Coach for Edinburgh. About 7 miles from Stirling we passed Torr-wood noted for the constant retreat and hiding place of the famous Wallace. A little way before we

came to Falkirk, which is 11 miles from Stirling, we passed under the great Canal which looks down into the Forth just below the Carron Iron-works, the most extensive in the Kingdom & which are situated abt two miles from the Road here. Still nearer to Falkirk is Calendar, the Seat of Mr Forbus, the noted Coppersmith before mentioned. It was formerly the Seat of the Earl of Kilmarnock, whose Estates were forfeited and sold. It is a fine venerable looking place and well wooded. Not far from hence is a newly built handsome house with a fine Eastern aspect belonging to General Maxwell. Everything abt this house is modern. The Plantations are extensive but all young.

But few remarks can be made by a traveller in a Stage Coach. The Country is a fine open plain over which you may extend the view a great way, the sight not being interrupted by Timber growing in the Hedge Rows. From this cause I think the Woods & Plantations growing upon the Hills and abt the Houses have a better effect and give the Country a more variegated and picturesque appearance. We arrived at the White Hart Inn in the Grass Market at Edinburgh at 2 o'Clock to Dinner.

Immediately after Dinner I began my perambulation. I had a direction to Mr David Cannon, son of Mr Jas. Cannon of the Shields & own Cousin to my wife. He is a private Tutor to the Sons of Colonel Fotheringham who resides in the center of the principal Street of the New Town of Edinburgh. Conceiving Mr Cannon would be more at liberty farther on in the Evening, I determined to walk down to Leith before I called upon him. I passed from the Grass Market into the Lawn Market & thence descended down the High Street till I came to the part where the North & South Bridges stand at right Angles with the High Street & directly opposite to each other.

Turning over the North Bridge which is the road to Leith, the Register Office appears before you. This is a most beautiful stone Building 200 feet in front & 40 feet deep. It is supposed to be the most beautiful of the late Mr Adams' designs. It was sixteen Years in building & cost nearly forty thousand pounds. I think it the neatest Building I ever saw & it is one of the principal Ornaments of the City. At the East end of this Building, turning a little to the right, you soon come into a fine open Road called the Leith Walk. An excellent footway carefully barred against Horses & Carriages conducts you from Edinburgh to Leith by a very agreeable Walk.

Leith is the Sea-port of Edinburgh & is situated at something less than two Miles distance from it. The old Town is remarkable for the strength & gloominess of its Buildings, such as was the fashion of former times when habitations were crowded together without regard to any other accommodation than mere security & shelter. Its Streets are narrow & dirty, but like all other towns were Trade & Commerce flourish, it has been enlarged & enriched by new Streets & Houses remarkable for their lightness, commodiousness & elegance. The Merchants here take an extensive share in the Greenland whale fishing. They trade likewise to a large Amount with Russia, Denmark, Sweden, Hamburgh, Ostend & the Sea-ports of Holland, likewise to the Coasts of the Mediterranean & to the West Indies & America, but their chief trade is with London & other Towns on the Eastern Coast of England & with the inland Towns on the Frith of Forth, as also with Glasgow & the Western Districts, by means of the navigable Canal making a junction between the Forth & the Clyde. I can say nothing in favour of the harbour of Leith, the improvement of which has lately undergone long & frequent discussions in Parliament & I believe Government have now consented to grant a sum of money for carrying it into execution. I returned the same way I went. The two Towns are now become almost joined together by the Buildings erected upon the Road-side & in all probability will in a few years be completely so if Commerce continues to flourish.

In my return I called at Colonel Fotheringham's where I fortunately met with Mr David Cannon who received me very politely & said he would accompany me during my stay in Edinburgh. In a very few Minutes he was ready to walk out with me. We spent the remainder of the Evening in traversing & examining the New Town.

The New Town of Edinburgh with most superb, extensive & regular pile of Buildings I ever saw & hath without doubt a superiority over every City in Britain. It consists of three Streets running parallel to each other & parallel to the old Town, that is in a direction from East to West. Each of these Streets is nearly a Mile in length. The most northerly called Queen Street is 100 feet broad. The aspect of this Street is directly to the Frith of Forth and from hence a full view is had, of the Leith Road as it is called, & of the Vessels lying there, or passing & repassing. Between this Street & Frith are rich Fields beautifully extending to the Waters' edge & on the opposite side of the Frith are the picturesque shores of Fife-shire. The Center Street is called George's Street & is no less than 115 feet wide. It is terminated at each end by two very elegant & extensive Squares, that on the East end is called St Andrew's Square, the other not yet finished is named Charlotte's Square. Near the Western extremity of this Street is a cross Street called Castle Street which commands two views of very different description. Looking Northward there

is a full view of the Leith Road as from Queen's Street Southward stands
the Castle perched upon a lofty & apparently inaccessible Rock, bold &
picturesque beyond description. Prince's Street is the most southerly &
points towards the old Town. This Street is not quite finished. The New
Town is built thro'out upon a regular Plan. There are no projections into
the Streets. The houses are all built of polished Free Stone & all of a
height in each Street & as uniform as that no striking difference is perceptible & yet there is such a variety of taste displayed in the fronts & finishing of different houses, as to destroy that dull uniformity which to the
eye of taste is always disgusting.

It was now growing dark. We went to my Inn & supped together. Mr
Cannon soon retired promising to breakfast with me in the morning.

June 17th
I arose early in the morning to take an excursion thro' the Southern part
of the Town before Breakfast. Southward from the Grass Market & thro'
what is called Lawriston, the Buildings are few and scattered. The first
building of note I came to was Heriot's Hospital the most magnificent of
the kind in Edinburgh. It owes its foundation to Geo Heriot, Goldsmith
to Jas. the sixth. He left to the Magistrates of Edinburgh £23,625 10s for
the maintenance, relief & bringing up of so many poor & fatherless boys,
pecunious sons of Edinburgh, as the above sum should be sufficient for. I
next came to George's Square, which is large & elegant as most in
London & very much in the same stile. Hereabouts are several Streets laid
out with tolerable regularity & seem to be generally inhabited by
respectable Families. Having passed thro' Twist Row, Bristow Street, the
Square & Buccleugh Street, I came into the Southernmost end of
Nicholson Street which taken altogether is the best & handsomest in all
the old Town. This makes now one Street with the South & North
Bridges; having the front of the Register Office in full view at the northern end of the last of these Bridges; thus forms a part of perhaps the most
interesting Street in almost any part of Britain. The wavy form which
Street receives from a gentle rise & fall near the College, & from another
rise & fall at the crossing of the High Street contributes greatly to improve
its interesting & agreeable effect to the eye of taste.

Passing up this Street & a little short of the South Bridge I was surprised
with sight of the most elegant & noble front of a stone building I had
almost ever seen. But still more surprised to see that the Building was
entirely unfinished & no appearance of workmen abt it. Upon inquiry I
found it to be the University.

The old Buildings being very mean, were thoᵗ. unfit for the dignity for so flourishing an University, & a few Years a ago a Subscription was set on foot for erecting a new Structure. But the Plan has exceeded the means & what if finished would do great honour to the City of Edinburgh, stands at present a disgrace to the Nation. The East & West Fronts are no less than 255 feet & the South & North Fronts 358 feet.

Almost adjoining to the University stands the South Bridge. It consists of 19 Arches, tho' only one is visible of 30 feet wide & 31 feet high. This Arch carries Nicholson Street over the Cow-gate which lies near 40 feet below it, & is a very crowded & populous Street. From this Bridge up to High Street are the best Shops in all Edinburgh. Passing directly across High Street you come upon the North Bridge. This is an amazing structure for the purpose only of a Road over a dry Valley. The whole Length from High Street in the Old Town to Princess Street in the New is no less than 1125 feet. The Piers & Arches are 310 feet. The width of the 3 great Arches is 72 feet each, the Piers are 13¹/₂ feet & the small Arches each 20 feet. The height of the great Arches is 68 feet, the breadth of the Bridge over the Arches is 40 feet & each end 50 feet.

It was now time to go to Breakfast. Mr Cannon was waiting of me at the Inn. Our first walk after Breakfast was to the Palace of Holy-rood House which stands at the Eastern extremity of the Old Town. We were first shewn the Abbey Church which is wholly in Ruins, the Roof being fallen in. The Ruins, however are still sufficient to shew the excellence of the workmanship. We were then carried thro' a set of Apartments, quite unfurnished & merely kept clean from Cobwebs. Here we were shewn a piece of Wainscott hung upon hinges, which opens to a trap-stair communicating to the Apartments below. Thro' this Passage Darnley & the other Conspirators rushed in to murder the unhappy Rizzio. Towards the outer Door of these Apartments are large Dusky Spots on the floor said to be occasioned by Rizzio's blood which never could be washed out. We were then shewn into the Apartments of the Duke of Hamilton which he possesses as hereditary keeper of the Palace. Here Queen Mary's Bed of Crimson Damask bordered with green Fringes & Tassels is still to be seen but almost reduced to Rags.

On the right hand as you first enter is the great Stair-case, which leads to the Council Chamber of the royal Apartments. These are large & spacious; in one of them the 16 Scots Peers are elected to represent them in Parliament. The rest have been painted & furnished in a modern Stile for the reception of the French Prince D'Artois who has resided in them upwards of two Years & had only left them a few weeks ago. While in these Apartments I could not help reflecting with what gloomy ideas the Prince must first have entered them. Banished from his native Country & from all hopes of ever returning thither in his own proper character, a Pensioner on the bounty of strangers & the Resident of a Building calculated above all others to be perpetually reminding him of fallen Majesty.

From the Palace we went to the Parliament house, where the Lords were assembled & each of them making a Speech previous to giving his Vote upon a question of importance which had been by then sent to the house of Lords in England & from thence remanded back for the final decision of the Lords in Scotland or as they are called the Court of Session. This is the supreme Tribunal in Scotland & consists of 15 Judges, who sit on a circular Bench clothed in purple Robes turned up with Crimson Velvet. After hearing the Debates for an Hour we went to the College where Mr Cannon had to attend a Lecture upon Natural Philosophy. It consisted chiefly of a dissertation upon Peat Moss which the Professor seem'd to handle with great Judgm^t. I was particularly entertained with one part of his discourse in which he treated of the antiseptic quality of Peat Moss. There was a tendency to prevent putrefaction & is a quality which I did not know that Peat possessed. To prove this quality several rare curiosities which had been dug out of Mosses ab^t. Dumfries & other parts of Scotland were laid upon the Table, particularly a large pair of Horns of an Animal of which none have been in Great Britain for upwards of 800 Years, & a Piece of Silver supposed to be the Ornament of a Roman Helmet, & if so must have lain more than 1200 years, it was so completely preserved that the inscription upon it was perfectly legible. After this we went into another Room in the College to attend the Chemical Lecture which was principally on Phosphorous with experiments. The Company which attended the Lecture was both numerous & genteel. Here I was introduced to a young man of the name of Cannon, Surgeon of an East-India Ship, a genteel well informed young man & a pleasant Companion. He agreed to go & dine with us & afterwards to take me to the Botanic Garden with the Keeper of which he was intimately acquainted. We had an excellent Dinner which with the Wine that followed we enjoyed so much as not to rise till 7 o'Clock. Tho' it was now beyond the time of admitting Company into the Botanic Garden we found an easy access. This Garden belongs to the University & is situate at the distance of ab^t. a Mile on the Road bet. Edinburgh & Leith. It consists of ab^t. five Acres of Ground & is furnished with a great variety of Plants, many of them bro^t. from the most distant quarters of the Globe. The Professor is botanist to the King & receives a Salary of £120 annually for the support of the Garden.

I have neglected to observe that before Dinner we went up to the
Castle. It is accessible only on the East-side. On all others it is very steep
& in some places perpendicular. It is ab^t. 300 feet high from its Base. The
entry is defended by an outer barrier of pallisadoes, within this is a dry
ditch, draw-bridge & gate defended by two batteries which flank it; & the
whole is commanded by a half moon mounted with brass Cannon carrying Balls of 12 pounds. Beyond these are two gate-ways, the first of which
is very strong & has two portcullises. Immediately beyond the second
Gate-way, on the right hand is a battery mounted with brass Cannon carrying balls of 12 & 18 pounds weight. In the upper part are a number of
houses in the form of a square which are laid out in barracks for the
Officers. Besides those there are other Barracks sufficient to contain 1000
men, 30,000 stand of Arms may be conveniently lodged in this Castle.
The Castle, from the natural strength of its situation, might be supposed
to be capable of sustaining a long siege, yet I conceive it could not with-
stand, even for a few hours, a well directed Bombardment. The view
from the Castle is grand & picturesque. The following are the principal
objects viz: the Town & Harbour of Leith, the expanse of the Bay, the
rich Parks & Villas between Edinburgh & Leith, Calton Hill, Salisbury
Craggs & Arthur's Seat, the palace of Holyrood House, & both the old
and new Town.

After perambulating the Botanical Garden the Evening was drawing to
a Close. My Companions bro^t. me to the Inn & as I was to get into the
Coach at 2 o'Clock in the morning I could not prevail upon them to stop
Supper for fear of detaining me out of bed. The Inn from whence the
Coach went stands upon the Leith Wall & just at the foot of Calton-hill.
Every hour of the day had been so fully taken up that I had no opportunity
of ascending this Hill, the views from which I was, are, from its height &
situation, most big & interesting. I determined not to lose the present
opportunity while Supper was preparing. The side of the Hill I had to
ascend was scarcely accessible. I never before attempted an ascent so difficult, at length the scrambling up more than half its height fell in with a
poor path ascending from the south side of the Hill which leads you in a
winding track around to its summit. Every step you advance the scene
slowly shifts & every advance produces variety. I thought I had never seen
any thing so enchanting. The objects seen from its summit, are, for the
most part the same as those that are perceived from the Castle but the
point of view being different the objects appear little less novel than if
they had never been seen before. On the top of this Hill stands the
Observatory, furnished with Telescopes &c. The Evening was now fast

closing in & I began my return. But the descent if not more fatiguing than the ascent was far more difficult & dangerous. I was obliged to stop at every step, to choose my Road with judgement & move with caution as one false step would have inevitably rolled me headlong to the bottom. I was frequently obliged to creep backward on my hands & knees. At length I arrived at the bottom entered my Inn, supped & ascended 59 stone steps of a hanging Stair-case to go to bed.

It may perhaps be proper here to make a few remarks of the City of Edinburgh in general. I conceive it to be upon the whole but an uncomfortable Town to live in particularly for the middle & lower Classes of people. The old Town particularly the High Street is built upon a Ridge running from East to West & sloping very rapidly & steep northward & southward. The part of the old Town, & a great quantity of Buildings adjoining which lie at the foot of the Ridge Southward are very full of Inhabitants, who, unless they reside in Nicholson Street or near the South Bridge have a very uncomfortable walk to get into the Center of the Town, the ascent up every Street & Wynde is so steep. The Street leading from the Grass Market into the Lawn Market & thence into the High Street is so steep & winding as to be dangerous for Wheel Carriages either to ascend or descend & the several streets & Wynds out of the Cowgate are the same.

This inconvenience is very much relieved abt the Center of the Town by means of the South Bridge which by an Arch of above 30 feet high carries you so far above the level of the Cow-gate of the lower part of the Town.

The Valley which lies on the North Side of the above ment. Ridge & runs between the old & the new Town is very deep & was formerly covered with water & thence called the North Loch. It is now drained & besides the easy passage over it by means of the North Bridge & before described, an Eastern Bridge or Road abt half way between the North Bridge & the Castle, has been raised by the Rubbish which was brought from the Cellars & Ground-works of the Buildings in the New Town. It may easily be conceived how inconvenient it must be to all persons passing and repassing to have to go to one or other of these Bridges.

The same inconvenience likewise attaches to the Houses here as in Glasgow, of a number of families living under one Roof. The Houses here are in general higher than in Glasgow & it is not uncommon to see 7, 8, or even 9 boards one above another in front of a house expressing the different trades of the different Inhabitants. This must be a source of much filth and uncleanliness.

June 18th
At 2 o'Clock in the morning I got into the Coach to leave Edinburgh for
Carlisle. At 7 miles from Edinburgh we passed the Park & Palace of
Dalkeith belonging to the Duke of Buccleugh. Report speaks highly of
them but no part of the House & very little of the Park can be seen from
the Road. About 20 miles from Edinburgh is a Gentleman's Seat near the
Road which I admired very much. It is called Nair & belongs to a Mr
Pringle. It is situated upon the Banks of the Tweed. The Turnpike road
runs easily two Miles upon the one Bank of the River & upon the other
are beautiful & romantic Pleasure walks amidst a fine venerable Wood.

From Langham to Haywich[23] for many miles together, the Road lies
quite in the bottom of a very deep Valley. The Hills on the right & left
are only separated by the Road & a small Rivulet. They are very lofty &
so steep that in many places not Cattle but sheep can stand to graze upon
them. They are well grassed & not a Bush or Bramble to be seen upon
them, & the surface almost as smooth as a Bowling Green. From Haywich
to Long-town the Country is in a good state of Cultivation. For a considerable way the Road lies upon the banks of the river Esk. A little way
below you arrive at Long-town, you have a fine view of Netherby, the
beautiful Seat of Sir Jas. Graham.

At 11 o'Clock we got to Carlisle after a most tedious long day of travelling,
having only had a pair of Horses at once all the way from Edinburgh & they
sometimes dragging us 20 miles at a Stage, tho' we were frequently 4
Passengers at once & the Roads often rough & hilly. Having secured a place
in the Mail Coach for four o'Clock in the morning, I wrote to L. Lilford &
then went to rest.

June 19th
Nothing particular occurred upon the Road. I quitted the Coach at
Westhoughton & walked home where I arrived at 10 o'Clock, after finishing a
very long Journey in which I had succeeded in everything I proposed, had gratified my curiosity beyond what I could have expected, had not been interrupted by an hour of bad weather, nor had suffered one single untoward accident.

Method of Making Mortar which
will be Impenetrable to Moisture

Take of unslacked Lime, & of fine Sand in proportion of one part of the
Lime to three parts of the Sand, as much as a labourer can well manage at

Plate 23 The ruins of Bildwas Abbey. 'As we were riding round the inside of the Walls, I do not remember so awful and dismal a scene. All was silence, except the Owl.': Richard Hodgkinson

Plate 24 Coalbrookdale by night, by P.J. de Loutherborg. 'It was now near midnight, the moon was set and the Furnaces flaming prodigiously . . . I stopped, I gazed and admired.': Richard Hodgkinson (Science Museum)

Plate 25 Ironbridge. 'Just below the Bridge was a view, which struck me particularly and which I stopped my horse to admire.':
Richard Hodgkinson (Ironbridge Gorge Museum Trust)

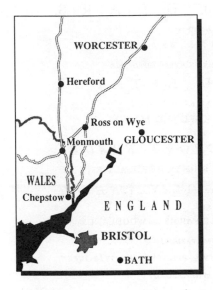

Plate 26   Richard Hodgkinson's travels to settle the Hereford estates

Plate 27   Langston Farm. Here was 'the residence of a worthy Family [the Gwillyms], honoured and respected by all who knew them, the boast of their friends, and the pride of Langston.': Richard Hodgkinson

P A R T I C U L A R S,

AND

C O N D I T I O N S OF S A L E,

OF SEVERAL VALUABLE AND VERY IMPROVABLE

F R E E H O L D E S T A T E S,

CONSISTING OF

The MANOR or REPUTED MANOR

OF

F R A G E E or *C R O F T F R A U D,*

With the QUIT-RENTS, RIGHTS, and ROYALTIES;

An ANCIENT MANSION called *LANGSTON-HOUSE,*

AND

Several CAPILAL FREEHOLD FARMS and WOODLANDS;

Situate in the several PARISHES of

LANGARRON, TRETIRE, ENTLAND, PITSTOW, and *LITTLE-BURCH,*

In the County of *HEREFORD:*

AND

A S M A L L F A R M at *T R E G A R E,*

In the County of *MONMOUTH:*

CONTAINING, IN THE WHOLE,

O N E T H O U S A N D A C R E S;

Let to Responsible Tenants, mostly from Year to Year, at very Improvable
Rents, amounting to

SIX HUNDRED and TWENTY POUNDS:

Which will be SOLD by AUCTION,

at the By *new Inn in* Mr. *Hereford* Y O U N G,

~~At Garraway's Coffee-House, Exchange Alley, Cornhill, London,~~

On the 2d Day of , 1794, at Twelve o'Clock.

IN SEVEN LOTS:

The several Tenants will show the Estates:—And printed PARTICULARS may be had of Mr. JOHN GREEN
at *Wilton Castle* near *Ross;* at the King's-Head, *Ross;* New-Inn, *Hereford;* Beaufort-Arms, *Monmouth;*
George, *Cheltenham;* Bell, *Gloucester;* at *Garraway's;* and of Mr. YOUNG, N° 58, *Chancery-Lane,
London,* where Plans may be seen.

Plate 28 Poster advertising the sale of Langston House and the Herefordshire Estates (Lord
Lilford: Hereford and Worcester Record Office)

Plate 29   Chepstow Bridge with the castle in the background. 'I had been told that the Bridge is 70 Feet above the surface of the Water and that the Tide rises here 40 feet.': Richard Hodgkinson

Plate 30   Entrance to Vauxhall Gardens. 'We immediately agreed to go to Vauxhall where it was . . . an extra night in honour of the Duke of Clarence's birth day. The appearance of the Gardens was brilliant beyond description and the company was very numerous.': Richard Hodgkinson

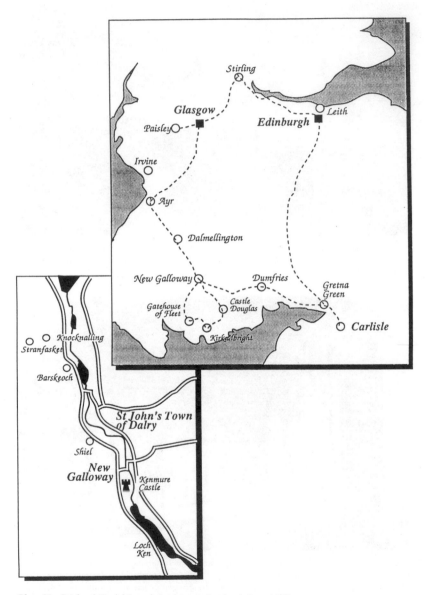

Plate 31   Richard Hodgkinson's journey to Scotland, June 1800

Plate 32   Gretna Green, where in 1800 the blacksmith, Joseph Paisley, who married runaways from all over England was an 'old sloven . . . so intoxicated as to forbid all attempts at conversation': Richard Hodgkinson, June 1800

Plate 33   Kenmure Castle on the shores of Loch Ken, New Galloway. 'I was soon within the Woods, the gloom of which agreeing with my present temper of mind put me perfectly in humour for contemplating the fate of the unfortunate family of Kenmore Castle.': Richard Hodgkinson

Plate 34   Cotton magnate, John Kennedy. 'Such carousing and drinking was quite unknown in our native glen', he wrote about his arrival in Chowbent

Plate 35   The farm, Barskeoch. Property and farms in the Glenkens, visited by Richard Hodgkinson in 1800, bear the same names today: Strangfasket, the Shiel, Knocknalling and, here, Barskeoch

Plate 36   Visit to St Mary Isle, Kirkcudbright, 1800. '. . . this is the house which John Paul Jones and his Crew plundered of all the plate in the American War.' Lady Selkirk's silver plate was later returned by Jones. The teapot here is the only surviving piece (Sir David Hope-Dunbar)

Plate 37 'It is not . . . a very delicate or a very decent sight to see a sturdy Scotch–wench bare foot and bare legged tucked up to the waist, splashing & trampling in a tub of dirty clothes.' (Glasgow City Council Libraries Department)

Plate 38   Stirling Castle. '. . . the Rock on this side and indeed all round form the truly grand sublime.': Richard Hodgkinson

Plate 39 Edinburgh Castle 'perched upon a lofty and apparently inaccessible Rock, bold and picturesque beyond description.': Richard Hodgkinson. The White Hart Inn in Edinburgh's Grassmarket, where Richard stayed, is on the left in this painting by Nicholson (Edinburgh Library Services)

Plate 40 Mary Queen of Scots' bedchamber in Holyrood Palace, Edinburgh. 'Dusky spots on the floor said to be occasioned by Rizzio's blood which would never be washed out.': Richard Hodgkinson (National Galleries of Scotland)

Plate 41 Wroughton Church. '. . . a lady of the Benet family, dying, had desired to be buried in her Wedding Clothes.' When the vault was opened for an interment, 'the silk stockings which this Lady had on, and the Ribbands which she had upon her head were in a state of perfect preservation.': Richard Hodgkinson

Plate 42 Salthrop House. 'Mr Pye has laid out not less than £3,000 upon the House and pleasure grounds.': Richard Hodgkinson (Picture: Michael and Jane Gould)

Plate 43　The Grecian Coffee house in London. 'They were so full of Company we could not have Bed in the House but they provided us 2 beds at the next House but one having already 14 beds engaged out of the House.': Richard Hodgkinson

Plate 44　Astley church. Scene of the bitter and tragic dispute between Joseph Hodgkinson and the parishioners

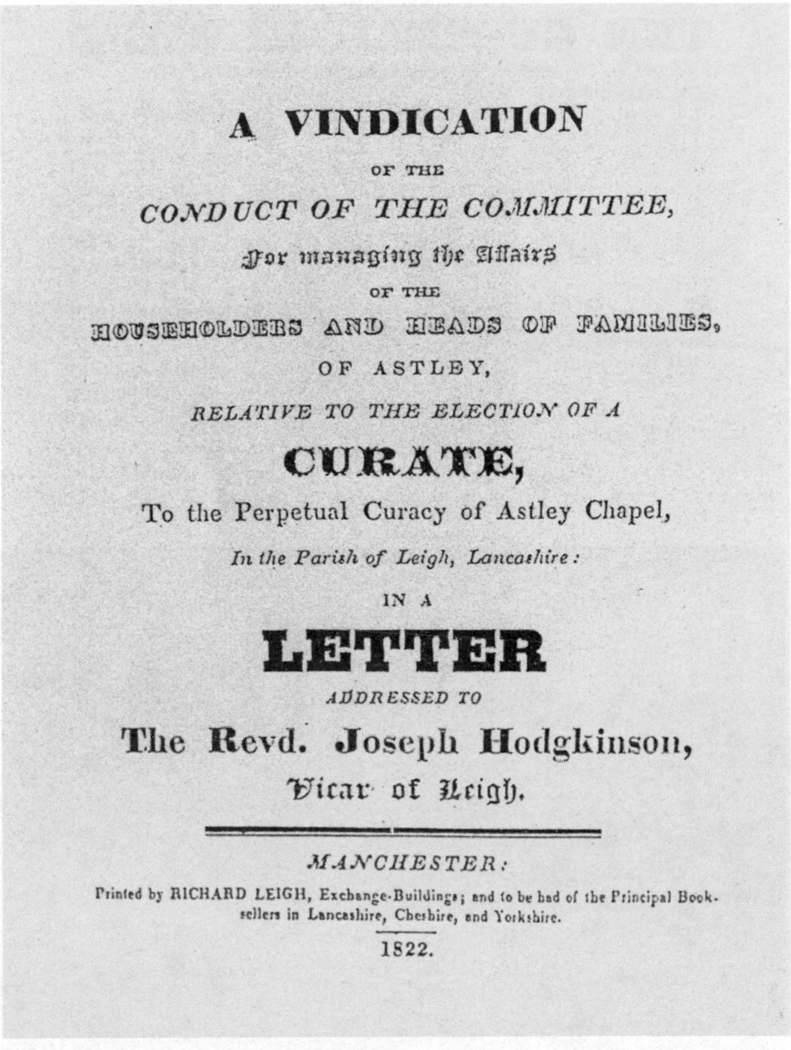

A VINDICATION

OF THE

CONDUCT OF THE COMMITTEE,

For managing the Affairs

OF THE

HOUSEHOLDERS AND HEADS OF FAMILIES,

OF ASTLEY,

RELATIVE TO THE ELECTION OF A

CURATE,

To the Perpetual Curacy of Astley Chapel,

In the Parish of Leigh, Lancashire:

IN A

LETTER

ADDRESSED TO

The Revd. Joseph Hodgkinson,

Vicar of Leigh.

MANCHESTER:

Printed by RICHARD LEIGH, Exchange-Buildings; and to be had of the Principal Booksellers in Lancashire, Cheshire, and Yorkshire.

1822.

Plate 45   Front cover of the vitriolic pamphlet sent to Astley parishioners in February 1822
(LRO DDX 211/6)

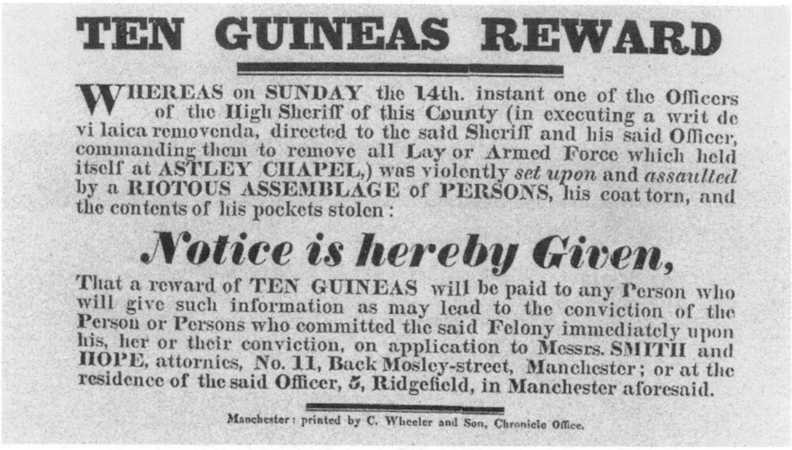

TEN GUINEAS REWARD

WHEREAS on SUNDAY the 14th. instant one of the Officers of the High Sheriff of this County (in executing a writ de vi laica removenda, directed to the said Sheriff and his said Officer, commanding them to remove all Lay or Armed Force which held itself at ASTLEY CHAPEL,) was violently *set upon* and *assaulted* by a RIOTOUS ASSEMBLAGE of PERSONS, his coat torn, and the contents of his pockets stolen:

Notice is hereby Given,

That a reward of TEN GUINEAS will be paid to any Person who will give such information as may lead to the conviction of the Person or Persons who committed the said Felony immediately upon his, her or their conviction, on application to Messrs. SMITH and HOPE, attornies, No. 11, Back Mosley-street, Manchester; or at the residence of the said Officer, 5, Ridgefield, in Manchester aforesaid.

Manchester: printed by C. Wheeler and Son, Chronicle Office.

Plate 46   A poster offering a ten guinea reward for information on parisioners who were claimed to have assaulted officers during the disturbance in July 1822 (LRO DDX 211/6)

Plate 47   This gilt snuffbox was given to David Hodgkinson as a token of esteem 'by a number of his friends in the Parish of Leigh'. Three of the thirty-nine subscribers came from Astley (Wigan Heritage Services)

once; & then adding water gradually mix the whole together, till it be reduced to the consistence of mortar. Apply it immediately while it is yet hot, to the purpose either of Mortar, as a cement to Broken Stone, or of Plaistere for the surface of any Building. It will then ferment for some days in drier places, & afterwards gradually concrete or set & become hard:–

Annual Register for 1771, Page 121.

Expences

1800	£	s	d
May 31st			
Paid Mr Middlehurst Coach fare to Carlisle	2.	12.	6
June 1st			
Breakfast at Preston		1.	3
Coachman at Garstang, Lancaster, Burton,			
Kendal,Shap, Penrith & Carlisle		3.	6
Guard at Lancaster & Carlisle		2.	0
Dinner at Kendal		3.	6
2nd.			
Expences Rossley Fair		3.	0
3rd.			
Expences at Carlisle		17.	10
Servants		2.	6
Coachmen to Dumfries		1.	0
Expences on the Road		2.	0
4th.			
Do. at Dumfries		3.	10
Servants		1.	0
Paid for ¹/₂lb Tea		3.	0
June 4th			
Hire of a horse to Newgalloway 34 Miles		12.	9
Paid a man for fetching it back		5.	0
Expences on the Road		2.	2
Expence of myself, Horse and Man at Newgalloway all night		6.	6
7th			
Paid at the Collection for the Poor at Kells Kirk		1.	0

8th
Expences at Castle Douglas	1. 7
Do. at the Gate-house	3. 6

12
Do. at Cass-fern	1. 6
Gave to Mrs Wallace, second Daur. of Wm. Sloan	10. 6
Expences at Damellentown	4. 6
Coach-fare fm Ayre to Glasgow	13. 6
Expences at Ayre	13. 0

June 13
Breakfast at Kilmarnock	1. 0
Coachman at Do.	6
Do. & Guard at Glasgow	1. 0
Paid for a history of Glasgow	5. 0

14th
Coach fare to Stirling	8. 0
Breakfast at Paisley	1. 0
Coach-fare to Glasgow fm Paisley	2. 0
Expences at Glasgow	12. 0
Coachmen to Stirling	1. 0

15th
Coach hire to Edinburgh	11. 6
Expences at Stirling	12. 0

16th
Coachmen to Glasgow	1. 0
Coach-fare to Carlisle	1. 17. 0

17th
Expences at Edinburgh	13. 0
Dinner Bill	5. 6
Tea & Chambermaid	2. 8
Bed	1. 6
Given to 3 women at Holyrood	2. 6

18th
Coachmen to Carlisle	3. 6
Breakfast, dinner & Tea	5. 0
Expences at Carlisle	4. 6

June 18th
Coachfare to Mancr	2. 2. 0

19th
Breakfast at Shap	1. 2

Dinner at Lancaster	4. 0
Tea at Preston	1. 3
Coachmen & Guards	6. 0
Paid for a history of Edinburgh	3. 8
Coachfare from Carlisle to Dumfries – omitted above	17. 0

Total £18. 18. 8

Notes

1 David Cannon M'Connel, *Facts and Traditions Collected for a Family Record* (1861).

2 Alexander Trotter, *East Galloway Sketches* (Adam Rae, 1901).

3 M'Connel, *Facts and Traditions*.

4 Alexander Trotter, *Last Galloway Sketches*.

5 John Lunn, *Atherton, a Manorial, Social and Industrial History* (1971), p. 170.

6 See the David Hodgkinson letters.

7 See the David Hodgkinson letters.

8 For many years, Sir James Lowther, Earl of Lonsdale, fought to control both of the Carlisle Parliamentary seats. The city was a freeman borough with an electorate of about 750 out of a population of some 7,000. In 1784, with Lonsdale in control of the corporation, 1,447 people were created freemen, mostly miners from Lonsdale's Whitehaven collieries and tenants from his Westmoreland estates. They were named 'Mushroom voters' from the rapidity of their appearance overnight. M.J. Smith, *Victoria County History of Westmoreland*.

9 In 1797 a Militia Act to conscript ablebodied males between seventeen and twenty-three years of age for military service led to riots in Scotland.

10 A forestaller is one who prevents or hinders sales at a market by buying up merchandise in advance for profitable resale.

11 William Forbes made a fortune in London in commerce and government contracts. 'It is stated that he was in the metal line of business, and receiving a hint from a customer (Admiral Byron is mentioned) that it was the intention of the Admiralty to copper the ships' bottoms, he immediately purchased up all the copper that could be obtained, and soon afterwards possessed the exclusvie right of supplying copper for the Navy and the East India Company's ships, for twenty years, thereby realizing a large fortune.' McKerlie, *Lands and their Owners in Galloway* (c. 1830).

12 In February 1800, Quintin Macadam of Craigengillan took Elizabeth Walker into his house at Waterhead and settled sixty guineas a year on her. The couple had two children and on the morning of 22 March 1805, Macadam called the again pregnant Elizabeth and three servants and declared: 'I take you

three to witness that this is my lawful married wife, and the children by her are my lawful children.' The same afternoon Macadam shot himself. The House of Lords later ruled that Macadam intended to marry Elizabeth and their children inherited his estates. John Paterson, *Reminiscences of Dalmellinton* (1902). Quintin Macadam was described as a rakish young man and was possibly the subject of Burns's 'Young Dumashire Laird'. 'History of Lands and their Owners', in McKerlie, New Galloway.

13 Paul Jones, born at Kirkbean on the Solway, is hailed as the founder of the American Navy. In his ship, the *Ranger*, he carried out raids in 1778 on .Whitehaven and Kirkcudbright during the American War of Independence. During the Kirkcudbright raid he had planned to take Lord Selkirk hostage, but his crew threatened mutiny unless they were allowed to loot the silver plate. Jones later wrote to the Countess offering to buy the plate off his crew and return it. A silver teapot is the only item left from the collection.

14 This property is now known as Cally House and adjoins Cally Lake and Cally Park.

15 To roup is to sell by auction.

16 Freestone is a fine-grained stone, usually limestone or sandstone, which is easily worked by masons.

17 Lammas is 1 August.

18 This is Carsphairn.

19 Scotland's famous Dunlop cheese was first made in the late seventeenth century to use the surplus milk from Dunlop cattle, later known as Ayshires. Muriel C Easton, *Kilmarnock Standard* (December, 1961).

20 King's Evil is scrofula, tuberculosis of the lymphatic glands.

21 The Cunninghams were landowners in Ayrshire and were involved in the early development of the coal and iron industry.

22 Researchers . . . are confident that mustard grown between crop plantings and ploughed back into the field will produce enough potent weedkilling chemical to dramaticallly reduce the need for synthetic chemicals. *The Guardian*, 1 December 1989.

23 Hodgkinson's route home was along the A7 to Carlisle via Galashiels and Hawick.

6

The Tangled Web: Richard's Visit to Wiltshire

Marriages between the landed clans, death's grim harvest of sons and heirs and an angonizingly prolonged court case were only recent history when Lord Lilford despatched Richard Hodgkinson to Wiltshire in 1803. His task was to keep an eye on the Powys family interests in complex issues of greed, inheritances and the valuation of the farms and lands on the Wroughton estate on the Downs near Swindon.

Lord Lilford (through his marriage to Henrietta Maria Atherton), the wealthy Legh family of Lyme Hall in Cheshire, and the Benets of Wroughton in Wiltshire were connected by family and marriage. Peter Legh (1706–1792) married Martha Benet, the 'worthy, but exceedingly plain'[1] daughter and heiress of Peter Benet of Salthrop, in 1737. Lady Lilford's direct connection with the Legh family and the Wiltshire estates came through her mother, the daughter of Peter Legh.

Peter and Martha 'were a somewhat dull, uninteresting couple, neither of them possessing any great charm or attraction'.[2] Notwithstanding his bride's lack of natural endowment, and Peter's personality expressed through a 'face which is weak and inexpressive',[3] their early life was not without interest. From 1748, Peter represented the Newton (south Lancashire) Division for twenty-five years and they entertained on a grand scale at their magnificent home in Lyme Park. After death carried away their two sons at early ages, the resulting stress and misery soured the marriage partnership to such an extent that, after forty-six years, Martha left her husband. She went to live in Weymouth before returning home to die in 1787. Disharmony between man and wife were exacerbated by the activities of Peter's sister Ann (1711–1794), who overrode Martha's position and authority at Lyme. The body of the unhappy Martha was taken from Lyme and buried at Wroughton Church, near her late father's home at Salthrop. A monument was erected to her by her daughter, Elizabeth Pye Benet.

Peter Legh died without male heirs and it was the disposal in his will of the Wroughton estate that led to court.

Following her mother's early death, Lady Lilford (Henrietta Maria) and her sisters were due to a share of the Wroughton estate, but their aunt Mrs Elizabeth Pye Benet and their great-aunt Mrs Ann Legh attempted to disinherit the three girls. This led to a court case in Chancery which dragged on for many years. It was finally resolved that Lady Lilford and her sisters were entitled to their mother's inheritance and Hodgkinson was sent to ensure fair play when the valuation was made.

Elizabeth Pye Benet lived at Salthrop Hall on the Wroughton estate. She appears to have been a woman of some resolution and eager to get her hands on what she rightfully considered hers. When her first husband, James Anthony Keck, died, she adopted her mother's maiden name of Benet and then married her second husband William Bathurst Pye, a lover of the sporting life whose unbridled assaults on local game aroused the ire of a noble neighbour.

To settle the affairs of the estate, Mrs Benet and Lord Lilford had the farms and land of the Salthrop estate valued. Each party appointed a valuer and Hodgkinson was sent by Lilford on the long journey south 'to satisfy himself of the real value which was to be taken of the property'. Valuation of the Salthrop property which had been inherited by Martha Legh was complicated by the position in its midst of Constables' Farm, a property bought separately by Mr Peter Legh.

Never averse to listening to gossip, Hodgkinson records an account of a visit to Lyme Hall, by Bathurst Pye and another gentleman, to confront Colonel Thomas Peter Legh with accusations that he had not for many years paid an allowance to his, by now, penurious Aunt Ann. As a result of her allowance not being paid by the new master of Lyme Hall, she died in Bath in some destitution after borrowing money and mortgaging her home. When the two visitors descended on Colonel Legh, who had inherited Lyme Hall after the death of his uncle Peter, he feared arrest and promised to pay the debts to his aunt's estate. Then, unabashed, he entertained his pursuers for a lavish week of amusement and pleasure.

Colonel Legh was a man of both military and extra-marital consequence. The father of seven children, all by different women, he gained his army title by raising at his own expense the 3rd Lancashire Light Dragoons and six regiments in Cheshire to fight the French. It was the complexities of his will following his death in 1797 that led to the family squabble.

Hodgkinson had modest, probably professional connections with the Legh family, who apart from their properties in Cheshire and Wiltshire also had extensive lands in south Lancashire at Haydock and Winwick, quite close to Atherton and Bewsey. In December 1813, Hodgkinson and his son David were invited to an entertainment at Haydock to celebrate the coming of age of Young Legh, the bastard son of the Late Col Legh. 'He has nothing striking in his appearance or figure and his Face is quite uninteresting.' Hodgkinson wrote to his friend Blundell. To celebrate the birthday and the young man's return from a three year absence abroad, an ox was fed for the occasion. 'He was seven years old and had worked in the plough to the last . . . his flesh was too fat to be eaten comfortably,' complained Lilford's steward.

The complexities of defining ancient parcels of land apart, Hodgkinson provides in the journal of his visit to Wiltshire an entertaining and informative account of life on the Downs, and notes the struggle for existence of farmers toiling on the poor soil.

Memorandums of a Journey into Wiltshire to Attend the Gentlemen Appointed to Value the Salthrop Estates

1803 February 25th
Left Warrington in the Coach at 10 o'Clock at night & arrived at Birmingham at 4 o'Clock in the Afternoon of the next day. After stopping an hour I got into the Bristol Mail Coach which set me down at the Bell Inn in Glocester at one o'Clock in the morning. I here went to bed and after breakfast in the morning I took a Chaise to Cirencester, a Stage of 17 miles & from thence a Chaise to Swindon, a Stage of 16 miles where I arrived at 3 o'Clock in the afternoon.

After I had dined I wrote a Note to Mr Bradford[4] who came to me immediately. He told me the valuers were to meet in the morning, but that most unaccountably they had fixed their place of meeting 7 miles from the Lands to be valued. We agreed to take a Chaise in the morning and go to Kenet, the place appointed for meeting.

28th February
At 9 o'Clock in the morning Mr Bradford & I left Swindon in a Post

Chaise to go to Kenet to meet Mr Gale appointed by Mrs Benet and Mr
Heath appointed by Lord Lilford &c., to value the Salthrop Estates. We
had not travelled more than 2 miles before we met Mr Gale who said he
had left word at Kenet for Mr Heath to follow him to Broad-hinton,
where he intended they shd begin their Valuation. We went together to
Mr Hughes's, the Manor Farm at Broad-hinton where having waited abt
an hour Mr Davis arrived. He is a young man, son of Mr Davis, principal
Agent to the Marquiss of Bath, and had measured & planned all the
Estates for the sole purpose of this Survey and Valuation. He attended to
value the Timber, as well as to give the Valuers any explanation of his
Plans that they might stand in need of. The morning was wet and we
spent a long time in investigating & finding out what part of the property
constituted Constables' Farm. This Farm was purchased by Mr Peter Legh
& of course did not descend with the original Salthrop Estates, but passed
into the hands of his Exors. or Trustees, to be by them disposed of and
the Purchase money arising there from to sink into & become part of his
personal Estate. It was therefore necessary to have this Estate valued separately, & of course carefully to trace out and distinguish what Lands did
belong to it. Mr Bradford had got a description of the property extracted
from the Purchase Deed & sent to him by Mr Maine. Comparing this
with the Plan, and assisted by the information of old Mr Hughes who is
near 80 years of age, & has long farmed Constables' along with Broad-
hinton, we did discover pretty accurately & satisfactorily what Land
belonged to that Farm. Mr Heath arrived now, it being 2 o'Clock & still
continuing to rain. Mr Heath said that in a Lett^r. he had rec^d. from Mr
Gorst he was informed that their was another part which had been purchased by Mr Legh called Hawkins'. This we found to be the case but cd
not learn what Fields it consisted of, only Mr Hughes said that he knew
the Purchase had been so made, and that it formerly lett for ten pounds a
Year, but that since that time a Cottage of thirty shillings a Year Rent had
been taken from it & leased for Lives. The rain now ceasing, Mr Gale &
Mr Heath began their Valuation & Mr Davis with his Clerk went to the
Timber. Mr Bradford & myself returned to Swindon. I stopped to Tea
with him as we had to talk over & endeavour to elucidate what appeared
to us an inexplicable difficulty. There are several Charities payable off
Quidhampton Farm to the Schools and the Poor of Wroughton and
Broad-hinton, charged upon the said Farm of Quidhampton by Mr Thos.
Bennett [Benet], the father of old Mrs Legh. There are likewise the sums
of £10.10s and £7 payable to the same Parishes off Constables' Estate.
How these sums shd be charged upon Constables' & yet it be a Purchase

made by Mr Legh we cd not conceive. We imagined that if this Estate were purchased by Mr Legh these two last mentd. sums were said to be charged upon it by mistake, when in fact they were charged upon some other part of the property, as Mr Benet cd not charge an Estate which he was never possessed of, or else this Constables' was not the Estate purchased by Mr Legh. It never occurred to us that Mr Legh wd, after the Estates had been so heavily charged by Mr Benet with Charities, go and saddle his own Purchase with such a Sum as £17.10s, and so early in his lifetime as they appear to have been. The thing must be found out and immediately, else the Valuers cd not proceed as they ought. We turned the question every way we could think of and at every turn found a difficulty. We parted without coming to a determination. I was to breakfast with Mr Bradford in the morning previous to our setting out on Horseback to go over the Estates I had not yet seen.

29th February
At 8 o'Clock I went to Mr Bradford's to Breakfast. As soon as I came into the Parlour, he exclaimed 'I have solved the Riddle,' & produced the 2 Wills, extracts of which are at the end of the Book. In the first Will, viz. Mr Thomas Benet's, he gives £300 to his executrix to be by her distributed to the Poor of Wroughton according to her discretion. This Executrix is his own Daur., the wife of Mr Peter Legh. In the secd. Will, Miss Eliz. Benet gives to her Bro. the said Thos. Benet, £200 to settle it for the purpose of fitting out poor Girls in the Parish of Wroughton for Service. The secd. Testator & Testatrix appears to have died abt the same time as his Will was proved, 9th December, 1754, & hers the 23rd Decr., 1754.

The £200 being paid by Miss Benet's Exor. to Mrs Legh as Executrix of her Father, Mr Legh, applies the whole £500 to his own use and charges his Estate of Constables' with an Annuity of 3½ per cent for it, applicable to the purpose directed in the said Wills.

After breakfast we set out for Salthrop. On our way we passed Wroughton Church in which I was told there was a Table, containing an acct. of the Benefactions of the Benet Family to that Parish. I wished to see it. A Copy of it is below.

'Benefactions of Thos. Benet, of Salthrop, Esquire, and his Sister, Eliz. Benet, to Wroughton in the year of our Lord 1743.
'A Charity School in this place endowed by the said Thos. Benet

with £20 per annum to be paid quarterly out of Quidhampton Farm. And also the interest of £300 at three and a half per cent per annum, to be paid out of a Farm called Constables' at Broad-hinton to the poor of the Parish.

'Given by the said Eliz. Benet the int. of two hundred pounds at three and a half per cent per annum, to be paid out of the said Farm called Constables' at Broad-hinton, to be employed for the use of poor Girls of this Parish in setting them out to Service.

'N.B. The said Thos. Benet at the death of his Lady gave £20, and at his own death gave twenty pounds, and his sister, Eliz. at her death gave £20 to the poor of this place, all which sums were distributed as they ordered.'

In this Church Miss Keck was married last Year to a Mr Cawley, a neighbouring Gentleman of good connections and handsome property. To this Church old Mrs Legh was brought from Lyme to be buried & lies interred near the Altar within the Communion Rails. The Clerk informed me that a long time ago a Lady of the Benet Family, dying, had desired to be buried in her Wedding Clothes, that when he opened the Vault for old Mrs Legh, he found that the Silk Stockings which this Lady had on, and the Ribbands which she had upon her head were in a state of perfect preservation and as complete as when they were put on, and that even when exposed to the Air it required a very considerable degree of force to tear them.

From Wroughton we rode on to Salthrop house. Mr & Mrs Pye reside here only in Summer and at Bath in the Winter. Mr Bradford informs me that Mr Pye has laid out not less than £3,000 upon the House & pleasure grounds. The House I perceive must have cost a large sum of Money, & still it is a little better than a heap of Ruins. New Sash Windows have been put into most of the Rooms. The Dining Room has been made out of no less than three Rooms & here a new Floor has been laid. The drawing Room is small but it is in tolerable good condition. The Stairs Case are the worst I ever saw in any house which at any time had been the residence of a Family and there is scarcely one step from bottom to top that is perfectly sound and lies as it shd. Turning to the right at the top of the Stairs is a Door leading into a Room which was the best Bed-room but is now undergoing a complete repair and alteration, and is fitting up for a Tea Room so that now they will only have one spare Bed-room in the whole house. The marble Chimney piece is set up and a marble Hearth laid in this new Tea Room, but no plaistering is yet done. The Door into this Room is not more than five feet from head of the Stairs, and yet at the Door the Floor is six Inches lower than at the Stairs. The Bed-rooms are very mean. The Kitchen & servants' Offices are low, dark, uncomfortable places. This part of the House will inevitably want taking down and indeed I understand it is Mr Pye's intention to take them down as soon as his Finances will admit of it.

The money has been laid out to better advantage in the Grounds than in the House. Mr Pye has taken down a Dove house & the Stables which stood within 8 Yards of the back door and inclosed the Sale on which they stood by a handsome new brick wall near 40 Yards long and eight feet high & is now making a grass Platt & Shrubbery there. He has likewise erected a very handsome square Portico at the back part of the House, supported upon Stone Columns and covered with Lead. He has grubbed up large tall Yew-hedges which grew close up to the House, not less than a quarter of a mile in length in different directions, and has inclosed a very considerable piece of ground for Pleasure ground, and encompassed it with a paling which cost more than two hundred pounds. In this Inclosure which is all planted, the Walks are laid out in a very tasty Stile, and the Shrubs flourish amazingly. Up to the new Wall, Mr Pye has erected a small Hot-house abt 12 Yards long of Glass. The making of a new Road to the House has been attended with very considerable expence. The Masons are now at work sinking the foundations for the new Stables, which with the Yard that must be made & paved about them, being entirely upon fresh ground, will cost a large sum of money. Mr Pye has paid £40 a year Rent for a few fields about the House, but has never paid any rent for the House or Gardens. There is a very considerable quantity of large, full grown Elm around, and within sight of the House. Indeed here lies the great weight of Timber which is upon the Manors. On the upland Ground there is very little Timber.

From hence we went to the Binal Wood. It consists of Hazel underwood growing upon the North-side of a steep and high Hill. It is exposed to the East, North & West Winds, and seldom grow large enough to make common Sheep Hurdles of. Its extent is about 23 Acres, but it is of so little value that tho it was included in Mr Hughes's Lease; he has given it up to Mr Pye without any consideration. It is surrounded entirely by Land belonging to Lord Bolingbroke and Mr Bradford gave me the following curious Acct of its coming into the Benet family. This family was always very much respected by the nobility & gentry of the County and indeed by all who knew them. One of the Ancestors of the Bolingbroke Family desired to stand Godfather to a Child of some of the Benets. The day after the Christening he gave this Wood to the Child and it has remained in the Family ever since. But by what Deed it was done, & where the Deed now is, cannot be told. And the only title which can now be set up for it, is uninterrupted possession for more than 60 Years. Lord Bolingbroke had it last Year in contemplation to dispute Mr Pye's title to it. It affords shelter to some little Game, which Mr Pye was so frequently pursuing that it gave offence to Lord Bolingbroke who has warned Mr Pye off all his Manors & it is doubtful whether Mr Pye can insist upon a Road to and from the Woods.

On our return to Swindon, talking about the probability of the valuation being completed time enough for the money arising therefrom to enable Lord Lilford to complete his engagements, Mr Bradford said that if it wd in any way be an accommodation to Lord Lilford he wd at Lady-day next furnish him with three thousand pounds upon his Lordship's Note or Bond until the Business cd be settled. After this we began to talk abt Mrs Ann Legh, & I was surprised to hear the distress to which she was reduced in her last Sickness. Independent of her sufferings, which Mr Bradford said, were extreme beyond anything he ever saw, she was reduced to very great pecuniary necessities. After leaving Lyme she purchased a House in Bath for £1,700. After being sick some time she wrote to Mr Bradford acquainting him with her distress and desiring him to come to see her. She told him that not having recd any part of her annuity from Col. Legh she was reduced to the last extremity & ever deprived of the necessaries of Life. After much pressing, he promised to lend her £500. This, by her own necessities and the plundering of her Servants, was soon gone. She applied to him again, when he furnished her with £300 more; this was managed with a little more economy but did not last long. She then sent for him again in greater distress than ever proposing, that if he wd make up the sum he had already lent her into £1,300 he shd have the House at her decease for that sum, which had so lately cost her £1,700. He told her he knew very well that the house was well worth the money she gave for it, but he did not like to be concerned in any such bargains. However, he said, he wd make up the sum already had into £1,000 provided she wd give him a Mortgage of the House and likewise make her Will. She consented and he made her Will & got her to execute it before he left her. There was at this time, & until her death, a great shyness between her & Mrs Pye on account of Plate & Furniture which Mrs Ann Legh had carried away to her own house from Salthrop. However she made Mrs Pye sole Executrix of her Will & gave her the house in Bath on paying off the Mortgage. Col. Legh never paid a shilling of her annuity during her life.

Soon after her death Mr Pye and Mr Bradford went to Lyme to wait upon Col. Legh respecting the arrears of Mrs Ann Legh's Annuity. Mr Bradford was to take the examination of two Servants at Bullocks Smithy[5] who lived at Lyme at Mr. Legh's death, respecting the confinement of Mrs Ann Legh, and of her being compelled while in durance to give up a great number of Life Leases which Mr Legh had granted to her, for an Annuity of six hundred pounds per Annum. If the evidence had been sufficiently strong, the intention was to file a Bill in Chancery agst the Col. to recover back these Leases. But their evidence not being satisfactory they contented themselves with demanding the arrears of the Annuity amounting to £2,700. There having been a quarrel and a shyness between Mr Pye and the Col., Mr Bradford waited upon the Col. alone leaving Mr Pye at Dishley.[6] Upon opening the business to the Col. he says he never saw a man so much startled & alarmed. However upon talking the matter over a little he soon consented to pay the money, that is, he wd give them a Bond for it payable at a certain time, as it was impossible for him to pay it immediately. Mr Bradford said he wanted some money at that time & if he wd give him a Draft at a Month for £500 he wd take a Bond for the Terms to which he immediately assented and seemed highly pleased to get off so well, for Mr Bradford, that the Col. apprehended, he was come to arrest him. The business being thus arranged he then informed the Col. that Mr Pye was at Dishley. He ordered the Carriage to go & fetch him immediately and though they intended to stop only a few hours, he kept them a whole week doing everything in his power to gratify and amuse them.

March 2nd
After Breakfast I set out alone and on foot, to take a further survey of the Estate. I called at Mrs Neatis' Farm which consists of both Salthrop and Quidhampton Farms. These are by far the most valuable part of the whole property. The House and Outbuildings are very extensive and in good repair and the distant parts of the Farm are very well provided with Sheds for Oxen and Sheep upon a very large Scale.

There is but little land of inferior quality upon these Farms & I am much deceived if Mrs Neatis' Farm will not average twenty shillings per Statute Acre throughout, which is in this neighbourhood a very uncommon thing. These Lands lie all round and close up to the house at Salthrop, Mr Pye only occupying a few small Inclosures at a rent of £40 a Year. I passed twice thro' the Yard at Salthrop. I had some conversation with the Carpenter. He told me that the wages of a common Carpenter here are 14 shillings per week. In the Timber Yard I found a pair of Sawyers at work. They measure their work pretty much in the same way as we do in Lancashire. There is Timber in the Yard sufficient to complete the new Stables, a good share of it is cut up. I think this ought to be valued.

I then went to the men who were digging the Foundation for the new Stables. They are unfortunate in having a bad bottom. The East and South sides are dug seven feet deep and at the bottom of these they are driving Piles of six feet in length. At the distance of 2 fields I saw Mr Davis valuing the Timber. I had the curiosity to walk to him just to observe his method, for I understood on Monday that he w^d measure every Tree, & not value by inspection. He has a small silk Cord with a knot at every foot and a mark at every 3 In; allowing for the Bark. With this he takes the girt of every Tree and a man with a ten foot staff takes the height. So much is this staff short of reaching the top of the body of the Tree, held up as high as the man can reach, he is obliged to guess at. He did not measure any trees while I was with him which were more than six feet higher than the top of the staff. There is no oak upon the whole Property worth mentioning. Elm is the universal Timber all over the Country. Below and about Salthrop House stand some very fine Trees. I noticed a great many of which had upwards of fifty feet in them and not a few which had more than sixty and some seventy feet of Timber in them. Yet they will raise but a little money compared with Oak. I suppose the best Trees among w^d not in this situation sell for more than 10 pence per foot. I quite enjoyed myself and my walk; it was the first time I had got out by myself and I was at full liberty to make my own observations. Salthrop house is situated on the North side and close to the foot of a very high Hill, which prevents you from seeing any thing Southward a hundred yards from the House. Up the side of this Hill Mr Pye has just been extending his Plantations very considerably. To the East, North & West, a very extensive tract of country lies open. There is no River runs thro' this Valley, but I understand a Canal is about to be cut, which will pass within a Mile of Salthrop and which will complete the inland Navigation from Bristol to Manchester. If it pass near the line which was pointed out to me, it will, in my opinion add much to the beauty of the place, as well as to the convenience of the Country, particularly with regard to fuel, which here is an article of the greatest necessity.

I now ascended the Hill to make my way across Country to Broad-hinton which is full two miles distant. As soon as you get to the top of the Hill, a wild bleak uncomfortable tract of Country lies before you. The land but rarely intersected with Hedges, and scarce a Tree to be seen, the whole exposed to cutting Winds in every direction. Tho' the Country was strange to me I steered pretty directly to Broad Hinton. This Manor Farm, Constables' & Hunters' are all rented by Mr Hughes. The old Gentleman has given up business to his two Sons, and has retired to the house which belongs to Constables' Farm. This is a large handsome well built brick house, but is not so good in the inside & one w^d imagine from its outward appearance. There are Outbuildings to it, sufficiently extensive, but like most of the Outbuildings upon these Estates, but in bad repair in the inside. This Farm of Mr Hughes is the largest I ever had occasion to look over. The Buildings abt it are immense & the Yards and Folds amazingly extensive. The House is of Stone covered with Slate and has the appearance of an ancient Mansion. At present it is large without convenience and ruinous in every corner. The best part of it is the Kitchen, which I conceive cannot be less than eight Yards square. The Court which was formerly the front of the House is separated from the Farm Yard by a high Stone wall in the centre of which is a handsome arched Gate-way. The side of the Court opposite the Stone Wall is inclosed by a large handsome stone building covered with Slate which in former times I doubt not was Servants' Offices, at present only filled with lumber. The bottom of the Court is likewise enclosed with a stone-wall. Beyond this Stone-wall is a piece of ground which was formerly, I conceive, a Lawn or extensive Grass Platt. It is now used as a Timber Yard for which it is very well adapted. On one side of it has been erected a long low thatched Building, one part of which is a Shop for a Carpenter, and the other contains a very great curiosity. It is a Well, the diameter of which is not less than seven feet, and its' depth no body c^d tell me. The present Chain is 52 Yards long, but is far short of the bottom, and the length of this Chain every bucket must go to fetch up water. The Chain is fully stronger than what we call the buckling Chain used in carrying Timber & I shd not wonder if every link weights a quarter of a pound. The Bucket may hold abt 30 Galls. of Water. The water is raised thus: Across the Well & abt six feet above it, a Shaft of fourteen Inches Diamr. lies horizontally. The end of this Shaft goes into the Center of a Wheel of 13 feet Diamr. and four feet upon the face. Over the Shaft lies the Chain with a Bucket at each end so that when one Bucket is at the top the other is at the bottom. When a Bucket of water is wanted a man steps into the Wheel, and setting his face tow^{ds}. that side on which the empty Bucket is, he begins to move his feet as if he were walking. This forces the Wheel round and of course the horizontal Shaft over which the Chain lies, and as the empty Bucket descends the full one rises. The Carpenter stepped into the Wheel & raised a Bucket of water to gratify my curiosity. The Water is very clear and is excellent for all culinary purposes & is so soft that it is preferred to rain water for washing with. I c^d discover no tradition of the making or the maker of the well, & all that I c^d learn was that it was never known to be dry. As far as I c^d see down, it is walled with free stone of excellent workmanship and in complete repair.

It now beginning to rain very fast I went into the house and found the Valuers who c^d not get off for the wet. The Weather had been so bad ever since they met, and likely to be no better that they concluded to adjourn the business until Monday fortnight. Mr Heath asking me whether I understood that they were to value the Yorkshire & Hampshire quit Rents, I told him most certainly. He then took out Mr Gorst's Letr in which he said no mention was made of the Quit Rents, & doubted this Authority. As I walked in the morning, I had unluckily laid all my Papers out of my pocket which I thot I shd not want and among the rest of the Abstract of the Agreem^t given me by Mr Gorst I found I c^d not satisfy him and as he meant going home to-night & I had no chance of seeing him again I was determined to fetch it. I desired Mr Hughes to lend me a horse, I set out tho' I was 6 miles from Swindon and it was raining. I was only an hour and a half away, but I was wet exceedingly. I came to Broad-hinton back just as the Gentlemen were sitting down to Dinner at half past 5 o'Clock. Abt 7 o'Clock Mr Heath set out havg 17 miles to go. I stopped [for] Tea, & abt 8 o'Clock I borrowed an Umbrella and in the Wind and Rain set out to walk 6 miles to Swindon thro' a strange Country in the dark. I got to my Inn abt half past nine.

March 3rd

Mr Bradford had said that on this day he shd be particularly engaged & I was happy to find myself at liberty again to pursue my enquiries my own way. As soon as I had breakfasted I took the direct Road to Broad-hinton. Abt a mile short of the House, a Gate stands across the Turnpike Road. And here the Manor and the Farm commence. The Turnpike Road passes thro' the Lands all the way to the Village, and is not fenced off from the Lands. The fields from hence to the House & for near a Mile to the right are all in grass, they are very large and have a very Park like appearance, having single Trees, and large single Thorns growing scattered within them. This Land upon examination is not as valuable as at first it appears to be. Riding along the Road one c^d not have the most remote idea of this Land being wet, it both lying high & sloping tow^{ds} the South, yet when upon it, it is very soft indeed. But it is not much poached being only pastured with Sheep and in the Summer with a few Horses. I believe the Grass is not sufficiently good for grazing their feeding Cattle even in Summer. I apprehend twenty shillings per Statute Acre will be as much as can be laid upon it. There are abt a hundred Acres of Meadows, which will bear something more per Acre, but the Hay is not of good quality. There are large Hay-ricks with Sheds and Folds for the Sheep and Cattle in different parts of the Farm. As they are now foddering all their Stock with Hay, most of the Ricks are cut into, and I had numerous opportunities of examining them. The Hay has almost universally been extremely well got, yet it does not seem nutritious or well flavor'd. This I conceive may partly be owing to it being impossible to cover so large a tract of Meadows with Dung as frequently as might be wished, and of course the Grass must become dry and tasteless. The Farmers use no Lime, or purchase any species of Manure whatever. Their Corn Land is manured solely by folding of Sheep, and without this they cd get no Corn. They fallow and fold for Wheat; then take a Crop of Oats laid down with Grass seeds, mow the Clover &c., the third year, & fallow & fold the fourth, & this is their Scale of cropping. Upon this Scale they say they only get a Crop in 4 years, that is, they are unwilling to call any thing a Crop but Wheat. Land which will only bear cropping in this way is of very inferior quality, and seldom letts for more than ten or twelve shillings per Acre. There is no Marl hear, but there is a white stone lying pretty near the Surface which answers the same purpose. But it is so expensive an operation that it is never resorted to but at the commencement of a long term. There is a very large Tract of this inferior Land, upon Mr Hughes' Farm lying between the Village and the Downs. It is hard to work, requiring in general five Horses to plough & when it is worked and even sown in fine condition either for Wheat or Lent Corn, shd heavy Rains fall soon after, the whole surface turns into a Cake which the young Corn cannot penetrate. The principal part of the plowing Lands lie in this tract, but some are in the uplands and are of a greater value. On the South side of the Turnpike Road mentd before to pass thro' this farm are some of the best grass Lands, part in Meadow and part used for feeding the Oxen in Summer, for the Butcher. The Downs are Hills not very high which lie in different parts of the Country. There are ranges of them on the South side of the Manor of Broad-hinton, on which Mr Hughes has I believe abt two hundred Acres. The Downs are never broken up; they are in fact Commons for grazing Sheep, but, tho' they are not divided into Inclosures or separated by any Fences, yet the Stock is stinted and every

Farmer knows his own Limits. When the Sheep are pastured here in the Summer they are always attended by a Shepherd in the day, and driven upon the above ment^d poor arable Lands to fold at night. The Downs I believe are never valued at more than five shillings per Acre.

March 4th

As I had not yet seen much of the Farm rented by Messrs Browns I hired a Horse at Swindon to go over it. In my way I had the curiosity to cross over Mr Hughes' Farm in a direction different from that I had done before. I found no reason to alter the Opinion I had previously formed of it, only that in examining more particularly the Grass-lands lying to the right of the Turnpike Road above mentioned I did not find it so generally wet as I at first imagined.

Messrs Browns' Farm lies up to and a little intermixed with Mr Hughes. It is by far the worst Farm of them all. The major part of their Arable Land lies up to the Downs, adjoining to and of the same quality with that of Mr Hughes in the same situation before described. Considering the size of this Farm it is much more detached than the others. The Meadows lie at near a Mile distance and are of very inferior quality. The Buildings are intolerable bad and wholly thatched. The Dwelling house, except a Pillar of Brick here and there, is composed of the Boards only to the Outside, lathed and plaistered within. The Housing & Outhousing, taken altogether, is I think, without exception, the worst I ever saw upon so large a Farm, and I do not see how a farmer can enter upon a new Term of this Farm without a new house. This House stands in the Village. One of the Mr Browns went with me & pointed out to me, I think 23 or 24 Cottages belonging to these Estates all of which are granted . . . upon Life Leases, several of them lately renewed. They are all thatched and may upon an average be worth ab^t 30s. apiece per Annum, except a Public House, the Sign of the Bell, which is a good Brick building covered with Slate & may be worth 8 or 10 pounds a Year.

It may be necessary here to remark two very great Drawbacks upon Mr Hughes' Farm. The one is the Land tax which is just three shillings in the pound upon the present stretch Rent. The other is the Tythe, which is not only valued in kind, but is gathered and taken off the Premises, the Tent. not having at present the option of retaining & paying for it.

The Timber upon the whole of these Estates, I apprehend, will scarcely be valued at two thousand pounds, tho' it sh^d not be much less.

On my return to Swindon I had the curiosity to call at the House of Mr Cawley who married Miss Keck. I am informed he has a very pretty landed Estate not less nominally than £4,000 per Annum, but by Incumbrances of different descriptions, is reduced at present to abt. £2,000 per Annum. He has a Park adjoining to his House, which is a very fine piece of ground containing abt 200 Acres and is stocked with two hund. head of Deer. Below this park lies a Wood of Ash, the best of its kind & the most regularly attended to of any I ever saw. It is regularly cut down at 18 Years growth, for Poles & Fire-wood. Its extent is abt 150 Acres and abt 6 or 7 Acres are cut down annually, and when any old stock is dead a new plant is put down. They sell it by the Pole, 160 of which Poles are in an Acre. The worst part of the Wood never sells for less than 5s per Pole & sometimes in the best part of the Wood it sells for 10 or 12 Shills. per Pole. There are abt 6½ Acres sold this Year which have sold for upwards of £400.

The House is handsome & convenient. It is abt. 70 feet square, with Attic story & a stone Cornice all round. It has been much neglected for abt 10 Years during Mr Cawley's minority, but whitewashing & papering seems to be the most that is wanted at present. Mr Cawley keeps a pack of Harriers. He is a remarkably good rider & is noted for having excellent Horses.

March 5th

I took a Chaise at 9 o'Clock to Marlborough, to meet the Bath & London Coaches. After waiting abt. an hour I succeeded in getting a place to London. After getting a few Miles out of Marlborough, the Road thro' Berkshire and all the way to London is the most level I ever travelled in my life for so long a distance. The watering or floating of Meadows is pursued to the greatest extent, & the most systematically all thro' the southern part of Berkshire of any place I have ever seen.

I arrived at the Bolt-in-Tun Coffee-house in Fleet-street abt. 2 o'Clock in the morning.

I stayed in London until 5 o'Clock on the Thursday morning following when I got into the Oundle Coach to go to Lilford where I arrived at 8 o'Clock in the Evening. I only stopped here until Saturday Noon when I got into the Cambridge Coach to go to Leicester where I arrived abt. 9 o'Clock. At 8 o'Clock on the Sunday morning the Coach Defiance from London to Manr. came in. For want of Room in the inside I was obliged to submit to an outside place to Ashburn. I had never ridden on the out-side of a Coach before. I took the Guard's seat, & we had not got more than half a mile out of Leicester before one of the hind-wheels came off & I was pitched into the ditch. The Coach lay entirely upon one side. With difficulty we got the Passengers out, none of whom were materially injured. But a young man who had taken his Seat beside the Coachman, had his leg so very much hurt that he c^d not proceed on his journey, & was obliged to be sent back to Leicester.

Notes

1   Lady Newton, *The House of Lyme* (1917).
2   Lady Newton, *The House of Lyme*.
3   Lady Newton, *The House of Lyme*.
4   Mr Bradford was agent at Lyme Hall.
5   Bullock Smithy was at Hazel Grove near Stockport, Greater Manchester.
6   This is Disley, Cheshire.

7

A Further Visit to London in 1819 Concerning the Canal Bridge at Leigh

In 1819, Richard Hodgkinson travelled more than two hundred miles to London to argue the case for a matter of one inch. Hodgkinson and his fellow trustees of the Bolton and St Helens turnpike wanted an easy gradient for a road bridge over the new waterway which was to connect the Leeds & Liverpool Canal at Wigan with the Bridgwater Canal at Leigh. This was opposed by the canal company who wanted a sharper gradient, thus reducing the capital cost and maintenance expenses.

For more than two decades there had been plans and counter-plans to give either the Leeds & Liverpool Canal or the Lancaster Canal a connection with the Bridgwater Canal, and thus with the markets in Manchester and the Midlands. Canal companies had courted and schemed with rivals with ardour and deceit.

Twenty-five years earlier in 1794, Hodgkinson had foiled the Lancaster Canal Company's plans to connect with the Bridgewater at Worsley by building a new canal from Aspull to Worsley through Atherton and Leigh. With the Canal Age now reaching maturity, the Lancaster's hopes of direct access to the Bridgwater were again dashed by an agreement between the Liverpool & Leeds Canal Company and the Bridgewater Canal Company to build a short link between Leigh and Wigan.

To bring this into effect a new Act of Parliament was required, and Hodgkinson and other turnpike trustees went to the House of Commons where the Bill was being examined to argue for an easy gradient approaching the new bridge at Leigh rather than the steeper and less expensive one the canal company wanted. How Hodgkinson solved the problem is described in his journal.

One of Hodgkinson's fellow trustees on the Turnpike was Col Ralph

Fletcher, lessee of the coal rights in Atherton and owner of other collieries in the Bolton area. A powerful political figure, he was notorious for his formidable opposition to the machine breakers of 1812 in particular, and other reform in general. Colonel of the Bolton Light Horse Volunteers and a magistrate, 'Fletcher [was] an inveterate hater of the Luddites and an unscrupulous hounder of them.'[1] Despite his high moral stance on public order, Fletcher was not averse to fiddling his expenses, and on this visit to London in 1819 he persuaded Hodgkinson to double his claim to the Turnpike Trust 'that it might correspond with the Bills of Col. Fletcher & Major Watkins'. Also in London on turnpike business with Hodgkinson were John Ravald, a Bolton solicitor, founder member of the Bolton Light Horse Volunteers and a member of Bolton Pitt Club, and Maj. John Watkins, bleachworks owner, also a member of the Bolton Light Horse Volunteers and Bolton Pitt Club and whose son married Fletcher's eldest daughter, Mary.

The days and hours Hodgkinson waited upon the dilatory offices of parliamentary procedure were not wasted, and in his vigorous and enquiring manner he pursued an old acquaintance who had fled to London 'in consequence of a young woman fathering a Child upon him', visited the theatre and art galleries, and viewed the new iron bridge at Southwark, built at a cost of forty-three lives. He also renewed his acquaintance with John Christian Curwen MP, the Workington colliery owner who farmed his large estate according to the most modern practice. Together, Hodgkinson and Curwen visited a large dairy farm out in the country at Paddington. On his way home, Hodgkinson travelled via Oxford and spent two pleasant days with his son Joseph, then just concluding his studies.

It was on this visit too that Hodgkinson endured a performance of Mozart's Marriage of Figaro, an experience he dismissed as 'ridiculous'.

Minutes of a Journey to London begun May 11th, 1819 to Attend a Committee in the House of Commons upon the Leeds and Liverpool Canal Extension Bill

Left home at 9 o'Clock & went on Horseback to Bolton, from there went in a Chaise with Mr Ravald to Manchester. We dined at the Palace Inn, from whence we set out at half past 2 o'Clock in the Afternoon in the Prince Cobourgh Coach, fare inside to London two Guineas.

The Road we came lay through Wilmslow, Congleton, Newcastle,

Stone, Woosley Bridge, where we paid four shillings apiece for Supper. Litchfield, Tamworth, Coventry, Dunchurch where we breakfasted at 6 o'Clock in the Morning, Daventry, Towcaster, Stoney Stratford, Dunstable where we had a very good Dinner & well cooked, St Albans & Barnett to London where we arrived at halfpast 6 o'Clock having been only 28 hours on the Road. The Weather was fine the Roads good without Dirt or Dust, & all the Country looking charming from the forwardness of the Spring, & some genial Rains which had fallen a day or two before.

As we passed by Trentham, the Seat of the Marquis of Stafford, the day was closing and I could see but little of that charming place. But during all the next forenoon after Breakfast at Dunchurch, from thence to Stony Stratford I was quite delighted with the Country. There was a deal of Grass Land all the way, and very well stocked particularly with Sheep. But whether the Land was Meadow or Pasture it was perfectly clean from Rushes or Rubbish of any kind & looked beautiful. The Farms were well attended to & I do not remember ever passing thro' so long a distance where there was so little of Common Land Waste or unimproved or even neglected Land. I observed several Fields which had been very lately drained in the manner we are now draining at Atherton & Bewsey.

At Towcaster was a very large Fair for Cattle & Sheep. I think I never saw so fine a Show of calving cows. We passed through one Lot just entering the Town which I was told consisted of a hundred all belonging to one Man.

While the coach changed Horses I stepped for a few Minutes into the Fair & was told that buyers were very slack owing as my Informant told me to both Meat & Butter having given way the preceeding Week. Butter he said was a shilling & a halfpenny per pound. The 12th of May seems to be a great day in this part of the Country. For 2 or 3 Stages on the Road from Towcaster we saw several very smart Garlands accompanied by Crowds of young people & even the Children had Garlands with which they went singing from Door to Door.

We were set down at the White Horse in Friday Street & taking a Hackney Coach we came to the Grecian Coffee house[2] in the Temple. They were so full of Company we could not have a Bed in the House but they provided us 2 beds at the next House but one having already 14 beds engaged out of the House.

13th May
After Breakfast Mr Ravald & I called upon Mr Watkins at No.9 Northumberland Street near Charing Cross and from thence I walked on to

Grosvenor Place to Lord Lilford. I returned by Hyde Park Corner up
Piccadilly, calling in again at Mr Watkins' Lodgings and found a Note
saying that he & Mr Ravald would dine at the Grecian at 5 o'Clock. It
being now only 12 o'Clock I thought I would go as far as the West India
Docks & set out for that purpose.

I stepped into St Paul's & there found that it was the Charity Sermon
for the Orphans of Clergyman. It was so crowded that I could not get
within the Chancel to hear the service, but I could very well hear the
Music which was very fine. Mr Greatlorne presiding at the Organ. Several
of Handel's best choruses were performed. After stopping here near an
hour, I went on up Cheapside & called in at the Bank & the Stock
Exchange and so many objects kept continually engaging my attention
that when I got to the Tower instead of proceeding to the Docks I found
I had only just time enough to get back to Dinner. I returned through
Lower Thames Street and keeping as near to the Riverside as possible I
was soon at Blackfriars Bridge & from thence soon to the Grecian Inn. At
9 o'Clock Mr Fletcher came to us having arrived in London about 7. In
the course of the Evening the Engineer of the Leeds & Liverpool Canal
Company joined us. From his Account his Levels of the Road & Canal
corresponded with what Mr Fletcher & I had taken on the Monday night
near Limbrick in Leigh. He said he thought our proposed Ascent of the
approach of the Bridge at one inch & a half at a Yard was too little &
would cause too much of the pavement of the Street to be taken up & of
course add to their Expense. But he said he thought by ten o'Clock next
Morning we should have a proposal from the Company.

14th May
This morning we were told at the Grecian that if we pleased we might
have Beds in the House some Company having left. This we thought
would be more comfortable & we had our Luggage fetched in.

At one o'Clock we went down to the Committee Room; it being the
first day the Committee sat. Almost the first person I saw upon coming
into the Room was Lord Lilford, he stayed all the while the Committee
sat. There were eleven Petitions presented against the Bill for extending
the Canal from Wigan to Leigh, but the principal opposition came from
the Proprietors of the Manchester Bolton and Bury Canal originating in
an Agreement made between the two Companies in 1794 for making a
junction of the two Canals at Red Moss near Blackrod & thereby opening
a way for the Leeds & Liverpool Canal Company to get to Manchester
through Bolton, but by joining the Duke of Bridgewater's Canal at Leigh

they would get to Manchester that way & thereby the Line to Red Moss would be abandoned which would be a serious disadvantage to the Proprietors of the Manchester Bolton & Bury Canal. After some preliminary Conversation of the Committee it was agreed that the Petitions against the Bill should go into their Cases first & accordingly the Bolton people began with reading the Agreement alluded to, after which Mr Fletcher was called into the Witness Box but before his Examination was finished it was 4 o'Clock & the Committee was obliged to adjourn.

It appeared to me that the Leeds & Liverpool people had much the larger number of Members in the Committee. I then got Mr Thomas Claughton to take me into the Gallery of the House of Commons where a very animated Debate took place on the Bill for altering the present Game Laws & making Game the Property of the person on whose land it was found. For the Bill the speakers were Mr Brand, Sir John Seabright, Mr Wilberforce, the Marquis of Tavistock, and Mr Long Willesby, agst the Bill the speakers were Sir John Shilley, Mr Parkinson & his son, & two more members whose names I could not learn & others. Upon a Division the Bill was lost by a considerable majority. At half-past 8 o'Clock I came to my Lodgings to Dinner not having tasted anything from Breakfast in the Morning to that time. I found Mr Fletcher, Mr Watkins & a Mr Farrand from Rochdale had been dining with Mr Ravald at 6 o'Clock. They stayed till 12 o'Clock & had drunk rather too much Wine. Mr Fletcher & I agreed to meet at Mr Watkins' Lodgings at 10 o'Clock the following morning to go & pay a visit to Lord Lilford.

15th May
We went at the time appointed. The principal conversation between Lord Lilford & Mr Fletcher was about continuing the Colliery Rail-way to the Canal at Leigh. Lord Lilford objected to its being continued on account of its crossing The Avenue at the Gates in Leigh until he had been in Lancashire & viewed the Ground again. Returning I called upon Mr Curwen, Member for ———.

He received me very kindly. We soon entered upon the Political subjects of the day & among others upon the Bills pending in Parliament respecting the Poor Laws. One of these Bills was to be discussed in the House of Commons on the Monday following. He gave me a Ticket of Admission into the Gallery & desired I would attend. He then proposed I should call upon him the following day (Sunday) at three o'Clock & he would walk with me into a large Dairy Farm in the country. At six o'Clock Mr Ravald & I dined with the Gentlemen from Bolton at the

Somerset Hotel where we stayed till ten o'Clock & then went to Covent Garden theatre, time enough to hear the farce of Roland For an Oliver.[3] It is a tolerably good thing in that way but I have no partiality for that kind of Entertainment.

Before we went to Dinner Mr Fletcher, Mr Ravald & myself took a Boat at the Temple Stairs to see the new Iron Bridge called the Southwark Bridge erected between the Black Friars & London Bridges. We sailed under the Blackfriars Bridge & then through all the three Arches of which the Iron Bridge consisted. It struck me as the most stupendous & indeed astonishing piece of Architecture that I had ever seen. We got out of the Boat on the Borough side and ascended the Steps and went upon the Bridge. The Battlements are all of Iron, the road over it and the approaches are excellent. The Waterman informed us that during the erecting of it 43 men lost their Lives & that 13 had unfortunately been killed at one time.

16th May
Being Sunday morning we went to Foundling Hospital intending to go to Divine Service there but being rather late the Chapel was so crowded we could not get in. We then walked on till we came to St.Martin's where we heard the Service very well performed. It was now one o'Clock & being half way to Mr Curwen's Lodgings where I was to go at three o'Clock I determined to walk that way which led me to the grand new Street now opening between Carlton House and the Regent's Park through Portland Place. Having amused myself hereabouts till the time appointed for calling upon Mr Curwen I then went to his Lodgings. He was out but came in about half an hour. We set out immediately & going through Portland Place & the Regent's Park we walked a considerable way Westward then turned into the Fields north of Paddington & soon arrived at a large Milk Farm belonging to a Mr Millan the place where Mr Curwen intended to take me. Here two hundred & sixty cows are kept of the Short horned breed for milking. They are kept all the year round. Their principal food is grains of which the manager told me they had eighty Quarters every day from Mr Whitbread's Brewery. But he said a quarter would not measure out more than five Bushels. Through the Winter they are fed with Grains, Hay, Turnips & Potatoes each given at a particular hour of the day. At present, instead of Hay of which every Cow has only two pounds a day, they have green Food viz: Vetches & Grass with grains as usual & Turnips or Potatoes. At this time they are buying Potatoes at fifteen shillings per Ton only. Before Christmas they paid 13

& since Christmas £2 & £2.5s. per ton & now only pay fifteen shillings per ton. The Cows are all in very good Condition & the Manager told me that they suffered great inconvenience from the Cows getting too fat for milking. They sometimes keep the Cows while they bear two or three calves if they be good milkers. These Cows are let out to the milk sellers in the town 10, 15 or 20 Cows to one person who sends his own Milkers & milks his own lot.

He gives 3 pence per Quart for their Milk & sells it at home at 6 pence. Cream is sold at the Farm at 5 shillings per Quart. Mr Millan was at the Farm waiting for us when we got there. He had his Curricle[4] & Pair with him. He is a Gentleman of large Property & resides about eight miles off.

Mr Curwen talking of his own Farm as we returned said he had sent the preceeding week two Heifers & a Bull to a Gentleman in America. The Heifers 40 guineas a pair & the Bull 50. They travelled from the Schoose Farm to Liverpool to be shipped. Mr Millan intended to begin to cut his Meadow Grass for Hay the following morning. I got back to the Grecian to Dinner at six o'Clock.

17th May

After breakfast I went into Oxford Road to call upon Mr Matthew Wilson, a Saddler. As I passed through his Shop I counted 15 men at work. I had some Refreshment & sat an hour with him. He told me that including himself & two Nephews who he had lately taken on as Partners, the whole numbers of men he employed was 25 because of a considerable quantity of work he had done out of the Shop as Piecework. He was when a young man a Journeyman to Thomas Sale a Saddler in Leigh and left Leigh in consequence of a young woman fathering a Child upon him which he would never acknowledge to be his & even now insists in the same disavowal. During our Conversation he told me that on his arrival in London he was a Month before he got employment & his money was reduced to half a Crown. He said that during all this time his Spirits never drooped. From a confidence in himself of his knowledge & skill in the business & his natural inclination to Sobriety & Industry, he was sure that if he could only once get a situation he should keep it. At the end of a Month he was engaged in a Shop of great business where he continued near eight Years. At the end of three Years he was made a Foreman & placed over a man who had been the Foreman ever since he came into the Shop. After he took a Shop of his own he did not immediately fall into full business but did a deal of Piecework for other Shops. Mr. Aston, of Aston, in Cheshire was the first man who brought him into Notice. He procured the work of all the Gentlemen of the Leicester Hunt, since which time he has never had any check in his business. He sends Saddles & Harnesses to all Parts of England, Scotland & Ireland & to the East & West Indies.

At one o'Clock I went to the Committee Room where nothing particular occurred. Lord Lilford was in the Committee Room & I got him to give me an Order for Admission into the House of Lords that evening to hear the Debates upon the Catholic Claims. I heard Lord Dunnoughmore speak who made the motion for going into a Committee upon the Catholic Claims. I heard the Bishop of Worcester, the new Bishop of Peterborough (Dr Marsh), the Lord Chancellor & Lord Liverpool speak against the Motion & the Bishop of Norwich & Earl Grey in favour of it. Tho' opposed to Lord Grey in my sentiments respecting the Catholic Claims I admired him most as an Orator. His Figure & Voice are good, his attitude was graceful, his action considerable, his language eloquent, his manner was impressive & he raised or lowered his Voice according to circumstances, was sometimes loud but never vociferous.

18th May
Our journey to London was in compliance with an Order of the Commissioners of the Bolton & Leigh Turnpike Road made at a public Meeting to get a Clause invested in the new Act of Parliament which the Leeds and Liverpool Canal Company were soliciting to enable them to join the Duke of Bridgewater's Canal at Leigh, to this effect that the Approaches to the Bridge to be erected over the Canal at Leigh should not be of a steeper Ascent than one Inch & a half at a Yard. The Parliamentary regulation is three Inches at a Yard & the former Acts of the Leeds & Liverpool Canal Company confine them to two Inches & a half at a Yard.

From different persons connected with the Canal Company whom we occasionally met & conversed with in the Committee Room we learned that the principle objection to our Clause was that by such an easy ascent the Approaches would be considerably lengthened at each end & thereby increase the expense to the Company at present & would in future also impose upon them the expense of keeping so much additional length in repair for ever hereafter. It was also proposed to us that the Clause would be agreed to, if we would engage that the Township should repair the additional length of the Approaches. This we could not certainly bind the Township to do. But from their making this proposal I thought some arrangement might be made between us without going into the Committee

& thereby the Expense of Counsel be saved to the Commissioners which would be ten Guineas per day. I was the more induced to adopt such a measure as I observed the Committee growing every day stronger on the part of the Leeds & Liverpool Company, thro' the influence of the Marquis of Stafford & Mr Bradshaw. I found too that several other Petitions had been settled in the same way.

Influenced by these considerations I went to the Lodging of Mr Watkins & Mr Fletcher to consult with them upon the subject. After some deliberation upon the subject we agreed to call a Coach & wait upon Mr Bradshaw at his Lodgings before he went in the Committee. We did so & found him just going to dress which made him a little impatient at being interrupted, however, he said, as you are here let me look at your Plans. We opened them & explained them to him and also the difference between our Proposals and those of the Canal Proprietors foundered upon the Clause for Bridges in their former Acts allowing the ascent to be two Inches & a half in a Yard. He became pacified, said it was very proper that we should have a good & commodious Bridge but at the same time it was equally proper that the Proprietors should not be put to any unreasonable expense & he concluded with saying that he would speak to the other Parties in the Committee Room.

As soon as the Committee was opened Mr Harrison, Counsel for the Canal Proprietors, began their Defence. He commented very severely upon the Evidence both of Mr Fletcher & Mr Darbyshire, said a great deal about the comparative advantages both to the Proprietors & the Public from joining the Duke of Bridgewater's Canal at Leigh rather than the Bolton and Bury at Red Moss and also the greater facility of executing the former than the latter. As to their agreement which had been entered into in 1794 between the Leeds and Liverpool and the Manchester Bury & Bolton Canal Companies for making a junction at Red Moss and which had been read in the Committee, he said his Clients would be ready to complete their part of the Agreement as soon as the opposite party would come forward with Parliamentary Authority & shew themselves to be in a condition to fulfill their part of it. He concluded without calling any Witnesses which prevented the opposite Counsel replying.

Strangers were then ordered to withdraw & a Motion was made 'That the Manchester Bury and Bolton Canal Company had not made good the Allegations stated in their petition.' Members began to pour in from all quarters & this continued for an hour when upon the question being put it was carried in the affirmative by forty against sixteen. The Committee then adjourned to the day but one following.

As soon as Mr Bradshaw came into the Lobby out of the Committee Room, I desired Mr Fletcher to go & speak to him, he was talking with Mr Birbeck one of the most active of the Leeds & Liverpool Proprietors, who, I suppose, had been talking with him upon our business for when Mr Watkins, Mr Ravald & myself joined them he was saying to Mr Fletcher that if the Clause was proposed to the Committee in the present form he would oppose it. But however, he said, let the Parties come together. Mr Birbeck go & fetch your Engineer & I will go with you into a private Room. After some time the Engineer was found & we went together into what is called the Long Room. Both Parties explained to Mr Bradshaw their respective wishes & after arguing the matter over for a considerable time it was agreed that instead of the approaches to the Bridge being one Inch & a half at a Yard as we proposed or two Inches & a half as they proposed, they should be two inches in a yard & that our Clause should be inserted in the Act in the words we had drawn it up except the alteration of the ascent for $1^1/_2$ Inches to 2 Inches in the Yard.

This being arranged I was at liberty to leave London as soon as I pleased. It was now four o'Clock & the House of Commons was assembling. Mr Turney was to make his promised Motion on the state of the Nation this evening & I was anxious to hear it but upon going towards the Gallery I found all the Lobbies so crowded that I saw no possibility of gaining admittance & I went out & walked to the new Vauxhall Bridge. This is an Iron Bridge over the Thames of nine Arches. This does not appear so stupendous as the Southwark Bridge but it is far more elegant & more pleasing to the eye. I do not know that I ever saw a piece of Architecture of this kind that pleased me so much. I went upon it, walked over it and spent a very agreeable half hour in examining it in its various parts & viewing the Country and the Objects from it both up and down the River. Near this Bridge is a very large building called the Penitentiary House where convicts are confined and set to labour whose Crimes are deemed not sufficiently atrocious to send them beyond the Seas. My curiosity was gratified here, I felt rather fatigued and taking a Boat at the foot of the Bridge I had a very pleasant sail down the River under Westminster Bridge & the Waterloo Bridge to the Temple Stairs where I was landed at six o'Clock just in time for dinner.

In the evening Mr Ravald went with me to the Opera.[5] I found the House as he described it to be splendid in the extreme and the Company both numerous & in their Dress elegant but I could not help thinking the whole performance an absurdity for an English Audience. The whole of the play is sung so that whether a man be in a rage at his Servant, jealous of his Wife, affectionate towards his Friends or fondling with his Mistress he expresses himself in Song which is ridiculous enough but to render it more ridiculous still the language is Italian which certainly not one in twenty of the whole Audience understands a single word of. But to render absurdity more absurd the After piece is a pantomime the whole of which is performed without one single word being spoken in any language whatever. The Pantomime concludes with a great deal of Dancing, in a stile which I suppose is considered elegant. It may be so & is well enough to be seen once but I cannot conceive how an audience can be amused or entertained night after night with a repetition of the same thing over & over again & I certainly cannot compliment them on their good sense for so doing.

19th May
Immediately after breakfast I went to wait upon Lord Lilford to inform him that I was now at liberty & should leave London as soon as possible. I hoped if I cd meet with him by ten o'Clock or soon after I should be able to get away in one of the Afternoon Coaches to Oxford through which place I intended to pass in my way home to spend a day or two with Joseph there having never been since he went to settle there & having received a Letter from him since I came to London, pressingly inviting me to return that way. When I arrived at Grosvenor Place, I found his Lordship had been out all night with his eldest daughter at Mrs Pattons Bold's Concert. As soon as he was informed I was there he sent the Footman to tell me the reason he was not up & to request me to call in again at one o'Clock. I now find it would be impracticable to get away this afternoon, so I walked to the Gloucester Coffee House in Piccadilly and engaged a Place in the Coach to Oxford at eight o'Clock the following morning and returned to Grosvenor Place to take my leave of Lord Lilford. On passing through Pall Mall I called in at the British Institution for promoting the Fine Arts in the United Kingdom founded June 4th, 1805, opened January 18, 1806, with a Catalogue in my hand which I purchased for a Shilling as I entered I found ample Amusement for an Hour though I have no particular taste for Paintings in general nor do I possess any scientific skill, whereby to judge of their excellence, or to form a comparative estimate of their respective Merit, I thought I would perceive a great difference as well in Execution as Design between many of the pictures and some I thought had not merit sufficient to entitle them to so distinguished a Situation. The Pictures are all numbered and the Catalogue is also numbered to correspond. After the number is a Column

with a description of the Painting and another Column containing the name of the Artist and a third Column with the name of the Proprietor who presented it to the Institution. The number of Pictures is one hundred & fifty-five.

From hence I went to the Exhibition of the Royal Academy, Somerset House. Here I found a vast assemblage of Persons in every Room where Pictures or Statues were exhibited. Here I purchased a Catalogue as I entered. Indeed without a Catalogue it would be impossible to understand anything of the very great variety of Paintings & Sculpture that is exhibited. Indeed the number & variety is such as to keep the ideas in a continual confusion and to leave but a very imperfect Recollection on the Mind of the Excellences of any particular piece of Sculpture or Painting. The pictures &c.,&c., are all Numbered as the Catalogue and though they are exhibited in several different rooms the numbers go on progressively to the end amounting to twelve hundred & forty-eight. Besides these there are in the Council Room sixty-eight which were presented by the Acadamecians on their Election.

Having half an hour to spare before Dinner I went to see the wild Beasts in Exeter Exchange. It is the largest Collection I had ever seen. The Elephant was an enormous size being ten feet high and upwards of four Tons in weight. But the most interesting Animal among them was called a Gnu. It was a singular Compound of Animals uniting the strong Head and Horns of the Buffalo, with the Mane, Tail and Body of the Horse. It was about 13 hands high, beautiful in its symmetry, & its Legs, remarkably fine.

Mr Ravald and I met at Dinner at the Grecian at halfpast five & at seven we agreed to go to Drury Lane Theatre. We only stayed during the Play to hear Mr Incledon sing a Song in the Costume of a Quaker.[6] Both this Theatre & Covent Garden had been burned down since I was last in London and rebuilt with equal if not additional splendour to the former ones.

20th May
The Oxford Coach took me up at The Grecian at halfpast seven and at eight we left the Gloucester Coffee House in Piccadilly and arrived at Oxford at three o'Clock. The rapidity with which the Coaches are now drawn is astonishing. The distance from London to Oxford is 56 miles which we were whirled over in seven hours including stoppages & changing Horses. Immediately upon leaving the Environs of London the country is very naked & barren for many Miles and I saw nothing in it till we came in to the neighbourhood of Henley upon Thames. Here the

Country assumes a wavy appearance, is beautifully interspersed with Hill and Dale & several Gentlemen's Seats lying about here. The Plantations and Woods enrich the Prospect very much. Being set down at the Mitre in Oxford, I wrote a short Note to Joseph who came to me in about half an hour. It was necessary I should sleep here and having secured a Bed I went to my Room to clean & dress myself while Joseph went to Prayers which he was obliged to do at halfpast four, it being a Holy Day viz: Ascension Day. His Lodgings are at a Widow's in a Street called Holywell a considerable distance from the College. He ordered Dinner from the College Kitchen to be sent to his own Lodgings at halfpast five. We dined by ourselves and the Evening being very fine we drank but little Wine and then went out to walk. The favourite Amusement of the Students is rowing in Boats upon the River. This Evening a great match was expected to take place between a party from Christ Church and one from Brazen Nose. We passed Christ Church and along the Christ Church Walk which is a very fine gravel walk between Rows of Elms of immense size which is a very great ornament to the Town. At the end of this turning to the right we entered another Gravel Walk which at length brought us to the Banks of the Isis where we found immense Crowds of genteel people anxiously waiting to see the rowing match. It did not however take place this Evening. After perambulating all the Walks which are very beautiful and of great variety, after seeing all that was to be seen and being assured that the Boat Race would not take place we returned about nine o'Clock to Joseph's Lodgings and after supper I returned to the Inn to sleep.

21st May
At eight o'Clock Joseph called for me at the Inn as he returned from Prayers and we went to his Lodgings to Breakfast. After Breakfast we began our perambulations of the City. We first called upon a very extensive Bookseller with whom Joseph deals. He showed us through his immense Shop and Store Rooms. He then took us to the Clarendon Printing House which is an amazing Establishment. There are separate Rooms and Presses for the different Departments of Printing, especially for printing Bibles & Testaments where the rapidity with which the work is performed and the quality done, excites a wonder wherever Purchasers are found for them and this wonder is greatly increased upon going into the Warehouses or Store Rooms to see the enormous piles upon piles of printed Sheets which are there stored ready for packing up and sending off to the London and other Booksellers.

We then visited the Theatre & the Radcliffe Library both of which well deserve the admiration of the curious and merit much more attention than we had time to bestow upon them.

We visited most of the Colleges in succession but they are so numerous and so various that after so hasty a view it is almost impossible to recollect any distinct idea of them individually. Of them a description would be best obtained by consulting 'The Oxford Guide.'

We occasionally stepped into the Schools where the Great Examination for Degrees was going on. I was desirous of seeing the mode of conducting these Examinations but as I take no pleasure in seeing young men tortured I was not anxious to stay long there.

We also spent a short time in the Room where the Vice-chancellor &c.,&c., were conferring Degrees. This seems to consist of mere Forms of Ceremonies and apparently to a Stranger of the most ridiculous kind. Here, Mr Gilbert, one of the Fellows and formerly Joseph's Tutor, invited me to dine with him the following day but I declined, as I intended to leave Oxford at two o'Clock on that day. Being pretty well tired we sat down to Dinner at Joseph's Lodgings at five o'Clock as I preferred spending this short time I should stay in Oxford with him alone, I could not permit him to have anyone to Dinner or to spend the Evening with us.

22nd May

This Forenoon we spent visiting those places we had omitted the preceding day. At noon we went into Confectioner's shop for a Lunch. While we stayed the Gown's men came in, in rapid succession some asking for Soup, some for Sweet-meats, Tarts, Jellies, Ice creams, as their respective Tastes and inclinations prompted. I concluded, from what I saw, this was an excellent place for stuffing the Stomach and for emptying the Pocket.

At two o'Clock the London Coach came in for Birmingham. There was no inside place vacant. Just as I was about to get upon the Coach which was very much crowded, an elderly Gentleman in the inside invited me in saying his son was desirous of going a Stage or two on the outside & I was welcome to his place that while. Though the Afternoon was stormy the young man continued outside for more than half way and when he came to resume his Seat another inside Passenger was at the end of his Journey and no one taking his place I remained inside all the way to Birmingham. We arrived at Birmingham about half past ten o'Clock and though it was so late the Market seemed to be at the height. the Butchers' Stalls and all the other Stalls and Standings were fully lighted and the Market place crowded with people. This was a novel appearance to me and having ordered Supper I took a walk while it was preparing. The number of the people in the Market place & streets adjoining was immense but I thought I had never seen such a poor miserable dirty looking set of people, especially the women, collected together in all my life. While at Supper I sent a porter to secure me a place to Manchester which set out at 7 o'Clock in the Morning. This being secured I went to Bed and leaving Birmingham next morning I arrived at Manchester about seven o'Clock in the Evening. I was set down at the Star Inn, Deansgate and while I took Tea I ordered a Chaise to be got ready which brought me home just as my Family was gone to bed.

Here, I found all well and thus I ended a long journey in which I met many Pleasures, Enjoyments & Gratifications without any untoward Accident, Impediment, Disappointment or Delay.

Expences of a Journey to London

1819

May 11th	£	s	d
Supper at Woosley Bridge	4.	0.	12
Breakfast at Dunchurch		2.	0
Dinner at Dunstable		3.	2
Coachmen fm Manchest. to London		5.	6
Guard who came all the way		4.	0
19th			
Repaid Mr Ravald Coach Fare to London	2.	2.	0
Coach hire		2.	6
Expenses at sundry times & places, exclusive of the Bill at the Coffee House		10.	3
Bill at the Grecian Coffee House	6.	15.	0
Coach fare to Oxford	1.	5.	0
20			
Refreshment at Henley		1.	6
Coachman to Oxford		2.	0
Guard to do.		2.	0
22			
Bill at Oxford		18.	0
Refreshment at Stratford		1.	6
Coachman & Guard to Birmingham		4.	6
Expences at Birmingham		6.	6

Coach Fare to Birmingh.	15. 0
23	
Fare to Manchester	1. 15. 0
Breakfast at Wolverhampton & Waiter	2. 3
Dinner at Talk o'th Hill	4. 3
Coachman & Guard to Manchester	4. 6
Tea at Manchester	2. 0
Chaise home	18. 0
Turnpikes & Postboy	4. 6
Total	£17 .15. 0

July lst At the annual Meeting of the Commissioners I gave in the following Bill instead of that on the other side [above] that it might correspond with the Bills of Col R. Fletcher & Major Watkins.

1819	£	s	d
May 12th			
Journey to London	3.	10.	0
Expences 14 days	22.	1.	0
25th			
Journey down	4.	10.	0
Paid Mr M only for 2 Plans	4.	14.	6
	£34.	15.	6

Notes

1 Malcolm Thamis, *The Luddites* (Library of Textile History, 1970).
2 The Grecian is first mentioned in 1709 and initially attracted such men of learning as Sir Isaac Newton and Dr Halley. By 1803 the coffee house claimed a clientele of 'gentlemen of law'. It closed in 1843.
3 The play, *Clandestine Marriage, A Roland for an Oliver*, was performed at the Theatre Royal, Covent Garden.
4 A curricle was a two-wheeled open carriage drawn by two horses, side by side.
5 Hodgkinson's criticisms are directed at Mozart's *Marriage of Figaro*, which was staged at the King's Theatre, the Haymarket, together with a short two-act ballet. The first performance of the *Marriage of Figaro* in England was at the Haymarket in 1812.

6   There were four items on at the Drury Lane that night: *Life of a Day*, or *Fun at Hampton Court*; Mr Incledon 'positively for this night only at the particular desire of several old friends and admirers of this favourite vocalist, will sing (in character) the celebrated song from the *Musical Farce of The Quaker*, called "While the Lands of the Village"'; *High Notions*, or *a trip to Exmouth*, and *Honest Thieves*.

8

The Affair of Astley Chapel & the Descent into Madness of the Revd Joseph Hodgkinson

Until well into late middle age, Richard Hodgkinson's affairs had flourished and progressed with little hindrance. From his modest beginnings as a schoolteacher he had become a wealthy and influential man. As land agent to the Atherton and Bewsey Estates he drew a salary of £200 per annum, collected rents from his own property in Atherton, Leigh and Westhoughton, and rented the estate's largest farm at Platt Fold for £150 a year. He was an Overseer of the Poor, a Turnpike Trust Commissioner and a pillar of the Established Church. In the absence of his master, Lord Lilford, he presided at the court leet and rent days and was the virtual lord of the manor of the Atherton estate, a position of great power and patronage.

In an age when childhood ailments, such as measles, whooping cough and diphtheria, could swiftly strike and kill, his family had been blessed with exceptional health. His daughters had married men of substance: his elder daughter Mary wed a prosperous farmer and his youngest daughter Jane married into the wealthy Guest family of Leigh. Hodgkinson's elder son David, following in his father's footsteps as a farmer and agent to another local landowner, was a prominent if not universally popular man in the community. All apparently stood fair for the fortunes of the Hodgkinson family.

If in the early months of 1822 Richard Hodgkinson had reflected on the bountiful rewards of his life, he would have been well contented with the progress of Joseph, his younger and favourite son. Joseph had led a sheltered life and had been encouraged to tread the path to Holy Orders denied to his father. A pupil at Manchester Grammar School between 1811 and 1814, Joseph proceeded to Brazenose College, Oxford, on an Exhibition. In 1816 he graduated with a second class honours degree in Literae Humaniores, Greek and Roman history, literature and philosophy, but an exhibition from the Hulme Trust[1] worth a handsome £135 a year kept him in Oxford studying for his Master of Arts until 1819. Richard Hodgkinson spent much time trying to secure a good curacy for Joseph [see the Blundell papers], but following his ordination in 1819 Joseph was invited – without his father's help – to take up a curacy at St Peter's, 'the most genteel church in Manchester' where the vicar, the Revd Jeremiah Smith, left the living in Joseph's novice hands for long spells. Smith was also the headmaster of Manchester Grammar School where Joseph returned to teach junior classes.

After Joseph had spent two years ministering in Manchester, Richard Hodgkinson achieved a major ambition in 1821 when Joseph was inducted Vicar of Leigh, giving the Hodgkinsons a large degree of control of matters spiritual and temporal in the large parish.

This triumph was followed in the spring and summer of 1822 by disaster and Richard Hodgkinson's well-laid plans and ambitions for Joseph lay in ruins. The father had helped to push his ill-equipped son beyond endurance and into deepening madness. Within months Joseph's mental health had been damaged beyond cure, and Richard's own life, together with that of his wife, had been blighted to the end of their days. The cause of this devastating reversal of fortune was the Affair of Astley Chapel, a battle of wills between a vicar and his parishioners, in which the military was called out to intimidate villagers and in which Richard Hodgkinson, according to one vituperative pamphleteer, played a Machiavellian role.

The affair began at the end of the second decade of the nineteenth century. An ageing and sick vicar of Leigh who owed certain favours to Richard Hodgkinson, and an even more aged curate of Astley Chapel, had made church affairs the gossip and speculation of Leigh parish. The vicar, the Revd Daniel Birkett, had owed obligations, possibly financial,[2] to Richard Hodgkinson for some years. As early as 1814, Birkett had complained that the expense of educating his two sons had exceeded his income. Birkett's sons, Tom and Will, were acquaintances of the Hodgkinson children, and when both entered the church they were given curacies by their father.

In July 1819, Hodgkinson, writing to his friend the Revd James Blundell, said that Birkett, 'whose obligations to me you know', had now also offered Joseph a title. Hodgkinson feared the Bishop would turn down Joseph because Birkett had made his own sons curates, but thought he could surmount this difficulty, should it arise, 'by a personal acquaintance which I have with Mr Slade, the vicar of Bolton, who is son in Law to the Bishop and the Examining Chaplain of the Ordination'.

In the event, all went well for Joseph and his nomination was accepted. 'By doing this for me in the handsome manner he has done, Mr Birkett has cancelled many obligations which he owed to my father', wrote Joseph to Blundell in September 1819. By now, Birkett was a sick man and when he died Joseph Hodgkinson was, in October 1821, presented vicar of Leigh by his father's employer, Lord Lilford.

Joseph had been popular and respected for his hard work at St Peter's Church, where he had been a particular favourite with women in the congregation and had plunged with great vigour into his dual roles as a pastor and schoolteacher. The young priest had become acquainted with William Simmons, senior surgeon at the Manchester Infirmary, and had written a well-constructed appeal for funds in the preface to the Infirmary's Annual Report of 1819, the troubled year of Peterloo, when the Infirmary was faced with an increasing number of patients and a diminishing amount of subscriptions. Joseph also fell in love with Simmons' daughter, Elizabeth, who was usually known as Bessy. On 4 June 1822, Joseph and Elizabeth were married in Manchester and began their brief married life in the newly furnished vicarage at Leigh. Their happiness was to last only one night.

Amid all the rejoicing surrounding Hodgkinson's marriage and newly acquired eminence, a volcano of discontent was about to erupt in the chapelry of Astley, a few miles to the east of the Mother Church, and engulf the entire Hodgkinson family. For fifty-three years since 1768, the incumbent at Astley had been the Revd Robert Barker. For some time before his death in March 1822, there had been speculation and strong feelings among his village flock, most of whom claimed an ancient right to elect his successor. Joseph Hodgkinson, the new and untested vicar of Leigh, thought otherwise and, most likely urged on by his father, planned to install the Revd Tom Birkett, son of the late Vicar of Leigh. Was it now time for Joseph to return a family favour to a long-standing friend and give him the living worth a generous £150 a year?

So traumatic did Richard Hodgkinson find the succeeding events at Astley that he could hardly bear to mention them, even to his friends, in later years. The affair, and the violence it engendered, was widely reported in the newspapers, and an anonymous pamphleteer, with a vicious dislike of the Hodgkinson family, published two accounts of the events which led to a riotous confrontation in the church yard.

The first anonymous pamphlet, signed 'A Householder' and widely distributed in Astley, claimed the parishioners had the right to elect their own curate under the will of Adam Mort, who on 19 May 1630 left to two certain trustees two farms in Tyldesley, and directed that the rents and profits were to be used to maintain a preaching minister at Astley Chapel. Adam directed his son Thomas to be responsible for appointing the preaching ministers during his own lifetime and then 'set down some plan or course to be observed in the nomination and appointment of the Preaching Minister; which plan or course, Adam Mort ordered to be for ever observed'. Thomas Mort failed to make this provision but, said the pamphlet, since 1716 four curates had been elected by the villagers. At each election the current vicar of Leigh had been present to give advice but not to appoint.

In stirring tones the pamphlet urged:

Men of Astley! The benevolent Adam Mort built and endowed a Chapel and a School for your good. He gave them to you by his last Will and Testament; and in that Will he ordered you to appoint the Curates & Schoolmasters. Will you pay no regard to his orders. Will you give up your own Rights, the Rights of Your Children, and the rights of your Children's Children? Rights that have been handed down to you from Generations immemorial, and which ought to go unimpaired to your remote posterity?

In a second savage pamphlet, 'A Householder' recorded the events following Barker's death and made vicious personal attacks on Richard Hodgkinson and his son David, dismissing Joseph as a weak-willed man manipulated by his father. This diatribe of destructive prose, with more than a suggestion of personal jealousy and revenge, also describes Joseph's meeting with the Committee of Astley men on the morning after his marriage and how he was berated by his wife of one day for not standing up to his parishioners. The pamphlet read:

To the Householders or Heads of Families in Astley

I congratulate you on the spirit and determination you have shown in the present contest about the right of appointing your Minister:

they are worthy of you. We have signally punished our enemies –
we have made their bed a bed of thorns – and driven sleep from their
pillows. We have foiled the artifices and deep-laid schemes of an old
man long acquainted with the management of mankind, and skilful
in bending them to his purposes. The honour of being the first to
stop his ambitious career, has been reserved for us. His ruling passion
is his pride, and the advancement of himself and his family; and he
wished to extend his patronage or his son's (for it is all the same) by
appointing a Curate of his own to be Minister of Astley. He is Agent
to a nobleman of large property, and by means of his two boys he is
(and will be so long as they all live) both the Agent to Mr Froggart,3
and the real virtual Vicar of the Parish; for he who thinks the youths
have anything to do with either of the situations but just perform the
outward duties, is very much deceived: they are only the Punches of
the puppet-show, to do as the wires are pulled by the Chief
Performer behind the curtain.

He has thus, from mending pens and setting copies, in short from
being the usher at a village school, got to such power as very few
men in private life have reached. In addition to all these, he wanted
to have been a Justice; and his obedient servile subjects at the Bent,4
who sit uncovered and silent in his presence, thought the best way to
flatter him would be to press him to be one. He would then have
been, if he is not now, the most powerful man in the Parish. But the
nobleman just mentioned, did not approve of grinding Stewards into
Justices, and so it was dropped.

Proud, and puffed up with his own self importance as he is, this
was a great check to him; and our spirited resistance has been another and more severe one. These are the only instances in which his
silent calculating schemes have not answered. We had luckily a
strong hold of him. He is afraid of his purse, and an expensive law-
suit; – his avarice has for once been a check to his ambition. The
horror of losing any part of his riches is without bounds, and has driven him into a conduct at once hesitating and censurable. He has
done us all the injury he could by appointing Mr Birkett in preference to the man of our choice; and his conduct has since been such
to Mr Birkett, that instead of being grateful for the appointment, Mr
Birkett must, if he feels like a man, heartily hate him as long as he
lives.

Act on the plain broad lines of honour and truth, and you have
nothing to fear; but if you get into the mazes of dissimulation, you

are sure to be lost. His pride, his fawning to those above him, and his lofty but occasional condescension to those below him, is pretty generally known; and the consequence is, as it always ought to be to those who mind nothing, care for nothing, and aim at nothing throughout their whole life, but their own interest.

I must not, however, in giving you the real character of him who is the main spring of all our troubles, nor even of the Son, who begins his Vicarship by an act of tyranny to his next-door neighbour respecting a paltry clothes-hedge, forget to give you an account of events of which any of you may be ignorant, and which is the main object of my Letter.

In November last, Mr Joseph Hodgkinson was appointed Vicar. The very first week after he was appointed, he sent his Brother to inform the Inhabitants of Astley, that as Vicar for the time he had the right of nominating the Curate of Astley Chapel; and that as the Curacy would soon be vacant, he would look out a proper person to give it to.

This communication was not approved by the Inhabitants; and their dislike to it was not lessened by the haughty and peremptory terms in which it was delivered. In the double capacity of Mr Froggart's Agent and his Brother's Messenger, he told them in very high language what he and his Brother would do — He do!! the empty headed boaster! — it was a dwarf threatening Sampson.

The Vicar seeing that he could not intimidate us, in the course of the following week sent another message to inform the Inhabitants, that if a Deputation of the principal Householders would wait upon his Father, he would in an amicable manner point out to them the plan intended to be pursued, and would give them his opinion upon the subject.

This was an insidious design to get to know what proofs we had to establish our claim. We knew who we were dealing with, and replied that we wanted no one's opinion as to the course we ought to pursue, and that we would neither be bullied or wheedled out of our rights. This answer was quite proper. The first was plainly an attempt to bully us through Mr Froggart's influence, and the second was an attempt of the enemy to spy into our quarters under the mask of friendship. At the same time it was intimated to the Vicar it would be highly indelicate to talk of appointing a Curate during the life of the venerable incumbent.

Mr Barker died in March.

A Committee being formed of our principal Householders, notice was given in the newspapers that the householders would, on the 25th April, proceed to elect a Curate. On the 22nd the Vicar sent his Brother requesting them to meet him at a public house on the 25th.

The Committee met the Vicar on that day, and he spoke as follows: 'Gentlemen, the business we are met upon is one of infinite importance; it is important to the cause of religion in general, to you in particular – you are part of my flock – it is important to everyone, and it concerns every one that is interested in it; it is important to me because I wish you to have a Minister capable of assisting me in the important task of watching over you. And if I should be guilty of the impropriety of allowing you to appoint, it would be highly improper. I am the Vicar, and you are my Parishioners. You must be aware of the high responsibility I hold over you; and as Astley Chapel is in my parish, it is under my church. I therefore have the right of appointing the Curate of Astley Chapel. I am aware that the Inhabitants of Astley have sometimes appointed, and on that account I wish to do everything in my power to give satisfaction to the Inhabitants.

Mr JOHN FARNWORTH, one of the Committee, replied: 'Sir, the business we are upon is certainly important. The Committee inform you, Sir, through me, that they have the right of appointing, and that they will appoint. Bent Chapel[5] is in your Parish, as you term it; Is it therefore under your Church? Have you the right of appointing the Curate of Bent Chapel?'

The VICAR – 'That Chapel was founded under peculiar circumstances: it is in my Parish, but not under my church. I have not the right of appointing.'

Mr FARNWORTH – 'Then Chapels are not always under the Mother Church and you have no more right to appoint to Astley Chapel than you have to Bent Chapel, Sir. Read that will, Sir.' (Here Mr Farnworth threw down a copy of Adam Mort's Will).

The VICAR – 'I have read it, Sir, and I think it an innocuous document. I wish to render every accommodation to the Inhabitants of Astley, particularly because the proceedings of the Committee have been open and candid.'

Mr FARNWORTH – 'Sir, if the Committee behaved with openness, be yourself open. Tell us, at once, what you mean to do.'

The VICAR – 'I will appoint the Rev. Thomas Birkett the Curate of Astley Chapel'. (Here there was a long pause).

Mr FARNWORTH – 'Then, Sir, we will not have him; and whilst you have been telling us you would render every accommodation to the Inhabitants, and do everything in your power to given them satisfaction, you have been deceiving us with plausible speeches; perhaps you have been sent here to pry into the temper and disposition of the Astley people? Go, tell your Father that we are not to be duped.'

On the 29th April Mr (Thomas) Bowman was elected by a majority of the Householders: two neighbouring clergymen[6] attended at the election. There are 305 voters: of these two did not vote. 287 voted for Mr Bowman and 16 for Mr Birkett. Everything was conducted with propriety and decorum, and every one hoped that so large a majority would insure peace and harmony to Astley.

As soon as the election was over, the two Clergymen accompanied by a Deputation of Astley Gentlemen, waited upon the Vicar. One of the Clergymen (Rev Mr Burton) addressed his as follows: 'Rev. Sir, I am desired by the Inhabitants of Astley to inform you that they have elected the Rev Mr Bowman to be their Curate. The Inhabitants wishing to remove all cause of uneasiness in this populous Parish, have resolved since you are Vicar of Astley Chapel, to submit the man of their choice to your approval. They make this concession to prevent discord and quarrels, not doubting that you will readily concur with them and second their views. I recur to the unanimous declaration of the inhabitants. Will you set your wishes against the united wishes of 287 heads of families? Your refusal to accede to the proposal now made will be destructive to the peace of the congregation, and injurious to the interests of religion. It will bring the character of the clergy into disrepute and fill the meeting-houses of the Dissenters. If you are a sincere Minister of the Church of England, you will on this occasion give up any inordinate views of patronage, and sacrifice the petty ambition of having a living in your gift, to the interest of that church which you have sworn to forward and uphold. 287 respectable Inhabitants have signed their names to a solemn Declaration that they will never enter the doors of Astley Chapel if Adam Mort's will is set aside. Will you, Sir, after having sworn to uphold the Interests of the Church, knowingly drive these 287 heads of families into the chapels of the Dissenters? You are a young man, and have probably many years to live; beware that your actions this day do not embitter the remainder of your life.'

The Vicar told the Clergymen and the Deputation he would give them an answer in two hours: in the mean time he flew to the Old

Counsellor for his advice. In the end he was ordered to go to Astley and tell the people that his determination was. You all know the event; the poor boy fainted.

The cruelty of the Father, in sending this inexperienced youth to encounter buffetings and contradictions which he was sure to meet with, and so little accustomed to, has been generally blamed, not only by us in Astley, but by grave and sensible men in the adjoining townships, quite uninterested in our dispute.

That the fainting scene was an artifice to make us pity him and induce us to comply with his views, I will not take upon myself to say; for I cannot think the young man has so much artifice and cunning about him.

The sequel to the fainting scene was a letter, of which the Brother was the bearer to Mr Birkett, in the middle of the night, telling him the Vicar was dangerously ill; and Mr Birkett must either give up the promise, or the Vicar would die. They did not shew much judgment in the choice of their messenger. It is well for us that he babbles and blusters in ale-houses, prosing over his glass and letting out the secrets of his party in the way he does. It has been of much use to us. September, 1820, taught us how to estimate this gentleman. Overseers of the Highway were chosen at Bent in the morning and at Astley in the afternoon. At the Bent[7] he argued that the highway leys ought to be applied to make good the bye roads, and through his influence it was ordered that the Lodge lane should be paved out of the highway leys. At Astley, in the afternoon of the same day, he argued that the highway leys ought not to be applied to make good the bye roads, and through his influence it was ordered that the road at the lower end of Astley Green should not be paved out of the highway leys. When the Old Counsellor goes, this man of consistency will find his proper level.

Mr Birkett was called upon from his bed in the night and was much agitated. He was told that a friend who had served him, lay at the point of death and that it was in his power to save him. Attacked at a time when he had just got up, and with scarcely time to recollect himself, it is wonderful he did not fall into the trap. He happened however to have the presence of mind to escape it.

The messenger lost his labour, like the calf that ran three miles and a half to suck a bull, and the next day the Vicar was out visiting, apparently as well as ever he was in his life. The messenger about a week afterwards, coolly laughed at the matter as a good joke. What think you of this? Is it knavery? Is it folly? Is it both? Though hostile to Mr Birkett, I feel for him when his friends and patrons can use their own appointed person so treacherously. It is better to have such men for open enemies, than as treacherous friends.

On the 5th June the Committee waited upon the Vicar by appointment. Mr John Lingard, one of the Committee, read the following extract from the Will of Adam Mort: 'And that to "person or persons", for his own or their own gain, profit, or the accomplishing of his own private ends, would seek to cross or hinder my good meaning, but every one which shall have to do herein, would chiefly have regard to the glory of God and the common good, as they will answer at the great day of judgment.' Mr Lingard then addressed the Vicar as follows: 'When you oppose the wishes of United Astley, do you think you have any regard to the common good? For this you must answer at the great day.'

The VICAR replied: 'I wish we could accommodate this matter. Let me appoint this once and I will never do so again.'

Mr LINGARD: – 'No, Sir, if we let you appoint this once you will obtain a right to appoint hereafter. If we once put on your fetters, we cannot afterwards throw them off. If we let you appoint, we shall act as Guardians of the rights which our townsmen have committed to our care? No, Sir, you shall not appoint: I have witnessed many shameful transactions; but never, from my youth up, did I ever see anything half so bad.'

Here the Vicar left the room crying; and after waiting some time, the Committee returned to Astley.

I cannot but feel some little pity that the young man's nuptial happiness should have been interrupted so soon after his marriage. Our Committee were too hasty in going the very day after the marriage. But it happened fortunately for him that his Fair Partner had the sense and courage to advise him to act like a man of spirit. When he retired whimpering into the yard, she went to him and said, 'Why don't you order them out of the house? Are you not master in your own house? You make yourself like dirt under their feet. Why don't you talk to them? You let them have all the talk to themselves. I'd have given it 'em. You are like the dog that can neither bark or wag his tail.'

Signed by A HOUSEHOLDER and the HEAD OF A FAMILY IN ASTLEY

Matters did not improve for Joseph Hodgkinson who found himself in the position of either having to make a humiliating retraction or of going ahead with his plans to install Tom Birkett as curate. The Astley villagers were equally adamant that they would not back down, and on Sunday 14 July 1822 a crowd of nearly one thousand people gathered outside Astley Chapel to oppose Birkett's induction. The events that followed were reported by newspapers throughout the country, most notably by the *Manchester Guardian*. On 20 July 1822 the newspaper recalled the circumstances of Adam Mort's Will and the rejection of the villagers' choice, and claimed that before the confrontation Joseph Hodgkinson had unsuccessfully attempted to persuade Tom Birkett to decline the nomination. In the meantime the villagers submitted the Revd Thomas Bowman's name to the diocese registrar at Chester as their choice, but the Bishop replied: 'Most gladly would I do anything in my power to restore peace and harmony between Astley and Leigh; but I can only advise and that I have already done to all parties concerned.' However the Bishop promised that if the villagers would send a proper nomination he would not licence Birkett until a court case on the rights of nomination had been heard.

The villagers were later astounded to find that their nomination had not reached the Bishop and had been left lying in an office at Chester. On 17 June 1822, an Astley gentleman was sent to London to plead with the Bishop who renewed his promise not to licence Birkett until the right of nomination was decided by a court of law. The Bishop also agreed to meet a deputation of villagers at Warrington on 2 July, when to their amazement, and notwithstanding his promises, he announced his intention to licence Birkett the same day. The Bishop later claimed that from the case submitted to him he was satisfied that the legal right of nomination was vested in the Vicar. The *Manchester Guardian* reported:

> The great body of the inhabitants of Astley were, however, unanimous in their determination not to receive Mr Birkett as their minister, and their disinclination to do so was, of course, increased by the manner in which he was thrust upon them.
>
>   Last Sunday was the day on which it was arranged for Mr Birkett to take possession of the Chapel, and he accordingly set out for that purpose about the hour of morning service, accompanied by some relatives and personal friends, by a constable named Turner from Warrington and a sheriff's officer of the name of Mather from this town. Some expectation had probably existed that opposition would be offered to his proceedings, for it is stated that the sheriff's officer had in his possession a writ de vi laica removenda. However, Mr

Birkett's intention being understood, a great body of the householders and heads of families of Astley, who constitute the congregation
and were hostile to his nomination by the Vicar, did, in fact assemble
outside the chapel yard. On the arrival of Mr Birkett and his party
near the gate, they demanded entrance, which being refused them by
the assembled multitude who were ranged around the outside, some
of them instantly exhibited pistols, and, presenting them to the breast
and ears of several of the respectable inhabitants threatened to shoot
them if any obstacle was opposed to their progress.

It is stated to us that some iron crows which had been disguised by
being covered with brown paper, were also produced and several of
the congregation violently assaulted with them. To what extent the
inhabitants might proceed in their opposition to Mr Birkett's
entrance into the chapel we do not feel able to assert. It is alleged on
one hand, and denied on the other, that they committed any actual
breach of the peace, though it is certain that in the scuffle the coat
skirts of the sheriff's officer were torn. They did however undoubtedly present such obstacles to Mr Birkett and his friends, that the latter for the time being desisted from attempting to obtain admission
into the chapel and retired from the place. But their departure was
not a termination of the contest; for two of the party straightway
proceeded to Manchester to obtain military assistance in order to
enable them to get possession of the chapel.

Meanwhile information of the proceedings at Astley was conveyed
to J.A. Borron Esq., a magistrate residing in the neighbourhood; but
some time before his arrival (indeed about three o'clock in the afternoon) a detachment of the 7th Dragoon Guards arrived from
Manchester. Under cover of their protection, Mr Birkett and his supporters again repaired to the chapel-yard; at this time a very considerable crowd was assembled, but they of course, offered no resistance to
the military. As, however, they shewed no disposition to leave the
scene of the action to the minister, the gates of the chapel yard were
forced and the people were speedily dispersed by the Dragoons. Two
persons are stated to us to have received sabre wounds, and several to
have been much hurt by being struck with crows. The doors of the
chapel were next forced open, and the minister and his associates
entered and took possession. The customary services and ceremonies
were then entered upon. During this performance, Mr Borron
arrived, but finding how things were did not remain long, contenting
himself with enjoining people to be peaceable.

The prescribed services were gone through, we understand, amid great tumult and confusion, and when they were finished Mr Birkett left the chapel under the protection of the soldiery.

A day or two afterwards, a very ill-judged handbill was issued by the minister's party, alleging the sheriff's officer to have been set upon and assaulted and robbed. In the publication of this handbill, the officer, we are informed, disavows all participation; and there does not appear to have been any pretence for charging any person with a felonious purpose towards him. On Wednesday warrants were delivered to Mr Lavender charging several individuals with riot and assault. Three persons, Joseph Rawson, James Thorpe and Joseph Beaumont, were, early on Thursday morning taken into custody and conveyed to Leigh for examination before Mr Borron.' The report concludes by noting that Beaumont was sent for trial accused of assault and Rawson and Thorpe were sent for trial accused of rioting and obstructing the sheriff's officer. Bail was offered and they were set at liberty until their trial.

At the end of the report the *Manchester Guardian* commented:

Such is the narrative which we have drawn up with considerable care, partly from authentic documents and partly from information derived from a variety of sources. On the legal question, with respect to the right of nomination we offer no opinion but we take the liberty of saying that the feeling and wishes of the inhabitants ought assuredly to have been consulted in the appointment of a minister and that amongst considerate or impartial men there can be only one opinion with respect to the propriety or the decency of a minister's forcing himself upon a congregation under the protection of naked sabres. There is surely not in the world one person disposed to contend, that regard for the spiritual welfare of the flock forms one amongst even the possible motives which could induce such conduct on the part of the pastor. The legality of calling in the aid of the military on such an occasion particularly without the sanction of a magistrate, is very questionable, and we hope the conduct of the officer in obeying the summons he received, will be strictly investigated.

Birkett, fearing the worst from the *Manchester Guardian*, requested a right of reply even before the report had been published. This was appended at the foot of the *Manchester Guardian* report of the riot and

Birkett's lawyers wrote their version of the encounter which indignantly claimed that Joseph Hodgkinson had even offered to solve the dilemma by nominating the man the villagers should vote for, namely Birkett. Birkett also claimed there had been threats to drag him through the brook and tear the gown from his back if he attempted to take up his post.

A week later another letter appeared in the *Manchester Guardian* under the *nom de plume* of Justus, championing Birkett's cause and challenging the newspaper's version of the events at Astley. The *Manchester Guardian* replied that notwithstanding the *nom de plume*, the letter had in fact been written by Birkett and reminded him of Christ's words: 'Whosoever will not receive you, when ye go out of that city, shake off the very dust from your feet as a testimony against them.' The newspaper tartly added, 'The Astley people, we have reason to believe, have no objection to Mr Birkett's literally fulfilling this Scriptural injunction.'

So ended the major confrontation between priest and parishioners. The villagers, though bloodied and bowed, were not yet beaten and on one day of worship, which became known as Frying Pan Sunday, they beat their pots and pans to annoy Birkett as he walked to church. As well as preparing a case to put to the High Court in defence of their rights, the men of Astley who had led the fight against Hodgkinson also published a long open letter to him in October 1822, claiming to have been much misrepresented, but pointedly heading their letter with three Biblical quotations, including one from Genesis, ch. 43, v. 30: 'And Joseph made haste, and he sought where to weep, and he entered into his Chamber, and wept there.' The villagers' committee wrote in firm but restrained terms, destroying many of the arguments of the establishment. The committee also revealed that, as a consequence of all the troubles, the chapel at Astley had been almost totally boycotted by the villagers, with not more than ten out of a population of 1,800 making up the congregation.

In another unpleasant incident in the village Joseph Hodgkinson had been made the subject of ridicule, but the committee put the blame for this on his brother, David. 'On the afternoon of Friday the 23rd of August, you [Joseph] came to Astley to inter a corpse, your brother David was in Astley that afternoon, taking his glass at Dunster's Public House, the sign of the Bull, when he heard of your arrival he left Dunster's. On his way from thence to the Chapel he met a drunken man and called out to him "Art thou a Bowmanite or a Birkettite?" or made use of other party words, which caused the man to swear at him. Whilst David was waiting for you, the man collected some of his neighbours, and when you came out of the Chapel Yard, after having interred the corpse, they began to hoot and shout at you, your brother more than once turned to the shouters, and dared them to follow you farther, and when he got to the boundary of the township of Astley, he challenged any of them to come across it. Now if any person connected with you chooses to come into Astley, and use irritating language, to people with minds agitated as those of the people of Astley are by the present disputes, we cannot see how it is for him or you, or any one else, to accuse the inhabitants of being riotous.'

The committee also invoked the name of Lord Lilford, saying, 'your patron and benefactor, he, from whom you derive all power of interfering in this matter, has disapproved of your conduct.' But in a letter to the *British Volunteer* on 7 December 1822, Lilford said there was not one syllable of truth in that claim.

The committee of eleven men ended their ten page letter by asserting the clamour raised against them was groundless and that they were the injured persons. They had tried to suppress the vicious address by A Householder and '. . . we trust that you will consider our discountenancing an over zealous partizan, and endeavouring to prevent his statement from being injurious to yourself and your family, proofs of our having acted towards you in the spirit of Christian Charity.'

When the villagers' claim on their rights of nomination went to the Lancaster Assizes in August 1823, great weight was attached to past precedent and there was jubilation when the jury decided in their favour. This turned to dismay when, in July 1824, judges of the King's Bench perversely reversed the jury's verdict and found in favour of the Bishop of Chester and the vicar of Leigh. Historian John Lunn, himself a native of Astley, wrote in his book, *The History of Astley*, 'It does not fall within the province of this limited work to question the wisdom of that strange decision.' By the time the final words had been spoken in court, the life of Joseph Hodgkinson was moving towards its tragic end; he lay incarcerated in a mad-house, periodically raging through the night and tearing at his clothes, until his death at the age of thirty.

As for the main characters on that particular stage, no one gained much credit or comfort. Joseph, lacking the experience to handle the devious manoeuverings that led to such an outburst of passion, died in July 1826. Little is known of his wife, Bessy, except that in 1829 she married a Manchester clergyman, the Revd Nicholas William Gibson, who later became a canon of the cathedral. She died in 1861 at the age of sixty-two. A window in the cathedral dedicated to her memory was destroyed in the Second World War.

Richard Hodgkinson's distress at his son's downfall was so great that there is only a single record of him ever visiting his stricken son. For a considerable time Richard's immaculate handwriting deteriorated severely, showing signs of stress and agitation, and in 1823 he wrote to his friend, James Blundell, keening his misery at the 'complete failure of everything I have done and accomplished for my poor son'. Hodgkinson's wife went into a decline and, until her death ten years later, Richard only wrote gloomily of her condition.

As for Birkett his ministry was an abject failure, and during his incumbency religion in Astley sank to its lowest depths, said Lunn. 'At first the curate was annoyed and obstructed; then he was ostracised and left to preach in an empty church.' Even though parishioners deserted the Established Church and flocked to the dissenting chapels, Birkett stubbornly refused to give up the living until 1838, but for the last years he moved from the neighbourhood and left a locum in his place.

David Hodgkinson shouldered most of the burden of Joseph's illness and corresponded in fond terms whenever it was felt Joseph was well enough to receive letters. He also looked after Joseph's affairs and received regular reports from Dr John Hill of the Leicester Asylum in which Joseph passed his last days. When Joseph died, David was by his side, and he escorted the corpse back to Leigh for burial. A month before, David was presented with a gold-lined snuff box made from an old mulberry tree at Atherton Hall as a token of esteem 'by a number of his Friends in the Parish of Leigh who know and appreciate the Worth of his Family and himself'. Three of the thirty-nine subscribers were from Astley.

The Letters and Accounts of Joseph's Incarceration in Dr Hill's Asylum in Leicester

In January, 1823, Joseph Hodgkinson was admitted to the Manchester Asylum, next to the Manchester Infirmary where his father-in-law, Mr Simmons, was senior surgeon. After three weeks he was transferred to the private asylum of Dr John Hill in Belle Grove, Leicester. John Hill was an urbane and hospitable man, who held very successful musical parties, but when he took over the asylum from the late Doctor Thomas Arnold in 1816 he had only recently qualified and was not a well-known psychiatrist. Under his supervision the asylum ran down and closed in 1840.

The Belle Grove asylum offered several grades of accommodation and for five guineas a week a patient had a large apartment, a servant and 'every proper and reasonable indulgence suitable to the disorder.' For one guinea a week the accommodation was in wards with patients 'not allowed tea, and their diet . . . more restricted than those of the superior Classes.' Joseph was admitted into the third class at three and a half guineas a week where the apartments 'are not quite so elegant; but each has a separate Room and Servant, and is treated in other respects nearly in the same manner as those who pay four Guineas per Week.

The first of the following letters is written by Richard Hodgkinson to Mr Simmons, advising on Joseph's transfer from Manchester Asylum to Leicester. Under a recent Act of Parliament no private patient could be admitted into an asylum without having an order in writing from a physician, surgeon or apothecary. It is likely that Simmons, Joseph's father in law, signed his committal.

Later letters trace the inevitable deterioration of Joseph's health; despondency being relieved by short-lived hopes for a return to well-being. Initially Joseph did not seek contact with his family and a touching letter from his father to Dr Hill was quickly followed by a tender and encouraging letter from Richard to his son. Some 18 months after his incarceration Joseph wrote a long and affectionate letter to his brother David, but within three months Dr Hill was reporting that his patient was 'in a violent state, very high and vociferous,' a condition which occurred until Joseph's death. Joseph's isolation in the asylum was relieved by occasional but welcome visits from the Revd James Blundell, his father's friend. (See the Blundell Letters, Chapters 12 & 13.)

The Letters

Richard Hodgkinson to Mr Simmons.   January 7th, 1823
After considering the Conversation which passed at Manchester yesterday, and examining the Terms sent by Dr Arnold, we think of poor Joseph being sent to him for the following reasons:
1st: Because the Journey is so much shorter, of course not likely to distress him so much.
2nd: Occasional Visits might be paid him if necessary with less inconvenience & loss of time.
3rd: Because he may have a separate Servant as well as Apartment.
And lastly because the Terms and Accommodations are so distinctly stated. We think of his being entered in the 3rd Class of 'Separate Apartments', viz: at 32 Guineas per week.

This determination of ours is intended to be subservient to any the Ladies may adopt, and if they have the least preference for Bristol it will be quite agreeable to us.

I shall give directions to the Coachman to call upon you at 4 o'Clock in the Afternoon for such Letter as you may have to send informing David whether you would wish him to come early on Friday Morning so as to begin the Journey on that day or whether he might come to Manchester at 3 o'clock in the Afternoon, in the Preston Coach to be ready for Saturday Morning.

My Spirits will not permit me to say more, only to add my Blessing upon Joseph, and Bessy, & my most earnest Prayers to the Almighty, that he will, of his kind Providence remove this heavy Calamity from us. Rd Hodgkinson

The Revd Joseph Hodgkinson's Account
with the Lunatic Asylum, Manchester

1823		£	s	d
January 17 to February 7				
To 3 Weeks Board at 2. 2. 0		6.	6.	0
To Medicines supplied by the Infirmary		1.	7.	10
To Cash Returned		13.	6.	2
	Total	21.	0	0
1823				
January 17				
By Deposit		21.	0	0

N.B. Out of the 6.6.0. charged for board, 2.4.0. was expended in wine and an extra Servant.

Expences in a Journey to Leicester with Joseph

1823			
Feby.	£	s	d
Chaise to Bullock Smithy 10 miles		12.	6
7th			
Postboys & Turnpikes		5.	0

Chaise to Macclesfield 10 Miles	12. 6
Postboys, Turnpikes & Refreshment	4. 6
Bill at Macclesfield including Chaise & four Horses	
to Leek 13 miles, Refreshment	2. 4. 0
Postboys & Turnpikes, Chaise & 4 Horses to	
Ashbourne, 15 miles, turnpikes	2. 6. 6
Chaise & 4 Horses to Derby 13 Miles, Turnpikes	2. 2. 0
Bills at Derby all night including chaise to	
Loughboro, waiters, postboys &c.	2. 17. 6
Expenses at Loughboro' & chaise to Leicester	
11 Miles, Postboys &c.	1. 2. 9
Bill at Leicester, 2 nights	1. 15. 8
Coachfare from Leicester to Mancr for Mr Boutflower	
& self	2. 6. 0
Coachmen & Guard	1. 0. 6
Expences of Dinner at Leek	8. 6

Total   17. 7. 11

From Joseph's friend, Thomas Johnson, of Prestwich to David Hodgkinson.

February, 22nd, 1823

You will not be surprised at receiving a letter from me when you know my warm attachment to your unfortunate Brother. I cannot think of him without tears, my heart bleeds whenever I recall him to my memory. I have adopted this exposition as the most delicate and at the same time the most satisfactory to my own feelings to make a few inquiries respecting my very dear Friend. I beg the favour of a letter from you and I sincerely hope that you will not object to particularise to me with his personal state of health, when it began to decline, whether he is convalescent and what is the opinion of his Medical attendants. I shall feel myself much indebted to you if you will satisfy me on these points. Pray tell me whether Mrs Hodgkinson is at Leigh and how she bears this awful visitation.

Thos. Johnson, Prestwich, near Manchester

David Hodgkinson to Dr Hill

1st July, 1823

Although your last report of my Brother was not quite so favourable, as the accounts we had previously received, still I entertain great hopes that time, aided with your skill in his distressing malady, will ere long restore him to his anxious friends. DH

Dr John Hill to David Hodgkinson

6th July, 1823

. . . my patient, Mr Hodgkinson, has been going on well since my last report. The apathy and inertness which has almost constantly marked his condition, seems of late to have given way more than at any former period, and though he is still very silent, he does occasionally speak a few words to me, and those to the purpose of reply to my observations. There is more exertion, more vivacity & consistency in all his actions, and though he is not free from delusions, they are easily overruled. His general health is good, his appetite and zest natural. He reads six hours or ten in the day, the bible, magazines, the Spectator &c., and seems to be amused. Under all these circumstances I am warranted in considering him to be steadily advancing towards recovery, to which I look forward with confidence. John Hills.

David Hodgkinson to Mr Simmons (Joseph's father-in-law)

October 8–13th, 1823

Herein I send you a copy of Dr. Hill's Letter received this morning. You will perceive that he has entered a good deal into particulars; that you may the better understand it I transcribe you a Letter which I wrote to him last week. In frequent conversations with Mr Blundell he seemed to insist that little was wanting to restore my Brother to convalescence but a direct communication & proper understanding with his friends. DH

Richard Hodgkinson to Dr Hill

1st December, 1823

Honoured Sir, I am the unfortunate Father of your unfortunate Patient the Rev Hodgkinson. I have some for time past meditated writing to you (but the last fortnight I have been prevented by the arrival of Lord Lilford who engages much of my time) but I never felt such difficulty as I do on this occasion. This may be owing partly to the distressing subject on which I am to write, partly to the great uncertainty that my writing may lead to any beneficial result, and partly to the conflicting Feelings that perpetually agitate my Mind and render me incapable of either Acting or Writing as I was wont to do.

In one last particular I am much relieved in making this my first address to you by knowing that my Friend, Mr. Blundell, has had repeated Interviews with you, in which I doubt not, he has acquainted you with my Situations, Prospects and Connections in Life, and also with the Particulars, how my poor afflicted Son was brought into his present calamitous Situation, which otherwise I would have thought it my Duty to do. As it is I will only detain you at present while I briefly state the purport of this which is to request you will have the goodness to give me a Letter stating whether it is your opinion that my Son would be able to bear without inconvenience the perusal of a Letter from his Brother from me or whether a personal interview with either of us would be too much for him yet.

Though I write this with the Fullness of a Parent's Heart I would on no consideration be premature in pressing one or the other. Probably an introduction or accidental meeting with some more indifferent a friend might in the first instance be more desirable.

I beg that your answer to this Letter may be addressed to me and that it may not prevent David receiving your usual Communication which he immediately inspects and sends to Mr Simmons.   Rd Hodgkinson

Richard Hodgkinson to his son Joseph

12th December, 1823

My Dear Joseph, It is with Feelings of a very pleasurable kind that I now take up my Pen to renew that intercourse between you and myself which has been so long interrupted by your Indisposition. And I am encouraged to this by the favourable Accounts I have for sometime received from Dr Hill on your regular and certain approach to Convalescence. All your Relations are even now anticipating the delight they shall experience on your Return among them and your other Friends are all ready to receive you with every mark of Kindness and Affection. I parted with Lord Lilford on the 6th inst at the Rectory at Warrington on his return into Northamptonshire. His enquiries after you are unremitted and of the most affectionate kind.

I can give you a good Account of all your Relations but at present will only send this short Letter which when you have answered, as I expect you will in a day or two, I will take an early opportunity of sending you a longer and more particular Letter.

Among the many Friends who will hail your Return among them with great pleasure, none will do it with more sincerity and kindness than your Loving and Affectionate Father,   Rd Hodgkinson

Dr Hill to David Hodgkinson

February 9th, 1824

Mr Hodgkinson has made more progress in his recovery during the last fortnight than in any preceding month during his residence in my house;

and on several occasions has appeared so perfectly rational & free from fancies of an erroneous kind that I have been able to keep a pleasant conversation with him for an hour or more at a time. In those conversations he has manifested such entire powers of recollection of reasoning on past, & on present circumstances, that it would be exercising an unnecessary degree of reason & caution, at long last to withhold from his family the certain conviction of my mind, that the evident convalescence which is now so considerable will proceed to his entire and perfect recovery. I say these remarks, as the honest impression of my mind with the view to relieve those natural feelings of anxiety which must pervade every branch of his family & connections.

Of late I have not importuned him to write, as it evidently oppressed him & rendered him thoughtful. I have furnished him with writing materials, & I consider it better to leave him to exercise his inclination than to urge him on the subject. He is proceeding so satisfactorily that I am desirous not to interfere with him in any way; the returning powers of his mind will naturally lead him to the exercise of his feelings & to begin a correspondence with his family, & to express a desire to see them. Whenever that is the case, I shall be most happy to convey to you either his letters or his sentiments. I have annexed my account for the year, and I beg to remain, dear sir, your faithful Servant, John Hill.

From David Hodgkinson to Dr Hill

19th February 1824

Your last report of your unfortunate Patient is very satisfactory & has been a source of comfort to all of us. We have derived equal satisfaction from a Letter my Father has received from Mr Blundell dated 14th inst. in which he says he has had an interview with my Brother; and enjoyed an agreeable chat with him of nearly two hours, during which conversation he evinced such powers of reasoning that we are led to hope for his restoration to us 'ere long. As the Ice has been broken by Mr B's introduction to him, is not the time approaching when he should come more directly into contact with his immediate friends, more particularly as he has been led into conversation about them. The method of bringing this about with the time, must of course as everything else has been since he was under your care, be left exclusively to you. D.H.

Joseph Hodgkinson to brother David at camp with the Militia. The 1824 letter is addressed to Gaskells Hotel, Blackpool near Preston, Lancashire

Leicester.   7th June, 1822 [*sic*]
My ever dearest Brother, I will write you a letter with the greatest pleasure in conformetry with your urgent request. You were very right in
saying that you knew I would do anything that would promote your
happiness. I would lay down my life for you, if it would do you any
good, but I know that you would not like that. I thank you with sincerity for your kind affectionate letter, it was a very well written one &
indeed the first scene of it quite overpowered me. I hope you will not
be fatigued with the exercise of your Yeomanry duties & I trust firmly
that you will distinguish yourself in the review on the Friday before Sir
John Byng. You will now be in the high glee of military exercise; enjoy
all your meals of which I have no doubt that you will partake most
heartily.

   Is not your birthday the 27th of June? My ever Dearest David, my
ever dearest brother come, come, come, the very earliest moment you
can to fetch me home for I am very well & in high spirits at the pleasing prospect of so soon getting home. I did yesterday administer to
myself the blessed Sacrament of the Lord's supper as I promised my
Mother. I am quite glad to have such an account of the flourishing state
of my dear Mother's poultry yard. And I am quite delighted that she so
stored my letter. It shall not [be] long before she receives another. It
will be Saturday night before which you cannot get home. You will
have warm work of it this hot weather, but this will have no effect on
your strong resolution. I suppose you are out 3 times every day. Good
drilling. There will be a good deal of drinking after it is all over. You
will be glad, I am sure, to get home again. And indeed your presence
will be absolutely required on Trinity Sunday in Leigh Church. There
can be no doing without you. You always take such strong interest in
it. I am quite delighted my dear Mother having such interest in the little work by Shenstones. She will equally rejoice to have & receive the
other letter which I shall very soon send her. She will have the same
feelings as before. You will have a great deal to do after being ten long
days from home away, and my poor Father will have a very busy time
of it whilst you are away. I often think of you & was determined in a
moment to take the first opportunity writing to you & therefore I
wrote it today that you may receive it on Wednesday morning. I shall
be exceedingly happy when I see you here, for I hope it will not be a
long time. I am assured that you will enjoy your excursions. I know it
is just the thing you like. You will tell my dear Mother all the circumstances of the time & give full account of every thing that occurred

during your absences. I am quite delighted with your last letter & hope it will not be the last.

This month promises that it will be very fine. There is not the least chance of having any rain for a long time. The crops of fruits here will be very abundant. There was never any thing seen as the display of the blooms. Every thing in these gardens flourishes with an exceeding degree. The asparagus about here abounds that I have some asparagus almost every day at dinner. I get on very well & have every day plenty of reading & of walking. Mr Slade, I think has been very judicious in choosing a wife, for the sake of his little daughter. He could not have done at all without her. But he must be in difficulties in expences of his family's arrangements since the value of the profits of the living is so small & trifling with an immense deal of labour. But he is a very laborious & active man. Poor Mr Robson, but I am very glad to hear, that he is going to visit his friends, he will (have) a very great pleasure in it from having been so long absent. He must have had a very laborious occupation for the last year and a half and that laborious occupation will commence again when he returns, for he is not, I think very strong. He will have warm work on Trinity Sunday but I hope he will get through it very well. You must give my best respects & warmest love to all of them. This is a most beautiful evening. My dearest Mother will be quite glad to have you back again. I should very much wish to see you on Friday in all your pomp & parade. And now accept the warmest love & fondest affection of your ever loving & affectionate brother,   Joseph Hodgkinson.

I hope that little Jane Jackson will be quite well when you get home.

Dr Hill to David Hodgkinson

October 9th, 1824

My poor patient has continued for the last fortnight in a violent state, very high and vociferous, but at times within the last six days, he has had intervals of greater calmness, than he had previously for near three weeks, experienced. His shouting & exertions have sometimes been so excessive as to cause great exhaustion, but luckily we have had no difficulty in giving him food to support his strength. We have some obstacles to contend with in the way of medicine. I hope & trust that the violence of his disorder is abating, his nights have been rather better lately, though he has almost come out Carter with watching; and I have difficulty in putting any other person to relieve Carter as Mr H is extremely irritable with others.   John Hill

Richard Hodgkinson to Dr Hill

12th January, 1825

Honoured Sir, With every feeling of respect for yourself and affection for my unfortunate Son I cannot but accuse myself, if not of neglect at least of procrastination in not writing to you before this time. But alas! You have (been) writing enough on this melancholy subject, and I have but little to say in any case where no effort of mine, either personal or pecuniary, can do anything more than has been done and is doing.

The afflicting Accounts which your Letters have now for a length of time given of my dear Son have abstracted materially from the little Comfort we had left, and to add to my Affliction, My Wife's Firmness & Resolution begin to give way and I tremble for the Consequences.

Our distress is not a little increased on our youngest Daughter's account, now 27 Years of Age, who has 4 small Children and her Husband in a declining state of Health. The Winter of 1822 he spent in Lisbon. His Wife accompanying him. Last Winter he went to Lisbon alone and for the last 2 Months he has been in London and we do not learn that he is reaping much benefit.

My own health continues very good which under divine Providence I attribute to that perpetual Round and Variety of Employments in which I am engaged and which call me much into the open Air. Were I to be wholly abstracted from Business I should be much more wretched than I am.

In the melancholy Case which has brought you and me acquainted I can unfortunately render no assistance. I can give no profitable advice. It is mine to submit to the wise though inscrutable disposition of Providence, praying that your best directed efforts may tend to restore Peace and Comfort to my poor distracted Son. 				Rd Hodgkinson.

Dr Hill to David Hodgkinson

February 12, 1825

I lament that the nature of my communications continue to convey to you and to your anxious family so little that is calculated materially to diminish your grief. My poor patient remains at times in a state of turbulence, though now he is calm and has been with very slight interruptions for eight or nine days. His irascibility is very much diminished and his nights are much more composed. The powers of his mind when calm are so much enfeebled that he cannot yet keep up a chain of association for many minutes, his ideas wandering from one subject to another, having no rational connection. It is comfortable to me however, to see him quiet, for the high paroxysms exhaust him, though his general health seems to have sustained so little injury the violence of his disorder, that it is rather a matter of surprise to me.

I received a box of linen for him from Mrs Hodgkinson a few days ago. I have not procured him any new apparel except a pair of Trousers, which he has not yet worn, as he had been at times inclined to tear his clothes, & those he has are sufficient till he improves, when I will procure what he requires.   John Hill.

Revd Joseph Hodgkinson's Acct with John Hill

To one year's board, lodging, washing, medical attendance & medicine and the use of a manservant, for one year ending Feby 8th, 1825.

£233 3s 0d

	£ s d		
Wine about two doz	6. 0. 0		
Paid			
Shoemaker	1. 14. 9		
Tailor	2. 2. 6		
Prayer Book	8. 6		
Alamnack	2. 6		
Reading from Library	8. 0		
Hairdresser	2. 0		6. 12. 4
Lavender	1. 6		245. 15. 4
Carriage of Boxes	3. 4		
For repairing hat	3. 0	Cash	100. 00. 0
6pr lambs wool hose	16. 6		———
3 pr drawers	9. 9		145. 15. 4
	———		
	6. 12. 4		

David Hodgkinson to Dr Hill

25th February, 1825

It has been a cause of great regret & anxiety to all his friends here, to find that your reports of late have been so unfavourable. We are all of us afraid though latterly they have been a little better that the affliction has continued so long, that there is but faint hope of his being restored to us.

Dr Hill to David Hodgkinson

February 27th, 1825

I had written to Mrs Hodgkinson yesterday (& my letter was in the Office before yours arrived) giving rather more favourable intelligence than for some time past, of my patient, which letter I dare say you will have received before this reaches you. I have at present nothing to add to that communication.   John Hill

David Hodgkinson to Dr Hill

19th August, 1825

It is with pain that I observe that the reports of your Patient continue so very unfavourable. I am happy to inform you that my Father is doing quite as well as we can expect from the serious nature of the accident. The fractured Bones have both been carefully examined and are to all appearances perfectly correct.   David Hodgkinson

Dr Hill to Joseph's wife

My patient, with the exception of pulling the sleeves of his coat & shirts, has been very tranquil and has shown more rationality in his general habits for several days. He has read correctly somethings to me & though without acute comment, I think his reasoning powers are a little improving. The change is on the whole more favourable since my last report.

John Hill.

Dr Hill to David Hodgkinson.

January, 28th 1826

I cannot . . . say that there are any favourable changes since my last report, all circumstances in regard to my patient being as nearly as may be in the same state as when I wrote to Mrs H this day fortnight. Perhaps you will lighten my labor of correspondence by communicating with Mrs H the substance of my present letters.   John Hill.

The Revd Joseph Hodgkinson's Acct with John Hill

	£ s d
From February 8th, 1825, to February 8th, 1826	
To one year's board, lodging washing, medical attendance & the use of a man servant	236. 3. 0

Paid for articles of dress & for repairing the same

for one year   11. 9. 5
                                                                ─────────
                                        Total   247. 12. 5

Dr Hill will send the particulars of the account for clothes at any time if requested.

David Hodgkinson to Dr Hill
                                                    3rd February, 1826
I sincerely wish you could give us more favourable Accts of him, but I fear the malady is now so established that it is vain even to hope.
                                                    David Hodgkinson.

Elizabeth, Joseph's wife, to David Hodgkinson
                                                    February 14th, 1826
My dear Bro David, I hope you all arrived safe at home after your visit to Manchester and that your Mother was not the worse for it. I am now writing from Medlock. I came here a week on Saturday to spend a week or two with my old friend.
    Give my kind love to Mr & Mrs Hodgkinson. I am afraid Dr Hill has lost some relative, his letter is sealed with black. I am yours affectionately,
                                                    B Hodgkinson.

Dr Hill to Elizabeth Hodgkinson and attached to the letter above (copied in Elizabeth's hand)
Leicester   February 11th, 1826
My Dear Madam, I regret to say that my patient Mr H has within these few days (after being more than usually calming) become very talkative and restless in the night with more than usual excitement and he has been so destructively inclined with his own dress & bed linen & that we have found it necessary to secure his hands. He rested better last night than for several preceding ones, and is calm today with his hands quite at liberty so that I hope the excitement is going off again.   John Hill.

[Joseph Hodgkinson died on 5 July 1826]

Richard Hodgkinson to David Hodgkinson who went to Leicester to bring home Joseph's body.
                                                    July 9th 1826
My dear David, I have just received your 3 Letters and I am happy to

inform you that your Mother bears the melancholy intelligence not only with fortitude but resignation.

I shall inform Mr Simmons and send William off to Manchester as soon as possible that he may get there time enough to put this into the Post Office. We have no objection to the opening of poor Joseph's head. Your Mother is reconciled to it as she knows the head of one of Mr McConnel's Children was opened for a similar purpose.

You say it would be well not to enter Leigh too early in the Evening. I know not that any thing was fixed about interring the Corpse when it arrives at Leigh, or bringing it home for the Night. Mr Simmons will determine this. I shall certainly meet you at Manchester. With respect to Hat-bands, in Hat Bands and Scarfs, Bessy may please herself. The only persons we think of giving to are Mr & Mrs McConnel, Mr G Murray, Dr Woodward, Mr Wharton and Mr Robson, except perhaps to Mr Marsh, Dr Smith, I suppose should have one. If my own opinion were asked I should think Hat-bands sufficient.

You will be aware I must write in great confusion. I wish Mr Simmons and Family to be particulary consulted about the Funeral and their Wishes complied with. William will wait for yours and Mr Simmons' Letter this Evening and Save a Messenger being sent over on purpose.

                                                                R Hodgkinson.

Your Mother is now with me, and seems to have let upon a very good idea about the Interment. She says, the Vicarage is the proper place for the Corpse to be placed in, and that if it were placed there for one hour on its arrival at Leigh, the Interment might take place the same Evening it comes to Leigh. This appears to me very proper and removes many difficulties.

Richard Hodgkinson to Dr Hill

                                                                July 15th, 1826
Hon'd Sir, The Die is now cast and this World with all its Miseries, is closed upon the mortal career of my unfortunate Son. It was a consummation devoutly to be worked. I have for many Months ceased to have any Hopes of his Recovery, and I believe my Wife's Hopes have been extinguished longer than my own. She has often bitterly complained of not being allowed to see him but she bears this new Dispensation not only with Resignation but Fortitude feeling as a Mother thankful his Sufferings are over. Poor young man his Lot has been a hard one to be buried alive in the very bloom of Youth and Health in the full Tide of Prosperity.

Under the Circumstance it is no wonder that he should be and I have no doubt he has been a troublesome Patient and I have now to thank you for all those kind and feeling Attentions which I have every Reason to believe he experienced uniformly at your hands. I will thank you to convey my best thanks to Carter for his treatment of and attention to his poor afflicted Companion, if I so may call him, and assure him they will not soon be forgotten.

The Corpse arrived at the Vicarage in Leigh at 12 o'clock on Tuesday night and remained there till 9 0'Clock on Friday Morning, when it was interred in a Vault I made a few years ago, in which no Corpse had been laid before, for strange as it may appear, I have been married 38 years and this is the first death I have had in the Family. I will thank you to remit your Account as soon as convenient, and believe me Yours,

Rd Hodgkinson

Dr Hill to David Hodgkinson

July 22, 1826

I received your Father's sensible and affecting letter a few days ago, for which I request you to offer him my thanks, and not him only, but to all those immediate connections of my late patient. I beg to express my sorrow at the afflicting loss they have sustained. I will only add that I shall be gratified to receive a call from you or Mr Hodgkinson Senr at any time when you come into this neighbourhood. The unhappy circumstances in which my acquaintance with your family began, & the still more melancholy duties which your confidence imposed upon me, have left an impression on my mind which will not soon be effaced.

I have sent the accounts to you, that I might not impose upon your Father the task of inspecting them. It is necessary that I should explain to you the charges for the surgeons fees, for attendance twice a day to use the catheter; an operation which I have for so many years ceased to perform, that I had occasion to require his assistance, having no confidence in my own expertise.

I have as you desired put down two pounds gratuity to the Cook and other female servants who contributed their share of solicitude to the poor sufferer.

I beg you to present my kindest compliments to Mr & Mrs Hodgkinson Senr and to the Lady, who tho' personally unknown to me I have often corresponded with during the severe and trying dispensation which she has had to endure. I trust Mr Simmons also will accept my respectful recollections.   John Hill.

David Hodgkinson to Bessy, Joseph's wife
Platfold   20th July, 1826
My dear Bessy, Allow me to offer you my most sincere condolence and
sympathy upon the mournful event which has lately happened among us.
But however mournful it may be, we should do wrong to consider it any
other than an happy event; but the hope of having him restored to us
again, had with me fled some time ago; and the satisfaction of supposing,
as we have every reason to do, that he is removed from this world of
affliction and misery, to receive the reward of a well spent life, must with
his friends, act as a soothing and consoling reflection, and reconcile us all
to a separation which under other circumstances might have been afflicting and distressing to a degree. You will have received all the particulars
through Mr Simmons. It will only be for me to state, and it will be I am
sure be to your satisfaction, that he shewed evident signs that he knew me
before his death, and that in the moment of death he went as tho' he were
going to sleep, and left this world without any extraordinary effort of
departing nature.

   You know my dear Bessy that you have always had the good wishes
and esteem of all of us here, and I am sure on your part we have enjoyed
yours.

   And the connecting link which immediately bound us together is sev-
ered and gone, yet I sincerely trust it will never interrupt our friendship
and unity; but the same good feeling will ever prevail, as well on our own
accounts as in remembrance of him who was truly dear to us but whom it
has pleased Providence to remove a short time before us. I am happy to
say that we all bear this dispensation, with more resignation and fortitude
than we could reasonably have anticipation, as I trust and hope you do. I
am desired by my Father, Mother and Sisters to say everything that is
Kind and consoling to you and to offer you their unaltered love and affection. Accept from me my dear Bessy my Brotherly love and esteem,

                                                                David.

David Hodgkinson to Dr Hill

                                                      23rd Sept, 1826
Dear Sir, Herewith you will receive a draft Value £111 7 0. As this is
very probably the last transaction we may have together, I cannot take
leave of you without expressing on my own part, as well as on that of my
Friends, the satisfaction which we have had in your conduct towards my
unfortunate Brother while under your care. I shall feel obliged if you will
convey the same expression of feeling to Mrs Hill. You will be glad to

hear that we all bear this dispensation of Providence towards us with almost more resignation than could have been expected. D Hodgkinson

Dr Hill to David Hodgkinson

Sept 24, 1826

I have to acknowledge your letter containing the draft for £111 7 0 which discharges my account against the late Rev^d J Hodgkinson and includes a kind donation towards the servant who waited upon him and which I have given to him; he begs to offer his grateful thanks for your attention.

I cannot but feel the deepest regret, that our intercourse, which commenced under circumstances of a melancholy nature, should have been characterised in its course & in its termination, by the same touching & distressing features, but I have some satisfaction in hearing that this dispensation is met with becoming fortitude by the friends of my late & lamented patient. To your intelligent & most respected Father, I request you to offer Mrs Hill's & my own kind regards, & assure him that I am sensible of the value of his good opinion & that of his family. I hope, when the day of sunshine shall return, that we may meet under happier circumstances, than that which have hitherto brought you to Leicester; it will give me pleasure to see you or any other of your family, whenever business or inclination may lead you into this neighbourhood. John Hill.

David Hodgkinson's Expenses in Going to Leicester to Bring Home Joseph's Body for Burial at Leigh

Joseph's Expences
Joseph was born 17th Jan^r 1796. He died at Leicester at 2 past one o'Clock on Sunday morning 5th July 1826.

Took with me	£
Notes	27
Gold	27
Silver	1
	£55

Expences in a Journey to Leicester to bring
Joseph's Corpse to Leigh, who died 5th July, 1826

	£	s	d
Expences at Mancr		4.	6
Coach fare to Leicester	2.	0.	0
Supper at Leek		3.	0
Coachman & Guard		5.	0
Bill at Leicester	1.	4.	0
Horses, Hearse & Chaise to Derby	10.	12.	6
Chaise from Loughboro	1.	5.	6
Toll bars to Derby		5.	0
Drivers to do.		11.	6
Hearse Horses & Chaise to Ashbourne	5.	1.	4
Breakfast at Ashbourne		2.	0
Drivers & Porter		6.	6
Hearse, Horses & Chaise to Macclesfield	10.	5.	4
Toll bars to Leek		9.	0
Expences at Leek		2.	6
Toll bars to Macclesfield		6.	0
Expences at do. including Men and Horses sent from Mancr		15.	0
Toll bars to Mancr		3.	0
Toll bars to Leigh		4.	0
Drivers from Macclesfield to Leigh, the same Drivers having come thro'		18.	0
Total	**£35.**	**3.**	**8**

July 1826

Money expended at Leicester when there
to take Joseph's corpse to Leigh

	£	s	d
Paid Bosworth & Parr for Hat bands & Gloves for Dr. & Mrs Hill & Carter	2.	0.	6
Paid Jane Sivinsen for Lead Coffin	8.	10.	0
Paid Thos. Hainy for Oak Coffin, Shell, Shroud, Plate, Black Cloth, Flannel, Ornaments etc	10.	0.	0
Sundry Expences		11.	6
Total	**21.**	**2.**	**0**

Expences at Leicester & of conveying corpse to Leigh	35.	3.	8
	21.	2.	0
Total	56.	5.	8

Inventory of Joseph Hodgkinson's Furniture at the Vicarage, Leigh

Drawing Room

6 and 1 arm'd Mahogany Chairs	8.	8.	0
Mahogany Pembroke table	3.	10.	0

Dining Room

Set of Mahogany Dining Tables	9.	10.	0
Sofa	4.	10.	0
Mahogany Card table	2.	10.	0
Side board & Oil case cover	6.	0.	0
Blue & White table service	4.	0.	0
Napkin press	2.	0.	0
Oak knife, Rose, Wine baskets & Lanterns		4.	6
Set of Tea china & sundry china	1.	0.	0
150 pieces of Earthenware	1.	10.	0
Taken by Mary		19.	0
7 Jugs & 3 Porter mugs		7.	0
6 Glass desert dishes	3.	10.	0
1 Large Jug		2.	6
Desert Service of Earthenware		7.	0

Kitchen

8 Flat irons, Italian iron and stands	13.	0
Marble pestle & Mortar	7.	0
do.	7.	0
Metal Coffee biggin & Tea pot	9.	0
Japann'd spice box	2.	0

Brass Tea Kettle & Stand	12. 6
Cleaver	1. 0
30 Table Knives and 30 Forks, 18 desert do., 3 Carvers	
& Forks with Ivory Hafts	4. 10. 0
6 Common Knives & Forks	3. 6
17 Table Knives, 16 Forks, 7 Desert do., 12 Forks,	
Carver & Fork, Steel & Oyster knife with black hafts	1. 0. 0
1 Set of Brass, 2 sets Steel fire irons	2. 0. 0
2 Sets of Common fire irons	7. 0

Back Kitchen

Dripping Pan, Iron Stand and tin hasliner	15. 0
Frying pan & 2 tin cans	7. 6
7 Iron pans	1. 4. 6
Iron tea kettle	5. 0
Tin fish kettle & coal box	8. 0
Iron Board	1. 0
3 Maidens	11. 0
Knife board & 3 Cleaning boxes	4. 6
Dolly tub & 2 washing tubs	1. 0. 0

Yard

1 Mash tub & soaking tub	1. 15. 0

Room over Kitchen

Mahogany Butler's Tray and Stand	18. 0
Mahogy Supper Tray	1. 5. 0
Japan'd Plate warmer	8. 0
2 Japan'd Trays & waiter	10. 0
2 Black tin pans	3. 6
2 Door matts	5. 0
Feather bed, bolster, 7 Pillows	14. 0. 0
Snap table	1. 1. 0
Paper tray & Waiter	1. 0. 0
8 Pair Blankets	8. 15. 0
4 Counterpanes	2. 0. 0
Bottle Rack	16. 0

Plate Basket		6. 0
Chopping knife, steak tongs, 2 brass pans & saw	1. 4.	0
3 Shaving Cans		3. 0
Dutch oven Cullender, egg slice, spoon Grater tin, Petties		9. 0
2 Small tin Pans		3. 0
Toasting Fork		1. 0
Iron shovel		3. 6
Lemon squeezers and Wood ware		2. 6
Iron Ladle		1. 0

Room over Parlour

Washstand & Dressing Table	1. 2.	0
2 Painted Towel rails		6. 0
Dressing Glass	2. 5.	0
Mahogany chest of draw'rs	4. 10.	0
Mahogy Bedstead printed Hangings and Window curtain	12. 10.	0
Feather bed, bolster and 2 Pillows	8. 10.	0
Flock Mattrass	1. 15.	0

Dressing Room

2 Painted Chairs		10. 0

Room over Drawing Room

3 Painted chairs and 1 cushion		17. 0
Dressing Glass	2. 0.	0
Mahy Night Commode	1. 15.	0
Tent bed Hangings, Window Curtains	5. 0.	0
Feather bed, bolster & Pillows	8. 0.	0
Straw Mattrass		12. 0
Towel rail		2. 0

Dressing Room

Painted Dressing table and 2 Wash Stands	1. 12.	0
Dressing Glass	1. 10.	0
Mahogany Pot Cupboard		10. 6
Do. towel rail		7. 0

2 Painted chairs	10. 0
Boot & Shoe rack	18. 0
Plate chest	1. 10. 0

Attic over Kitchen

4 Painted chairs	1. 0. 0
Painted dressing table	10. 0
Mahogany Bedstead, Green Moreen Hangings and	
window curtains	8. 10. 0
Feather Bed & Bolster	8. 0. 0
Straw Mattrass	12. 0

Attic over Dining Room

4 Painted chairs	1. 4. 0
1 Brass Fender & Set of fire Irons	2. 12. 6
Coal pan	4. 0
Flower pot stand	5. 0
50 Pieces of Chamberware	2. 10. 0
Flour Chest & 2 back screens	1. 2. 0
Sofa and cover	2. 5. 0
Brussels carpet and Rug	7. 10. 0
2 Buffets	8. 0
2 Tea Caddies	15. 0
6 Brass Candlestick	15. 0
Hearth brush	3. 0
Linen Chest	1. 10. 0

Attic over Drawing Room

Chairs given to the Clerk

Back Attic

3 chairs	15. 0
Painted Chest drawers	1. 15. 0
Dressing table and Ironing glass	1. 1. 0
Night lamp	3. 0
Linen	

12 Table cloths & 6 Breakfast do.	10. 16. 0
26 Diaper Towels and 38 Huckaback[7] do.	3. 8. 0
12 Dinner Napkins, 12 Breakfast do .	2. 8. 0
12 Pillow cases	1. 1. 0
15 Common Towels, 4 roller towels, 3 Dresser cloths & 20 Dusters	1. 9. 6
5 short blinds, 6 Toilet Covers, 7 Pincushion do.	15. 0
3 Dressing table cover	3. 0
2 Table covers	1. 10. 0
26 Bil case table mat	13. 0
12 Pair of Sheets	8. 8. 0
24 Doyleys, 11 Doyleys	8. 9
45 feet Brussells bedside Carpet	3. 0. 0
44 do. do	3. 4. 0
230 feet Venetian	11. 8. 0
Paid by Mr Topping 7. 4. 0	4. 4. 0

Cellars

2 Drippers	8. 0
Long Neck and Tun dish	3. 6
Dish tub and Piggin[8]	3. 6

Library

Library table	3. 16. 0
4 Cane seated chairs	1. 12. 0
11 yards of narrow Lobby Oil cloth at 2/6	1. 7. 6

Wine

150 Bottles of New Port at 2/9	20. 12. 6
26 of Old Port at 3/4	3. 6. 8
20 of Sherry at 3/	3. 0. 0
9 of Old Hock at 5/-	2. 5. 0
Total	303. 10. 1

Goods at Platfold valued by Jos^h Warburton 10th April 1827

Room

Mahogany drawers	5.	0.	0
Desk & Drawers	2.	0.	0
Bedstead & Hangings	2.	15.	0
Feather bed, bolster & 2 Pillows	5.	0.	0
Mattrass	1.	10.	0
2 Sheets, 2 Blankets & Quilt	1.	1.	0
Mahogany desk	5.	0.	0
Eight days Clock Mahogany Case	5.	0.	0
Buffett Cupboard	2.	2.	0

Pantry

Oak Chest	1. 0.	0
Flags	10.	0
Two barrels	10.	0
Coffee Mill	2.	6

Kitchen

Iron oven, Grate, Fender, Poker & Grid	3. 0.	0
Dining table	15.	0
Cupboard	7.	6
4 Rush bottom'd Chairs	10.	0
Iron tubs	8.	0
Brew Pan Brass & Lead	2. 0.	0

Milk House

Cheese press	2. 0.	0
Tub and Heshon	6.	0
Irish Cheeseboards, Tub & Handleboard	4.	0
Chesfoots	16.	0
Ale Can	1.	6
Small Cheese Press	4.	0
12 Cream Mugs	10.	6
4 Flags	1. 0.	0
12 Pan Mugs	4.	0
Mug, Tub & Tin Sieve	4.	0

Butter Scales etc		2.	0
Two Basketts		2.	0
Churn Waggon		5.	0
Churn Staff etc	1.	1.	0
5 Cans		5.	0
Barrell		4.	0

Barn

3 Barrells	11.	0
3 Tubs	18.	0
Churn	7.	0
24 Cow Chains	15.	0

Books

Johnson's Lives of the Poets 4 vols	10.	0
Smith's Wealth of Nations 3	9.	0
Robertson's Hist. of Scotland 2	6.	0
do. Charles the 5th 3	9.	0
Moore's Travels in Italy 2	6.	0
do. in France 2	6.	0
Poems etc	2.	0
Letter to Mr Peel	2.	0
Pursuits of Literature	2.	6
Police Report	3.	0
Anecdotes of the Founders of the French Revolution	4.	0
Knox's Essays 2	5.	0
Teleuco 2	4.	0
Rural tales by Bloomfield	2.	0
Spectator 8 Vol	16.	0
Barrow's Essay on Education	4.	0
Reports of the Society for bettering the condition of the Poor 5 vol	7.	6
Byron's Poems 2 Vol	3.	0
Bloomfield's Farmer's Boy	1.	6
Young's Night Thoughts	2.	6
Iunius 2 Vol	4.	0
Pope's Works 8 Vols	12.	0

Travels of a Philosopher	1.	6
Atherstone Green 3	4.	6
Satirical View of London	2.	0
Doctor Syntax	2.	6
Fables	1.	6
Journey to Paris 2	3.	0
History of Glasgow	1.	6
of Edinburgh	1.	6
of Liverpool	1.	6
Plays	1.	6

Literary Miscellany Vol 20	2.	0.	0
Shakespear 14	2.	2.	0

Watts Improve^t of the Mind	2.	0
Watts' Logick	2.	0
Agricultural Chemistry	3.	0
Savory's Travels in Egypt	5.	0
Marshall on Landed Estates	3.	0
Burke's Peerage and Baronetage	3.	0
The Subaltern	2.	6
The Young Rifleman	2.	6
The Plain Englishman	3.	6
Hall's British Flora 2 Vol	3.	0
Early Education	3.	0
Memoirs of Rd Cumberland 2	7.	0
Gisborne's duties of Women	3.	0
do. Sermons 2V	6.	0
do. Sermons on Christian Morality	3.	0
Fordyce's Sermons to young Women	4.	0
do. Addresses to young Men 2	4.	0
Cooper's Sermons 5	7.	6

Mant's Bible	5.	5.	0
Percy's Anecdotes 4 V	3.	0.	0

Telemachus	2.	0

Farming Stock
Valued by Thos Smith

Cows

Cherry	7.	10.	0
Rosa	7.	10.	0

Slingsby	9. 0. 0
Juno	10. 0. 0
Spot	8. 0. 0
Smirk	5. 6. 0
Beauty	12. 12. 0
Tulip	14. 14. 0
Daisy	10. 10. 0
Bullneck	6. 15. 0
Cockett	9. 0. 0
Lucy	5. 10. 0
Stella	8. 0. 0
Young Flora	9. 9. 0
Leigh	11. 0. 0
Nutt	15. 15. 0
Sprightly	12. 0. 0
Maria	12. 10. 0
Flora	13. 0. 0
Spanker	9. 9. 0
1 Bull, 3 years old	11. 0. 0
1 Bull, 8 months old	4. 10. 0
3 Two year old Heifers	21. 0. 0
1 Do. out calf	5. 10. 0
3 Calves	10. 10. 0
Total Horned Cattle	250. 0. 0
1 Churning Machine	20. 0. 0
3 Tons of Hay at 6.10s. per	19. 10. 0
Total	289. 10. 0

These Accts examined and found correct – Richard Hodgkinson, David Hodgkinson.

Joseph's affairs lingered on for many years after his death. His widow, Elizabeth, renounced all claims on his estate and in July, 1850, the Bishop of Chester gave power of admininstration to what was left of his estate to Robert Jackson, Joseph's nephew.

Notes

1   William Hulme (1631–1691), who was buried in Manchester Cathedral, left
     most of his money to enable four 'poor' graduates to prolong their studies at
     Brazenose to attain MA degrees. The fund became extremely wealthy and in
     1814 fifteen exhibitioners received £135 a year. From an article in *The Times*
     (1879), reprinted in the Manchester Grammar School form lists.
2   According to one of his cash books, Hodgkinson had for many years lent
     money to various people. Unfortunately the book has been damaged and the
     debtors are not known.
3   David Hodgkinson was agent to Mr Froggart for many years.
4   Bent was the local name for Atherton.
5   This is Chowbent Church.
6   The clergymen were the Revd Mr Brocklebank, vicar of Deane, Bolton, and
     the Revd Charles Burton of All Saints, Manchester.
7   Chowbent.

9

Richard's Last Visit to London, 1824

Richard Hodgkinson's last and saddest visit to London, in the spring of 1824, was overshadowed by the grief he felt for his son Joseph, who was then spending his second year in an asylum for the insane in Leicester. Adding to Hodgkinson's misery was the main object of his mission: to arrange the demolition of Atherton Hall and thus bring to an irrevocable end six hundred years of the lord of the manor's residence on the Atherton estate.

Hodgkinson's master, the 2nd Lord Lilford had a London home in Grosvenor Place and they spent many hours discussing estate business, the removal of furniture from Atherton Hall, the small matter of a tenant farmer's dispute with a gentleman on a neighbouring property, and grossly underestimating the value of coal which lay under the estate. In his spare moments he passed the time of day with Lilford's daughters and paid his customary London visits to those places that offered education, entertainment and interest, an art exhibition and the zoo. After a visit to the Theatre Royal in Drury Lane for an evening of mixed entertainment, including an opera, Hodgkinson showed no change in his musical views from the time when he heard Mozart in 1819. After enduring Thomas Arne's opera, *Artaxerxes*, the farce *Deaf as a Post*, and *Zoroaster, a New Grand Tale of Egyptian Enchantment*, he wrote in his diary: 'Of all species of stage Entertainments the Opera is to me the most disagreeable and disgusting.' In a crowded House of Commons he stayed briefly to hear Sir Henry Parnell speak on the Irish Question. Almost by chance, Hodgkinson paid a fascinating visit to Greenwich where he struck up a passing acquaintanceship with a pensioner from the Hospital, and the result was a remarkable and quite lengthy record of life for the veterans of war, even down to details of their daily rations and mortality rate, and the strange significance of a yellow jacket worn by inmates who had disgraced themselves in drink.

On his way home, Hodgkinson spent two days visiting Joseph in the Leicestershire asylum and kept details in a special journal, which is now missing from the collection of his papers.

Richard Hodgkinson's visit to London in 1824

May 7th

Set out on a Journey to London, to consult with Lord Lilford about what Estates were to be offered to Sale this Year, to arrange about taking down the Hall and on other matters connected with his Lordship's property.

I left home in a Chaise for Manchester at 10 o'Clock where I transacted some business and at a Quarter before six in the Evening I got into the Defiance Coach at the Bridgewater Arms and after a safe and not unpleasant journey I arrived in London at half past six the following evening. Fare £3.3s.0d. Took up my Quarters at the Grecian Coffee House.

May 9th

In the Morning went to St Paul's. Being the beginning of Term the 12 Judges accompanied by the Lord Mayor attended Divine Service there. I afterwards went to Grosvenor Place to wait upon Lord Lilford. We just took a short Notice of the Subjects which wd engage our attention during my stay in London, especially such as we shd have to attend to with Mr Gorst, who it was agreed shd accompany me at 11 o'Clock next morning to Lord Lilford.

May 10th

Mr Gorst and I took a Hackney Coach to Grosvenor Place. It having been previously arranged what Estates in Sankey & Burtonwood were to be offered to Sale this Year & it appearing that their Values fell short of the Amt of Money present wanted. Mr Gorst & myself endeavoured to prove to his Lordship and succeeded in proving to him, the great Sacrifice that must necessarily be made if the deficiency was to be made up by Sales of Land in West Leigh, where there is Coal under every Estate. By the existing Atherton Coal Lease (which will not expire for fifty years to come) Mr Fletcher has the power of preventing the working of these Mines during that period. I had with me a Calculation of Mr Fletcher's in which it is stated that the Coals under Lord Lilford's Property in West Leigh viz: a hundred Acres of Land; are only worth £1600 with the power of getting them immediately, but if they are to lie to the end of the Atherton Coal Lease, viz: 50 years; their value in present Money is only worth £140. It was at last agreed to adopt a Plan, which I had suggested to Lord Lilford some time ago viz: to sell the Estates in Sankey & Burtonwood & to make up the deficiency, if any, by the sale of the least objectionable parts of his Lordship's property. The next subject for consideration was the Policy and the Propriety of Letting out Land in Atherton for building upon for 999 Years. His Lordship was prepared for entering upon the subject, by previous discussions had upon it when in Lancashire last Year. Mr Gorst now read to him the powers he had of granting such Leases. It having before been determined that the Hall at Atherton sh^d be taken down, and of course no Family Residence w^d be there, his Lordship determined upon granting such Leases in future. But to carry this in to full effect it was necessary that another very important Act sh^d take place, viz: the exonerating of the Tenants in Atherton from paying the Levies and Taxes of all the Demesne Lands there. To this his Lordship, with the advice of Mr Gorst, was prepared to agree and it was settled that steps sh^d be taken to carry it into effect as soon as matters c^d be conveniently arranged for that purpose.

We then took into consideration a Plan of the Diversion of the Turnpike Road in Chowbent, proposed by the Trustees, accompanied by a Copy of the following Resolution passed by them at a Meeting held at Chowbent on the 6th inst. at which I was present and argued with some degree of warmth the impropriety of passing such a Resolution and the unpleasant situation it was placing Lord Lilford in with respect to Mr Sanderson.

Resolution

In pursuance of the Order of the last Meeting, the Plan of Mr John Albinson, of the diversion of the Road from near Mr Sanderson's House being produced or Ordered that the same be adopted, and that the diversion be made as laid down in the said Plan but it also appearing that if the said Diversion be made as laid down in the Plan about a Statute Acre of Land belonging to Lord Lilford opposite to Mr Sanderson's House might be afterwards be made use of for building upon or to the annoyance and injury of Mr Sanderson's House and Property adjoining Ordered that Mr Hodgkinson be requested to apply to Lord Lilford, that his Lordship (to prevent this inconvenience) would grant and convey to Mr Sanderson the said Land on such Terms as his Lordship's Agent and Mr Sanderson may agree. And also the making of the said proposed Diversion be not commenced until next Spring unless before that time the Negotiation between Lord Lilford and Mr Sanderson be concluded to his Lordship's & Mr Sanderson's Satisfaction.

Upon reading this Resolution both Lord Lilford & Mr Gorst said it was the most extraordinary Resolution they had ever heard & that the attempt by it to interfere with private Property was most unwarrantable. Lord Lilford said he had no objection to the Line of the Road proposed; as stated in the Plan, but to the suggestion contained in the latter part of the Resolution he could by no means accede.

May 11th

Waited upon Lord Lilford at eleven o'Clock and continued with him till two. We recapitulated what we had gone thro' the day before and confirmed the determinations we had then come to.

I then, upon a Plan of Atherton which I had with me, pointed out to Lord Lilford, a line from a Farm in Atherton called Meanley's, thro' which the Tenant of that Farm claimed a right to pass into the Land of the late Thos Johnson Esq (now Mr Ormerod) and thro' that Land into the Bridle Road from Tildesley to Leigh with Horses & Carts. This right the Tenant has occasionally exercised, with a view, as he said, of preserving the right which his Landlord, old Mr Meanley, who had a Life Lease of this Farm, told him the Farm was entitled to. Supposing the right to exist, it is only for this one Farm and is of no possible use. Mr Johnson always locked up this Gate leading out of this Road into Tildesley & Leigh Bridle Road, when and as often as he thot proper and Lord Lilford's tenant asking for the Key, has had it given to him to pass thro'. Soon after Mr Johnson's Death, the Tenant John Caldwell came to inform me that Mr Ormerod had put a Lock upon the Gate and was for stopping the Road. I wrote to Mr Ormerod informing him of our claim and the practice of the old Tenant, Wm Pennington (whose Daur the present Tenant John Caldwell married) passing thro' that way for thirty Years, in my knowledge, occasionally, for the purpose of keeping up the claim. Mr Ormerod sent me a long and civil Letter stating that the Tenant had in passing thro' left all the Gates upon the Road open so that the Cattle could not only pass out of one Field into another on his land but could also pass over into Atherton and commit Trespass upon Caldwell's own

Farm and this neglect he persevered in not withstanding Mr Ormerod's personal Remonstrations. The fact is that Caldwell was at that time building some Cottages at Tildesley and carted the Materials thro' the Road in question which he had no right to do, tho' the claim of the Road for the Farm might be ever so well established. Mr Ormerod went on to say, that in consequence of my Le^t. he had made enquiries abt the right of Road but could not find that the right had been acknowledged, nor could he find anything among his Uncle's Papers to that effect. But he concluded by saying that the thing itself was of very little consequence to him and that the Tenant conducting himself properly might have a Key for asking for and pass thro' as usual. He observed in his Le^t. that he could not help noticing that in my Letter to him I relied upon the practice of the old Tenant exercising the Right for a number of Years rather than stating any specific Right confirmed by a Deed, Conveyance or Writing. Mr Ormerod was leaving Tildesley till the month of June and it was agreed that neither he nor I sh^d take any further steps in the matter till his return.

On stating this to his Lordship he said he could not see that the right of Road being limited to that Farm only could be of any essential use, and its being relinquished might be a convenience to Mr Ormerod and on that account he had no objection to it being given up.

In the Morning I visited the Exhibition of Painting at Somerset House which is very splendid. I also called in at the Exeter Exchange to see the Menagerie there. No fresh or uncommon Animals had been added since I saw it four years ago. The same Elephant is there now as was then, it has been there fourteen years. It is a most enormous Animal, said to be four tons weight & is a stupendous production of Nature.[1]

In the Evening I went to the House of Lords, and heard the Debates upon the Aliens Bill. Lord Grosvenor's manner of speaking is tame in the extreme. Lord Holland's, violent in the extreme. Lord Liverpool, the best speaker, both in language, manner & voice. After leaving the House of Lords I stepped into the Commons to hear the Debates upon Lord Althorp's Motion to inquire into the State of Ireland. Sir Henry Parnell was speaking, but the Gallery was too crowded to afford any room and I soon left.

May 12th
Went to Lord Lilford's at 11 o'Clock to meet Mr Wyatt, the Architect, to arrange ab^t taking down the Hall at Atherton and to fix upon a Plan for disposing of the Materials, Mr Wyatt was accompanied by a person from the Board of Works conversant in the mode of selling the Materials of

Buildings to be taken down. After considerable discussion it was determined that the Hall only shd be taken down at present without meddling
with any of the Offices, Outbuildings or adjoining Walls, that the
Biddings shd be by sealed Tenders and sent to me at Atherton, and that
twelve months shd be allowed for removing the Materials and that the
Advertisement founded upon these Principles shd be forthwith drawn up
by Mr Wyatt and sent to me to be inserted in the Newspapers.

Lord Lilford also determined that no Fixtures that were fastened into
the walls nor cupboards so situated shd be taken down but remain to be
sold with the House. He said that in all probability when taken down they
wd be found rotten and decayed, that they would in general be too large
for Bewsey & that it wd be more convenient to provide new, what was
wanted of that kind, than be at the expense of taking down, carting away,
and altering what at best was of little Value.

After Mr Wyatt was gone I consulted with Lord Lilford about the
removing of the Books & Pictures all which, he said, must be packed up
in Cases & sent to Bewsey and remain so packed up there till the Family
came there. The Picture of Mr Rawstorne I am to pack up as soon as I
get home and send it to Lord Lilford in London for the purpose of having
a copy taken of it to give to the Rawstorne family. The stuffed Birds must
not at present be sent to Bewsey but placed in the little Room formerly
used by the Ladies as their Bird Room, the Road to which is thro' the
Corn Room. The Plate Chest must be sent to the Bank at Warrington, if
the Bankers will take the charge of it.

I had this Morning an interview with Miss Powys and Miss Eleanor to
see if they had any directions to give abt the Furniture or say what particular Rooms at Bewsey, they would have any particular Bed or piece of
Furniture placed. They had very little to say but I requested them to put
down in writing, what they had to say that I might give [it] to Mrs
Standish. They wrote a few directions about the Beds and also abt the
Baby House in the Hall, which is to be sent to Mrs Hornby at Winwick
for Captain Phipps Hornby's children. The Pea-fowl, they said, must be
given away.

The Curtains and Carpets are to be cut and made to fit the respective
Rooms & Windows at Bewsey and an Upholsterer is to be got to assist in
doing them.

Neither his Lordship nor the young Ladies could give any directions
about the packing up of the Pictures and I am left totally in the dark on
that head.

On my return I called in at Mr Kecks' house in the Park Crescent, top of Portland Place. Mr and Mrs Keck not being expected in town before Saturday I stopped an hour with Mrs Mather and told her I would call again if I stayed till the beginning of the week. Mrs Mather informed me that the day before Nancy Davies, widow of Bryan and mother of John Davies, had called upon her and being informed I was coming to Town said she was very desirous I shd give her a call. Mrs Mather informed me I shd find her in Brook Street leading out of Bond Street. She also informed me that John Davies had been married abt a year and a half to a young lady of large fortune who at the time she fell in love with him resided near Mr Keck's in the Crescent and her first knowledge of him was from seeing him frequently pass her Father's in his way to a house in the neighbourhood, which he was furnishing and fitting up. She commenced the Acquaintance by writing a letter to him. By Mrs Mather's account she was not the first lady of Quality who had addressed letters to him on the same subject.2 He keeps his close Carriage and Gig, and resides in a House not far from Piccadilly and has left his mother in the house and shop3 in Brook Street which he visits for a short time every day but which is kept on solely for the sake of his mother.

In the evening I went to the Covent Garden Theatre, no particular performance.

May 13th
The Morning being wet I shd not have gone to Grosvenor Place but I expected to find there Thurston Peak's Conveyance which I had directed Mr Littler to address to me there. It had just been left by the Postman and finding his Lordship very much engaged, I went up stairs and sat half an hour with the Young Ladies. On quitting them I went into the Housekeeper's Room and having there got some Refreshment, I set out in my return and in my way to call upon Mrs Davies. Being pretty well acquainted with Bond Street, and having some idea where to look for Brooke Street, I soon found both it and the Shop. On entering I saw a person in a small counting house at the upper end of the Shop engaged in the Books. On enquiring for Mrs Davies he called her into the Shop, she soon recognised me and took me upstairs. Her dinner was just coming up. I declined taking any, but said I had no objection to a draught of Porter. The foreman came & sat down to Dinner. I took the opportunity of talking abt removing the Pictures, Looking Glasses, &c., from Atherton and enquiring how it could best be done. He said the smaller ones could be very easily packed into Baskets, but the safest way of removing the Pictures is in a Carriage upon Springs, such as Mr Pickford uses for carrying

up small parcels, called a Van. Ab^t packing them I could get no information so much depended upon the size of Frames &c.

For half an hour after the Foreman had left us, we had been talking over old affairs when John came into the Room. He seem'd glad to see me. I congratulated him upon his Marriage. He had not sat long but he complained of being indisposed from his last night's Excess. He said he had only got to Bed at 2 o'Clock. He had been dining in the Bourough with a Member of Parliament, Sir Jacob Astley, he said, was of the Party, and that he had bro^t Sir David, in his Carriage and set him down at his own Door when the Party broke up. He said they had drank a deal of Wine & finished up with 2 Bottles of Sherry Brandy, a Guinea & a half per Bottle, which they took in their Coffee. Port & Sherry being Common Wines, by his acc^t, did not come on to the Table. He asked many Questions about the Culcheth Hall Property & said he had often thought of writing to me about it, after he had seen the Advertisement for its Sale. He said he wanted to invest some Money & had thot that the Purchase of it might ans^r his purpose. He said he now only kept the business on on his Mother's Acc^t. She must have a Living and she preferred attending to the Shop rather than having nothing to do. His Wife, he said, did not like it. He did not talk in any boasting stile of his fortunate Marriage nor make any allusions to his Carriage or Horses or Servants. When I got up to come away he invited me to fix a day for dining with him. This I at once declined, well knowing that I could not be introduced to his Wife without bringing to their recollection Circumstances which it must be unpleasant for both of them to be reminded of.

In the Evening I went to the Theatre at Drury Lane. An Opera was the first part of the Evening's performance. Of all species of stage Entertainments the Opera is to me the most disagreeable and disgusting. How unnatural it is to hear a person singing who is acting the part of a person in a most violent Passion, singing when in the extremity of Misery & Distress, singing when ab^t to administer the poisoned Cup or to commit Murder by more violent means. The Tedium was somewhat relieved, now and then by Miss Stephens in the exercise of her superior vocal Talents.[1]

May 14th
I went to Lord Lilford this Morning, to take my leave of him, so as at last to be at Liberty to return home as soon as I had made all the necessary arrangements with Mr Gorst, having previously settled with his Lordship all that he and I had to do together. I wished briefly to recapitulate some

of the more important points we had touched upon.

I first said, I presume that now I am at liberty when I get home to inform your Tenants that it is your Intention to grant building Leases upon Long Terms of 999 Years; he answered, Certainly. I then mentd. that he had some time ago said I might give the clock at the top of the Hall at Atherton to the Chapel at Chowbent; he ansd. that I might give it now. I then observed that as such very great changes were now taking place at Atherton it might be necessary to examine whether any bargains that had been entered into were not completed on his Lordship's part, or any promises made which had not been fulfilled. As an instance of the first, I mentioned that Mr Jackson had never had a Lease of the Lodge, which he was entitled to expect, previous to any change taking place with Respect to the Demesne. And of the second that the new School at Chowbent had not yet been built; both of which he said ought to be done.

I told him that much expence wd necessarily be incurred in the making of the different arrangement of the Land at the Hall, the Old Hall and Plat Fold, that it could not in the future be occupied in the Large open Fields it had been, that Inclosures must be made and several new Fences planted; but if this was to be done much advantage might be made by taking up the Fences round the Plantations in the Great Wood and applying them for the purpose; which he said might be done, they might all be taken up. I likewise observed that I thought it wd be necessary to have a new Plan taken of all the Demesne Land belonging to the Hall and the Old Hall before a proper arrangmt. could be made. This he said might be necessary. In talking of the Old Hall, he mentd. he intended Building there and said it did not offer ansr. to add new Buildings to old; he thot it wd be best to take the old Building wholly down and make an entire new one as was done at the Lodge.

May 15th
The Rain was incessant from Morning till Night. I never was out the whole day except for an hour with Mr Gorst.

May 16th
Being Sunday, after Breakfast I called upon Mr Gorst as I had promised. I then walked along the Strand looking for some place of Worship to go into. But having strolled as far as Charing Cross, I saw a Coach just setting off for Greenwich. I paid my Fare, two shillings, and got into it. Greenwich is only five Miles from Charing Cross. We went over the

Westminster Bridge. It is a continued town almost all the way. Deptford, where much ship-building is going on joins Greenwich, together they entertain about twenty-five thousand Inhabitants. At Deptford Bridge, about a quarter of a Mile short of Greenwich, a great Crowd of people were collected, viewing the Ruins of some Building which had been washed down in the Night by the Flood occasioned by yesterday's Rain. On one side of the Stream, a Dwelling house was thrown down & on the other side a Warehouse, out of which many Hogsheads of Sugar were washed away. Damage estimated at £1,400. Getting out of the Coach I did not go into the Inn but began my Perambulations.

Having walked some time in the Streets without knowing where to look for the objects most deserving of attention, an elderly person in a coarse blue Coat and three-cocked Hat over took me. I asked him the way to the Hospital. He said he was going that way and would shew me. As I went along the Streets I observed many others dressed in the same way and began to suspect they were Pensioners. I asked my Companion and he said they were. He said as soon as divine Service was over, which wd be at one O'clock (it then wanted abt a quarter) he said he could take me in and shew me thro' the College. We were now passing thro' a narrow Passage as a near cut to the Hospital and observing a public House I asked him if he would take a draught of Porter. We went in and he took me into a back Parlour which was close to the River. The Tide was nearly at the Height and had a full view of the River covered with Vessels of all sizes and denominations. On the opposite side of the River is the Isle of Dogs; & on the farther side of that nearer to London are the famous East India Docks. In the conversation over the Porter I discovered my Companion had formerly lived in the neighbourhood of Manchester & Bolton. He knew Major Pilkington, and the Ainsworths and Ridgeways. He had also known Mr Booth and Heywood and almost anyone I could name.

We now entered the Hospital Yard & at half past one he said they would be sitting down to Dinner and in the meantime he would take me into the Wards, that is the sleeping Rooms. The Room I went in had abt thirty Beds on each side with a space up the middle of about four Yards wide. Each Bed is in a separate Recess and only one person sleeps in a Bed. There are two Fires kept in the Room and everything was very neat and clean. Some of the men had ornamented their little Hammocks with Pictures, The sleeping rooms are all alike throughout.

When we came down stairs the Men were seated at the Tables in the Hall and the Servants were bringing in Dinner. Each man brought in a

large deep Pewter Dish full of Broth with a piece of Mutton in the middle
which I understood was a Mess for four men. They continued to fetch
fresh supplies from the Kitchen till the Tables were full. The Servants had
smock Frocks on. All seemed to be conducted with great Order. They
have flesh Meat every day of the week, Mutton 4 days and Beef 3.
Allowance three Quarters of a Pound to each man every day. The whole
number at present in the Hospital are two thousand seven hundred. There
are three halls for dining in. In that where I was there were seven hundred
and ninety-two at Dinner. There is a separate Building at the other side of
the Court which is called the Hospital for the Sick & Helpless to whom
their Provisions are carried. I saw abt a hundred of these men in the Court
Yard who appeared old and infirm but I saw very few Cripples. On the
opposite side [of] the Road is a spacious Lawn at the top of which is the
School (a very handsome Building) for the Children of Seamen brought
up in the Naval Asylum. At present they amount to abt 450 Boys and 350
Girls. Near this is the Infirmary, as a relief to the Hospital from the sick,
which is calculated to hold 256 Patients. My Companion told me that
more than one Pensioner upon an average dies every day. The Hospital
consists of four grand Buildings separated from each other, yet forming
one entire Plan, especially when viewed from the River to which the
main Front presents itself.

The Pensioners have many indulgences & but little personal restraint.
There is a very spacious Lobby in which they are permitted to Smoke.
On each side of the Lobby are small Cupboards in which each man can
put his Pipe and Tobacco and his Beer, of which he is allowed two
Quarts each day. On Sundays they are allowed to go to their own places
of Worship and every day they are permitted free egress & ingress as often
as they please. I observed to my Companion that when in the Town they
might occasionally meet with temptations to Intoxication. He said when
this was the Case, if the person would go quietly to his Ward no notice
was taken, but if he made any noise or disturbance he had to wear a yellow jacket for a certain time as a mark of Disgrace.

Their Breakfast consists of a Pint of Cocoa each, with Sugar, Milk and
Bread & Butter, and at 5 o'Clock in the Evening they have each a pint of
Tea with similar allowance. It takes 17 Gallons of Milk at each of these
Meals.

Besides the Governor there are two Chaplains and three medical
Gentlemen who have Residence in the Hospital.

We now went into the Park, which adjoins to the Hospital and is contiguous to Black Heath. It is stocked with abt 600 head of Deer. The

Trees, the Grass and the Walks are beautiful. Soon after you enter the Park you begin to ascend a Steep Hill, which affords some fine Views of the Metropolis, and of the Thames filled with Shipping. On the top of this Hill is the Royal Observatory, a conspicuous and celebrated Object.

Having perambulated the Park in various directions I began to feel a want of both Rest and Refreshment. We descended into the Town and going to the Public House we had been at before I ordered a Beef-stake & Potatoes, we had another Quart of Porter and each a Glass of Grog, for all which, with the Quart of Porter we had first had, I only paid 3/6. During Dinner I had a full view of the River, and it being then high Water, a fine day and the Vessels of every Denomination all in motion, the Scene was delightful. At this time two of the large Steam Packets from Hull and Newcastle passed up the River for London. At six o'Clock I got into a Coach, which brot. me to London by a different Rout from that I had gone in the Morning and coming over Black Friars' Bridge set me down at Temple Bar at 7 o'Clock.

I after this called upon Dr. Cartwright who resides in Bloomsbury Square. I found him alone. His wife, he said, had been in Lancashire a Month. I declined taking Tea and only stopped an hour with him.

May 17th
Called on Mr Gorst who was going out early to called upon several Gentlemen whose Assistance he wanted at the Committee on their Road Bill which was to sit at one o'Clock. He desired, that on my way back from Grosvenor Place I would come round thro' Grosvenor Sqr. and upper Grosvenor Street & endeavour to find out Sir Robt. Peel, or to get to know whether he was in Town or no.

I had no business wth L. Lilford this Morning, but I had told him on Friday that if I did not leave Town before Monday or Tuesday, I wd. call upon him again. He said he had just had a Physician's Opinion upon his Daur. Mary's health which stated that she wd. be able to be one of the Party in their Excursion to Paris; that he has now determined positively upon the Journey; that they sh. only be absent three Months viz: July, Aug & Sept. In returning I passed Hyde Park Corner and entering the Park went on to Grosvenor Gate. Traversing several Streets, I at length found my way to Grosvenor Sqr. and into upper Grosvenor Street where Mr Gorst said Sir Robt. Peel used to reside. I went from bottom to top on one side and very near from top to bottom on the other, but cd get no information abt. Sir Robt. or his House. As a last resource I stepped into a Confectioner's Shop and upon enquiring was told his House was No. 16.

I soon found it and was told by his Servt. that a week ago he had gone to Brighton, where he w^d. stay a fortnight yet & that his Lodgings were N°. 16 Regency Sq., Brighton.

I returned to Mr Gorst's Lodgings completely tired. Having waited more than an hour for his Return from the Committee, Mr Woodward came in and said Mr Gorst was gone with a party to Dinner & w^d. not return till Night. On coming from Mr Gorst's Lodgings to my own, I met in the Strand, young Mr Ditchfield f^m Hindley & his two Sisters. He said they had arrived in London 4 days before & were then going to the Opera-house to hear Madam Catalani.

May 18th

On going into Mr Gorst's Room this Morning to take my leave of him he shewed me a Let^r. he had just rec^d. from Mr Gaskell saying that his & Mr Morris' Conveyances wd be sent off on Monday night and he insisted on my staying to examine them with him. He deemed this so necessary that I must forfeit the Coach Fare I had paid to Leicester rather than go. I had then to go to Lord Lilford to fix a Meeting with him for signing all the Conveyances at 12 o'Clock on Thursday and to request him to get Col. Rawstorne to attend at the same time.

In the Evening I went to the Drury-Lane Theatre to see the Play of the Merry Wives of Windsor.

May 19th

I called upon Mr Gorst & while I was with him the Conveyances arrived. While he looked them over, I took a Coach and called upon Mr & Mrs Keck, who expressed themselves very glad to seem me. Mr Keck is very indignant at Atherton being pulled down. I then went to Lord Lilford to inform him the Conveyances were come and we sh. certainly have them ready to be executed the following day. Returning to Mr Gorst, I examined the Plans with him and the several Descriptions of the properties in the body of the Deeds. At 3 o'Clock I left him & went to 4 different Coach Offices to get my place for the following Evening but all were full. I returned to the Grecian at 6 o'Clock, tired and disappointed. As soon as I had dined young Mast. Lythgoe came to see me. I took him into my Bed-room, gave him two Glasses of Punch & when he left me in ab^t 2 hours I went to bed in no very good Spirits.

In the Morning I ment^d. to Lord Lilford that we hd omitted to say any thing ab^t. the Organ. He said he supposed it not to be worth much but its' value must be ascertained as well as we could & it must be sold.

May 20th

I got up at 7 o'Clock and went to the Bull & Mouth Inn where I took
my place in a Coach which runs no farther than Leicester & wh w^d set
out at a quarter past 5 on Friday Morning. From thence I walked up to
the Mansion House, the Bank, the Exchange and the Stock Exchange and
returned to Breakfast about 9 o'Clock. Mr Gorst having requested Mr
John Marsh, Solicitor of Wigan, who lodged at the Grecian to go with us
to be a Witness with me to the Execution of the Conveyance, I arranged
with him to meet me at Mr Gorst's Lodgings at 11 o'Clock. I then went
to Mr Gorst & settled all I had to do with him before Mr Marsh came.
Ab^t. a quarter past 11 we took a Coach; went to Lord Lilford, got the
Deeds executed by him, and then came to Mr Law^cr Rawstornes'
Lodgings in South Audley Street and got them executed by him. In coming from thence we had to cross New Bond Street, and here a Scene such
as never can happen in the Country engaged my attention for more than
half an hour. Today was the Drawing Room at St. James' Palace in honour of the King's Birthday. It had been more than once put off on acct. of
the King's Indisposition. When our coach came up a bye-street to cross
over Bond Street it was arrested by one continued range of Gentlemen's
Carriages so closely following each other that it was impossible to cross
the Line. These cd. only move ^when those at St. James' moved on, & the
distance from us to there we computed cd not be less than three quarters
of a Mile. This space of course was full of Carriages, and to the top of
Bond Street as far as we c^d. see, was also full, and in some places a double
row of Carriages. So that we computed that including the Carriages
which had set down their Company at St. James and gone on and those
which were not yet come into sight at the top of Bond Street, the whole
Line could not be less than two Miles long. This interruption was not disagreeable to us. Our position was such that we had a full view of the
company in every Carriage that passed us, and we had full time to view
them, sometimes as they stood for five Minutes, they then would move
slowly on for a Minute or two, then stop again. After waiting ab^t. half an
hour, the Coachman spying a momentary opportunity, whipped his
Horses and dashed thro'. When we got to Mr Gorst's Rooms it took us
till 3 o'Clock to write the various Attestations and sign our Names. I then
took my final leave of Mr Gorst and walked down to St. James' to spend
half an hour in seeing the Company leave. The sight was very imposing,
but wd have been much more interesting if I had had any one with me
who could have named the Owners of the Carriages as they passed along.
Those of the Lord Mayor & of the Sheriff were pre-eminent.

I returned to the Grecian at 6 o'Clock and dined. As soon as I had dined the Waiter came to tell me that all the Mail Coaches were passing by in procession. I went to see them and the sight was very pleasing. Each Coach drawn by 4 fine Horses, many of them in entire new Harness, Coachmen & Guards in new scarlet Liveries, and the whole followed by the Postboys, on horseback in new scarlet Jackets.

May 21st

Having taken my place in the Union Coach for Leicester to set out at 5 o'Clock this Morning I took care to be at the Bull & Mouth Inn from whence it set out in good time, and after a safe Journey arrived in Leicester at 6 o'Clock in the Evening. I here spent two days with my unfortunate Son, Joseph, the particulars of which will be found in another Acc^t.

May 24th

I left Leicester at 5 o'Clock arrived in Manchester at 5 the same Evening, where I stopped all night and taking Chaise early the following Morning got home to Breakfast. Rd. Hodgkinson.

Notes

1 Chunee the elephant was a prime attraction at the Exeter Exchange. In 1826 the beast threatened to destroy its cage. Civilian and Military firing squads failed to kill the unfortunate animal, but before a cannon could be brought to bear, Chunee was killed with a harpoon.

2 John Davies is noted in *Boyle's Court Guide* and lived at 18 Upper Berkeley Square.

3 A London directory says the business was that of jeweller and silversmith.

4 Hodgkinson's ire is directed against Thomas Augustine Arne's most popular opera, *Artaxerxes*. The performance on the day of Hodgkinson's visit was followed by a farce, *Deaf as a Post*, and an extravaganza called *Zoroaster, or the Spirit of the Star*, and described as a 'new grand Egyptian tale of enchantment'. Madam Vestris sang the male lead and Miss Stephens sang the role of Mandane.

10

John Hodgkinson, Sailor in the French Wars

HMS *Intrepid*: Thursday, 23rd November, 1797. Wind SSE, Course N26 degrees. Lat: 44' 46" North. Long: 30' 40" West.

For four days the sixty-four-gun HMS *Intrepid* had been driven before a raging autumn storm in the North Atlantic. Fresh gales increased to strong and as the warship plunged through a heavy swell hands were sent aloft to shorten sail. At 6am in the cold dark hours before dawn the mainsail and stay sail split in the wild winds. A few hours later tragedy struck.

The Ship's log records: 'At 11 in a heavy roll Shipped a great Quantity of Water. A few Minutes later a more heavier Sea threw the Gangways under the Water at which time Captain Parker being alone in his Cabin endeavouring (as was supposed) to save a Portable Desk in which his private Papers were kept, fell with it thro' the aftermost Port.

'He was first seen swimming by the Gentlemen in the Ward Room who instantly ran up and gave Orders to set away the Life Buoys and to throw out any thing which might be of use to save him. He was seen several Minutes in the Water, yet it was thought improfitable for a Boat to live if lowered down. Thus finished a valuable Officer and a worthy Gentleman. (Signed by) J. Clementson, Ext. of Capt. Parker.[1]

One witness of this tragic drama was nineteen-year-old John Hodgkinson, the nephew of Richard Hodgkinson. John had been destined for the life of a handloom weaver in a Chowbent cottage until, 'on thursday the fifteenth of December in 1796, ten Minutes before seven by my Grand Father's watch', he secretly left home and ran off to Liverpool to join the Royal Navy. Orphaned in childhood, John was pursued by his

Aunt Wright (Richard Hodgkinson's older sister) who was anxious to take him back home, but the weather was stormy and she could not get out to the recruits' rendezvous vessel, HMS *Actaeon*, anchored in the River Mersey. The *Actaeon*, with its complement of eighty crew and 485 conscripts garnered from towns and villages throughout Lancashire, set sail for Portsmouth where John had a dramatic introduction to life in the Royal Navy.

On 1 April 1797 he was drafted to serve aboard the third rater HMS *Intrepid*, at anchor at Spithead after refitting. Little more than two weeks later the Channel Fleet was sundered by mutiny. Abominable food, low pay and brutal discipline, with too many officers forsaking leadership for the lash, had brought festering discontent to the lower decks. After a month of high tension limited concessions were made, the mutineers were pardoned and on 15 May the Spithead warships were again under Admiralty control – just days after a new mutiny had begun at the Nore. This second mutiny brought down the terrible wrath and revenge of the Admiralty and ended in much bloodshed, with twenty-nine sailors being hanged.

During the Spithead Mutiny the *Intrepid* was moved to an anchorage at St Helen's, off the Isle of Wight, and its crew was reported as being in 'a very refractory state'. The mutiny over, *Intrepid* was ordered to St Helena in the South Atlantic to escort a fleet of East Indiamen. On the return voyage the *Intrepid*, after a skirmish with a French privateer, headed far north into the Atlantic and into the storm that led to the death of Captain Parker.

Before joining the Navy, John had been an apprentice machine maker in the business owned by William Cannon. He had also been left a watch by his grandfather Hodgkinson with instructions to sell it and use the proceeds to set himself up in business as a handloom weaver. The tedium of life in a Chowbent cottage had little appeal for a healthy young man, and no doubt he was seduced by thoughts of glory and an £18 bounty into joining the Navy. He enlisted as an ordinary seaman, but on 1 July 1800 was promoted to able seaman. For two years he was Captain of the Afterguard, stationed on the poop to work the aftersails. Then for three years he was Captain of the Forecastle, a position given only to the best seaman. He was also at some time Bowman, the leading oarsman, of the Captain's barge.

The young Hodgkinson experienced the rigours of being at sea for weeks on end when, in April 1798, the *Intrepid* was despatched to the China Station where it had a mysterious and unresolved encounter with enemy warships. In January 1799 the British ships, *Intrepid, Arrogant* and *La Virginie*, sailed out of Macao Road in line of battle to seek two large Spanish frigates and two French frigates. Both squadrons anchored in the night, said a British report, and in the morning the enemy was not to be seen, 'their running away from a force so much inferior to their own is not otherwise to be accounted for, but from their dread of a conflict that would in all probability have terminated in their disgrace . . . '. The enemy account differs and the *Manila Gazette* claimed it was the English ships that had turned tail.[2] Young Hodgkinson's view was that 'They chased all day but in the night we lost them.'

John was an observer of momentous events in May 1799, when the *Intrepid* cruised with a British fleet off the coast of western India, a threatening presence which kept the French Navy at bay while British troops destroyed the army of Tippu Sultan, the Tiger of Mysore.

The Spithead Mutiny might have eased the lot of the lower deck but brutality and fear of the lash were still a force for discipline. After nearly eighteen months away from home, and while sailing off Trincomalee, the Ceylon naval base, the *Intrepid* was a deeply troubled ship. During the month of August 1799, seven men were fastened to gratings and flogged with the cat-o'-nine-tails before the assembled ship's company for offences against naval discipline. On the first of the month, Jas. Beason received twelve lashes for sleeping at his post. Three days later, Jacob Cornelius was rescued by a ship's boat after jumping overboard, an indiscretion he compounded with insolence and paid for with twenty-four lashes. On 6 August, Jas. Freason and Wm. Piper each received twelve lashes for fighting, followed on 10 August by a dozen lashes each for seamen John Poor and Thomas Ayres for a similar offence. On 31 August a terrible example was made of John Short who was brutally flayed with forty-eight lashes of the cat for 'mutinous expressions and insolence'. This savage demonstration of authority appears to have had a salutary effect on the crew and no punishments were logged for the succeeding weeks. John Hodgkinson later recorded: 'I never had the misfortune to be punished, tho often deserving it.'

The *Intrepid* stayed away from her home port until 1803 but John was taken from the ship at Cape Town suffering from a leg ulcer. After twenty days in hospital, and just before the Cape was handed back to the Dutch, he was invalided home on HMS *Brave*, formerly the *Braave* when captured by Elphinstone at Saldhana Bay in 1796. John's naval days were not yet over, and in the second French War he served aboard the guard ships *Puissant* and *Royal William* at Portsmouth.

John Hodgkinson and his sister Mary were the children of Richard Hodgkinson's elder brother, Joseph, who married Catherine Norris. Their parents' lives were short and by 1791 John and Mary were orphans, with little education to ease their lowly lot. Their uncle Richard appears to have shouldered some responsibility for their welfare, even though he did not accept the children into his house. Mary, badly burned in a childhood accident, drifted away from Chowbent and worked in mills in Bury and Oldham. Before her death in 1826 she visited her uncle annually, but only rarely contacted her brother.

With his seafaring days over, John became a waterman at Gosport, ferrying passengers to and from Portsmouth for a few coppers a trip, making a wage of 10s a week when times were good. John and Richard Hodgkinson carried on an intermittent correspondence for more than forty years. There was a strong bond of affection from John towards his uncle's family and his sentimental memories are very moving. Apart from family news and gossip the letters make mention of John's naval service, the lingering plight of the handloom weavers, the arrival of the Penny Post, John's later life as a waterman at Gosport and the threat to his livelihood from the arrival in 1844 of the first steam ferry. Despite being pressed by his uncle, John was a modest and God-fearing man and reluctant to boast about his naval service. He wrote laconically of the events he witnessed which helped to change the face of the world forever.

In the correspondence that follows, Richard Hodgkinson's letters are, as usual, models of composition; John's letters are reproduced, so far as possible, just as they were written.

The Letters of John Hodgkinson

Braave, Spithead   May 31, 1803

Dear uncle, I have the pleasure to infaurm you that I am safe arrived at Spithead in H.M. Ship Braave from the Cape of good hope. I had the misfortune to be left in the hospetal at the Cape when the Intrepid[3] sailed. I got well six weeks after, we left the Cape the 5 of march. I am verry sorry to hear that we hare going to war with the french so soon but howheaver I keep my spirits up in hopes of seeing peace one day or other. Dear uncle, I got invalided at the cape and I expect to be sent to the hospetal every day to stand the over haul, and wat ship I shall be drafted on bord of I can not tell.

Dear uncle, when I was in Spithead last you wished me to make a will to my Sister, but at that time it did not lay in my power for Captain Hargood would not sign a will or power to anney one excepting a mother, wife or child, but you may depend upon it that as soon as I am on bord of my respective ship I will make one out and send it to you. I had allmost forgot to inform you that we Captured a french east indiaman in the Chanel valued at one hundred thousand pounds.

Dear uncle, as soon as our Ship is paid I shall remit the most of my wages home. Dear uncle if you posable can, inform me where my sister lives . . . your afectionate nephew,   John Hodgkinson.

La Puissant, Spithead   June 12, 1803
I am very happy to hear that your fammaly hare In good health as I am at presant. Thanks be to god for it. Dear uncle, I will explain to you wat is maint by invalided when I was left at the Cape of Good hope. Our Ship sailed and left me and more sick in the hospetall and wee was sent on bord of the braave before wee got well, and doctor patterson, who was the head doctor, Invalided us on that accaunt because the Cape was delevered to the dutch.

Dear uncle, it was my intention to have sent my aunt wright four or five Pounds but as she is married to Thomas Hindley I have haltered my mind. Dear uncle, I am verry glad to hear that my sister was at plat fould and in good health but I think she could get a place that would be much better for her than a factory. Dear uncle, I expect to receive my wages on tewsday next and I shall remit the most of it to the wire ofice in Leigh, where you can recaeve it, and if my Poor unfortunate Sister should be in want I will be verry glad if you will remit her wat mony you think nececary. Dear uncle, I belong to the Le Puissant Sheer hulk at spithead.

John Hodgkinson

Portsmouth   June 28, 1803
I as have remited forty Pounds wich you will resaive at the Wire ofice in Leigh,   John Hodgkinson

Puissant, Spithead   September 23, 1803
I have been 8 weeks on bord of our Schoner in the channel and I left my clothes on board and when I came back all my Cloths were stolen, and if you will send me five Pounds, for I am in great distress, I shall do verry well.

Dear uncle, I am verry much obliged to you for your kind atention to my Sister and me and all that I am afraid of is that it will never be in pour to return your kindness . . .   John Hodgkinson.

Plate 48 The old parish church at Leigh, with the vicarage in the background (Wigan Heritage Services)

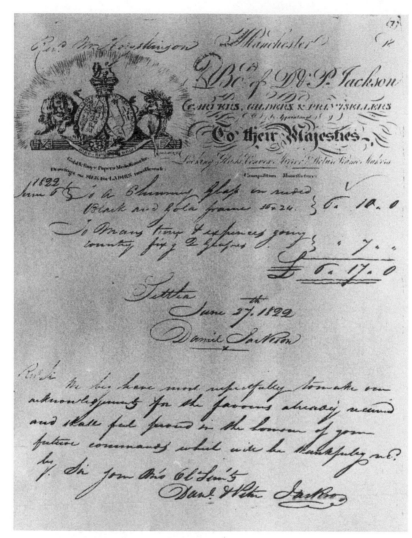

Plate 49a   (and opposite) Accounts from a Manchester shop where Joseph Hodgkinson bought furniture for the vicarage at Leigh (LRO DDX 211/1)

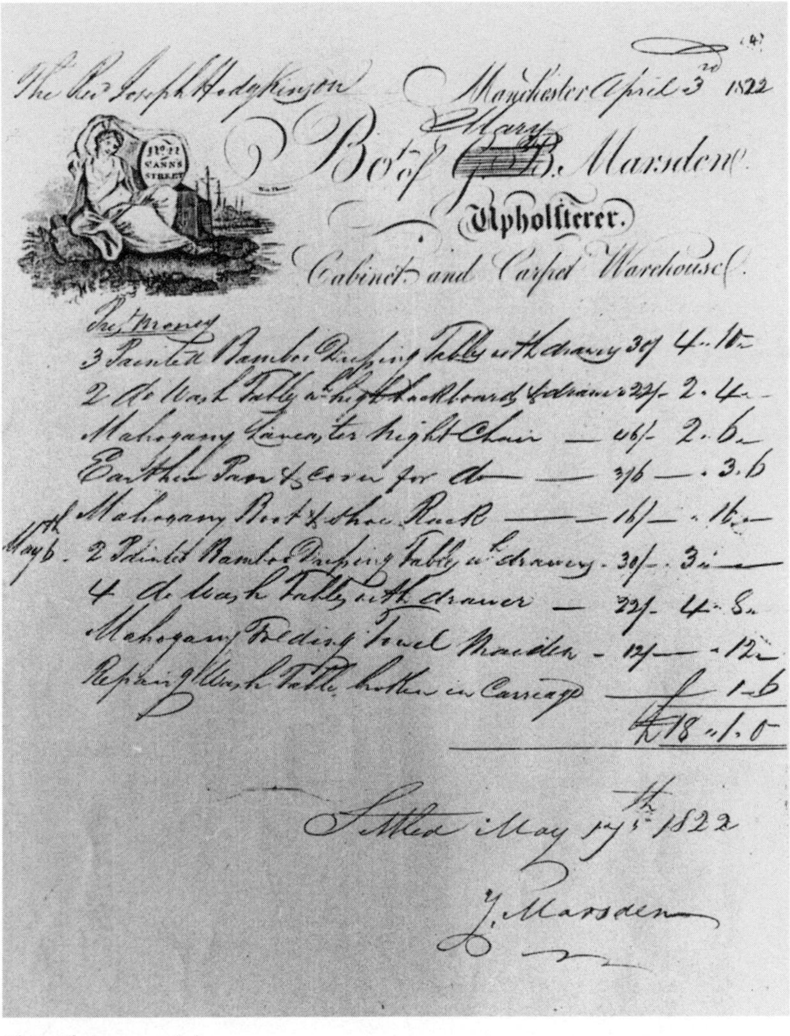

(4)

The Revd Joseph Hodgkinson Manchester April 3rd 1822

No. 11 CANN'S STREET

Bot. of ~~J.~~ Mary B. Marsden

Upholsterer.

Cabinet and Carpet Warehouse.

Recd Money

	3 Painted Bamboo Dressing Tables with drawers	30/	4.10.–
	2 Do Wash Tables with high backboards & drawers	22/-	2.4.–
	Mahogany Lancaster Night Chair	46/-	2.6.–
	Earthen Pan & cover for do	3/6	.3.6
	Mahogany Boot & Shoe Rack	16/	.16.–
17th May 6	2 Painted Bamboo Dressing Tables with drawers	30/-	3.–.–
	4 Do Wash Tables with drawer	22/-	4.8.–
	Mahogany Folding Towel Maiden	12/	.12.–
	Repairing Wash Table broken in Carriage		1.6
			£18.1.0

Settled May 17th 1822

J. Marsden

Plate 49b (see opposite)

TERMS OF ADMISSION
OF INSANE PATIENTS, OR LUNATICS, UNDER THE CARE OF
DR. ARNOLD, and Dr. Hill

At his House for their Reception, adjoining to his own House of BELLE-GROVE, LEICESTER.

I. *Separate Apartments.*

1. FIVE GUINEAS PER WEEK.——They who pay this price have the largest and best Apartments. Each Male is allowed a Man, and each Female a Woman Servant; and every proper and reasonable Indulgence suitable to the disorder.

2. FOUR GUINEAS PER WEEK.——These have the same privileges and treatment as those at five Guineas per Week, excepting the difference of not having the best Apartments.

3. THREE GUINEAS AND HALF PER WEEK.——Their Apartments are not quite so elegant; but each has a separate Room and Servant, and is treated in other respects nearly in the same manner as those who pay four Guineas per Week.

II. *Associated Apartments:*

TWO GUINEAS PER WEEK.——These have convenient Rooms allotted to them; but not separate Rooms, or separate Servants.

III. *The Lodge.*

This is a detached Building, with Wards for each Sex, and Courts for air and exercise.
Of this Department there are Three Classes.

1. ONE GUINEA AND HALF PER WEEK.——These have neither a separate Servant, nor a separate Room; but are more nicely dieted and lodged than those in the under-mentioned classes.

2. TWENTY-FIVE SHILLINGS PER WEEK.—These are better dieted than Patients at——

3. ONE GUINEA PER WEEK.——These are not allowed Tea, and their diet is more restricted than those of the superior Classes.

When it is suitable to the state of their disorder they walk in Courts or Gardens, appropriated to *each Class and Sex, who* are upon all occasions kept entirely separate. The three first Classes are attended in their walks by their several Servants.

All Patients are allowed Tea to Breakfast, excepting those who pay only one Guinea per Week. None are allowed Tea in the Afternoon, but such as pay for that indulgence, which in general is improper.

No Patient of any kind is taken for less than a quarter of a year. If therefore any be taken away for any cause whatever, whether cured or not, before the expiration of the first Quarter, the whole quarter must nevertheless be paid for. The same rule is observed in case of Death.

INCURABLES.

INCURABLE PATIENTS in the SEPARATE APARTMENTS, pay, 1. *Four Guineas and Half per Week.*—2. *Three Guineas and Half per Week.*—3. *Three Guineas per Week.* In the ASSOCIATED APARTMENTS *Thirty-six Shillings per Week.* In the LODGE, 1. *Twenty-seven Shillings per Week.*—2. *Twenty-one Shillings per Week.*—3. *Forty Pounds per Annum.*

BELLE-GROVE, LEICESTER, January 1, 1813.

Plate 50   Terms of admission to Dr Hill's asylum in Leicester (LRO DDX 211/6)

Plate 51   Memorial to Joseph Hodgkinson in Leigh parish church

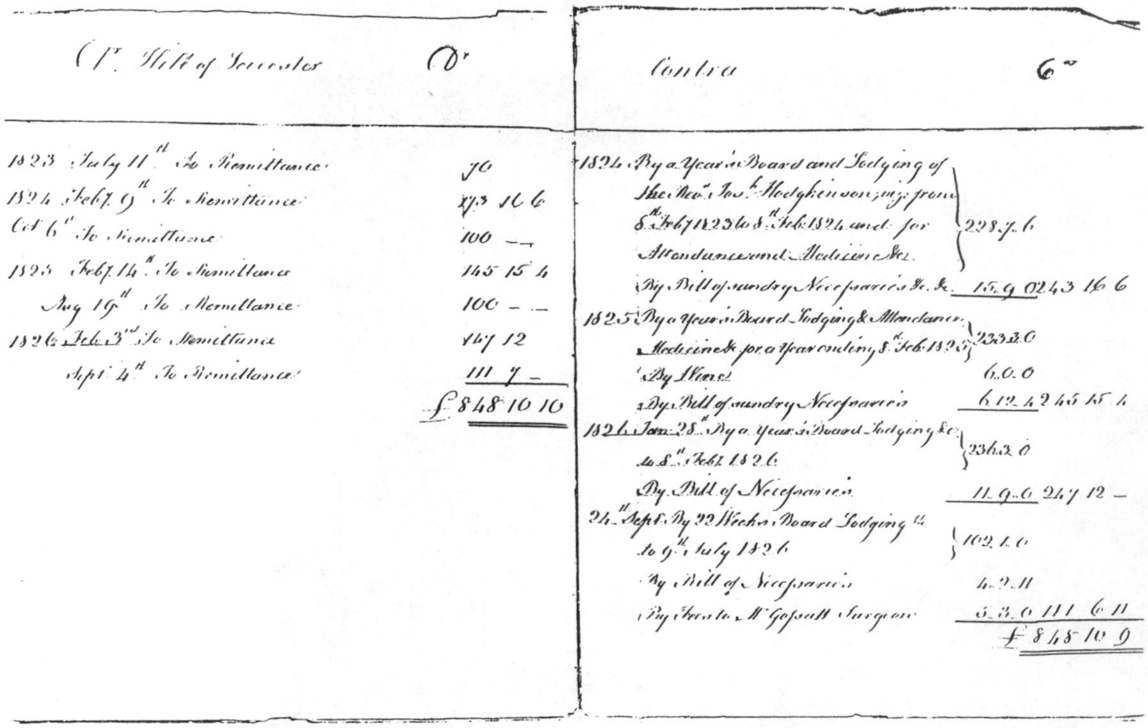
Dr. Hill of Lancaster Dr

1823 July 11th To Remittance	70
1824 Feby 9th To Remittance	173 16 6
Oct 6th To Remittance	100 – –
1825 Feby 14th To Remittance	145 15 4
Aug 19th To Remittance	100 – –
1826 Feb 3rd To Remittance	147 12
Sept 4th To Remittance	111 7 –
	£848 10 10

Contra Cr

1824 By a Year's Board and Lodging of the Revd Jos. Hodgkinson, viz. from 8th Feby 1823 to 8th Feb 1824 and for Attendance and Medicine &c.	228.7.6	
By Bill of sundry Necessaries &c. &c.	15.9.0	243 16 6
1825 By a Year's Board Lodging & Attendance Medicine &c. for a Year ending 8th Feb 1825	233.3.0	
By Wine	6.0.0	
By Bill of sundry Necessaries	6.12.4	245 15 4
1826 Jan 28th By a Year's Board Lodging &c. to 8th Feb 1826	236.3.0	
By Bill of Necessaries	11.9.0	247 12 –
24th Sept By 22 Weeks Board Lodging &c. to 9th July 1826	102.4.0	
By Bill of Necessaries	4.2.11	
By Fees to Mr Gossatt Surgeon	5.3.0	111 6 11
		£848 10 9

Plate 52 The price of tragedy – Richard Hodgkinson kept meticulous accounts of the cost of keeping Joseph in Dr Hill's asylum (LRO DDX 211/6)

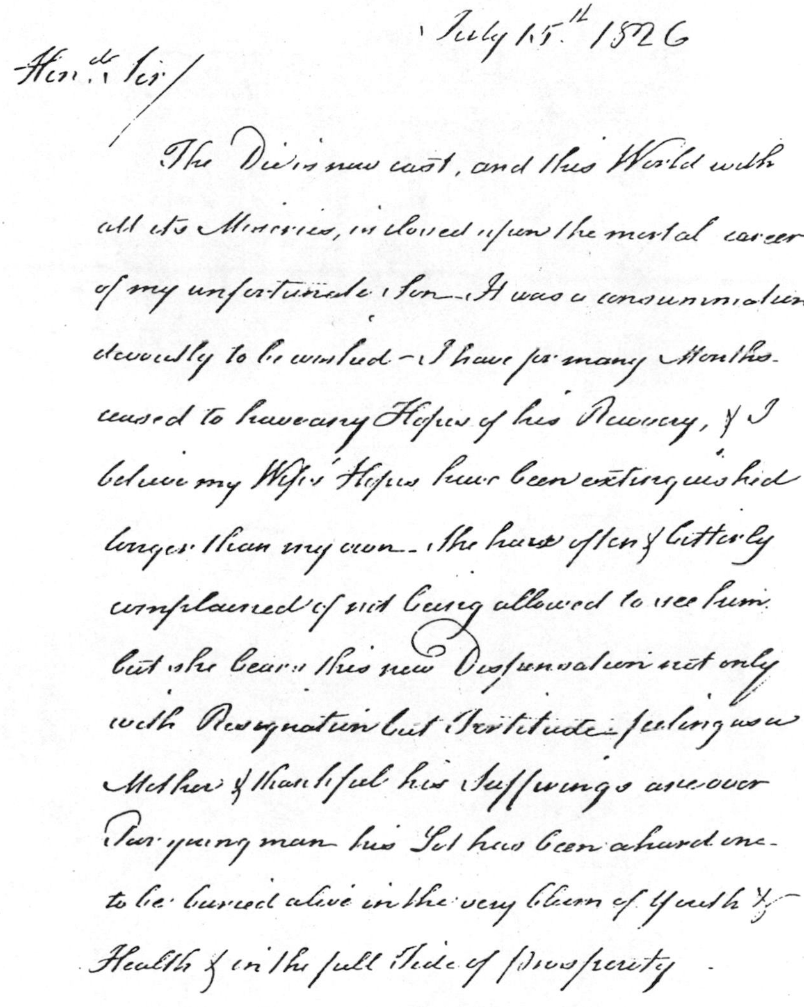

July 15th 1826

Honod Sir

The Die is now cast, and this World with all its Miseries, is closed upon the mortal career of my unfortunate Son — It was a consummation devoutly to be wished — I have for many Months ceased to have any Hopes of his Recovery, & I believe my Wife's Hopes have been extinguished longer than my own — she has often & bitterly complained of not being allowed to see him but she bears this new Dispensation not only with Resignation but Gratitude — feeling as a Mother & thankful his Sufferings are over Poor young man his Lot has been a hard one — to be buried alive in the very bloom of Youth & Health & in the full Tide of Prosperity .

Plate 53   Richard Hodgkinson's letter to Dr Hill reflecting on Joseph's death owes more than a passing acknowledgement to Shakespeare's _Hamlet_. The letter begins, 'Hon. Sir, The Die is now cast, and this World with all its Miseries, is closed upon the mortal career of my unfortunate son. It was a consummation devoutly to be wished.' (LRO DDX 211/6)

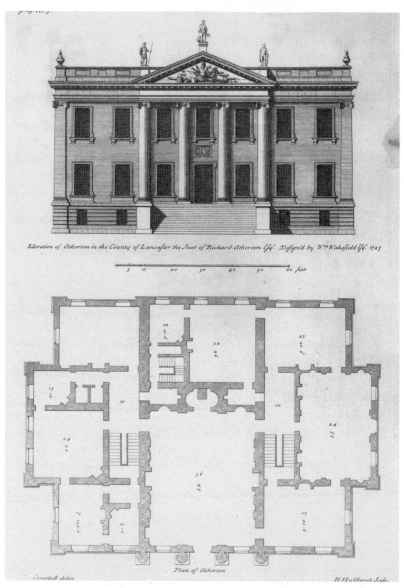

Elevation of Atherton in the County of Lancaster the Seat of Richard Atherton Esq. Design'd by W.ᵐ Wakefield Esq. 1723

Plan of Atherton

Plate 54   An architect's drawing of Atherton New Hall, completed in 1742 and demolished in 1825 (Manchester Public Libraries, Local Studies Unit)

Plate 55 Procession of the London mail coaches. 'As soon as I had dined the Waiter came to tell me that all the Mail Coaches were passing by in procession . . . the sight was very pleasing. Each Coach drawn by 4 fine Horses, many of them in entire new Harnesses, Coachmen and Guards in new scarlet Liveries, and the whole followed by the Postboys, on horseback in new scarlet jackets.': Richard Hodgkinson (British Museum)

OF PENSIONERS.

THE number of Pensioners now maintained in the Hospital are 2,710. Every boatswain is allowed 2s. 6d.—every mate, 1s. 6d.—and every private man, 1s. per week, for pocket-money.

They are also allowed, in the space of two years, a blue suit of clothes, a hat, three pair of blue worsted hose, four pair of shoes, four shirts, and a great coat, if necessary. Their diet consists of one loaf of bread of sixteen ounces, and two quarts of beer, every day,—one pound of mutton on Sunday and Tuesday,—one pound of beef on Monday, Thursday and Saturday,—pease-soup, cheese, and butter, on Wednesday and Friday.

Persons admitted into the Hospital as Pensioners are examined at the Admiralty-office (at present on the first and third Thursday in every Month,) and are selected from seamen and marines recently discharged in an extreme state of debility, or from such of the Out-Pensioners, as from age, long service, or debility. are no longer able to contribute to their maintenance or support.

Plate 56   Greenwich pensioners 'have flesh meat every day of the week, Mutton 4 days and Beef 3. Allowance three Quarters of a Pound to each man every day.': Richard Hodgkinson (National Maritime Museum)

Plate 57 'Pensioners have many indulgences and but little personal restraint. On each side of the Lobby are small cupboards in which each man can put his Pipe and Tobacco and his Beer, of which he is allowed two Quarts each day.': Richard Hodgkinson (National Maritime Museum, 9036)

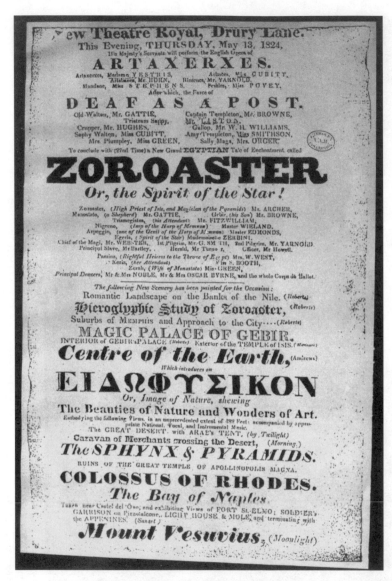

Plate 58 'Of all species of stage Entertainments the Opera is to me the most disagreeable and disgusting.': Richard Hodgkinson (collection of the Theatre Museum, by courtesy of the Victoria and Albert Museum)

Plate 59   Daunted by the prospect of becoming a cottage handloom weaver in Chowbent,
John Hodgkinson left his Chowbent home in secret in 1797 and joined the Royal Navy

Plate 60   A sixty-four-gun third-rater similar to the *Intrepid* on which John Hodgkinson
served (National Maritime Museum, C342)

Plate 61 Life below decks on a warship in port. While serving for some weeks on a schooner in the Channel in 1803, John Hodgkinson had all his clothes stolen after leaving them on the *Puissant* at Portsmouth (National Maritime Museum, B2629)

Plate 62   Tipoo Sultan. In the third Mysore War, ableseaman John Hodgkinson served on
board the *Intrepid*, part of the fleet keeping the French at bay while General George Harris
attacked Seringabatam. The campaign ended in victory for the English forces and the death
of Tipoo Sultan (Victoria and Albert Museum)

Plate 63 Heavy weather for a waterman making the crossing from Gosport to Portsmouth, (*Portsmouth*, by J.M.W. Turner, 1825). In 1833, John Hodgkinson earned one penny per passenger in fair weather and threepence in foul (City of Portsmouth Leisure Service)

Spithead   October 5, 1803
I resaved the five pound note wich you was so kind as to send me. I
whold not have sent for it if I had not met with that misfortune, but I
shall take your advice and keep myself to myself. We have verry little
news hear except that the french is expected hevery day and great preparations hare making for there arival, wich I hope if they do come they will
get it to there hearts content. We hare prepared for them and if they make
that bold atempt to land upon our little spot of ground I am afraid they
will forget to find there way back. We have a good captain and good ofi-
cers and I like the Ship verry well and am verry well content in my
Station.   [Not signed]

Puissant, Spithead   November 6, 1803
I am under the necessity once more of trobleing you for money, for to tell
you the plain truth I am going to be married, and if you will be so kind as
to send me twenty five pounds I shall take it as a grait favour. Dear uncle,
the young woman is of a verry respecttable family and of good carrector.
The remaining ten Pounds I shall lave with you for my Sister to buy her
cloths. I am verry sorry that I should be so troublesome to you but this
will be the last time.
    Dear uncle, it was my Intention if I had been Discharged from the
Service to Settle at home, but now I think I shall follow the Sea. Give my
kind love to my aunt and cozens.   [Not signed]

Puissant, Portsmouth   Aprill 12, 1804
. . . it has been my Intention this som time back to have gone to the East
Indies, but I am in hopes it will be a peace Shortly, and here I intend to
Settle here. Dear uncle, I am under the necessaty of Sending to you for
five Pounds wich I hope you will be so kind as to send me.
                                                                      John Hodgkinson

Spithead   May 25, 1804
I resaved the five Pounds wich you was so kind as to send me and am
verry thankful for the same, but I have much raison to think that you
must be verry angry with me for not writing an answer sooner, but I had
the misfortune to hurt my right hand three days before I resaved your letter. But thanks be to god, it is got much better and I hope you will be so
kind as to forgive me for the same.   John Hodgkinson.

Puissant, Spithead   May 15, 1806
I hope this will Find you and Family in Good Health and hope your
Goodness will Excuse me my being a Stranger to you at presant: and hope
it will not be so long. I write to Inform you my Husband and myself are
very Well and shall be very happy to hear from You and all Friends. I
much wish to know how Mary Hodgkinson is, whether She is Dead or
Alive, and Sincerely hope you will Excuse my Husband for his being so
Neglectful in not writing. He has Often thought of writing but knowing
himself Guilty of Neglectfulness has hindered him from doing himself that
Pleasure. Therefore I take it upon Myself and hope you will forgive him
and that we may have the Happiness of Receiving an Answer from you
soon.

I beg leave to Inform you that I have been married to your Nephew 12
months next 28th of May coming, and my Family belong to Halifax in
Yorkshire and hope soon that the War may be over as it is Our Intention
to come home, and hope with the blessing of God we may be happy
among Our Relations, and I have the Pleasure, Dear Sir, of Remaining,
                                      Elizabeth Hodgkinson, humble servant

Gosport   January 26, 1815
. . . I have nothing to say in excuse for my long neglect notwithstanding
wich I have not forgot my friends . . . . I am happy to inform you that I
am discharged from HM Service after 17 years and 9 months servitude. I
Shall go to London the first thursday in march to pass the admiralty board
as I understand I am intitled to fourteen Pounds per year.

Dear uncle, it grieves me at this moment that it is upwards of 18 years
since to think how I left you when I had neither father or mother, when
you was so richly supplying there place, but I hope your goodness will
forgive me. I was young and inexperienced in the world. I am at presant
working as a waterman. My wife died three years ago in a decline. I am
married again, we have had one child a little girl wich died in october last.
I am told that trade is in a flourishing way in Lancashire and in hopes with
a peace with America will Improve it.   John Hodgkinson

Atherton   3rd February, 1815
Dear John, Since the last correspondence we had together which is now
many years ago, I have not met with anyone who had seen you or could
give any acct. of you, nor have I been able to learn whether during the
last War you have been chiefly resident in England or employed in foreign service. I should be glad to be informed whether you ever received

any wound in the Service and whether you have at present the perfect use of all your limbs and whether your general health has suffered in any material degree from the length of your Service, change of climate &c.

Your Sister, Mary, has been to see us generally once in a year at least. When she was last with us, which is a few months ago, she was employed in a Factory at Bury, abt six miles from Bolton. From the serious injury she received by being so severely burned in her infancy, she is not capable of doing the best sort of work in a Factory and of course cannot get the best Wages. She will be very glad when she knows I have heard from you.

Your Aunt and Myself are both in good health as are all our Children, all of whom are living that we ever had. Mary, David and Jane are resident at home and Joseph is a student and lives at Oxford, preparatory to his going into Holy Orders. Your Aunt Wright is in a very distressed situation. She was severely struck with the Palsy 4 or 5 years ago and about 2 months since had another stroke which has deprived her of the use of her speech and she is yet very far from being able to speak intelligibly. She has been married many years to one Thos. Hindley, a Weaver, and lives as all other poor people do.

Trade is not so flourishing as one might expect. The Wages of a Weaver are one third less than they were last year at this time. It is very much feared that the Cotton Manufacture will meet with great Rivalship on the Continent.

You need not pay the Postage of your letters when you write.

Rd Hodgkinson

Gosport   25th March, 1815
I have been principaly employed on the Royal William and Puissant guardships at Spithead during the late war and I am sorry to say I have been very neglectful in not writeing to my friends at home. I am happy to inform you that I enjoy a good state of health and never had the misfortune to be wounded.

I received a hurt about 12 years since in my left Leg but I got the better of that in a bout 6 months. Four weeks ago I went to London, I was there 12 days. The Lords of the Admiralty gave me 14 Pounds height Shillings per year, with this restriction, in case of another war breaking out I must serve again when called upon or throw up my Pension.[4] I am afraid it will not be long before that will be the Case, as I understand our old friend Bonaparte is come back to Paris. It was my intention if the Pease had been established to have come down to Lancashire and followed the weaving business.

I should be verry happy to hear from my Sister. I very well remember the time she was burnt. It is 30 years since I had the pleasure of seeing an only Sister. John Hodgkinson.

Gosport 2nd March, 1819

It is upwards of four years since I wrote last . . . . Please god, in april or may I intend to come down to see you for a few days. I mean to come alone as it will two long a journey for my Wife and family wich is now increased with two Children a boy and a girl. I still follow the imployment of a waterman it's a dull trade at present like all others. I heard from my Sister about two years ago. She then lived in Oldham. I met a young man a short time since, a native of Chowbent. He informed me that you was well in health and that he saw you about 3 months ago. You mentioned that my Cousin Joseph was at oxford and as I intend walking my way to manchester lays through that City. I should like to see him if he is still there, if agreable to you. John Hodgkinson.

Haslar Road, Gosport June 1, 1819

I am happy to inform you that I got home safe on Wensday, 26th. My Mother's relations would not let me leave manchester before monday. I slept in London on teusday night and next evening landed in gosport . . . . John Hodgkinson.

Gosport 14 May, 1831

I defered writeing to you from time to time until I was Ashemed of my self. I have been unwell for this five or six weeks with a voilent pain in my back, but am recovered. My Situation in Life is nearly the same as when I was with you. I follow the Employment of a ferry or Waterman. It is 12 years this month since I was down in Lancashire. I was informed of poor Joseph's Death in a letter from my Sister.

. . . I wrote two Letters to my Sister 2 years ago and got no answer, wich makes me conjecture she is removed or dead. If you have heard let me know in your answer. Give my kind love to my dear Aunt and tell her I Should be glad to see her once more. I believe she is 68. It appears to me as yesterday that I saw her going in the North Door of the Church to be Married with a Cheek like a Rose. Excuse my noncence. Your afectionate Nephew, John Hodgkinson.

Atherton   May 23, 1831

Dear John, I was not aware that you was unacquainted with your Sister's Death which happened at the place she was working at near Oldham five years ago. I was informed she was sick and I sent Richard Wright over to her with some Money, to provide for her which she might be in want of. In a short time after this she died and I sent Rd. Wright again with Money to pay all Funeral Expenses and to stay and see her decently interred, which he did. She had been in the same Lodgings several years of which she always spoke as being very comfortable.

David is married and has 2 little Daughters. He lives at Plat-fold, I and your Aunt having given it up to him when he was married, and I have now no Farm but I retain the Stewardship.

Your cousins Mary and Jane have both large families, each having had 9 children out of which Mary has buried one and Jane two. So you see tho' I had a small Family of my own I am likely to have a large one at last. The respective Families are all well and the Children healthy and all perfect in Senses, Limbs and Eyesight. I am very sorry to inform you that your Aunt is very far from being as well as her Friends could wish. She is not feeble or decrepit in her Limbs, in that respect she is stouter than most women of her Age, but she is afflicted with an internal Complaint, the palpitation of the Heart, which keeps her in constant agitation depriving her both of Appetite and Sleep. She will be seventy years of Age the first of next Month.

Your cousin Wrights are as poor and as helpless as ever. They have Sickness in the House at present and David and I are assisting them daily. It is only last week that I have had to pay their Rent. I suppose you know your Aunt Berry is dead and your Uncle yet living. His son John is an idle character. James is carrying on an extensive Trade as a Corn Flour Dealer and I have reason to believe he has already acquired at least two thousand Pounds.

Enclosed I have sent you a £5 Bank of England Note which your Aunt joins in presenting to you for your three Children.   Rd. Hodgkinson.

Gosport   28th May 1831

I return you my most sincere thanks with Gratitude for the 5 Pound note you had the goodness to send me. It came on my berth Day, I am 53 years Old. I am very sorry my Aunt enjoys a poor state of health, but the Almighty is alsufficient, he never puts more than we are able to bear that put there trust and faith in him. My Sister, my Aunt Wright, My Uncle Berry and his family and I myself have been a burthen to you, but I know you find the reward in your Breast, knowing you have done a father's part to the fatherless and widow, and the Lord will reward you for it.

John Hodgkinson

Gosport   9th October, 1833

Honorored Uncle and Aunt, This comes with our kind Love . . . hopeing John, Jane and David are fine healthy Children. John works with me in the boat and is turned of 15. Jane assists her Mother and was 17 last june. David I keep at School and he will be 13 next march, and they all attend the Sunday School of the established Church. Have the goodness to let me know how trade is in Lancashire.

John Hodgkinson.

Atherton   30th October, 1833

Enclosed I have sent a £5 Bank of England Note to enable you to keep David at School a little longer than otherwise it probably might not be convenient for you to do.

Silk Weaving is now carried on to great extent in Leigh Parish, a weaver may earn from 7/s to 12/s a Week. A Cotton Weaver not more than from 5/s to 8/s. I am very sorry to say that the Masters are beginning to reduce the Wages of the Weavers in both Manufactures.

Richard Wright continues in the same low circumstances as heretofore. The Health of his Family has certainly not been good. His Sister Mary has been dead some time. John Wright died at Sea a great many Years ago. Joseph deserted his family I should think 20 years ago. It has been said he resides at Glasgow, but I believe nothing certain is known of him in his Family.

I should like to know what parts of the Globe you have sailed to and how long you were at Sea. I think you once told me you had never been wounded.

Rd. Hodgkinson

Haslar Road, Gosport   November 5, 1833

I will now tell you what I did with five P Note you had the goodness to send me in May, 1831. My Boat was old and out of repair, in fact she was passed it. Upon averige I earn about ten Shillings per Week but a good deal of our work depends upon Chance.[5] My Wife goes out two or three days in the week to wash and oirning and I belong to a Bennifit Socioety. In Sickness I receive 10 shillings per week. At the Death of a Member the Wife receives 10 pounds, and the Death of the Wife, the man has five, and whenever I am passed my Labour I Shall receive 5 Shillings per week for Life, and my Pention is fourteen Pounds Eight Shillings. If you remember I shoed you my Pention ticket and two or three certificates of

Charrecter, but you went to London sometime before I left your house and most likeley it slipt your memory.

If I lives untill the 11th of next month it will be 37 years since I left Chowbent. At this a tear is running down my cheek for my Ingratitude to you. I have before me now your first Letter dated January 21, 1798. You stated you was sorry at my manner of leaving the Country. It gave rise to ill natured reports concerning your conduct towards me, wich I should have been much hurt to have heard knowing them to be falce. This Letter has been my Companion ever since to put me in mind of my ingratitude. I see in this Letter that Mrs Guest was about Six weeks old so she must be very near 36.

The first 7 years I was in the Intrepid, 64 Guns, princepally in the East Indias, Chinia, the Cape of good hope and St. Hellena. The second War I was on the Home station belonging to the Puissant and Royal William, but Dureing the 18 years of Servitude I did my Duty as a Seaman and Petty officer to the satisfaction of my Superiors. I served some years as Captain of the forecastle and Captain of the Mast and seven years I was Bow man to the Captain's Barge and dureing the whole of the 18 years I never had the misfortune to be punished tho often deserving it. So you see tho a noughty boy I hope I have made a better man. I hope you will excuse me for I am not one of them that like to boast of there good deeds, it is better to come from others. At all events I have never disgraced the name of Hodgkinson and my Boys, I hope, will do the same.

God Bless you, my Honoured Uncle and Aunt and when you lays upon your Death bed you will have that Consolation that you have been a father to the fatherless and a Husband to the Widdow.

John Hodgkinson.

Atherton   26th August, 1836
. . . it appears that yr. last letr. to me is dated the 5th Novr. 1833, of course nearly 3 Years ago. In that time many Changes have taken place and probably some in your Family. In my own I have to inform you of the death of my dear Wife, your affectionate Aunt. She died on the 27th of July after a gradual Decline in health, I may say, almost ever since we so hastily retired from the Farm on giving it up to David on his Marriage, now 10 years ago. My own Health continues as good as ever tho' I am in my 74th year.

To the following Queries I wish you to send Ansrs. in a subsequent Letter at your Leisure as I wish to have them before me in one view.

What is your own Age now and what is the Age of your Wife?
At what time did you leave Chowbent? [Crossed out line reads:
'and what at that time was your particular reason'.]
How long was you a Sailor?
In what Ships did you serve and in what Quarters of the Globe?
In what Capacity was you in board of any of the Ships – if in any
other Capacity than a common Sailor?   Rd. Hodgkinson.

                                                       August 29, 1836
Dear Honoured Uncle, I received your Afflicting letter acqainting me
with the Death of my Beloved Aunt. The Lord Gave and the Lord as
taken away, Blessed be the Name of the Lord. It is hard to poart, you
sufered one great Afliction in the Death of Joseph and now the Partner of
all your Cairs and Troubles is gone to that Blessed abode of the Just, made
Perfect through the Blood of our Saviour Jesus Christ, where I hope we
shall all Sing Hims to Him that Shed is Blood on the Cross for all
Mankind. I must drop the Pen to Shed a few Tears to the Memory of her
who was a Good Wife, a kind Mother and a hard Working Woman.

Jane is a fine healthy young Woman. Her age was 20, the 17th of June
last. She is at home but Princepaly at work in a Neighbours at Waistcoat
making. John, a fine Healthy Strong Lad, the Picture of is Cousen David,
is in a gentleman's yatch caled the Noran, Belonging to one Major Mill.
He was Wounded at the battle of Waterlew. They are in the North of
Ireland. He was in her last Summer Six Months, I expect him home in
about 3 Weeks. He will work with me in the winter as I have got a
Licence for him. His Age is 18, the 14th of August last. William David,
my youngest boy, is not so stout built as John. He is growing fast. He as
been at a Linen Drapers Shop a few weeks, but there Sumers stock being
sold he came home on Saturday and I have sent him to School this morning. I think is Inclenation is towards the sea, like is brother John. He was
fifteen the 11th of March last.

I am a Member of the Hants County Sociaty and pay 1s 9d per month.
Bennifits 10s in Sickness, ten Pounds at the Death of a Member, five
Pounds at the Death of is Wife. My son John as been a Member upwards
of 2 years. He insures for six shillings a week sickness, six pounds on
Death, by paying 1s.1/2d per month.

Dear Uncle, Excuse me for Stateing these trifeling things but I think it
right that every Working man ought to provide something against sickness and not lean to heavy on is Neighbour.   John Hodgkinson

Haslar Road No 14, Gosport   September 3rd, 1836
As I have plenty of room I will Give you answers to the best of my
Recolection to the Queries in your last letter. [In the margin here is writ-
ten '58 last May'.]

In the First Place I was Born in Bolton on the 26th of May, 1778 and
cristened on the 14th of June, as I have my Register before me. My Wife
is a Native of Bury, 2 miles from Gosport. We where Married at
Alverstoke, in the county of Southampton, on the 12 of November,
1813. She was born August, 1788.

On thursday, the fifteenth of December in 1796, ten Minutes Before
seven by my Grand Father's watch,[6] I left Samuel Gregory's, God Bless
Him and his Family for is kindness. I went Direct to Wigan and ingaged
with two overseers, belonging to Rainford, for eighteen guinies to serve
in is Majesties Navy. They mounted me behind one of them and about
nine that Evening got to Rainford. Next day we walked to Liverpool and
fitted out with sailor's clothing with one third of the Bounty. I was found
serviceable and sent on bord HM Ship Action[7] laying in the River. In
your first Letter, my Aunt Wright, you mentioned, came to Liverpool but
the wether was so bad she could not come alongside. On the first of April,
97, I was drafted on bord the Intrepid 64 at Spithead, Commanded by
Captain Robert Parker and proceded to Saint Hellena with a fleet of East
Indiamens. We retook an Irish Brig in the Bay of Biskey from a french
Privateer, but retaken afterwards. In Short, we arived in the Downs
December following. Unfortunately on the Outer Banks of Newfound-
land Captain Parker was washed overbord out of the after-Port in is
Cabbin in a Gale of Wind and was Drownded. When the ship paid at
Spithead I received the remaining two thirds of my Bounty and fooleishly
made a way with it insted of sending part to my Sister, but we cannot put
ould heads on young Shoulders.

From Spithead we sailed for Chinia in april, 1798; arived there in
November with a fleet of East India men. January, 99, in Company with
the Arrogant 72 and Virginia 44 fell in with four Line of Battle Ships,
Spanish, and 2 large french Frigats. They Chased all day but in the night
we lost them. From Chinia we found Admiral Renior[8] on the Mallabar
Coast. At this time General Harriss was Besiageing Serringabatam and the
Admiral in the Suffolk 74, the Victorious 74, the Trident 64, and the
Intrepid 64, was Cruising of Mangelory,[9] the only Seaport Tippos Seab[10]
had left at that time, untill the place was taken by storm by the Troops.
Tringubar belonging to the Deans we took without fighting, it went as a

Droit to the Admiralty. May, 1803, we arived at Spithead after giving the Cape of Good Hope to the Duch. In february, the War being renued, I was kept in the Service untill the Peace.

I was seventeen years in is M Service and eight months; 3 years as Captain of the Fourcastle and 2 years as Captain of the Afterguard. This last war I was in the Puissant and Royal William Guard ships at Spithead.

Dear Uncle I have given you the outlines of my life During the time I was in the Service and if I was young again I would go at my Country's call if wanted.   J. Hodgkinson.

Atherton   September, 1836

My H. continues very good but not so my Spirits, and I perceive that my Powers for Business are beginning to relax, so that I am sometimes more than half inclined to think of retiring altogether.

As a Memorial of your departed Aunt who had always a kind feeling towards you, I inclose a five Pound Bank of England Note, which you will not fail to acknowledge the Receipt as soon as this letter comes to hand.

Mary and her 9 children, David and his 2 and Jane with her 8 are all in good Health. You see I have a goodly Race of Grandchildren, 19 in number, among all of whom there is not a single Defect either in Feature, Limb or Intellect, which calls for my daily Gratitude to the Giver of all Good.   Richard Hodgkinson.

Atherton, near Manchester   20th February, 1838

I finally retired from the Stewardship last Midsummer, Lord Lilford was very reluctant to let me retire but after much Solicitation he consented. A few Months ago he gave a public Dinner to about 140 of his Tenants. His Lordship presided at the table and after Dinner proposed my Health, prefacing it with a long and very flattering Encomium on my Character, acknowledging the great and weighty Obligations himself and his Family owed to me for my long and valuable Services. I continue to live in the same House I have done ever since I left Platfold and I have the same Servant I engaged soon after my Wife's death. She is a very respectable person (a Widow) abt 40 years old.

Mr Jackson's oldest son Robert is out of his Clerkship and is going to London in about a Fortnight to complete his Education as an Attorney. Mrs Jackson has had no more Children nor buried any since I last wrote to you. Mrs Guest has the same number she had having had one born and buried one during the last year. David after being 5 or 6 years without any increase in Family had another Girl born a few Weeks ago making 3 in all. Richard Hodgkinson.

Gosport 28th Febuary, 1838

I enjoy my Pension, Fourteen pounds Eight, and shall dureing Life expect this whig ministry shortens it, as they are cutting everything to pieces. Me and John belongs to the Hants County Society and if he goes to the Mediterranean I will make is payments good.

It is in contemplation to make a floating Bridge from Portsmouth to Gosport. If it takes place it will considerably injure the Watermen and most of the Old men served His Majesty in the War and Fought their Country's Battles. We have two good Advocates against it, Loyds and the Trinity Board. John Hodgkinson.

Gosport May 26, 1838

I received your hansome Preasent, the Five Pound Note. My two Boys Sailed the 3rd of April for Gibralter and Mallega in the Mischief yatch, Captain Lyon owner. In the Hants telegraph of last week she was in Cades. I expect her home in a few days and from there it is thought they will go to Rusia after the Queen's Corranation this 26th of May. I am Sixty years of Age and by looking this morning at the Register of my Age, wich I got when I was in Lancashire last, it sais John the son of Joseph and Catherine Hodgkinson of Great Bolton and was Baptized in Bolton Church on the 14th of June in the year 1778, and on this day 19 years I arived home from Lancashire. John Hodgkinson.

Atherton 23rd Sept 1839

My own Health continues very good but the Infirmities of Old Age are creeping on & gradually increasing. The Families at Plat-fold & Bedford are pretty much in the same State as when I last wrote, but Mr Jackson has had an awfully sudden death in his family. His youngest son, 7½ years, was thrown off a Poney, his foot sticking in the Stirrup and his head on the Ground. He was dragged off the Poney at full gallop over a rocky surface a considerable distance. His head presented, when taken up, a dreadful spectacle, but not a ray of Hope that his life cd be saved. He lingered 36 hours without shewing one single Sympton of Reason or Sensation and expired at 4 o'clock on the Morning of Sunday the 8th inst Sept. Richard Hodgkinson.

Gosport   27th September, 1839
I mentioned in my last letter that John and David was gone to Gibralter in
the Mischief yatch. They returned in about four months, David not liking
the Schooner left, and he prefering a man of war I got a Letter of recommendation from Admiral Patterson, one of my old Captains, to the
Commander of the Victory in ordenary in the Port, the Ship Lord Nelson
lost is life in. He remained in her 12 months and then Drafted in to H M
Ship Curacoe, of 28 guns, bound to Jamaica from thence to South
Ammerica for 2 years. John left the Mischief last saturday week being laid up
for the winter; he was up the medeteranien last winter.   John Hodgkinson.

Atherton   28th October, 1839
I now write inclosing a Bank Note value Five Pounds . . . I do not send
you this supposing you really stand in need of so small a Sum, but it may
nevertheless be usefully employed in the Purchase of some additional
Article of Furniture, or a Article of Dress, and it keeps up a Connection
with the Family. I continue in my usual good Health but I daily feel the
Infirmities (in a slight degree as yet) of old Age creeping upon me. I rise
early as usual, I live temperately, and take moderate Exercise, all of which
no doubt contribute to the maintenance of my Health.

   The Country is in a very unsettled State here, trade bad, Bankruptcies
daily taking place, Factories beginning to work short time and it is thot
but few of them will be lighted up at all thro the Winter.

                                                            Rd Hodgkinson.

Haslar Road, Gosport   2nd November, 1839
I received your . . . five Pound Note. I mean to apply it to the purpose
you intended in getting me a new suit of Clothes. My own health is good
but I was taken about a fortnight since with a severe pain in the calf of my
leg which has quite laid me up. I have had on two blisters wich I hope
will have the desired efect.

   Dear Uncle I hope that a correspondence may be kept open betwen
our familis when by the course of nature you and me shall be gathered
unto our fathers, nothing in this world wold give my Children greater
pleasure. The Contemplated Bridge is daily expected from Bristol to ply
from Portsmouth to Gosport wich will make a diference in the prospects
of the watermen I am afraid.   John Hodgkinson.

Haslar Road, Gosport   November 7, 1841
My eldest son John as been in a Gentlemans yacht this somer. He was in

expectation of going to Liverpool; if he had he would have came to see you and all is relations. He is now in London in the Eastindia Docks on bord of a Schooner Named the Liffey as an able Seaman. I expect he will be gone two years if he likes the Service; she is a Merchants Paquet. My youngest son William David is at home, he has been in Her Majesties Service two years and a 1/2. He was in the west Indies and South Americia Eighteen months and was Paid off from HM Ship Stag of 46 guns. Since that he has sailed in an Irish Trader from London to Waterford and the Vessel being paid off he came home. He is at work in the Boat with me this winter, most likely in the Spring he will be off to sea again.

John Hodgkinson.

Chowbent, Mancr.   16th Nov, 1841
The long delay (more than two Years you say since I last wrote to you) has been caused by various Circumstances chiefly connected with our own Family; some of greater and some of less Importance. Of the former is the death of Mr Richard Guest of Bedford who died on the 26th of May last after a long illness, by which melancholy Event your Cousin Jane has become a very young Widow with a Family of 8 Children, five sons and three daughters, the youngest only 4 Years old. present. Her eldest son is at home carrying on the Business of the Brewery. The Second is Apprenticed to his Uncle, an eminent Surgeon in Manchester. The other 3 boys are together at Boarding School near Halifax in Yorkshire and the 3 daughters are at home. Richard Wright is as he always will be, steeped in Poverty. He is sober but has no Inclination or Exertion, consequently he is too often troublesome to mc without affording me the least Satisfaction.   Rd. Hodgkinson.

Lodge, Chowbent, Near Manchester   22nd Nov 1841
One Reason for my long delay in writing to you was on account of the new Post Office Arrangement.[11] From the immense increase of Letters passing thro' the Post I thot the Danger of a Letter arriving safe at its destination was also increased. I never was comfortable when I had to remit Money by Post, and as neither you nor I could well afford to lose five Pounds I have from day to day kept procrastinating, but as I have no other way of transmitting it to you I must run the Risk at last, and I now inclose you a £5 Bank of England Note which if you receive safe I desire you will give me early information. It is the first Bank Note I have sent by Post since the new Arrangement.   Rd. Hodgkinson.

Haslar Road, Gosport   November 24, 1841
Honoured Uncle, I am sorry to here of the death of Mr Guest, poor Jane
as her troubles before her, but the Lord will be a Father to the fatherless
and a husband to the widow, that put there trust in him.

John Hodgkinson.

Atherton, near Chowbent, Manchester
As I am writing to you I will just mention that I wish you to write to me
as soon as this comes to hand, informing me what was your Mother's
Christian Name and her father's Name and Surname. I think the family
Name was Norris.   Rd. Hodgkinson.

Haslar Road, Gosport   1 of December 1841
In answer to your Questions conserning my Grandfather and Mother's
Chistian names, in looking at my Indentures wich was rote by my
Honoured Grand Father Mr Joseph Hodgkinson, I found her name not
there. Her maiden name was Cathrine Norris, my Grandfather had ten
Children, five sons and five daughters, and there Christian names I know
but my Grand fathers name I do not recolect. Is oldest son's name was
Richard and he was a tailor in Bolton and died 21 years ago in Spring
Gardens.   John Hodgkinson.

Haslar Road, Gosport   17th December, 1843
When I Wrote last I informed you my Eldest son John was going to the
West Indies. He is returned in good health after an absence of nearly two
years, a few weeks ago he Sailed to the Mediterranean in a Gentlemans
yatch. I expect him home in April or May next. David arived yesterday
from Malta and the Ionian Islelands, being absent six Months. My daughter Jane is living in a Gentlemans Family as upper Nurse Maid, about two
miles from Gosport. She as been there about eighteen months.
     . . . it is Forty seven Years this day I embarked on bord HM Ship
Action at Liverpool. Many changes of life as hapened to both of us in that
space of time.   John and Mary Hodgkinson.

                                                               1 January 1844
I am glad to find that you and your Family are in good Health, which has
not been the case with me for near two years. On the 12th of March,
1842, I went in a Omnibus to Manchester evidently in as good Health as
ever I was in my Life. The morning was fine and I had a very pleasant
ride but when I got to Manchester and I attempted to rise from my Seat, I

could not stand from excessive pain in my left Leg and it required three Men to convey me to the Inn. I was come to Manchester by appointment upon special Business with a Gentleman in the Law and I sent for a Stand Coach to convey me to his Office. I had no pain as long as I sat still, so I desired we might proceed with our Business which took us from one to four o'clock. As soon as I attempted to get off my Seat the Pain was as acute and I was as helpless as ever. There was a Descendant of old Doctor Guest of Leigh practicing as a Surgeon in Mancr, his brother had married your Aunt Jane. The Gentleman I was with had unknown to me sent a Note to him to inform him where I was and the State I was in. He immediately sent his own Carriage for me with Directions to his Coach man to take me to his House. On coming there Mr Guest had got with him another Surgeon, they examined me and immediately bled me by Cupping between my Shoulders, and had me in bed in half an hour, where I lay from 5 o'clock on Saturday afternoon till 12 o'clock on Monday, scarcely conscious of what was going on about me. On Monday noon I sent for a coach which brought me safely home. A Bed was brought down into the Parlour where I was confined five Weeks without being able to get to my own Front Door. At the end of 7 weeks I could walk about the Room and in ten Weeks I could walk a little in the Garden. I have gradually improved ever since, the Pain in my Leg has subsided some Months ago and I can now, and for a long time since, have been able to walk to Bedford and Plat-fold. This Attack has not seriously injured my bodily Health but it seems to be rather hastening the Feebleness of Old Age. I have completed my eightieth year.

We are in a wretched condition here — all cotton, both in Spinning and Weaving is down in the Factories and the poor Hand Loom Weaver cannot get half employed and when he has Work the Wages are so miserably low that with his utmost Industry he cannot earn a Living. Inclosed is one half of a Five Pound Bank Note which you must acknowledge the Rect of as soon as it comes to hand, and when I receive your Letter I will remit you the other half.   Rd. Hodgkinson.

Haslar Road, Gosport   3rd January, 1844
I am Sorry to hear that trade is so bad in the weaveing line but we have our troubles. The floting Bridge that go by Steam from Gosport to Portsmouth every 1/4 of one hour from seven in the morning untill half past nine takes half of our work away. This year the tols of the Brige is let for 2000 five Hundred Pounds but with my Pention and what I earn in the Boat I can do better than in the waveing Business.   John Hodgkinson

10th January 1844

Dear John, In your letr you twice mention Weaving, by which you mean of course Hand Loom Weaving, which is now done, I may say, universally by Power in the Factories, where a Girl of 15 or 16 years of Age will attend four Pair of Looms at least. Hence there is nothing for a Family to do at home. Children and very young persons are preferred in the Factories and the Father of a Family is left idle at home to be supported by the Wages of his young Children. This is a severe blow upon the Owners of Cottage Property by rendering the Weaving Shop, the most valuable part of the house and where the rent was expected to be paid from, perfectly useless and depriving the Tenant of the means of paying any Rent at all. I with hundreds of others in this District suffer serious Loss from this Cause. This with other Consequences necessarily attendant upon our present State of Society, viz the Increase in Rates and Taxes, the Income Tax etc etc., cause very serious Deductions from a limited incomes like mine. I regret very much the irresistible opposition upon the River which you have in the Floating Bridge but it is what might be expected in the now extensive application of Steam.

Your pension being retained and your Family grown up will be a great relief to you, and perhaps you may have laid up a small Fund against a rainy Day.   Rd Hodgkinson.

Haslar Road, Gosport   January 12th, 1844

I have the same Boat that I mentioned to you some years ago. My son David is at work with me this winter. In the summer he goes 3 or four Months in a Gentlemans Sailing Yacht. John is on the Luise, a vessil belonging to Sir Hide Parker. John as followed the Sea this eight or nine years and at times as left half Pay to me wich I have paid into the saveings Bank in is own name to the amount of Forty three Pounds. I have Thirty pounds of my own in the same Bank at Gosport. My Wife she goes to Cook now and then in Gentlemens Families. My daughter Jane I mentioned is in a most respectable family, the gentlemans name is Mr Powel he is from Yorkshire they live at anglecy 2 miles from Gosport. Jane as 14 Pounds per year.   John Hodgkinson.

Haslar Road, Gosport   December 22, 1845

My oldest son John is gone on a voige to the East Indies and China. He is second Mate of a vessel named the Mischief. My daughter is living in a Gentlemans family of the name of Powel in the town of Ashbourne in

Derbyshire. She went with them from here near two years since. My youngest, David, works with me in the Boat as I begin to find I cannot do without help. In regard to the state of employment here the Railroad makes a great bustle in the town but the floating Bridge gets half the profits. But thank God we continue to rub along as well as we can expect.

John Hodgkinson.

Green Bank, near Chowbent, near Manchester
You will think your last letter has been long unanswered . . . principally from my own Reluctance to Letter writing which is very troublesome to me on account of the gradual decay of my Eyesight, and my Friends must in future be satisfied with few letters from me and those very short. Another Cause has been that our Post Office at Chowbent will be authorised to grant Money Orders which we are at present obliged to get at Manchester. After much Trouble and delay you must send me your Christian name and Surname written at full length with a particular Direction of your Residence viz the town, the street, and the number of your house if it have any and also your vocation and employment.

[No Signature]

Richard Hodgkinson's Memoir:

Account of Bank Notes or Notes sent to John Hodgkinson

1831 May 23; 1833 Oct 30; 1836 Sept; 1838 May 26; 1839 Oct 29; 1841 Nov 22; 1844 Jan 10; 1846 Jan 31 and 7 Feb.

The last few letters in this collection were very brief, usually only enclosing the gift of a banknote. Richard Hodgkinson died on 9 May 1847, and his nephew, John, died at his home in Hoskins Row, Gosport, in 1864 at the remarkable age of eighty-six.

Notes

1 Details from *Intrepid*'s ship's log, Kew Record Office.
2 This account of the affair is condensed from C. Northcote Parkinson, *War in the Eastern Seas, 1793–1815.*

3 John Hodgkinson was taken off the *Intrepid* suffering from a leg ulcer. After twenty days in hospital, the night before the Cape was handed over to the Dutch he set sail in HMS *Braave*, a fifth rater of forty-four guns, for the passage home to Portsmouth. Cape Hospital log, Kew Record Office.

4 On 23 February 1815, John Hodgkinson was granted a Greenwich Outpatient Service pension of £14. 8s a year for Life by Lord Henry Paulet.

5 In 1823 the fare between Gosport and Portsmouth was, in fine weather, 1d for every passenger not exceeding six or 6d for the hire of a wherry for one passenger and a maximum of six. In foul weather the fares were 3d for each passenger, 1s for a maximum of four people hiring the boat and 1s 6d for five or six people. *The Portsmouth Guide*.

6 This watch was left to John by his grandfather, Joseph Hodgkinson, with the proviso that it was to be sold and two looms were to be bought for John with the proceeds. After John ran away to sea, Richard sold the watch for £3 and sent the money to his nephew.

7 HMS *Actaeon*, a fifth rater with forty-four guns, was a 'rendezvouse ship'. After leaving Liverpool she called at Lancaster before returning to Portsmouth with 1,613 recruits, vastly outnumbering the crew of eighty. Almost all were volunteers and not pressed men, and were entitled to a joining bounty of £5. Details from ship's log, Kew Record Office.

8 This is Admiral Rainer.

9 This is Mangalore.

10 This is Tippo Sahib, also known as Tipu Sultan.

11 In January 1840, Rowland Hilll, father of the modern postal system, introduced a standard charge for a letter regardless of distance. The basic letter charge was one penny for half an ounce.

11

Farmer Hodgkinson & John Curwen of Workington

Before the Industrial Revolution gained momentum, Britain underwent a transformation in agriculture. In the early eighteenth century, pressure from a growing population created demands that were met by dramatic changes in land use, concentration on root crops, scientific stock breeding, and the introduction of machinery and lighter and stronger farm implements. These changes swept away the agricultural practices that had altered little over the centuries and had led to the enclosure of millions of acres of land.

In the last decades of the 1700s, migration from rural areas to cities and towns increased as manufacturing became concentrated in factories. Despite the pioneering work of such innovators as Jethro Tull, with his seed drill and other iron implements, and Charles 'Turnip' Townshend, who introduced clover and turnip crops, England became an importer of grain. During the French Wars the supply of food became a chronic problem when Napoleon introduced his Continental System. This barred his allies from trading with Britain and brought the country perilously close to losing the war for lack of food.

On all his journeys, Richard Hodgkinson kept a farmer's eye on the land through which he travelled. In 1794, on his way to London, he particularly noted the fertile pasture and meadowland of Lichfield with its many fine fields of turnips. He recommended those with time to spare to visit the grounds of Windsor, where the King, 'Farmer' George III, indulged his great interest in agriculture. In 1800 on his way to Scotland, Hodgkinson expressed surprise at the price demanded for poor land. In family letters written in 1807 he described himself as a farmer, for apart from his duties as Steward to the Atherton estate, he also had his own farm, renting Platt Fold and some 170 acres from Lord Lilford. When Lilford was re-organizing his estate in 1824, Hodgkinson made a point of saying that, in keeping with current trends, there would be larger fields with hedging, fencing and drainage. New ideas abounded in the world of agriculture, and Hodgkinson had been impressed by the work of John Christian Curwen, of Workington, who in 1809 had written *Hints on Agricultural Subjects and on The Best Method of Improving the Condition of the Labouring Classes*, and introduced many new ideas to his Schoose Farm.

Curwen, who married his cousin and then adopted her surname, took over her family's extensive land and coal-mining interests. His enthusiasm for modern farming arose in 1804 because of the cost of feeding pit ponies on oats, an expense he sought to reduce by a change of diet for both horses and cattle. Curwen called his new system 'soiling', feeding horses on steamed potatoes and carrots and supplying his cattle, which were kept in stone pens all the year round, with root crops, cut grass and cabbages. This method of feeding, a precursor of intensive farming, required much less acreage to supply food for his stock, and, with cattle no longer grazing, land was freed for the production of grain. One beneficial side effect was that Workington had unusually healthy children, thanks to a liberal and year-round supply of milk from Curwen's herd.

Schoose Farm was a very substantial enterprise, with imposing stone buildings, a windmill for grinding and threshing, and a mill pond which drove two wheels. Curwen, who also experimented with different breeds of cattle and sheep, kept an abundance of manpower on the farm, as well as teams of oxen for ploughing, milk cows in their pens, and scores of horses. Curwen not only had the drive and ability to improve agricultural techniques by implementing his ideas on a grand scale, but also the capital and patience to wait for a return on his investment.

Hodgkinson had not forgotten the lessons learned during the French Wars and was eager to improve the productivity of his own modest property. In 1815, with this new prophet of agriculture then being acclaimed, he wrote to Curwen asking if David Hodgkinson, his eldest son, could visit Schoose for a few weeks during the spring to observe the new techniques at first hand. Curwen replied with alacrity and extended a warm welcome. During David's stay at Schoose, appalling weather brought farming to a standstill and he went to spend a few days with his grandparents in New Galloway, sailing from Whitehaven to Kirkudbright.

The Curwen Letters

Atherton Hall, near Bolton, Lancashire.   15th Febr. 1815
Honoured Sir, Being an entire Stranger to you, I have to apologise for troubling you with a Letter. It is on acct. of the management & mode of cultivating your Farm at Workington and of raising food for your Cattle, & the mode of applying it that I thus address you.

I am Land Agent to Lord Lilford for the Property which he acquired by his marriage with Miss Atherton of Atherton, in which situation I have been more than twenty two years.

I hold a Farm under his Lordship of abt one hundred & seventy Statute Acres, which lying in a populous neighbourhood, I employ a considerable part of it as a milk Farm, raising a large quantity of Meadow hay. I breed my own Cows chiefly. One piece of Land of abt 25 Acres I stock with Ewes bot at Chester Fair the last Thursday in Feby & sold at Michmas., never wintering any Sheep. I grow abt 20 Acres of Wheat &d Oats every Year & abt 6 Acres of Clover, but have not hitherto been in the habit of raising much green food for the Cattle, having only a very small patch of Potatoes, anr of Carrotts, anr of Cabbage & Potatoes anr Turnips yearly, in all not much above a Couple of Acres.

I have a Son 23 Years of Age who is fond of Farming & is desirous of seeing some of the improved methods & the purport of this letter is to request that you would permit him to spend a few weeks upon your Farm during the busy part of this Spring. It is not intended that he shd be any inconvenience, trouble or expence to you, Sir, or any of your Servants. He will provide his own Lodgings at some neighbouring Farm house if it can be done, if not, in the town. All that is desired, is your permission & authority for him to accompany your Bailiff or Farming man in the various operations upon the Farm, to inspect the Cattle feeding, to see the uses of the improved Instruments of Husbandry &c., &c. and if he can, in any way, make himself useful he will be very glad.

I have for some time hesitated abt making this application to you, thro, my friends Col. Fletcher of Bolton or the Rev Mr Blundell of Croyland in Lincolnshire, but have at last determined to venture to address you myself.

Shd my request meet your approbation I shd wish to send my Son as soon as the Spring work fairly begins, and for him to continue till Seed time is over & if you will have the kindness to let your Steward or Bailiff answer this letter it will particularly oblige.   Yours &c. Rd. Hodgkinson

Workington Hall   February 22nd, 1815
I shall be very glad to render any service to your Son & to give him every
facility & opportunity of seeing the whole proceedings at the Schoose. He
may be boarded with the Bailiff if he wishes . . . . Yours sincerely,

J C Curwen.

Workington   7th March, 1815
You will think I have been rather tardy in my motions when I inform
you that I only arrived here last night. I did not come thro' Ulverston.
The fact is that Ab^t three o'Clock on Friday I called upon Mr Higgin
with the letter you gave me, with whom & his family I spent a very pleasant evening. In the course of conversation I mentioned where I was
going, what my motive was & the route which had been pointed out to
me. Mr H. immediately said he w^d advise me to go thro' Kendal as the
road across the Sands[1] was not altogether safe at this season of the year &
moreover that there was no public conveyance from Ulverston, adding
that if I w^d stop at Lancaster untill Saturday evening at 5 o'Clock, (which
w^d make no difference in my progress as there is only one Coach a day
from Kendal to Workington which sets out at 5 o'Clock in the morning)
he w^d provide me a Horse & ride with me to Mr Gibsons' ab^t 3 miles
from Lancaster, where he said was kept the best stock of short Horned
Cattle at least in the County if not in the Kingdom. All these arguments
induced me to change my rout & I consented to remain untill the following evening. On the Saturday I was gratified with a sight of a Stock of the
best bred cattle I ever saw in my life without exception. There are ab^t 170
Head, 40 of which are milk Cows, fed in the winter entirely upon the
new system, Steamed Potatoes, Turnips and Straw. On Saturday even^g I
proceeded to Kendal, when to my great disappointment I discovered
there was no Coach forward untill Monday morning, I had no creature to
speak to the whole of Sunday except a Quaker from L'pool, who was
under the same circumstances as myself. On the Monday morn^g we set
out as fellow travellers. We had to be sure a most delightful ride. It is
scarcely possible for a person who has not enjoyed the scene to conceive
anything so romantic and picturesque. We drove for 8 or 10 miles within
view of the famous lake Windermere. We passed & saw several of the
minor lakes & was within a stone's throw of the high mountain of
Skiddaw. These things with being quite new to me struck me the more
forcibly. Ultimately we arrived safe at this place. Methinks when I look at
the number of lines which I have written, I must have been as tedious in

dragging you to Workington as the Horses were which brot. us from Cockermouth. It being 5 o'Clock when we got here I thought it w^d not be proper to go to my lodgings last night. I sent a Note to Mr Aikin, (for that is the Bailiff's name) wishing him to come down that we might make some arrangements ab^t my removal on the morrow. After I had sent this Note I conceived if the Bailiff called upon Mr Curwen in his way to me, he might not be pleased that I had not myself apprized him of my arrival. I therefore wrote a short note to him saying that I sh^d be happy to make my respects to him in person at any time today or any subsequent day he w^d be pleased to appoint. In ab^t a quarter of an hour I heard a person enquiring for me who proved to be Mr C's Bailiff with a request from him that I w^d either go & take a Glass of Wine with him then or breakfast with him this morning. As I expected Mr Aiken I declined going last night. I accordingly went to breakfast this morning, when I was most kindly rec^d by Mr C. During Breakfast he told me his library was quite at my service while I stopped in the Country, that my home shd have been at his own house only for the inconvenience of his house being a full mile from the Farm which might cause a great loss of time, that he had taken care to have everything as comfortable for me as it was possible, if there was any one thing that I wanted I must not fail to send immediately to him or Mrs C for it, and that if I wanted a Horse he had given directions to have one bro^t up to the farm for my use at any time. He desired that I w^d dine with him at least every Sunday & he particularly requested that I wd dine there today at 4 o'Clock which I shall accordingly do. Since the morning I have been taking a general view of the farm Yard & Stock. He has up ab^t 30 milk Cows, ab^t 22 working Oxen & a straw Yard full of young Stock & Horses innumerable. He told me this morning he had above 200 Horses at work. The Bailiff has to superintend above 100 workmen. This will give you some idea of the magnitude of the concern. Please to present my duty to my Mother & tell her that one satisfaction I enjoy in my absence from her is that I am got into the hands of a Scotch woman.

D. Hodgkinson.

Barley   20th March 1815
You will no doubt be surprised when you see the date of this letter to find that I am in Scotland. The case is this. If the weather has been the same with you as it has in Cumberland, I need not say it has been very wet since I left home. I was apprehensive Mr Curwen was making some sacrifice of time for my amusement as scarcely a day passed on which I did not

receive a verbal or a written invitation to dine with him & always when I saw him he was regretting the bad state of the weather saying he wished to make my time pleasant, but he was sure it must be heavy upon my hands. On Wednesday last as you will recollect the day was uncommonly bad. On that evening I dined at the Hall. In the course of the evening I mentioned that I had an inclination to cross the water to see an aged Grandfather, who in all probability, if I did not see now, I perhaps never might have so good an opportunity of visiting again.

He said he approved of the motive, & as it was impossible to do anything upon the farm for 10 days or a fortnight, he w^d forward it as much as possible; for that purpose he w^d send a servant to Workington and Harrington to enquire if any vessels were lying there for Kirkcudbright & he w^d inform me in the morning when he sh^d call upon me to take a ride with him. He accordingly called, but informed me there were none in at the time, adding you have never seen Whitehaven; if the morning is fine I w^d advise you to ride there, yet will most likely meet with one there if not it will only be a pleasant ride. On the Friday morning I went & found one likely to sail on Saturday at 2 o'Clock. In that Sloop I sailed from Whitehaven to Kirkcudbright and in less that 24 hours I arrived at my Grandfather's. The old man as well as my Grandmother were much pleased to seen me. They are both enjoying a good state of health & quite as stout as I expected to see them. Please to inform my Mother that Sarah Swan is still with them. I took tea with them & then proceed to this place which is likely to be my home whilst I stop. The length of my Stay will entirely depend upon the weather, as soon as the weather will permit I shall return.   D. Hodgkinson.

Schoose farm   5th April 1815
You & My Mother will no doubt be impatient to hear of my safe return to this place. I arrived here yesterday morn§, but being much fatigued with my journey & want of sleep, having come by the way of Dumfries & Carlisle, I deferred writing untill today, for wh^c I am very sorry, as upon recollection I find you will not receive my letter before Friday evening on your return f^m Warrington.

I do not know one circumstance in the course of my life that has given me more inward satisfaction than my late journey into Scotland. The very flattering attentions that I rec^d from all my friends w^d appear a sufficient recompence for the trouble of going so far. But it is not that to which I allude. It is the consciousness of having performed a duty, a last duty I apprehend to a dear & venerable Grandfather, fast verging to 80 years of age, but still nearer in all human probability to the grave! It is the opinion of all his friends that he is wearing very fast & that a short time, a year or two at most, will terminate his earthly struggle.

Our meeting was affectionate, our parting was affecting. On Sunday I went down to take leave. He seemed pensive & serious the whole eveng, frequently asked if I was obliged to leave so soon. After supper he pressed my hand & said, David this is the last time I shall ever see you in this world, I hope & trust our next meeting will be in Heaven. The old man's feelings overpowered him, he wept. He says it seems like repining at the will of heaven or he shd pray to be removed. He looks upon his afflictions as a punishment for the sins of his former life & therefore bears them with fortitude & resignation.

There has scarcely been two fine days since I left this place. Mr C is just beginning to sow Oats, there were twenty three teams at work this morning, but they are again stopped by the rain. I fear the wetness of the weather will have thrown you rather late. I am afraid that the money which you have been liberal enough to bestow upon me for the purpose of prosecuting my favourite study will appear to you, as well as my friends & neighbours, to be thrown away if some of the new system is not adopted. I mean only as far as it is practicable and evidently beneficial. I wish not to run to any length & to avoid even the appearance of extravagance, but as it is requisite that a certain number of Horses must be kept upon our farm it is equally necessary that these horses should be constantly employed: & likewise it is evident that cleanness is essential as any other improvement.

I have addressed a note to Mr C enquiring the probable expence of certain implements which will have the double advantage of reducing manual labour and effectually cleaning the land. The last time I dined with him he mentioned he had received my letter & he wd take an early opportunity of answering it. As I wish to do nothing without your entire concurrence & approbation, as soon as I receive his answer I will send you a Copy of it, that you may yourself judge whether it is probable that any benefit may result from the purchase of all or some of them. It will be very beneficial to have a Straw-Cutter as a farming apparatus, but of these I will say more in my next. D. Hodgkinson.

Schoose 14th April 1815
If the weather had continued as favourable as it has been for the last ten days this wd have informed you of my speedy return home. I purposed to leave this place abt the middle of next week, but a sudden change in the

weather has done away that arrangement. I intend to remain here untill
Mr C has finished planting a field of Potatoes (ab^t 40 acres). Yesterday
morning he began with great spirit. There were in the field at 6 o'Clock
nearly 100 Horses & at least 150 people all busily employed. Some were
ploughing, some carting dung, others laying setts &c. It was a most animated scene. The morning was rather gloomy, but we were all in hopes
that it might clear off: when lo! between 8 & 9 o'Clock it began to rain
most tremendous & continued for 2 hours. In the evening it again rained
heavily. You will be aware that this will put a stop to all work for the present. After this is finished there will be nothing worth my while to stop
for; all the work then going on will be preparing the ground for turnips
&c., the preparation for which is so like to that for potatoes (which I have
particularly detailed) that one will answer for the other. I am more anxious to see the end of the potatoe planting, as if all is well I hope to have
an opportunity of seeing the Crop before it is gathered.

In the course of a very pleasant conversation which I had with Mr
Curwen in the field a day or two ago, he said I hope you will be able to
say the next time you come here, that this is the best & cleaned Crop of
Potatoes you ever saw in your life. I answered it w^d give me a great pleasure, but I did not think it at all likely that I sh^d see it again. He said you
must come to the Agricultural meeting. I can have no denial. I wish you
to make my respects to your Father & tell him it w^d give me great pleasure to seen him at that time. I shall be very glad to see you a day or two
before the time that you may have an opportunity of looking round
before the Meeting. I hope you understand that there is a Horse at your
service at any time. Your Father & yourself have paid me a compliment. I
do not mean our acquaintance to drop here, I shall certainly come to see
you in Lancashire. You may be sure this was very gratifying to me. I hope
it will be a proof to you that your kind precepts & fatherly admonitions
are not thrown away entirely. I have taken every opportunity by a
respectful behaviour to Mr C to shew him how much I am indebted to
him for his kind attentions; & I hope my general conduct here has been
such as to keep me blameless.

You will observe that I carefully avoid mentioning any thing abt the
Farm or the system. I do it from this motive that the few memorandums I
make may retain their interest by being new to you.   D.Hodgkinson.

April, 1815

By an Acc^t I rec^d from my son a few days ago, I learn that in a short time
now he means setting his face homewards, that is, as soon as your planting

of Potatoes is over. But I cannot let him leave you without delivering to
you this Note expressive of my thanks for the handsome manner in which
you complied with my request & of my gratitude for the very kind & liberal treatment my son has experienced at your hands. I have only to add
that I hope he has conducted himself in such a manner as to shew that he
is as Sensible of the obligation conferred upon him is as, Your very much
obliged and respectful Servt.   Rd. Hodgkinson.

Workington Hall   April 27th, 1915
I cannot let your son return without conveying to you the satisfaction I
feel from the attention he has paid to the various objects carrying on at
the Schoose. I flatter myself I shall have the pleasure of learning he has
imbibed a spirit that can promote the improvement of the practice of
Agriculture on your [land]. He has seen the best there is of farming I am
[sure] the expence has been great but will, I flatter myself, amply repay
them.

   I could not send the Sheep by this Ship, but it will come by the next.

                                                        May 10th 1815
My son arrived at home last Thursday having spent a few days with his
Uncle in Liverpool. I sh^d have addressed a line to you sooner but by some
accident you directed to me the Note intended for Mr Dutton & vice
versa.

   The visit which my son has paid to the Schoose Farm, short as it has
been, has completely ans^d my expectations. It has enlarged his ideas upon
a subject, of all others the most interesting, & most vitally so to England as
she is now circumstanced. It has confirmed his dislike to weeds, docks &
thistles; it has convinced him of the absolute necessity not only of making
but of keeping the Land perfectly clean; and also of the policy of raising
the greatest possible quantity of Manure upon the Farm. These (with
draining) I take to be the first principles of good husbandry and they are
applicable to all Soils and all situations.

   But theory alone will make but a sorry farmer. The man who turns his
attention to Agricultural pursuits with the least degree of seriousness will
soon find it is not to be learned by inspiration or intuition, there is no
royal road to it, we must pursue the scriptural maxim of laying line upon
line, precept upon precept, & I may add experiment upon experiment,
and after all too often reap only disappointment. It seems strange that a
science upon the exercise of which has depended the existence of every
human being since the creation of the World in every civilized Society at

least, sh^d be so little understood. But be that as it may, its' practice & its improvement will now be forced upon us.

The present state in which the disproportionate encouragm^t given to Manufactures, Commerce & Colonization has placed us cannot be of any very long continuance and we must, whether we will or no, have recourse to Agriculture, the only solid & permanent foundation of national greatness & security. I have often tho^t it fortunate that our distresses with respect to Corn began so early as they did, after the commencem^t of the French war. What w^d have been the consequence to us if Buonaparte had carried his continental System² into execution previous to the year 1800. Necessity is said to be the Mother of invention, she is undoubtedly the parent of human exertion, & thus we have been compelled to turn our attention to what sound policy ought to have directed it long ago. The result however has been fortunate, much has been done in a few years & much is doing, altho' very much remains to be done, we have seen enough to give us the greatest encouragm^t & the greatest hopes when Agriculture shall cease to be conducted by Poverty & Ignorance & shall receive its fair proportion of Talent & Capital.   R^d. Hodgkinson

Notes

1   Stagecoaches crossed several miles of treacherous sands in Morecambe Bay from Hest Bank to Grange-over-Sands. Bodies of travellers caught by the tides are buried in churchyards around the bay.
2   The Continental System was Napoleon's trade blockade of Britain.

12

James Blundell, Parish Priest

James Blundell, parish priest, was a man of strong contrasts and his relationship with Richard Hodgkinson was one of contradictions. Hodgkinson, the composed, articulate and calculating man of practical virtues, contrasted with the apoplectic, pompous and flamboyant cleric whose letters, impatiently dashed off in a fury of energy, sometimes defy transcription.

Blundell, eager to add to his tythes and holdings of land, frankly acknowledged that his progress from humble schoolteacher to rector of a wealthy country living owed more to his cultivation of benefactors than the spiritual endowment of the Almighty. Always dominant and at least once violent towards his wife, he was a generous father to his six children and probably understood his afflicted godson Joseph Hodgkinson better than anyone.

Richard Hodgkinson had known Blundell's brother John as a contemporary at Standish Grammar School in 1780, but his friendship with James began in the schoolrooms of Leigh Grammar School in 1792. Hodgkinson gave up teaching after pledging himself to serve as steward to Henrietta Maria Atherton for a trial year, and the nineteen-year-old Blundell was put in charge of the thriving school on a temporary basis. In the event, Hodgkinson did not return to his pupils and Blundell took his place as headmaster and eventually taught at Leigh Grammar School for a total of sixteen years.

Blundell was ordained as a priest in May 1807, after first being licenced as a Clerk in 1804 and ordained as Deacon in June 1806. He continued teaching despite being granted the curacy, with a stipend of £45 a year, of Newchurch.

In 1808, Blundell, by judicious use of friends and acquaintances, was given the wealthy living of Crowland, a village in the Fen country some seven miles from Peterborough. In this tranquil and little visited part of England parish life was centred around the beautiful ruined abbey and church of Crowland where Blundell spent twenty-six years as rector. Despite an estimated lavish yearly income in 1822 of £800, Blundell spent much of his life in financial crisis and made energetic efforts to increase his revenue from tythes and allotments of land during the enclosure of the Fenland. Despite this he appears to have been well respected by his parishioners.

The distressed state of agriculture and a decline in rents, together with the injudicious purchase of a horse or two, added to Blundell's financial troubles. From time to time, Blundell resorted to borrowing money from Hodgkinson and in his last years Blundell's reluctance to repay £50 threatened to end their long friendship. By 1834, Blundell was plagued by ill health and never did repay the debt; he took it to the grave after dying in a fit of apoplexy when death 'bathed his fatal Javelin in . . . [his] . . . breast'.

During his years at Crowland, Blundell was in attitudes and aspirations probably typical of many a country parson, and the stranger from Lancashire was accepted and settled comfortably into rural life. No doubt flattery and obsequiousness had eased his path to Crowland and it was flattery that no doubt eased his acceptance into the community. Electioneering for Lord Milton in 1818, the off-comer was called upon to give a stirring speech to the native Fenmen. 'An Englishman of the genuine breed,' he declared, 'is still the same whether sheltered by a Willow or an Oak.'

Blundell appears to have been troubled by some aspects of his calling which others in equally comfortable situations may have let lie unchallenged. He wrote pamphlets on the *Necessity of Ordination* and the *Principles of the Church of England*, and in 1813 he confided to Hodgkinson that he had had long conversations with admirers of Emanuel Swedenborg, the Swedish mystic, who had created a following in Bolton and Manchester and included Samuel Crompton among his disciples. On this latter matter he urged discretion on Hodgkinson and asked him not to mention it to more orthodox priests. His doubts about the Holy Trinity were expressed to a friend: 'To prove that the Three were not one individual person, I brought forward our Saviour's baptism in which Christ was in the Hands in Jordan, the Spirit seen like a Dove descending: & the Father was heard in Heaven "This is my beloved &c."'

Blundell had been born into trade – his father was an innkeeper from North Meols near Southport – and although he courted the gentry and the high offices of the Church for personal and family preferment, he felt uncomfortable in the company of his betters. 'The truth is I always feel awkward with such People under existing Circum^s. as I may be supposed to have risen, I always fear any officiousness may be deemed presumptious & the want of it to a certain degree a summary want of Gratitude. I always however endeavour to reconcile the conflict by feeling a consciousness of the latter, & leaving the other to such opportunities as seem to elicit & make the advance reciprocal', he wrote to Hodgkinson in a moment of candour.

A friendship founded at Leigh between Blundell and the Hodgkinson family lasted a lifetime. Richard Hodgkinson was best man at Blundell's wedding in 1798 when he married Mary Anne Radcliffe, daughter of an established and prosperous local family. Blundell was Joseph Hodgkinson's godfather and Mrs Hodgkinson was godmother to Thomas, the Blundells' second son. After the Blundells left for the Fens, Hodgkinson kept a watchful eye on Mrs Blundell's ageing parents.

Not long after the Blundells' marriage, a violent disagreement with his brother-in-law distanced Blundell from the Radcliffes for some 20 years, and he only became reconciled to them on the death of his wife's father when her mother went to live at Crowland Abbey. Even this charitable gesture led to violence when elderly Mrs Radcliffe died and left a bequest to her daughter, money that Blundell felt should have fallen into his hands. Blundell resorted to physical coercion, and only a timely visit by Hodgkinson, in the role of mediator, brought this unhappy affair to a close.

One of the causes of Blundell's oft-repeated financial decline was the expenses he incurred in educating his three sons and three daughters, five of whom were born while the family lived in Leigh. Blundell hired a governess for his daughters, Mary Ann (born in 1799), Elizabeth Dorothea (christened in February 1808) and Frances (christened in July 1808).

Of the sons, George Peacock (born in 1800) entered the Church and his father drew extensively on all his connections to find him a lucrative living. With the connivance of Richard Hodgkinson, George was given the curacy of Cowbit, near Spalding, while probably still under age. He later went to Cambridge and was ordained in 1823.

Thomas (born in 1803), after showing a youthful talent for the sciences, studied in Dublin and Edinburgh and in 1825 became President of the Royal Medical Society in Edinburgh. Hodgkinson persuaded the young doctor not to start up in practice in Bolton because of the stranglehold certain doctors had in the town. In 1832 Thomas wed his 'matrimonial prize', just two years before it was his sad duty to inform Hodgkinson of Blundell's sudden death.

James Whitsed Blundell (born in 1811) received his middle name from his father's sponsor to the living at Crowland. Twice injured in accidents with animals as a child, James was treated by Dr Hill in whose asylum in Leicester resided Joseph Hodgkinson. Tragically, the Blundells and Hodgkinsons were united by grief when James died in 1825 and Joseph in 1826. James was nursed in his last days by his two sisters, and his father wrote tenderly of the youngster's great suffering and the devoted attentions of the two girls.

Blundell's true worth as a friend to Richard Hodgkinson was expressed most deeply during the tragic years of Joseph Hodgkinson's incarceration in the asylum. After Joseph had cut himself off from his wife and family, it was Blundell, Joseph's godfather, who persuaded the demented young man to reforge the family bonds. Blundell journeyed to Leicester without complaint to visit Joseph and lifted the young vicar's spirits to the point where a temporary respite from his illness was noticeable. Encouraging letters from Blundell must have been the only ray of light for the Hodgkinson family during those bleak years. There are, too, in this first collection of letters the first signs of Joseph's mental illness. In the autumn of 1819, and with Joseph's university days at an end, Richard Hodgkinson enlisted the help of Blundell and other men of the Church within his social sphere to find the young man a curacy. Joseph wrote to Blundell turning down one offer in a letter which, according to his father, was written 'in a perturbed state of mind'.

During their prolonged correspondence Blundell and Hodgkinson discussed many matters. Economic misery brought from the priest a novel way of solving the nation's distress in which the National Debt would be eliminated, prosperity restored and each man, high and low, would conveniently maintain his station in life.

Of particular interest in this collection is the letter drawn from Hodgkinson after Blundell wrote enquiring about Sir Richard Arkwright and John Horrocks, another textile pioneer. Hodgkinson's condemnation of Arkwright, 'a barber of the lowest order . . . whose morals were loose and his conduct profligate and debauched', was likely based on sympathy for Eyes (or Highs), a Leigh man who had accused Arkwright of stealing his ideas to make his fortune. To further his own fortune, Arkwright, said Hodgkinson, had defrauded investors in new mills 'which when set work he caused by one means or another to render so unproductive and apparently hazardous as to induce the parties to sell their shares at any price he would give for them'. Richard Guest of Leigh, later to be Hodgkinson's son-in-law, also published a justification for Highs's claim.

Despite his differences with his wife during his lifetime, Blundell ensured in his will that she would be amply provided for. After small bequests to his children he left his estate, valued at £4,000, to 'my dear wife Mary Ann', with the admonishment that she in turn should provide in her will for their children.

Blundell's letters do not flow easily, and sometimes change direction in mid-sentence as his mind darts from one thought to another. To save postage he added to Hodgkinson's problems of decipherment by sometimes writing cross-hatched – writing a letter the normal way and then turning the paper through ninety degrees and writing over the earlier script.

The Blundell Letters: Part I

Atherton Jany 11th 1813

Not having rec^d a line from you or you from me since you left Lancashire, I feel desirous of exchanging a Letter with you at the commencement of a new Year. The short period of a Year makes great & important changes even within the narrow circle of our own families & connections & neighbourhood & who shall say what a another Year may bring forth.

I have no doubt but you have been very much engaged since your return home & that in your present elevated situation you must ever expect to be so, but you are now fast approaching to that time of life when, like me & thousands of others you will find that, elevation of situation, increase of wealth & of influence take away from our leisure &c., rather diminish than increase the sum of our enjoyments. . . . you & I have been fortunate men, & having families, it is not permitted us to relax in our industry, or suppress our exertions for bettering their condition. Enough of moralizing.

Jane has finished her Schooling & I suppose Joseph will be with us a fortnight yet. For anything I know he will enter College at Easter. I wish him to have remained at School an^r Year. My Wife is better & stouter than ever. RH

Crowland Jan 23rd 1813

Were I to express the pleasure at receiving your unexpected Favour, you w^d suppose I was returning your own Comp. on my late Accession of Fortune.

That very Even. I had returned from a troublesome Business at Spalding. The Towns of Boston and Spalding were originally in the same Charter. And like rival Powers, when justly prosperous they now begin to now to have separate Views & to think of Liberty and Independence. But unfortunately their Custom House had but one Bourse and it is too small to make into two & I fear too old also.

Spalding is all Bustle, Spirit and Opposition. Boston is rich, has pre-scription &c., & bids defiance. On Friday Month there was a Meeting to name a Committee & form Resolutions. I had this Honour conferred & if you may judge my Trouble I cannot get out these Plagues.

Whaplode Drove Inclosure & drainage goes well. The Commissioners have allowed my two Rights from Lands of the regular Claims so that it w^d be handsome but Claims are so numerous that I cannot divine their worth. Over 400 hundred Acres are to be tried, of these I am not san-guine. If they be got, my share w^d be more than double the pres. Living. The Tythe of the least 5000 Acres of continued Crop Land seems in ques-tion and that of the whole Parish probable, & the small Tythe belonging to my other Parishes, strongly presumptive. And the defendants must bind themselves to pay even my own Expenses before they can take . . . into Court. I propose to go to London in the Spring to consult farther, but, I am satisfied & as I believe are the Parishioners. S^hd like your sentiments on this point.

Providence has been bountiful & it would be a pity to embitter Life with Cabal & Law. Besides my Dear Friend, if something assures me this w^d counteract those purposes for which my unmerited Success might be given.

You perhaps may not Know th^t Mr Clowes[1] of Manchester who is my Recommender thro Mr Hornby to my Friend[2] here. I am no Sweden-borgian, no Sectarian, & yet were I to explain various Favours from all description you w^d wonder how a mere Youth becomes so desirable. Mr C & I had some serious Conversations, some strong Arguments on the Trinity & he told me that Landaff & myself are of the same Sentiments. To prove that the Three were not one individual Person I bro^t forward our Sav^rs Baptism in which Christ was in the Hands in Jordan, the Spirit seen like a Dove descending: & the Father was heard saying in Heaven 'This is my beloved &c.'. He was puzzled, tho pleased.

A Letter from him (Mr Clowes) . . . in which he spoke in terms most flattering . . . and expressed his wish to see me a Convert. And from him I suppose the whole Fraternity almost adore me. S^hd wish you to be careful of ever noticing this to Mr Hornby or Mr Bullock or anybody.

Some letters have passed between me and our worthy Bishop on extended Publication. His Lordship encourages me to execute forthwith. It will come out in the Spring without name. It is 'On the Necessity of Ordination to give proper Validity to the Christian Ministry' and of course will be a general Refutation of our Modern Situation. It will be my endeavour to unite strong Evidence with Liberality, Candour & orthodox Principles, I have some other ready. You shall see them by and bye.

The Reflections you made on our Successes are very true, mine, however, has been truly fortunate, yours certainly has been principally the result of your good Management and Activity. Hope we shall both live to enjoy the Fruits. James Blundell.

Crowland Rectory July 25th 1813
My Letters of late are only Packets of something concerning myself. Indeed, when I consider I have been most unusually busy in pursuing & occasionally of seizing Adam Fortune. Mrs B w^d inform you (a long story) of the 400 Acres Common. I have now only till tomorrow to determine whether I w^d risk £100 on the question. The Counsel gives it to be within the Parish, but prescription is against the right of Soil. I am now in hope of settling the point without dispute, & the Claim is likely to be valuable. Counsel are of opinion it will extend over several Parishes w^h were formerly dependant on the Abbey. This seems too much, but my Family have demands w^h I sh^d otherwise not endeavour to inforce.

There seems nothing wanting to make every thing very complete but the Acquisition of a literary Neighbour. Non onmes omina pophumas.
James Blundell

Atherton Sept. 13th 1813
Mrs H . . . has been to visit her Father whom she has not seen since she became a Wife & Mother.

I find by your Letter that your Tythe Causes &c are not yet bro^t to issue. I fear the 400 Acres Prescription being against you, will be a Bar to your reaping much advantage from them. Will you at all events be intitled to Tythe from them? I am very glad to hear you are likely to arrange your other Tythe claims to mutual satisfaction, particularly as far as regards your own Parish but sh^d your claims extend to other Parishes will they comply without a struggle? Tythes are seldom acquiesced without reluctance.
R^d Hodgkinson.

Atherton   17th Jany 1814

For the last four or five Months, my engagements from one cause or other, have exceeded those of my any period. . . . the Business at Atherton is increasing progressively & from the advanced value of land, a greater degree of strictness & attention in the management is requisite. My own Affairs too & those I have in Trust, are directly the reverse of diminishing tho' I frequently threaten to contract them.

For the last three weeks I have wished to spend my spare time with Joseph, previous to his going to Oxford. He set out last Wednesday morning from Manc. & I hope by this time has made his appearance there. After the public speaking at the School last Oct he was appointed an exhibitioner by the Trustees and will receive £40 a Year from Manc for 4 Years, at which time he will be elected to the Hulme's Exhibition of £110 a Year.

Of Mr & Mrs Radclife I need say nothing, you hear so frequently from them. I am this Afternoon going to the Funeral of their neighbour Hannah Robinson, old Betty Jolley's Dau[r]. She had but indifferent health for some time, but she died rather suddenly last Thursday.

Miss Lewen & Lydia went with our young folks on Friday night to a Dance at Chowbent, a large party ab[t] 30 Couples I hear. Mr & Mrs Birkett[3] are as usual, Mr B lamenting that his Expenses with his two sons have lately exceeded his Income. It is whispered that Tom after being 3 Years in a Law Office is disgusted with it & wishes for the Church. This is entre nous.

Young Legh the Bastard son of the Late Col Legh[4] arrived at his Age of 21 Years on the 3rd Dec. At that time he was under quarantine in a Vessel lying off Plymouth which had bro[t] him from the Mediterranean where the Plague has been raging long. He came last from Rosetta. He has been 3 Years in the Grecian Isles, Egypt etc etc. I understand he intends to set out again in March on his Travels thro' the North of Europe. He gave an Entertainm[t] at Haydock on 31st Dec. None went but those who received Cards. I & David had each one. The Company at Dinner was ab[t] 250. The Dinner was superabundant. Ale Punch & Wine no less so. We were introduced to the young Gentleman. He has nothing striking in his appearance or figure and his Face is quite uninteresting. I am told he is a young man of great curiosity & fond of visiting foreign Countries, but not possessed of Learning sufficient to make the most of such a propensity. His income, I presume, cannot be less than £30,000 p.ann. He has 2 Brothers & 4 Sisters, but all the seven Children are by different women.

An Ox was fed for the above occasion, the particulars of which may amuse some of your Neighbours. He was seven Years old & had worked in the Plough to the last. He weighed 25 score the Qua^r, had 12 score & a pound of Chandler's fat in him & his Hide weighed 8 score, his flesh was too fat to be eaten comfortably.

Of public News you know as much as I . . . I hope ere long the Sword will be sheathed in Peace, and the dreadful scourge of divine vengeance which has so long afflicted mankind, will, I trust, & sincerely pray that it may, have taught the Nations Wisdom. R^d Hodgkinson.

Crowland Rectory   Feb 12, 1814
Your esteemed Favour came duly to & deserved an earlier answer, but one thing or other has daily prevented. Among other Causes that of collecting the Contributions to buy Coal for the Poor is one. It has cost me some trouble but the Cheerfulness of the Giver & the Thankfulness of the Receiver are ample recompence. In a very short time indeed I collected £70 to be given to the most indigent, sell to others for a third, & to others for half Prime Costs. On this plan our Fund will continue to supply all in a way proportioned to want thro the whole Winter. Hence this small Cloud is likely to diffuse extensive Blessing.

Am happy to hear Joseph has so fair a prospect & so likely to profit by the flowing Tide. It is very customary with Cambridge Students to take Orders & retire on a Curacy for a short time before and after they become Fellows & in my opinion whatever the Fortune, the plan is a good one. Godly Men, by that acquire the habit of Writing & Preaching which if neglected young are seldom acquired to any popular degree, whatever may be the subsequent attainments in Letters &c. If he wishes to adopt this I can probably help to a Curc & need not say that everything else I may be able to do w^d be a great pleasure.

We are just now in some danger, the immense Snows in Leicester and Rutland have filled our Wash so full that I presume the Water is in some places 12ft above the adjoining Land. A Wind w^d be fatally disastrous.

Poor Birkett is always wrong, but your remark on his exceeding his Income I sh^d think hardly correct. He had formerly as much to say against the Church that the situation of Thos seems judgematical I wonder how a sensible Man c^d as far mistake the Bent of nature as he has. Thos always seemed the better fitted for Church & W^m for the Law.

My Tythe Question remains in Status quo & some of the Principal Proprietors have agreed to make me a Compromise, at the final Inclosure of the Wash which be good Land for Summer. I however, neither desire nor expect a full equivalent. Have offered to accept a Bonus of £365 per Ann. Perhaps the Claim is worth £2000. My Friends at W. Drove met sometime last Spring & doubled the Rental within it, which has made handsome addition. I every day expect also an Allotment of Common, but what I cant say have determined to increase the Amount of the Allotment wh probably at my death w. bring 3 or 4 thoud to my Family. Indeed my dear Sir, when in thus writing I contemplate the Chain of Events I am lost in wonder.

Have just finished a Pamphlet on the Principles of the Church of England, which has been read & sanctioned by some literary Friends. It is my intention to submit it to the Inspection of our worthy Bishop to whom I long since communicated the Plan and received a Letter to encourage in the work.

Am really amazed at the Manner in which Mr Farrington lived with so handsome a Fortune it was inexcusable. Tho perhaps however, there were Circumstances in his Family which he might think made Obscurity the more prudent. But the Character of the Man, the Respectability of his Cloth, were certainly lost in the Shade. He was a shrewd, clever & sensible Man. I was very partial to him and perhaps the more as from his noticing me when several of his Brethren treated with neglect.

Hope the Cloud wh so long distilled its baneful poison on Europe wd shortly dispel & be succeeded by Happiness, Peace & Good. We have been particulary favoured. We heard the Thunder at a distance but saw the desolating Bolt fall first on one side and then another.   Blundell

Atherton   Augst 2nd 1815
Your great Tythe question, as it approaches towards a Crisis must engage very much of your attention as well as of your time. You must have found it an Herculean Labour to wade thro' all the musty Records of all the musty Offices in London, and the Expence cannot but have been very considerable. It seems the parties are unwilling to consent to pay, by any means, less than compulsion. I sincerely wish you a speedy & successful termination of the question.

My two sons are upon a visit to Mr Curwen at Workington. They went last Wednesday & will stop two or three weeks. They will also visit the Lakes. David spent the Spring with Mr Curwen upon his large Farm called the Schoose, to learn his System of modern Agriculture & of feeding Cattle. By his attention to the business and his skill & experience in it, he became the favourite companion of Mr Curwen, who wd not part with him without a promise that he wd attend his large annual Agricultural meeting which is held today, and at which the leading Agriculturists in England, Scotland & Ireland are expected to attend.

He sent me a very polite & pressing invitation to accompany him, but this being impracticable I have indulged Joseph with the journey. Joseph has some tho^t. of standing for his Batchelor's degree next Easter, tho' the Rules of the College do not require it before Michaelmas. The female part of my family are all well and desire their kindest respects & best wishes to Mrs Blundell & yourself. R.H.

Crowland Rectory   Oct 25 1815
As you suppose public and private Concerns so multiply that I have little time for demands of my Friends not however that I forget or willingly neglect them. My great Cause proceeds slowly but I am willing to hope surely, of course troublesome and expensive. It has drawn me frequently to London, and has made me acquainted with almost, I s^d think, every Tythe Connoisseur in Great Britain. The Annuls of the Abbey are so curious that I have only to announce my Residence and Function to a Virtuoso to become his dear Friend.

Was much pleased to hear how handsomely Mr Curwen praised your Cows, it may turn to good since he ranks first among Agriculturists. What Revolutions in a land of Politics! I suppose your Manufactures are lifting their heads, ours are drooping. I fear to use no more.

As I have written in great haste I had entirely forgot to offer my Congratulations &c.,&c on your daughter's marriage and wish it may rank in the Calendar of happy days to her yourself and Connections.

Have frequently intended to write to my Godson at Oxford. Hope he is steady and serious. As Matters now stand much will depend on the rising Generation of the Clergy. The old unvaried Way, I almost said, will not do. Men must be engaged to be roused and both to be taught. And it gives me great pleasure to find that we have reason to hope a Spirit equal & adapted to Exigencies.

Biblical learning is recovering very much in Cambridge. The Young men who now come out are creditable to the place & themselves. Should wish you to enforce on Joseph the necessity of daily reading his Bible especially the Epistles with some good Commentary. The best I know & which has been to me a real Treasure is Dr Taylor's Key to the Romans & his treatise on Original Sin. Your advice also may have weight to influence him to begin writing short Sermons in order to habituate to what will be the highest satisfaction to himself and advantage to others. It is a sort of conscientious Rule to write every week. One thus can catch current Circumstances, & Edification disposes much Interest. Sermon writing is one of my favourite Amusements I may say Obsessions.

Crowland   March 1816
   I have ventured to send the Feathers as directed wh I hope will come safe and give satisfaction. They are warranted to be Live Feathers seasoned & of the first quality. Mr Jackson may remit me whenever convenient.
   Was considering the other day that Joseph be nearly of age for Orders, as I had an opportunity of helping him to a Curacy of £200 a Year near Boston. It has been accepted by the Son of the General through whom I was invited to Lincolnshire, who wd be ordained in May. Had he passed it I had thought it might suit young Birkett. And by the bye I should like to know when you write whether a situation would be acceptable. You will smile at my Concussions but we must forget Grievances & return Good for Evil. NB I wish you to take no Notice to the Vicar on the Subject.   Blundell
   PS I see by the Papers Mr Curwen is busy in canvassing for Carlisle. As matters stand, his Return seems desirable. Ld Lilford & my Neighbour Wilton have been canvasing Northampton on the Income Tax, and the clamour is almost general on all sides. The Ministers must give it up. I hope for private reasons they will, it wd seem to me they will. It wd see me to France, Lancs &c.
   Was very sorry to hear of the death of young Dr Heath, with all his Eccentricities he had many good Qualities & his worst proceeded more from Head than Heart.

[The following is a bill for a box of feathers]

    The Revd J Blundell for Mr Hodgkinson. Bot of J Yarday
          1 Box of Best Geese Feathers   £20. 8. 0
          1 Helpen Box 5 at 1/4   6. 8
    Directed by Order
    Mr Hodgkinson, Atherton Hall, Leigh, Near Manchester
    Carriage Paid to Stamford
    To be kept Dry

Crowland Rectory   April 7th 1816
A few days ago two Lancashire Gentlemen were describing to a Party over Wine the Amazing success of Mr Horrocks &c of Preston & Richd Arkwright, when one concluded with observing that not withstanding all

this, they were not on the whole to be envied. For that Horrocks had a quarrel with his Wife, parted, & died in a few days; and the other had a Wife whom he c^d not cohabit on account of her Vulgarity, & that he was obliged to board her out, &, in fact, she never attained in a domestic Capacity, beyond Washing Dishes; by w^h he meant to imply (& this construction is admitted) that she was extremely Low. An Argument was raised & Mrs Blundell who was present was appealed to, but cd not determine nor cd I. The purport of this therefore is to request you will state whether Horrocks about 25 years ago did not quit the Occupation of Journeyman Stone-Mason, commence Manufacture, has not been known to confess than he has been many days without other help than in a Choice in prosecution of his Plans, whether he did not employ more men than any in his day, & did not in 15 or 16 years after his Commencement defeat Lord Derby & die as here states.

And the other, whether he was or not a Linen Draper, in his early Years a vagabond & guilty of some things not to his Credit, whether he was assisted in the Discovery by another, whether his Wife was not somewhat in the way here mentioned & whether much Improvement has been made on his Plan of Spinning Twist? An Answer to this containing as much of their Histories as you know or can learn in a few days, would much oblige for those interested, My dear Sir Your   J Blundell.
PS I think the party mistook a Mrs Seddon for Lady Arkwright.

Atherton   15th April 1816
I have received yours of the 7th inst. respecting Sir Rd. Arkwright and Mr John Horrocks. First of Sir Richard. I can inform you that he was a Barber of the lowest order in Bolton, where he lived till his Credit and Finances were so low that he thought proper to make what is termed in Lancashire a London Flit, that is, to quit his House and carry off his Goods in the night to avoid paying his rent. Even in this low state his morals were loose and his conduct profligate and debauched. His first efforts in mechanics and machinery were assisted, and I believe in a manner directed by a native and inhabitant of Leigh of the name of Eyes[5] whom he defrauded of the just rewards of his ingenuity and contrived to get quit of as soon as his plans became productive and profitable. This practice he pursued several years getting persons of Capital to join him in erecting Mills & which when set to work he caused by one means or other to render so unproductive and apparently hazardous as to induce the parties to sell their shares at any price he would give for them. Several of his first Mills were acquired in this way. His wife, I believe, never shared

any of his good fortune even at the commencement. She was boarded at or near Blackrod at 5s a week until one of Sir Richard's sons, when he grew up, increased it to £40 a year. In Poverty and in Riches, Sir Richard never showed himself to be possessed of one single amiable quality.

John Horrocks was the son of very honest parents residing in Turton. I have seen them both often at my friend, Mr Cassons, in Bolton and my Wife drank Tea with a Sister of his there last year. His father rented a small stone Quarry near his own House in which his sons were employed, sometimes working as Masons, and sometimes driving the Cart with Flags and Stones to their Customers. In the Hills above Bolton there are many Rivlets on the Streams of which small Buildings were erected when Machinery was first applied to the working of Cotton for the sake of Carding etc., by water. At one of these I believe Mr Horrocks first commenced his Cotton business. I think he went to Preston about 1785 or 86. Here the progress he made in erecting Factories, building houses for his Work-people, extending his business both as a Spinner and Manufacturer, astonished all who saw it and very shortly rivalling in both those Branches the great Mr Watson who was supported by the Earl of Derby and was his Lordship's electioneering friend.

In 1796 he was proposed by the Corporation of Preston to be one of their Representatives in Parliament in opposition to the Earl of Derby who had always claimed the Right of returning both the Members. In this first attempt he failed. But at the next Election which was not I think more than two years after, Lord Derby found it advisable to compromise with him and to admit him as one of the Members without opposition. He continued in the House as long as he lived and at his death his Brother Samuel was elected in his Room and is now the sitting Member along with Mr Hornby's eldest son Edmund the Lawyer. Soon after he became a Member of Parliament he parted from his Wife. She was fixed in a very good house in Leyland. I have passed it often while she lived in it. He did not die for several years after the separation. The reverse of Sir Richard Arkwright, his Character was that of kindness, benevolence and liberality. His dutiful attention to his parents was exemplary and to his poorer relations he was charitable in an eminent degree.						R. Hodgkinson

PS I have heard our friend Colonel Fletcher say that the parting from his wife was the only blot he ever heard of in Mr Horrocks's Character. It is said he suspected her of infidelity. She was of a respectable Family near Bolton, her Father renting a Farm of Sixty Cheshire Acres which in that situation you know is considerable.

Atherton   December 17th, 1816
I have deferred writing a week or two that I might be able to inform you
of Joseph's return from Oxford. He arrived at Platfold last Friday night.
He had just been taking his Batchelor's Degree and I learned from various
quarters that his Examination has been very creditable to him. And for
your entertainment I have got him to put down the Books he was examined in:

'Divinity & Logic to a certain extent as things of Course, Aristotle's
Ethics and Rhetoric, Herodotus, Thucydides, Zenophon's Hellinus,
Polybius, 2 first Books Pindar, Sophocles, Homer's Iliad and Odyssey,
Livy, Virgil, Journal of Persius.'

The miserable and alarming state of this Country I have not language to
describe. The poor in many instances are literally starving, except when
they receive a pitiful and temporary relief from the Contributions of their
more fortunate neighbours whose means of assisting them must very soon
be swallowed up in the Gullets of the Poor Rates. In the last Month the
poor in Atherton alone cost £270. For the same period in my time I have
known them supported for less than £40. The very unseasonable weather
of this whole year has contributed in a large degree to increase the distress.
The Potatoes are a most failing Crop and our own Corn, particularly
Wheat, is universally damaged, I may almost say spoiled and unfit for
making Bread. I will thank you to inform me of the state of the Corn
Crops in your part of the Country & whether as much Wheat has been
sown this Season with you as usual.   Rd. Hodgkinson.

Crowland near Peterboro'   December 27th, 1816
I much hasten to congratulate you on the Success & Promising Prospects
of my Godson in the path of Science & Refinement. Should certainly recommend you to encourage a College Life, at least till his Alma Mater
confer a some thing worth acceptance. My Friend Jackson, by doing this
is, now at the head (tutor) of St. John's & in the High Road to, tis said, a
Mitre. He has also had a Money Fall by the death of Calvert Esq., of
Preston.

Mrs Blundell's Friends, in London, are all in Law, and one with whom I
am very intimate . . . is (I think) Marshall to the Chancellor, all Warrants for
Elections pass through his Hands, and is Agent to the Marquis of Hertford.
George was on a visit with him last Xmas to be led into temptation, but
came unfixed. He is returning on a visit to the son of Mrs Radcliffe's oldest
Brother who is a Bachelor, & very rich, & has been pleased to take a fancy
to George, & may probably bring him to a definite Purpose.

Am truly concerned to hear so much on the State of Trade & the Poor. And we, who, heretofore, were differently in circumstance, began to feel the Effects of the same Cause. Our Harvest was very much injured, I suppose, indeed from the usual Bulk of the Crop, much worse than in the Upland District and the Wet has certainly interfered with Seeding. Indeed things can't long continue with^t. some Change. I fear the Violence of Party-spirit in one Class, continued with the Impulse of Necessity in another, will, in the end, bring on something disastrous to existing Establishments.

I humbly conceive a Sale of Crown Lands should be made, in order to pay off the national debt. Next I wd recommend a regular acct. of Property to be made, & a certain proportion to be taken from it, which would not only exonerate the Nation, but wd continue all Ranks in the same relative position & consequently, each Individual, with less nominal Property, wd virtually be equally as rich, as he was with more under present Incumbrance. If something like this, with a Reduction of Placemen &c.&c. I begin to fear we are on the Eve of some Dreadful Commotion. As this would mean a Universal reduction of Rents of Land by the just Proprietors, this would enable the Occupier to sell the Produce cheap, that the Mechanic to work for less, &, in the end, its effects, it wd revert to the Landlord himself by reducing the expence of his Establishment. Little People would also be able to reduce theirs & thus all wd be ultimately benefitted by the temporary defalcation.   J. Blundell

Atherton   Jany. 4th, 1818
. . . an occurrence happened on Friday night which has induced Mrs Radcliffe to request me to send you an acct. of it, rather than that you sh^d receive it in a garbled state from any other hand. It is neither more nor less than that Mr Radcliffe's House again been attempted to be broken into, but Mrs Radcliffe, by that cool fortitude and resolution which we all know she possess in so eminent a degree, succeeded in keeping the Robber out of the House, tho' she was compelled to give him some money thro' the Window.

But you will be shocked (though you need never be alarmed) to hear the Villain had the audacity to fire a pistol at her while she was springing a Watchman's Rattle to alarm her Neighbours. She received a slight wound in her right Breast. All this happened ab^t 2 o'Clock in the Morning, and strange to tell was heard by none of the neighbours until after the man (for she says there was but one) had gone away & she sprung the Rattle a third time.

You may at present make yourself as easy as you can after so alarming an acc^t for we have provided for future safety by having 2 men to sleep every night in the House whom I have provided with Pistols.

But one main purport of this Letter is at the special request of Mrs Radcliffe to desire you to look out & provide for them a small comfortable House at Croyland where she says she shall endeavour to move to in ab^t two Months. This is at present made known only to me. I shall write to you again before long.　　　　　　　　　　　　　　Rd Hodgkinson

Crowland Abbey　　　　　　　　　　　　　　　　　　　　Jany 15, 1818
Mrs B & myself beg to offer our sincerest thanks. We feel very happy the affair has led them [the Radcliffes] to the voluntary current of our own wishes, as their present Residence is every way improper & nothing on our parts will I am sure be wanting to smooth & stop their declining Steps to the Bourn of Life.

I purpose to come over about the 20 of April when the Days will be longer, the Roads and Weather better, & accompany them here. We have been very busy in a County Election on the presumption of a dissolution in Spring. It is out of my way, but Lord Wilton was so importunate in his Calls & Entreaties that I sallied forth, & have been very successful to the apparent Approbation of his Lordship. Nay, conceiving that Mediocrity on this occasion, is allied to Indifference & that to Thankfulness I have been very active, and tell it not! Made a Speech at the Committee Dinner to eulogize the Spirit of Fen-Men (who had been previously been complimented for their Liberality & Independence) which no little gladdened all present, as you may suppose from the metaphorical conclusion. An Englishman of the genuine Breed, is still the same whether sheltered by a Willow or an Oak. My Candidate & I may almost call him Friend, is the eldest Son of Ld Yarboro, the intimate friend of Ld Milton.　　　J Blundell.

Atherton　　　　　　　　　　　　　　　　　　　　　　April 2nd, 1818
. . . since the outrageous attack upon Mrs Radcliffe I told you that I w^d make a point of seeing her as often as my numerous Avocations w^d permit. I have done so and have not omitted calling upon her once or twice a week. During all this time I have observed a gradual falling off of Mr Radcliffe's Mind & Memory, so much so, that he now does not know the days of the week, and will frequently in the middle of the week insist upon having his Prayer Book & being dressed for Church & on Sunday Morning, after the usual preparations he will set out & in half an hour return without having been as far as the Gates. Upon a Mind so

enfeebled you will be quite aware that Argument can have no effect.
You may succeed at the mom^t but very soon all ideas are obliterated &
you have the same Ground to fight over & over again. This has been the
case with poor Mrs Radcliffe respecting their Removal from Atherton
& my Heart has bled for her as she has from time to time & times innumerable repeated to me the ill success of her repeated attempts to prevail
upon Mr Radcliffe.

At first he repeatedly promised to comply with her wishes but latterly he purtinaciously & perseveringly objects to the Plan. . . . sh^d Mr
Radcliffe, by a force was ever so gentle be removed from a situation he
loves to one when all w^d be strange & unknown and the probable consequences ensue, which from my observations upon Mr Radcliffe I am
confident w^d ensue viz a willfulness & dissatisfaction which w^d make
him miserable & be a perpetual source of alarm & distress to his
Friends.

I am quite convinced that the Removal of Mr Radcliffe, with his present ideas w^d answer no good purpose but w^d place the comfort of your
families at a very great risk.   RH

Crowland Abbey   August 26, 1818
Such is the force of appreciation that, in despite of former habits, I daily
become more & more attached to Farming & have lately intended my
pursuits that way with considerable success. This year, indeed, I understand, is likely to be unusually productive to agricultural Enjoyment, &
especially to growing wool.

About 6 weeks back we were in the midst of Electioneering for the
County. On those occasions all who have interests have Court & I had
the honour of being first made active & then sent for expressly to Lincoln;
& what is worth all, happened to side with the prevailing party the Lord
Yarborough. During the time all was bustle & activity, I seldom enjoyed
anything more.   J Blundell.

Crowland Abbey   Sep 29, 1818
This very day I have been 20 years married and just 10 years Rector of
Crowland & tho' I have a Son who is no small Momento, yet in spite of
all I can't conceive how such progress has been made by those whom I
left in their Infancy. Had I not seen your Dau^r. last Sum^r. I shd have picture in my mind a Girl in Teens; & Friend David, a boney Youth of 16.
You will readily conceive then the almost Electrification I felt, when I
heard him gravely discounting on his Citizenship with Old Bachelors. I

suppose he does not mean to buckle to.

As I understand Lady Lilford is over, I wish, if opportunity offers, you wd convey my acknowledgem^{ts}., & express my Concern for not recognizing her noble Lord when I saw him at a little distance last Summer.

The truth is I always feel awkward with such People under existing Circum^s. as I maybe supposed to have risen, I always fear any officiousness may be deemed presumptious & the want of it to a certain degree a summary want of Gratitude. I always however endeavour to reconcile the conflict by feeling a consciousness of the latter, & leaving the other to such opportunities as seem to elicit & make the advance reciprocal.

J. Blundell.

Crowland Rectory   March 12, 1818

I suspect the late unpleasant Proceedings must have also contributed to mortify, sour, & disgust both yourself and every one who felt for the miseries of the distressed, & I witnessed the abuse of the best means for Relief. I have long tho^t. the Opposition were doing great injury both in Religion & Politics. In order to strengthen their Cause, they have endeavoured to incorporate the restless, disaffected, ambitious, impoverished and such discordia Semina as can never amalgamate with producing a Monster. But I now begin to hope this was either the Bale of the day, or men have seen their error & with it the necessity of Reform. The late Election has made the parties define Creeds & it seems the Revolutionists were but a feeble party among the Reformists. The real Whigs in consequence, will rise in estimation & I trust, the examination will extend from Political to Religious Opinion, & Morality will be the general Result.

I have been looking out for something that might promise to make Joseph a Fenn man, and I hope in success in a Curc. not far distant, but an arrangement was made which rendered it below notice. If he intends to take a Curc. let me know a little before & I will do my best for him. My Friend Jackson, now Calvert,[6] Tutor of St John's, is made Margaret Professor & in consequence will shortly be instituted to a living in Norfolk, about 20 Miles from here, of £1500 a year. Besides other Emoluments, report says he wd. shortly be on the Bench of Bishops. He is coming shortly to see me, & seems to express much anxiety to assist George who, at his particular request is now at Oakham under the celebrated Dr Doncaster.

J Blundell.

Atherton   21st July, 1819

Joseph came home ab^t a fortnight ago, having taken his Master's Degree on the 3rd June. His Hulme's Exhibition does not expire before next Easter till which time he intends staying in College. This he wished the more on acc^t. of receiving ano^r. Year's allowance of £20 worth of Books from the Exhibition wch he cannot do unless he be resident on the 25th March, on wch day they become due. To effect this, & at the same time to get into Orders as soon as possible, he was desirous of procuring a Title from some one who might dispense wth Residence till next Easter. As present Emolum^t. was no object to us we hoped to prevail on some Friend to assist us, Confident that we might expect from you every assistance in your power. Joseph & I were sat down the other day to write a Let^r. to you, when David came out of the Hay field to his Dinner, and to our very great Surprise told us that Mr Birkett had just been with him and said that he was ready to give Joseph a Title whenever he wanted one. David said he believed it ^wd not be wanted before next Year. However in a day or two I called upon Birkett, & told him our views, when he ans^d. he was ready to do it now. Two little doubts still remain upon my Mind: lst. The College sometimes hesitates in giving Testimonials so long before hand, but Exhibitioners are allow'd to reside six months in Orders before their Exhibition expires, so I hope this will be got over. The other is that perhaps the Bishop may have some scruples on acc^t. of Mr Birkett having given two Titles to his Sons so lately (and this was the reason why I did not apply to Mr Birkett, whose obligations to me you know) but I hope I can surmount this difficulty sh^d it arise, by a personal acquaintance which I have with Mr Slade, the Vicar of Bolton, who is son in Law to the Bishop & the examining Chaplain of the Ordination.

You may think me a little singular but I am rather desirous that Jos^h. sh^d settle at a distance from home & therefore I shall draw upon your Friendship for any assistance you may be able to lend us sh^d any thing worth attention offer itself in your neighbourhood.

I have lately been in London, being sent up with your Friends Col. Fletcher & Major Watkins to watch the progress thro' the House of a Bill for making a junction of the Canal at Leigh with that at Wigan, and to procure the insertion of a Clause to protect our Turnpike Road. After 8 days attendance we succeeded in getting the Clause inserted. I returned thro' Oxford & spent 2 days with Joseph. I had a safe & a pleasant Journey, being from home just a Fortnight, receiving a Guinea & a half per day, and Coach fare paid both ways.

We are threatened with fresh Riots & Disturbances here. I am going this morning to meet all the Magistrates of the Division at Warrington to deliberate upon the best Measures for preserving the public Peace & strengthening the hands of the Civil Power. R.H.

Crowland Feb 21, 1819

By a letter from George today I have the pleasure to learn that he has procured from his Master, Dr Doncaster, the offer of the 2nd Mastership with 3 Curacies, val. £200 a year, for your son Joseph, till next Mid Summer; with the farther promise of the utmost exertion to do everything to promote his future advancement & the certain promise of the Curacies belonging to the person who will then become Master. To use George's own words, it will make his fortune, & I really think would be the very thing. The Dr is a most excellent man; the neighbourhood good, & every thing in favour.

If this meets Joseph's Ideas, had he not best come over? A Coach from Leicester run thro on Tuesdays, Thursdays, & Saturdays. If therefore he proceeds from Manchester on the Evening previous about 3 o'Clock he will be in Leicester at 6, the Oakham runs ab^t 7 and arrives at 12. If he cannot come or doesn't accept this he will write immediately as the Dr keeps it open. J Blundell.

Atherton 25th Sept, 1819

Joseph is now at Chester for his Ordination which sh^d take place to-morrow. He had his Testimonials sent from College without delay, but we anticipated some demur by the Bishop, on acc^t of Residence & also on acct. of Mr Birkett having given Titles to his two Sons so lately. In a very civil Let. we had from the Bishop to Joseph a few weeks ago, he says, 'I am ready to receive you as a Candidate for Orders upon Mr Birkett's nomination, but I hope you intend to reside, as I cannot admit any other Candidate from him for sometime to come'. Joseph expressed doubts when he left home whether, upon investigation, the Bishop, w^d under the circumstances, ordain him at all at present, for you will recollect I mentioned in a former Let. that, Joseph intends to continue at Oxford till Easter. Should he be ordained to-morrow it will be Monday Evening before he can get home of course. Till that time I must remain in suspense & till his return I am quite uncertain what injunctions the Bishop may lay upon him. I have now only just time to thank you for your exertions, the Post is coming up the Yard. R.H.

Atherton   Sept. 28th, 1819
I only returned after my Ordination last night when My Father gave to
me your two last Letters, the former he'd delayed acknowledging the
Rec^t. of an acc^t of the uncertainty of my being ordained, for I had determined to give up my Ordination, at present, rather than not complete my
time till Easter at Oxford. I had two motives for my determination to
continue there, one, that I might not lose twenty Guineas worth of Books
which I can only claim by being resident there on the 25th March; the
other and principle one, was that I might employ the time for my own
Reading, having for the last three years been too much engaged with
Pupils. As a Master the taking of Pupils is optional with me; as a Bachelor,
the College could compel me. I was anxious to be ordained at present,
that I might be enabled to take my Priest's Orders soon after quitting
College. But this c^d only be done by getting a Title from a place where
my Services c^d be dispensed with for a time. By doing this for me in the
handsome manner he has done, Mr Birkett has cancelled many obligations
which he owed my Father. The Bishop . . . was not very pressing on the
Article of Residence so that my remaining at Oxford is an arrangement
solely between Mr Birkett and myself.

   Under these Circumstances . . . I think it will not be prudent to Quit
the Diocese before I take Priest's Orders for which I propose to offer
myself a candidate at the next Easter Ordination. After which I shall be
happy to accept any such situation as you have now so kindly mentioned
in your Let of the 21st.   Joseph Hodgkinson.

Atherton   Oct 25th, 1819
From the very embarrassed state in which our neighbourhood is now
placed as you will perceive by all the public Prints, you will naturally feel
some anxiety for your old friends and acquaintances who are placed in the
midst of it and are so circumstanced as not to be able to quit it. Among
these you will conclude that I for one am not sleeping on a Bed of Roses.
The great extent of Lord Lilford's Property and Concerns necessarily
involves me in all the inconveniences and distresses of this populous
Parish. Guilty of two offences, unpardonable at this present day, viz: of
being possessed of Property myself and of managing the property of a
Nobleman. I am of course supposed to be Foe to Reform. This however
has not as yet subjected me to any personal insult or inconvenience nor
do I find that any violence or threats are denounced against me as they are
against some of my neighbours who I really think are in personal danger.
The state of the Country is very alarming. All sense of Morality and

Religion seems totally to have forsaken the great Mass of the People. Led by appetite and passion alone they are ripe for all the horrors of a French Revolution and Bloodshed, Rapine and Plunder, forms the general topic of familiar Conversation. And they are sedulous by arming themselves with offensive weapons of every denomination.

Riches are made in great number by all the Smiths hereabouts. We have one in Custody now whose Deposition (with the dts. of a Pike made by him) we have sent to Lord Sidmouth with a request to send a Troop of Horse to be stationed at Leigh. By a letter I received from Lord Lilford yesterday who has had an interview with Lord Sidmouth, it appears doubtful that no Troops can be spared for us. An armed Association is talked of but this I think cannot be effected and if it cd I leave to your judget what a state we must be living in. Every Individual who comes forward with spirit instantly becomes a marked man and the grossest language and the coarsest epithets are heaped upon him with threats of savage import, whatever his Rank in life may be. The higher his Rank the more violent the Abuse. Next Monday is said to be the day fixed for a general Rising of the Mob. If it be so some Blood will necessarily be spilt and when civil War begins who shall say where it will end.

By the blasphemous, seditious & rebellious cheap publications which issue daily from the Press, the People are persuaded that they do not occupy their proper position in society. That Property is unjustly withheld from them. That they have a right to a full share of all Property and to seize it by force is only to take their own. Of the consequence of such doctrines as these in a neighbourhood like this, overflowing with people & poverty, you will be well aware.   R.H.

Crowland Rectory   November 22nd, 1819
A circumstance has occurred wh has given me just pleasure. Mr Warren, the Gentleman appointed to the 2nd Mastership of Oakham, & to whom Joseph was to have been temporary substitute, was so much pleased, it seems, with the interest George took at once to serve him as the Friend of his Father, that the other day, wrote to offer George the nomination to his two Curacies wh wl be vacant in January. Elated with success George wrote immediately & in great haste to me, requesting I wd lose no time in communicating the offer to Joseph, wh I accordingly did by a special Messenger to Peterboro (It not being our Post-day) and made such Comments as time allowed. 'It is,' says George, 'a most desirable situation for a single Gent. who wished to be free from HouseKeeping. There are two Curacies, salary £120 inclusive of House Keeping. It is I believe a

most delightful Situation etc etc.' It is Winkfield Rectory, Bradford, Wilts. There is one Item, I mean the exclusive HouseKeeping, rather ambiguously expressed. But if it turn out, as I suspect that this means Free Commons with the Rector . . . it strikes me that this w^d be an eligible Introduction for Joseph.

Was sorry to find the Radicals were proceeding to such lengths. I fear the thing is but in Embryo, unless a something, at present, not known of, occurs to prevent.   J Blundell.

Atherton   26th November, 1819
Joseph . . . informs me of the Receipt of your Let, his serious deliberations upon the very handsome offer it contained, the result of those deliberations, and his reasons for that result. In the Ans^r which he says he has written to you I take for granted he has assigned his reasons, and if, from the perturbed state of mind, in which I am sure he wrote, they sh^d not appear sufficiently clear & cogent to you, I hope he will be able to explain them more fully when you see him at Croyland, which, I suppose will be in the course of a fortnight.

Upon the first perusal of your Letter, I was much pleased with the offer, and tho^t it altogether very eligible. Upon farther reflection I began to be staggered at the distance it w^d remove him from us & quite into a strange district and still without his Priests' Orders. But all these sh^d not have weighed a Straw with me if he had chosen it.   RH

St Guthlais   Decr 20, 1819
I c^d not allow your Son to quit the Fenns without charging him with a Congratulation on his attainments, deportment & what is to me a most favourable trait, his manner, of performing the professional duties. Being conscious that manner is a first step to eminence & notoriety, I have drilled him perpetually on the subject. As far as I can judge there is every indication of the qualities which form the Man & Christian, and had he continued much longer I perceive it w^d have been his own fault if he did not bring with him, if not a Golden Fleece, what would have been equally valuable, some of our Shepherdesses.

Your Accounts of Lancashire are shocking, but hope the present Exposition will lead the Government to do every thing to repress Rebellion, & to remove Want. Am willing to hope the former proceeds from, & will subside with, the latter. But the Spirit seems infectious, as we begin to hear of embryo Radicals in our own Neighbourhood. The present Administration have certainly brought a convulsive War to an honorable conclusion, & therefore, seem entitled to respect & approbation. But as, from cause or other, they have incurred the dislike of so many. I begin to wish, they w^d allow the experiment of Change. Without, however, anticipating the Result, as to amelioration, it appears doubtful whether, in the present state of affairs, an alteration for the Better wd satisfy those who have been most active in promoting the question. It seems one of those Political Diseases w^h cannot be cured till some violent effort has at once passed & shaken, the Constitution. J Blundell.

Atherton 10th Feby, 1820
I write to inform you that soon after Joseph's Arrival in Oxford after the Christmas Vacation, Dr Smith, of Manchester, called upon him . . . to make Joseph the following Offer, viz: to be his Assistant in the School at £150 per Ann., and to be his Curate at St Peter's Church. Joseph did not like to undertake more than half the Duty of the Church and for that he is to have £50 a Year. Subject to my approbation and the Bishop's permission for him to give up his Curacy at Leigh he closed with the Doctor's Offer. We rec^d the Bishop's permission last Friday in a Let. to his son in Law, Mr Slade, the Vicar of Bolton, who had written to the Bishop at my request. He says 'Under the circumstances Mr Hodgkinson presents himself I cannot object and he has my full permission to accept Dr Smith's Offer with my warmest wishes for his success.' The situation altogether will be arduous but I think it will for young men to be so placed that the whole strength of their Talents must necessarily be exerted. This will be the case both in the School and the Church. I suppose the Congregation at St Peter's is the most genteel of any in Manchester, and in the School he will have the two Classes immediately below Dr Smith's first Class that is, he receives the boys from the second Master and prepares them for the highest Class.

I was at Manc^r on Tuesday witnessing the Marriage of my old Friend, Mr Nuttall. I observed to my family when I returned home yesterday, that when any of my friends wished to play the fool I sh^d be glad they w^d not send for me to help them.

I am just going down to Leigh to assist in proclaiming King George the 4th. The procession is expected to be numerous, we dine at Isherwoods.

RH

Crowland Abbey June 2, 1820
I suppose Friend David is still an Old Bachelor. I have a Shepherdess, that I laid out for his Bro^r with the thous^d Charms & Pounds, that I think w^d just suit him.

I was very sorry to hear from Mr Fred. Powys, who took a Bed with me a little time back, that Lady Lilford is very seriously ill. Hope she is better. Fortune can ill supply her place to such a family.

The accounts from Lan^r are very distressing, but hope trade survives & the Current has found its height and begins to flow back. Tho I fear it subsides only to rise with more fatal effects, when the latent Breath of Fury begins to operate. You must have been in a most alarming predicament. Here we know little of misery, excepting the objects who stray down to seek a refuge from distress, or an Asylum from Justice. Hope the King by a Change of Ministry, if even the Change produce no food, or something that might shew a wish to conciliate, will endeavour to check the growing principle of dissatisfaction. I think a sale of Crown Desmenses and a general Sacrifice of property en masse wd not only be an useful expedient but w^d at once disencumber the State, and leave all ranks in the same proportion to each other that they were before. And tho' there wd be a surrender there w^d no loss, since we may presume the reduction of taxes and direct & indirect, make up the sacrifices. J Blundell.

Written by Mr H. after the death of Mr Radcliffe, Mrs B's father
Atherton   August 22nd, 1820
I apprehend you may begin to think the Ladies rather long in coming but to wind up a whole concern, however small, cannot be done at once. The alterations at the House took up a considerable time, and some time was spent in considering what was best to be done, & Mrs Blundell's Indisposition was a severe blow at the last.

I hope Joseph will find time to write to Mrs Blundell but he has had a busy Summer. Dr Smith left home the Morning the School broke up & only returned on Saturday night previous to its re-opening on the Monday, so that Joseph had the whole Duty of the Church during the Vacation; of which he only spent four days at Plat-fold. He had also to write & preach a Charity Sermon at Sankey Chapel near Warrington. And that he might have no leisure at all during the Vacation he was requested by the Board of Trustees at the Infirmary to write the Preface to their annual Report. This he delivered in ab^t a fortnight ago & I daily expect the Report coming out. (He is also preparing for his second appearance before the Bishop). He likes his Situation and I like it. He is closely engaged and young men sh^d be so, and to the extent of their Talents too. The Dr is kind, civil, friendly & attentive to him. He dines with the Dr every Sunday. It is no small credit to be under the wing of such a Man. Mr Elsdaile, the 2nd Master is also very attentive to him.

Joseph is much attached both to him & his Lady. The Congregation at St Peters' continue to be partial to Joseph. Were not his time closely taken up, I sh^d fear some of them being too attentive to him and engaging too much of his time. There has been a Confirmation at Man^r on the 10th inst, he pleased the Congregation much by giving them a Sermon on the subject in the Dr's absence.

The public Prints will have informed you of the death of Lady Lilford, an event for which you w^d be prepared by the Acc^t which I understand Mr F Powys gave you of her when he was at Croyland. The loss of her must in her Family be most severely felt.

Mrs Blundell will inform you of Mr Birkett's altered state of health as she will of any little local news we may have here. The Newspapers will supply you with abundance of public News, which is, and I fear will continue to be of a very acrid and gloomy cast, till some great Convulsion take place not only in England, but throughout Europe and indeed thro' the known World. The restlessness and irritability of public Feeling I do not attribute to anything peculiar to our own State of Nature. It must be something more general, as it extends far beyond our Limits & our Influence. I rather attribute it to the general diffusion of Learning, and the facility of Communication between one place and another. Learning (I will not call it knowledge) has changed its characteristics since Cicero's time. Instead of softening men's manners, it renders them fierce and intractable. Instead of opening and expanding the better feelings of the Heart, it contracts & poisons them & instead of reasoning up from Nature's Works to Nature's God it begets Scepticism, Atheism & every evil Will & every evil Work. We must not then wonder at Riots, Rebellion and Revolution. But enough of this.

Crowland Abbey   Sept 8 1820
From what I have been able to observe, Joseph w^d become an eminent Pastor, if he will only have perseverance & Confidence. You will & must agree with me that the Clergy in general fail more from the want of these than profound Learning. This I have always endeavoured to impress upon his mind; & from his remarks, I begin to hope not without producing the desired affect. Was sorry to hear of the decline of Mr Birkett's Health. He has frequently been ill & recovered but I understand he now exhibits symptoms of real decay. Hope you will be able to place my young Friend in his Shoes.   J Blundell.

Atherton   Jany 8th, 1821
Mrs Jackson is just come out of her confinement having had another son,
& Mrs R Guest is still in her confinement of a Dau^r. The Lads fortunately
keep out of the matrimonial noose.

At present Joseph is spending part of each week with us here, but as the
Doct always absents himself during the Vacations, he has all the Church Duty
upon his hands. Having to go to Manc^r at the weeks end and sometimes not
getting back before Tuesday, & having two Sermons to prepare weekly, he
has but little time to devote to his Friends. I have a nice little Horse for him
here, so that he is not unaccommodated for want of Conveyance & the
exercise does him good. I hope he will find time to address a few lines to you.
He left us early on Saturday & is not returned. David is as usual; he is very
partial to his Brother and affords him every accommodation in his power.

Your friend Mr Calvert, I suppose, will find some opposition before he
is quietly seated in the Rectory of Wilmslow. It is said the Catholics will
encourage Mr Trafford to resist the appointment, with what prospect of
success I know not. I have heard nothing of it for some weeks past.

I suppose George has made his debut at Cambridge, shall be happy to
hear he finds himself comfortable there. I imagine your Plans respecting
Thomas are settled by this time. Tis no easy matter to fix ones' sons in the
right place & to our own satisfaction.   R^d Hodgkinson.

To Mrs Radcliffe, Mrs Blundell's mother, from Hodgkinson.
                                                          Jany 28th, 1821
Hon^d. Madam, Lord Lilford . . . has been at Winwick more than a fortnight
but does not intend coming to Atherton at all at present. This has given me
no little trouble, as I have had to go to him nearly every other day since he
came. He returns on Tuesday & tomorrow I am taking Mrs Standish with
me in a Chaise to pay her respects to him for the first time. I think you had
left Lancashire before Mrs Standish & I rec^d each a Ring in Memory of Lady
Lilford. Hers is a large plain gold Hoop, mine is a real mourning Ring; I
understand fifteen were made for Gentlemen all of the same Pattern.

Mr Birkett's health does not improve. We have had his Son Thomas
doing Duty to-day. Mrs Birkett is quite well. Miss Lewen returned from
Liverpool ab^t a week ago, where she had been living gayly & yet left half
her Visits unpaid.

If the weather has been as fine at Crowland as it has been here you will
have had a very favourable Seasoning in the Fens. I shall be happy to hear
that your health has not suffered by the change. I shall also like to hear
that the little Invalid[7] continues to improve.   Rd. Hodgkinson.

Notes

1   The Revd John Clowes, rector of St John's Church, Manchester, is said to have presided over the followers in Bolton, including Samuel Crompton, of Emanuel Swedenborg. Gilbert J. French, *Life and Times of Samuel Crompton* (1859).

2   Blundell's friend was probably James Whitsed, his patron for the living of Crowland.

3   Mr Birkett was the vicar of Leigh.

4   These were the Leghs of Lyme Hall near Stockport.

5   In Arkwright's trial, and in several other works, the name is spelt Hays, but Mr Guest says it is written Highs in Leigh Church Register, and is so pronounced by his family and neighbourhood. Edward Baines, *History of the Cotton Manufacture in Great Britain* (1835), p. 142.

6   Thomas Jackson, whose principal home was in Ardwick, Manchester, adopted the name Calvert in 1817. Norrisian Professor of Divinity (1815–24), he was Lady Margaret Preacher with an annual stipend of £8 from 1819 to 1824. He died in 1840 and was buried in Manchester Collegiate Church.

7   This is Blundell's son James who was injured in an accident with a sheep.

13

Richard's Visit to Crowland, 1822, & more Blundell Letters

On 15 August 1822, with his son's struggle with the parishioners at Astley Chapel at its height, Richard Hodgkinson went on business to the Lilford Estate in Northamptonshire and on his way home made a visit of reconciliation to the Revd James Blundell at Crowland. Blundell, a spendthrift and in a state of high anxiety, had feuded with his wife's mother, Mrs Radcliffe, since soon after their marriage. Following Mrs Radcliffe's death, Mrs Blundell had inherited her estate, a circumstance that angered James Blundell who turned to violence in his desperation to get his own hands on the money. How Hodgkinson, mainly at the expense of Mrs Blundell, solved this delicate problem is related below.

On his way to Lilford and Crowland, Hodgkinson discussed the current state of the textile industry with a local manufacturer and gossiped with a fellow traveller on the misfortunes of a landed family brought to penury at the gaming tables.

Journey to Lincolnshire
by Richard Hodgkinson

Thomas Smith of Bedford, manufacturer, informed me that there are at this time thirty thousand Pieces of Cotton Goods produced weekly by Power Looms, and that ten thousand workmen are employed in weaving them which allows three pieces weekly for each person.

He says that the Wages for weaving a sixty Reed Muslin Piece with one hundred and sixty picks to the Inch is 8/6 and one fourth of that sum to be deducted for Outgoings viz: Looms and Winding etc., that to weave one of these Pieces is a fair average week's work for one Weaver and tho' some Weavers will do much more he reckons that taking all the Weavers together, Men, Women and Children, they do not average more than half a Piece per week. He himself has 800 Weavers, but does not take in more than 400 Pieces in each week.

He says that in the last Year one hundred and twenty seven millions of pounds of Cotton was spun into Yarn in the Country, of which seventeen Million was exported in the Yarn, and about eight millions of it was used by the power looms.

The thirty thousand Pieces which are made weekly by the power Looms, he says, is only one fourteenth of the whole quantity manufactured weekly.

Mr Johnson Eden, of Manchester, who travelled in the Coach with me from Manchester to Ashbourne said he had been informed by a Gentleman from London that in the Parish of Marylebone, three hundred and seventy Gentlemen's Carriages had been laid down this Year. We had been talking on the subject of the low price of Corn & other agricultural produce, the consequent reduction of Rents and the necessity landed Gentlemen would be under of reducing their Establishments & contracting their Expenses. I ment Sir Rich. Brookes having begun to contract his Expenses. Mr Eden says he was well assur'd, indeed knew it for a fact, that Sir Rd. Brookes Father in Law, Sir Foster Cunliffe had laid down his Carriage. And he went on to say that Sir Watkin Williams Wynne had entirely broken up his immense Establishment at Wynnstay and was removing himself and his whole Family into Switzerland. The Cause was this; that the Reduction of his Rents had so contracted his Income that when he had paid the Interest of the large Sums of Money he owed, and the heavy Annuities with which Estates were encumbered, he had not one shilling of clear annual Revenue left, and I said this must have been the foundation of a report I heard about a fortnight ago that Sir Watkin was completely ruined, but it was said by gaming, but I observed that I had never understood that Sir Watkin did gamble. But Mr Eden said he did very deeply some years ago and that our Present King had many thousand pounds of his Money. He added that a Gentleman told him who had frequently met Sir Watkin at the Gaming Table, that he has often seen him come into the room half drunk and sitting down at the Table, pull a large Rouleau of Bank Notes out of his pocket and laying them before him, wd in a short time sink his head upon them and be fast asleep. And when he had a throw to make, or any thing to say in prosecution of the Game his companions would slap him on the shoulder, saying, Come

Wat, what do you do next, and thus half drunk, half asleep and half awake, he suffered himself to be plundered without mercy & without end. Mr Eden said that the Debts upon Sir Watkin's Estates amount to no less that four hundred thousand pounds.

Mr Eden also said that being at Liverpool last Saturday he met with a person from Stamford in Lincolnshire with whom he had been acquainted many years. He inquired of him the price of sending Articles of farming Produce and among the rest of Barley, the Gentleman answered there were various prices of Barley and on acct of the very inferior quality of last Year's Barley, some of them were very low, in short they had all prices from ten to sixteen shillings per Quarter, so that the very highest price was only two shillings per Bushel.

As proof of the reduction of Labourer's Wages he said he had twenty Statute Acres of good Meadow Grass near Stamford to cut and he had set it to a man to cut at the low price of fifteen pence and one Quart of Ale per statute Acre.

On talking on this subject with Mr Selby[1] at Lilford he said he had no doubt that Hay Grass had been cut this Year at the price before mentioned but the usual price this Year had been two shilling per acre. 2/3 had been the usual price before and in good times 2/6 but whatever the price was in Money the allowance of the Ale was only one Quart per Acre.

Aug 21st
I left Lilford. Mr Selby furnished me with a Horse to Oundle and a man to carry my Portmanteau. At Oundle I took a Chaise to Peterbro' and from thence to Crowland where I arrived at 2 o'Clock. Mr and Mrs Blundell were both at home. Mrs B was very well but Mr B had for a few days been very unwell. On the preceding Saturday he had been suddenly taken ill and a Physician from Peterbro' had been called in, and copious bleeding had been found necessary both by cupping bleeding in the Arm, and Leeches on the Temples. He says he had for some time been over exerting himself, the Bishop having a fortnight ago held a Confirmation at Spalding for which he had to prepare his young Parishioners.

On the day after the Confirmation the Bishop had to consecrate his Church at Waplode Drove which had been rebuilt and at the same day dined with him at Crowland and last of all the sudden and most awful death of the Marquis of Londonderry had a most serious effect upon him and quite overcame him. The Fact is Mr Blundell is become very nervous, and often on very trifling matters, his feelings are excited and his

Mind disturbed in a very distressing degree and I find his family are not without weariness on his account.

Aug 22nd

Mr Blundell was better this Morning than the preceding day. He had not resolution to ride out with me but a Horse was procured for me and his son, George, and I rode as far as Thorney. The Country being very flat there is not variety of prospects and the scene was the less interesting as the Corn Harvest was just closing no Corn uncut and scarcely any uncarried. Thorney is a small neat Town, with a good Church and Parsonage & House in it. The Clergyman is a Mr Wing whose Brother lives in a very neat house just opposite the Vicarage and is the agent to the Duke of Bedford for his property here. The Duke is the sole Owner of the Town of Thorney, of the Church & of that vast tract of land called Thorney Fenn containing twenty thousand Statute Acres of Land within a ring Fence. The Tenants I understand are very liberally treated by the present Duke. The Land is of the most fertile quality and the Rent below twenty shillings per Acre. For some Years past this Rent was about 25/- per Acre from which an abatement was made last Year of 25 per Cent. It is well known that all this immense Estate was formerly belonging to the Church and was so secured in the general plunder of the Abbeys and Churches by the Duke of Bedford in the time of Henry the Eighth.

In the afternoon Mr Blundell was still better and in tolerable Spirits. My journey to Crowland was undertaken in great measure to bring about a reconciliation between Mr and Mrs Blundell whose peace had been very much interrupted since the death of Mrs. Radcliffe in consequence of her Will. Mrs Radcliffe had left all her property to Mrs Blundell and had made me Executor and Trustee. Mr Blundell was very indignant at not being men^t in the Will conceiving it to be the result of Mrs Radcliffe's revenge upon him in consequence of very serious quarrels between him and her son after the Marriage. He became quite violent upon knowing the Contents of the Will, and certainly for some time used Mrs Blundell very ill. He then came into Lancashire last Summer and spend a few days with me at Plat-fold, during which time it was agreed, by the desire of Mrs Blundell, that I should resign the Executorship and she would then have to administer her Mother's Personality, whereby Mr Blundell, as her Husband, would necessarily become Administrator and thereby be entitled to the Personality in his own right which might amount to about four hundred pounds.

I conceived this to be reasonable as Mr Blundell had a family of six

Children all of whom at that time were receiving an expensive Education, & Money was wanted. I still retain the Trusteeship of the freehold Property, Mrs Blundell having the power of receiving the Rents. Mr Blundell, I find has already drawn out of the Funds what Money was there and also what was in the Bank and has taken possession of all the Personality. He appears now to be pretty well reconciled, but I have no doubt that the phrenzy of Mind, into which he threw himself on acct of Mrs Radcliffe's Will, and in which he continued after some Months added to that irritability of Temper and excitement of Feeling to which he ws ever too prone, has tended in no slight degree to subject his Constitution to that malady under which he is now labouring.

His domestic expenses are very great. He has a Governess in the House for his three Daughters to whom he gives 30 Guineas a Year Wages besides Maintenance. His eldest son George is now at Cambridge where his Expenses exceed two hundred pounds a Year. He has lately paid a large Fee with his second Son Thomas to a Chymist and Druggist in Peterborough; and his youngest Son James, a boy of twelve years old is at home, who has scarcely commenced a regular Education. He is just now loosing Money by several of his Tenants who on Acct of the very distressed state of Agriculture cannot possibly pay their Rents. He has also lost some Money lately by a Horse or two, which he has been unfortunate in purchasing. All these things press upon his Mind, and the anxiety he appears to feel respecting money matters, I fear he has not made such annual savings from his large Church Revenue as prudence might suggest and they fairly might afford to do.

I am told Crowland is worth three hundred pounds a Year. There is a good Parsonage house upon it, amply sufficient for the accommodation of all his Family. To this living he was appointed in 1808. He tells me himself that the living of Waplode Drove is full five hundred pounds a Year, to this he was appointed in 1810. And he has the curacy of Cubbets[2] for which he receives as much as he gives to his Curate, so that he appears to have an Income of at least eight hundred pounds a Year. Mr Blundell has always maintained himself and his family very respectably but such a Revenue as above stated, for such a length of time, shd have provided a Fund for Contingencies more than enough to prevent any uneasiness abt money matters.

Aug 23rd
This morning as Mr B was about to get up he was seized with the fainting Fits and was unable to come down to Breakfast and Mrs B was so uneasy

that she sent for the Apothecary. He said they were nothing more than he expected and that probably they would continue occasionally for some time, till his strength was restored from the excessive Bleeding he had undergone.

Mr Blundell not getting up, I had opportunity of walking out alone after Breakfast. I went thro' the Town and to the Banks of the Wash.[3] This Wash is a very low lying piece of Ground; extending sixteen Miles from Spalding past Crowland to Deeping and is enclosed by an Embankment on the North and South sides, varying in breadth from half to three quarters of a mile. The use of this Wash is, that as the Country here is very flat, and the River which runs through the Wash meets the Sea-Side at Spalding ten miles below Crowland, cannot discharge the Waters at its Mouth as rapidly as they descend from the High-lands as they are called, above Deeping towards Leicestershire, this Wash is to retain the surplus Water which comes down in immense quantities in rainy Seasons, until it gradually discharges itself into the Sea.

In the Winter Season this vast tract of Land, sixteen Miles long and nearly a Mile in breadth is frequently filled with Water to the tops of the Banks, and last Winter it ran over the Banks in many places. When it is full the depth averages sixteen feet at the least. When I was in Crowland in 1812 and at this time of the Year a considerable quantity of Water was in the Wash, and the great part of it appeared like a soft springy Morass. Since then it has been divided like a Common and allotted to the respective landowners and now appears like the surrounding Country, the various Allotments being stocked with Cattle, converted into Meadows or even into Corn Fields. I walked more than half-way across it at the back of Crowland and found it firm as any of the surrounding Lands and certainly it is surprising when viewing it in its present state to be told that as far as the Eye can carry will be a complete Sea for weeks together perhaps in the course of two Months.

In returning I passed thro' a different part of the Town and could not help observing that all the Houses, however mean in appearance, were clean to a degree in the inside. This may in some measure be accounted for, from a knowledge of this fact that the men are mostly if not altogether Agricultural Labourers, and are out of the House all the day, making no dirty work by any in-door occupation, or passing to the Fire numberless times in a day as is done in the Weavers' Cottages in Lancashire, raising a dust every time they put their drying Iron into or draw it out of the Fire.[4] Passing by the Inn where I had put my Horse and Gig in 1812, I called in for a Glass of Brandy and Water. I found the same Landlady there as

before and she soon recognized me, when I ment^d the circumstance. I
was very sorry to hear her remark that several of Mr Blundell's Friends
had observed that he had changed much in appearance and were apprehensive that his Health was gradually declining. She said that Mr Blundell
and his Family still kept up the respectability in their situation which they
had ever done, and still met with the same Civilities and Attentions from
their Neighbours.

When I returned about one o'Clock I found Mr Blundell got up and in
pretty good Spirits. We dined at two. In the course of the Afternoon I
proposed a walk into the Abbey saying I was very desirous of seeing the
place where Mrs Radcliffe was buried. We went at four o'Clock. After
the Sexton had unlocked the Doors Mr Blundell desired him to retire and
leave us. Upon entering the Abbey after some observations on several
Monuments affixed to the walls and some remarks upon the curious structure of the Cieling (sic) Mr B led me up to the Communion Rails within
which he pointed to the place where the Remains of Mrs Radcliffe were
deposited in a Vault. Close to the Rails on the North side of the
Communion is a Vault which Mr Whitsed[5] had made for himself when
Mrs Radcliffe died, and close to it on the South and nearer to the Altar is
the Vault in which Mrs Radcliffe is interred, and where her Dust may
probably mingle with the Dust of Kings.

Here was a favourable opportunity (which I had sought indeed by
wishing to come to the Abbey) of entering upon the subject which had,
in a great measure, induced me to visit Crowland. I had learned by a letter
from Mrs Blundell rec^d some Months ago, that Mr B after his return from
Lancashire last Year, continued very indignant about her Mother's Will
and with a temper truly indignant used every means to make her unhappy, treating with the most marked contempt everything that had belonged
to her Mother and insulting her Memory on every occasion. From the
hostile Spirit which he had shewed when in Lancashire I had determined
not to give up the Trusteeship and thereby leave Mrs Blundell wholly at
his Mercy, and by my visit I intended to shew him the injustice of his
Conduct and to induce him to restore Peace to his Family if his own
good sense had not already led him to do so. I began by observing that I
felt a great satisfaction at viewing the burial place of Mrs Radcliffe at
Crowland and that I should have felt a great disappointment if she had not
lived to come there. He knew how much I possessed the Confidence of
Mrs Radcliffe, and I could assure him that in all her difficulties and in all
her trials, the idea of spending her last days at Crowland and in the bosom
of his Family had ever been her great support. That alone had enabled her

to bear with fortitude the melancholy situation she was placed in during the two last Years of Mr Radcliffe's Life, when all energy of Mind had failed him, his Memory was gone, and his understanding as imbecile as that of an infant. And I could with equal Truth assure him that with respect to that unhappy Misunderstanding which took place soon after his Marriage Mrs Radcliffe had repeatedly told me she had most sincerely forgotten and forgiven all, many Years ago. I then proceeded to state that with respect to the principles upon which she had made her Will they were perfectly consonant to all Rules made in our Neighbourhood with regard to Daughters, part if not the whole of whose Fortunes was, by all prudent Parents settled upon them and their Children, otherwise amid the Changes, the Chances and the Losses attending the Fluctuations of Trade and Commerce they would often be reduced to absolute Penury. And tho' his own Income was now large and not subject to much Fluctuation yet this depending upon his Life alone was liable to the greatest and most certain Contingency of all.

Cost of Trip	£10. 14. 4
Charged to Lord Lilford	8. 8. 2
My own expenses in going to Crowland	2. 6. 2

The Blundell Letters: Part II

This second series of letters in the prolonged correspondence between Richard Hodgkinson and James Blundell has two dominant themes. The two friends shared mutual hopes and then deepening pessimism over the fates of their two ailing sons: Joseph afflicted with mental illness and young James Blundell doomed to a lingering death following a commonplace accident.

The second major topic is Blundell's desperation to borrow money from Hodgkinson, even though the rector's pleas for help perhaps lack the eloquence of his excuses for breaking his promises of repayment. Blundell on occasion refers to Richard's son, David, paying the debts; this is probably a reference to DH collecting rents for property in Atherton owned by Blundell.

Wisbech   December 11, 1822
What w^d man be without conscience, and yet what a conscience has man!

To explain the remorse I have experienced at so long delaying to answer your very kind inquiries will scarcely obtain credit, because, you will conceive the remedy was always at command. The fact is, since my indisposition, I have been almost constantly on the wing, first at the sea-coast, & then to visit several of my friends. The result is, thank God, a restoration to health, & I hope, with no symptoms of a relapse. It arose, I only believe from an anxiety about many things which at the time unfortunately concurred with a press of professional duties.

Among other, one of great importance has bro' me to Wisbech. My living of W. Drove[6] I presume you know, is invested in Trustees. They are now reduced to 4 at w^h number the feofment enjoins, a renewal. In consequence of one or two warm friends among them, I have been induced to hope, the new ones may be so chosen as to secure the next turn to my son. It will now be decided in a short time & I at present, have reason to hope, in my favour.

By a letter from Joseph, and an incidental hint from a friend, I fear the contest with Astley is a sad Load. You of course know better than I the inducements & the grounds of the warfare. But as he is nervous & makes the molehills mountains, I sh^d recommend a speedy decision. I wish he w^d bring his new companion for a few weeks into the Fenns; I think we sh^d drive away care. He & I are fortune's spoiled children, but we must recollect that if we serve God we must with it, as antidote, if for nothing also see evil.

Thomas is come home for a few Months to repeat his experiments which are really astonishing & much beyond my ideas. He can take alloys of Gold and in a short time separate the component Gold, silver & brass into their respective and most pure and genuine states; analyze air; any drug & what is still more, can manufacture every thing he wants as nitric acid, muriative ammonia, phosphorous &c. He will shortly proceed, I know not where, but somewhere.   J Blundell.

PS George had two Churches contiguous & with single duty each offered him the other day at £150 per annum, but he is too young for orders.

PS If I secure Whap. Drove Income to purchase the next Cure of Crowland & the next after that is already promised to me by my friend and Patron.

Crowland Abbey   May 21, 1823
Tho I think I wrote last, I yet can no longer resist the strong impulse of sympathy in your unfortunate son. A hint was given us some time since

by a mutual friend but such strong injunctions of secrecy that I c^d not in honour communicate. But another has been so explicit as to leave no doubt of the melancholy reality. . . . as it is the will of Him in whose hands are the pieces of Life & Death we must submit. I much fear that untoward business of Astley has been too much for his sensibility of mind. I hope however the malady will be only temporary & that I sh^d shortly to congratulate you on a convalescence. A friend of mine here, some time back, was violent but is now as completely restored as ever. One of our friends says he is supposed to be near Leicester, from which I thot he may be at Greatford with Dr Hills & if so I may be of service. If he is ever at Leicester I w^d with pleasure ride over to make inquiries and execute any commission.

I am now waiting with anxiety for the ordination of George in September, tho he graduated only in Feb, in order to have opportunity of paying you a visit. He has distinguished himself a little in divinity & I have hope will make a useful Parish Priest.

I am at present in troubled water respecting the appointment of Feoffees to Whap:Drove, and the business is referred to the Lord Chancellor.

Am also equally engaged in an opposite concern the revival of a Market here, which, at present, promises to be of the first description for Cattle &c. I have taken the Chair at various meetings, made speeches, been in the News Papers & what not to effect this desirable & very useful object & begin now to see a prospect of success beyond my most sanguine expectations.   J Blundell

Atherton   May 31st, 1823

I have received your very sympathizing Let & feel grateful for the kind Wishes & Offers of Service it contains, but your best efforts can avail nothing in favour of my unfortunate Son in his present lamentable situation. The subject is one in which my Feelings are so highly excited, that I cannot bear to talk ab^t it & much less to write and I assure you, it has cost me many an effort before I c^d summon up Resolution to take up my Pen now & but for fear of apparent neglect to so old a Friend as yourself I sh^d have remained in Silence. The variety & violence of Passings which are eternally working in my Bosom, unfit me for Society, at which you will not wonder, when you contrast the Circumstances in which I now find myself placed, with those which I had every right and prospect to suppose myself placed in on the appointment of my Son to the Vicarage of Leigh. On this subject I can write no more.   R^d Hodgkinson

Crowland Abbey   July 26th, 1823
Being just arrived from a second ride to Hinckley within the month with
my youngest son who I have placed there at School, to be under Dr Hill
from an accident that was afflicting the spine, I lose no time in seconding
the favourable report you will have intermediately rec^d. from Dr Simmons
respecting your son. Dr Hill, with whom I dined on Tuesday, assures me
he is gradually convalescent & as an instant mentioned having at his own
request lent Joseph a Vo^l. of popular Sermons, Theo. Assums. Of varied
merit, these are usually admired as masterpieces both in matter & manner
& Joseph had no sooner read them than he pointed out these as being
greatly superior to the rest. This I mention to you, as it was to me, as an
instance of ever increasing reason and the dawn of approaching light. I
understand he seems very comfortable & I trust and hope ere long he w^d
be restored to the bosom of his friends with 'not a neck behind'.

It was from accidentally calling to inquire after Joseph that I was
induced to place James under the care of this excellent & worthy man.
The unfortunate circumstances first occurred 3 years back, by seizing a
lamb, & suffering himself to be drawn after for some distance which gave
a twist to the spine. He however was almost well when he was unfortunately riding a Pony given to him by Mr Whitsed and thrown on his
back. Since that his form has changed, his health declined, & his limbs
slightly paralysed, & I suppose, he shortly would have lost their tone and
use. The Dr, however, gives me every reason to hope a short and complete renovation of all the usual functions without the least fear of relapse.
It will be very expensive, as he is braced in steel-stays which must be frequently altered to accommodate the growth and changes of the body.

Owing to an unacceptable Curate in my parish of Whaplode Drove,
there has been a complete Row between the inhabitants & the Feoffees . . . .
In order to terminate the unpleasantness, I have determined to place
George in it & Cowbit, which together will be a fair start.   J. Blundell

Atherton   3rd August, 1823
I am unhappy to hear of James very serious misfortune. Alas! what family
is exempt from sufferings & distress. The afflictions of my unfortunate son
& the Consequences have inflicted such a Wound upon the Peace and the
Comfort of myself & Family that no Time, no Circumstances, I fear, can
heal.
[The following paragraph is lightly crossed out.]
The Disappointment I am deemed to experience in the complete failure

of everything I have done and accomplished for my poor Son, has cut up by the Roots every present enjoyment and every future hope. I have lost all ambitious Views for the advancement of my Family, and if I had them I have lost all zeal for carrying them into effect. I go through my Business indeed (and it is well perhaps that I have so much upon my hands) but it is mechanically, as it were, the usual Energy & Activity are fled & everything is tasteless and insipid to me. Company is irksome to me & if I read it is without either Improvement or Amusement.

Joseph's Recovery (if it so please God) w^d be a great blessing to us, but when that happy event shall take place, I almost fear, here he will support (if I may so express myself) the shock of returning Reason. With ideas so delicate as his, and with feelings so exquisite, I cannot contemplate without some anxiety how he is to quit his personal Abode to associate with his Family & Friends, to resume his Functions & mix with Society.

Crowland Abbey   10th November, 1823
As a temporary excursion invites an appetite for home & gives a zest for all one's interests and connections, my return [from Lancashire] on the present occasion you be glad to hear, was peculiarly augmented by the high ecomiums pronounced on my Son. Till of late I had my doubts of his qualities as a speaker but as I made him read the lessons and Psalms I soon found reason to think better, but certainly no idea he would equal what the event has proved. He left us this morning for Cambridge & will probably not return till he has taken his degree, when he will proceed to his Curacy of Cowbit, w^h both in respect to Salary and situation, for a year is most desirable.

James I fear is in a precarious state, & if not better soon I must have him home. I called upon and took Wine with Dr Hill who continued firm in his former opinion of a regular tho' but slow convalescence in your son. We had some conversation on the subject of a correspondence and interview with some of his friends. From what dropped incidently, I was the more convinced that this, if once affected wd conduce to allay that secret anxiety & mental distress w^h (as I can speak from experience), I fear, is too frequently the cause of continuing the paroxisms of the malady. The Dr I thought was much struck with the remark & promised to use every endeavour to assey this desirable object. As he now walks out & is perfectly sane, the ring of hypochondriac, I s^d apprehend no fear from the introductions of a Letter or some Friend. This might prepare and fortify the mind for the admission of his Relatives. Hence towards Christmas I sh^d recommend his Brother to pretend Business thro the place and contrive to see him. The Dr says he reads & can minutely detail & discriminate Sermons &c.,&c., & points out to him in the clearest terms & correctest manner what is excellent or otherwise & what is more comfortable still, says he has no doubt of a complete cure. Allow me therefore to recommend you to bear up with patience & imagination & to clear your mind under the incumbent gloom by casting an eye to the ray of light which I trust will progressively increase more and more to enhance your future Comfort by the contrast you have suffered. The present is not a state of enjoyment, we must therefore in some shape or other expect to experience sorrow. Tis a part of wisdom to be resigned.   James Blundell.

Crowland Abbey   February 14, 1824
I called upon Dr Hill & found his accounts still more favourable than before. And having expected me for some days, he had mentioned such his expectation to Joseph for this purpose and preparing him for an interview. The plan appeared to be so much to the Doctor's wishes, that, on my coming, he said I shd see Joseph on my return.

    Accordingly I called this morning & had two hours Chat in a very pleasant, &, after a time in familiar and becoming general subjects. And I have much pleasure in saying I found him very composed, & with the exception for what might to a stranger have appeared diffidence, perfectly himself. But after some enlivening reminiscences of past time & events even this diffidence or shyness vanished. When this was affected, I began to enquire when he had written home, to which he said, Not at all. In consequence I affected much surprise, especially, I told him as I knew you & his Mother were extremely anxious to hear from him.

    Pretending to reprove his negligence for selfish purposes, as I also had to complain of his inattention. He turned round and said he wrote last. After some banter I gave up the point on the condition that he would answer my sent. and we shd forthwith renew our correspondence. He agreed & not only so but promised also to write either to you or his Mother. Dr Hill during this had been out & when he returned we were talking about the propriety of making extracts from Books wh he read. It seemed to carry conviction & the Dr further improved the hint by recommending these extracts to be Sermons in order to provide my friend when he shd want them. This had such an effect that he actually asked the Dr for a Vol to recommence his career & hope, as the Dr says, the consequences will be useful. On telling him I expected David & asking him if he sd like to see him, he answered with much rapture, Yes! When I told him I had seen his Lady he seemed pleased & rejoined that she was as he expressed it, an excellent girl or young woman, can't say which, & spoke of her very rationally & affectionately. On the whole had I not known his situation, I do honestly and most conscientiously assure you I s^d have discovered nothing, but the diffidence in question, that would have led me to suspect a dereliction of mind.

Fear my poor son is in a very precarious state. Found him very comfortable in the house with Dr Partner along with a son of Sir John Piggott. The family are very kind and attentive but I fear all will not do; we are all born into trouble, Nihil abomni parte beatum.

PS I have forgot to say Joseph looks particularly well, rather fatter than when I saw him last. We had a good laugh at his Bachelor Dinner & I pretended his sending me off with too much wine.

Atherton   3rd July, 1824

Though I have neglected writing to you so long to enquire after your little afflicted Son that I am quite ashamed, yet, I assure you, it now requires no little exertion to summon resolve to take up my pen to address you.

Pray let me know how James is, I trust he is living, if he be not, it w^d be rather a subject of ungratulation than of condolence that he is released from his sufferings. Mrs Blundell must have suffered much on his acc^t. & whether she has yet to minister to his wants or to regret his Loss I doubt not she will find Resolution to support her under either Alternative.

The Accounts of my poor unfortunate Son are not such as to hold out any very sanguine hopes of his ever joining his Family. Surely such an Affliction from such a Cause never visited any Family in the World situated as mine was. The Reflection unmans me & I cannot pursue it.

But beside my domestic afflictions, my employment in my public capacity is of the most unpleasant kind. As soon as I arrived at home after parting with you at Leicester I began to strip the Hall at Atherton of everything useful or ornamental. All the Furniture and Pictures I have removed to Bewsey. The House is now a mere Shell & I am this week issuing Advertisements for the Sale of it as it stands to be taken down at the expence of the Purchaser and the Materials to be removed in twelve Months.

We last week followed our old neighbour Thos. Isherwood to his Grave. He had the misfortune some Months ago to fall down the Granary Steps in the yard at the Bull & has been confined ever since. . . . with the exception of the children at the Lodge having the Hooping Cough my Family are, generally speaking, well.

Crowland Abbey   August 1st, 1824
I have felt some degree of anxiety on your account. But as, I am confident, you believe in a superintending Providence, who, in his mysterious wisdom, frequently raises the storm to enhance the future pleasures of the calm, you will not only submit with patience and resignation: but will steal from some till-then unforeseen or latent consequence, derive some good from the apparent evil. For as He smiteth but to heal.

The time, I trust, will soon come when I shall have to congratulate you on the perfect recovery of your son; and mourning would be turned into joy.

My unfortunate son has continued to linger a most miserable existence with a patience, firmness & composure that have been truly astonishing. On Tuesday, his Birthday, we had over a Surgeon from Peterboro to perform an operation to assist his absess, but all in vain. He is now as low as the will can be, and, unless he rally very soon, his desolation must shurely [sic] terminate his sufferings and our anxieties. There seems to have been much mercy even in sparing him thus, as he will die in the bosom of his friends & those friends, tho deeply wounded with the blow, will yet find relief in the reflection that after every thing has been done to restore or to alleviate his afflictions are over. I have always considered myself peculiarly fortunate in the temper, dispositions, & general deportment of my children & this incident seems likely to knit them, if possible, in a still stronger bond. Their solicitude & attentions have been great in the extreme & every thing has given way to administer to the comforts or the wants of a beloved Brother.

I have on some account or other been much plagued to obtain remittances from Manr. having more than three quarters in arrear and money is seeming short in consequence of my enormous expence this last year. I fear my Friend David has not much if he has it w^d be useful and if not I s^d feel obliged, if convenient, by your inclosing me as soon, may be, a 20 or 30 draft and take what David may make at Michaelmas & I w^d send the Bal. with Interest or order it from my agent whenever you may want it.

J Blundell.

Plat-fold   6th August, 1824
On Tuesday morning early I went in the Leigh Boat to Manchester and in the Afternoon I took a Coach from thence to Bolton where I had an appointment yesterday and in the Evening walked home, where I found your Letter. The Acc^t. it gives of poor little James is just as I expected if he were alive, his Release from his sufferings w^d be a happy change.

We have each of us had a Letter from Joseph since I saw you, but I have nothing particularly to remark on them. The favourable change has not been as great as I then expected.

Judgement was given last Monday but one in the Astley business by Judges Bayley and Hullock in favour of the Defendants, upon all the points & but this, you know, is a subject I cannot enlarge upon.

My expences like your own have of late been enormous and my sources of Income have been very much curtailed by the reduction of Interest, of Rents, and of Farming Profits. Inclosed I have sent you a Draft value £20.   Rd. Hodgkinson.

Holme Vicarage, Market Weighton   August 14, 1824
Permit me to thank you for your kind attention to my request; and to assure you that I shall return it when ever required with Interest & many Thanks for the indulgence.

Was sorry to hear that the convalescence of poor Joseph is not so rapid as you were led to suppose, tho' Dr. Hill in a letter a little time since said his progress was very satisfactory. It appears the present cause of your conscience results from a sort of hypochondriac affliction produced in some measure by the tenseness of this disorder; & if so, I trust time will gradually wear it away.

Poor James continues much the same; & when I left we had some serious apprehensions that Thomas, either from a cold by being overheated in London; or, as I suspect, from making an experiment with poisonous ingredients, was seriously indisposed. He looks must ghastly; but hope to find him better on my return.

As I am out & travelling is always of service, I am not sure whether I may not visit Harrogate for the prime purpose of visiting Sir Wm. Ingelby, our Member, to whom I have rendered some service & for which I have reason to hope he entertains a disposition to remunerate with something more substantial than verbal Compliment.   J. Blundell.

Crowland Abbey   7th February, 1825
As my Paper I presume will announce, an event on which, while you sympathize with the parents, you will congratulate the Friend. My unfortunate son, after a long and most appalling sickness, borne however with patience & submission was most happily & under the most happy circumstances, released from his sufferings on the 29th. He had been confined entirely to bed since the beginning of August & I believe had nearly the whole of that period been deprived of all use, if not of all sensation in his

limbs. His sisters from first to last were his Nurse & Physician. They never left him & he would suffer none else to touch him. Hence when I tell you of four most virulent abscesses &c.,&c., you will not wonder that our solicitude is, for a time, likely to be transferred from him to them. We, however, on the whole, feel happy that they are no worse. We of course have long been placed in the most painful suspense and anxiety, though he did everything that patience, fortitude or resignation cd affect to mitigate our feelings & during the last fortnight dwelt almost exclusively on his hope & confidence of a joyful futurity.

I shd have written sooner but the very day he died, two situations were announced to my eldest Son which required immediate inquiry. One was the Curacy, with a hint at a probability of the living of St. John's in Manchester, by my friend Calvert: the other is one still more important in the northern part of Lincolnshire by Sir William Ingelby, the Member, who has been pleased to take great notice of him; &, I have reason to hope will do something for him. But he is already serving in a Church not far distant from me, that is in the hands of Feofees, and has been so acceptable to all in the concern, that, as the Living is very good & the Incumbent infirm, I know not after all, what will be done. He is very popular, & it is a pleasure to say not without reason.

Tho' Cash literally has melted with me for the two years past, if you are pushed I shall be most happy to order my Agent in Manr. to settle the Balance: I wd however say, that, if it will produce no inconvenience I had rather let David pay, when he can, principle and interest.   J. Blundell.

Platfold   February 17th, 1825

Poor little James, what must he have suffered during the length of time since I saw him put into the Coach at Leicester, with scarcely a hope on my part that you cd get him home alive? The distress of yourself and Family must have been great but you had the satisfaction of personally attending upon him, ministering to his necessities and soothing his distress.

Thus, alas! are all denied to us; my poor unfortunate and afflicted Son is buried alive, immured in Walls which his Disorder renders impenetrable to Friend or Relative. In the Autumn of last year his Disorder took an unfavourable turn and has continued so to the present time. This state of poor Joseph connected with the Circumstances that led to it and have and are consequent of it, have cast a Cloud over my Family of such dense and malign obscurity as to exclude every ray of Comfort and every prospect of Hope.

By the Rec^t of some of your Rents, this Morning David has been enabled to pay me the whole of the £20 I lent you last August. The Int. is not worth calculating. At present he is very much engaged in the Affairs of the last and only Son of the late W. Barker, of Astley. W. Barker married a young woman ab^t 34 years of age a few Months ago and he died since Christmas. He has made David one of his Executors with a legacy of £400 free of Legacy Duty and an Allowance of £40 a year during the Trust which is to continue as long as his Wife lives and seven years afterwards.

I write this early for fear delay might occur for it is not improbable but I may be called to London before the end of the Month to appear before a Committee in the House of Commons respecting a Rail Road from Leigh to Bolton.7   Rd. Hodgkinson.

Atherton   December 23rd, 1825
For a month past I have been forming the Resolutions to write to you but have delayed carrying them into effect. The fact is, that the Blow I received three years ago was so sudden, so unexpected and so severe, that it blasted my every present enjoym^t and every future hope and as I then anticipated the Gloom has thickened about me ever since. In this state of Mind one has but little to Communicate to a friend that can afford him any satisfaction, but indeed, ever since July till within a very few weeks, I have been incapable of writing at all having broken both my Arms by a fall of 18 Feet high in a new House we are building at the Old-hall.

What has roused me at present to take up my pen and write to you is the reading of the paragraph which David copied out of a Newspaper a few days ago giving an acct of your Son Thomas's elevation to the President's chair of the Royal Medical Society at Edinburgh, and I could not delay in congratulating you and Mrs Blundell.

The case of my poor afflicted and unfortunate son at Leicester has been growing worse ever since I saw you there last Year.   Rd. Hodgkinson

Crowland Abbey   January 4th, 1826
Your long-expected and long-wished for Letter came & tho' I in some measure, anticipated the main points of its formation, I was willing to hope time would have reconciled so far as to render tolerable, a wait which nothing I fear can absolutely remove.

And as the ways of Providence are not only inscrutable but invincible, it comes at once a duty and a consolation to submit with: Not my Will, but Thine to be done.

I shd . . . recommend you to reverse the plan you have fallen in with rather than chosen . . . look at some counteracting dispensations of Providence. For instance contemplate your more than common success in life; the high respectability He has suffered you to attain and permanently enjoy; the ever brightening gleams on the other branches of your family; the improved health of a kind and amiable wife;

You will see from the Papers we have had a terrible blow up in almost all our Banks. For a week all work was at a stand-still. The panic now begins to subside and commence pursuance of its course. For the first time for the 5 years past, I had begun to accumulate and now I am liked to have a little use from it, for three or four months, tho it is merely locked up, for the Bank is unquestionably solvent.

This is a reason I shall return it a favour if David will forward to Thomas at No 23 St James Square, Edinburgh, what he can collect and spare as it will save time and I fear that he will be run, for these honours are expensive, or as he says, very flowing distinctions.   J Blundell.

Peterborough   August 10th, 1826
Thomas's honours have been, as to the expence, what he calls most flourishing, and like men of his time, he had not collected & ascertained the Amount till the last, so that time is short. Yesterday George was out to collect; but only rec^d a small part as expected. Today I have come here to repeat disappointment, and if I go elsewhere, it may be with no better success.

I have therefore resolved to request you will, once more, & I hope for the last time, give me a lift by making what my friend David may have in hand, £25, and sending it to 23 St James' Square, Edinburgh, as soon as you can.

All I want is a mere temporary lift, only a few days if it would subject to inconvenience, or at most to a few weeks when I shall have plenty & if therefore, you will indulge me with the loan on these terms and mention to Thomas when you want, it should be punctually repaid either personally or thro' our Agent in Man^r.   J Blundell.

Atherton   August 13, 1826
I propose being in Warrington tomorrow and will call in at the Bank and get a Dft at a short date for £25 and inclose it in a Let. to your Son and put it into the Post Office there.

My Wife bears the late calamitous event better than cou'd be expected. As for myself I cannot say so much, all appears gloomy, melancholy and

sad. The Cloud that has hung over me for the past four Years has been so
severe as not to leave my eye a spot to settle upon. Enough of this,

R^d Hodgkinson.

Crowland Abbey   February 23, 1828
As between friends, domestic affairs are of most interest. I have now, on
the other side to observe that Geo. is most eligibly fixed in one of the
pleasantest villages just three miles from Wisbech, which is a Town of
great trade & some respectability. He still retains with this Curacy the one
he held before, & which there is reason to presume he will, ere long,
become Vicar making together something more than 200 a year. It is cur-
rently reported he is married, which leads to the presumption that he
shortly will marry a most amiable Lady with a very handsome Fortune.
One thing is certain, he is a very excellent & most gentlemanly youth.
Tho' of not the most brilliant talents, his acquirements are, perhaps the
very best for a brilliant Parish Priest. I am very proud of him.

As to Tom, since his return, he has been settled in a delightful house &
nice neighbourhood about 12 miles from us, where he has been doing
great things as a general Practitioner. Had he been less flattered at College,
he s^d have neither desired nor looked for more. But he fancies the Laurels
of Edinburgh can flourish to perfection only in a more respectable
Hemisphere. I feel unfixed by his determination to remove. In consequence he is at this moment disposing of the concern (a good 500 a year)
to speculate, after a short study in Paris, perhaps also at Lyden, on the
bounties of Providence. I fear he is going from home: but Flattery excites
ambition, & that sometimes achieves wonders; he also, it sometimes
reverses the proverb.

What do you think of Bolton for general Practice (I mean as a
Physician & Apothecary or a Physician)? This I ask merely from a wish to
keep him, for some time, in the country. From having light hair, buoyant
spirits, & a small figure, tho' four & twenty, he seems too much the Boy
to fix in London. In this profession appearances are of moment, but he has
been taught to depend so much on talent that his Motto is 'Nil desperan-
dum'. He is certainly clever but I fear the honours he has rec^d (I understand unprecedented in the annals of College) will lead him to expect too
much, & that success in his profession, will have conduced to fan the
flame, till disappointment will close the cause. I don't know his forte or
his predilection, but he shines in Chemistry & hence, before he goes to
London, I feel anxious to find him in the Country, & if you think there is
an opening at Bolton for 8 or 10 years of tyroship, I apprehend he w^d be

in his element. Will you enquire and give me your opinion? A
Manufacturing or Bleaching district might illicit some discoveries of the
first importance to both himself and the public.   J Blundell.

Atherton   6th March, 1828
Tho' I was surprised to hear that Thomas was sitting down to general
practice so soon, I am sorry to find he is already giving it up. I by no
means think he wd improve his situation in Bolton. You know something
of the peculiarities of Society there and generally speaking, I think you
will agree with me they are not of that kind which wd exactly suit
Thomas. There has certainly been a change in Society there within the
last 20 Years, but be no improvement, I think especially for Strangers.
The higher Classes have flown off at a Tangent, if I may so express myself
and keep quite aloof from their less fortunate Neighbours, tho' their
Elevation is only in degree, as you will know they are all sprung from the
same Stock, Trade.

Mr Bedford (whom I think you may remember) was considered an
eminent Surgeon, but tho' he married in Bolton, and had good connections, he was obliged to leave the Town some Years ago & settle in
Liverpool. A Mr Moore who has long resided in Bolton has the leading
Practice as a general Surgeon and Apothecary & has the best Families but
there are those who vie with him & some of inferior Rank. A Dr Black
some years ago settled in Bolton as a Physician, he married but died
young & was succeeded by anor Dr Black (no Relation I believe) who, on
his coming, was so violently attacked by the whole body of medical men
in Bolton that he was obliged to turn upon his Assailants & fairly write
them down in the public Prints. The common Surgery business is all
engrossed by a man of the name of Taylor, a Relative of the Oldfield
Lane Doctor, whose Practice he imitates.

My giving up the Farm, as far as my Wife is concerned does not seem
to have ansd well, she pants for her usual Employment, the want of wch is
but ill compensated by Rest & Retiremt. God knows whether her Health
wd enable her to continue her Labours but since she gave them up it has
much declined and she is at present very unwell.

David has settled your Acct with me, as under:-

        Bill remitted to Dr Blundell 14th Aug:1826   £26 15s 6d
        Feb. Recd Cash from David   17 0 0
        1828 March 6th   9 15s 6d

I fear you will not perceive any improvem^t in my Let. writing either in Style or Spirit since my last. I cannot help it.   RH.

Crowland Abbey   June 19, 1828
. . . a little time past, on finding myself eased from the immense weight of College & other expenses, in a liberal mood I jocosely told Mrs B she w^d now have her Atherton Rents for Pin Money. Shortly after, our Friend David, in writing on another subject, said he had in hand & command about £10. Without more ceremony, during my absence in Notts, she wrote to say the Rhino^8 w^d be very convenient: in a post or two it came, & the only reward for my generosity is the act of acknowledging the receipt, with, of course many thanks, enhanced by every token of gratulation from the whole company of Females in the family, who I suppose will share in the spoil.

I hear no complaints respecting trade among you; but from the reduced prices, some great change must have occurred in the process of making. Our Farmers are very feverish from the vacillation of Parliament on the Corn Question. Since we have risen into a Market, we have generally been very prominent & mainly on my own suggestions, on that & similar questions, in Petitions &c.,&. I have long been Chairman & Correspond with the Central Committee in London & we are now at it again respecting Wool, One Pound Notes. This serves to give support over to the Towns; & we find our account in a general progression of improvement.

I suppose you are busy in hay. I have done, but generally the harvest is only just beginning. I fancy we improve your system of making or managing Hay. We usually let the grass lie in the swaithes, two, three, or more days before we move. If the weather be fine we then turn & make into plats & the next day seen into cocks. Hence, if the weather be fine the hay is well made without lashing the seeds & if otherwise, the parallelism of the strawy part shoots off the wet and thus saves from harm.
                                                            J Blundell.
    PS It is about 36 years since we first met.

Atherton   August 18, 1828
I am very sure you must think me tardy in not having ans. yours of the 19th ult before now, many impediments have intervened, but one principal cause of delay has been waiting for Lord Lilford's arrival at Bewsey on his way to Scotland, where he has taken 17,000 Acres of Moors for shooting on. He arrived at Bewsey at 3 o'Clock in the Afternoon of Tuesday the 5th inst and left the following day at Noon. During the short inter-

view I had with him I took the opportunity of mentioning your application for a renewal of your Lease. As every Tenemn^t abt the Mill, and all the way to Howebridge, is out of Lease and nothing betwixt the Hall and Leigh and the Hall and Howebridge remaining in Life Leases but this small tenem^t of yours, he does not think it advisable to renew the Lease, and the rather, as it is desirable that some part of the Building shd be ultimately taken down. We have already built a very large and excellent House at the old Hall and what his Lordship's future determination ab^t building one on the Site of that which is taken down is at present uncertain as a Rail Road is abt to be made near Bewsey-hall which will render a Residence there everything but comfortable.

The Weather here at present is very unfavourable and I am fearful of the consequences. It is also unfortunate for me as I shall have to look after David's Farm for a Fortnight. He is summonsed upon the Jury at Lancaster Assizes which commence on Wednesday and is this Morning gone to Oldham upon a special Summons to view some Premises there which are the Subject of a Law Suit and to meet 11 other persons there who with himself are to compose a special Jury on the Trial.

I apprehend I must give up all thoughts of ever seeing Crowland again. I feel no inclination to leave home. My wife with Mrs Guest's little Dau^r have been a fortnight at Southport, but I am not myself going to any Watering Place this Season.

My Business as Agent (I have withdrawn myself from all other) has increased to a very great extent and is regularly increasing by the rapid falling in of Life Leases, none of which are renewed and tho it does not yet feel burdensome to me I experience great reluctance, and of course some uneasiness in meeting and contending with difficulties to which I have hitherto been a Stranger.   Rd Hodgkinson

Atherton   26th February, 1830
A long time has now elapsed since any direct Communication has passed between you and me but I cannot forego the opportunity of congratulating you and Mrs Blundell on the marriage of your Daughter and the addition to your Family Connexions, of, as I am informed, a very respectable and worthy young man. My Wife and myself desire you to communicate to the young couple our hearty congratulations on their happy Union and our sincere Wishes for their Health and Happiness.

I fear the opening at Leigh for a Surgeon will hardly hold out sufficient encouragem^t for Mr Thomas. The Society too at Leigh is far from what it was in your time.

You will have heard that Tildesley with its National Church is dubbed a Parish and Marriages are now solemnized there. I do not approve of this Division of Parishes, in my opinion it is a step towards Disunion & Separation in the Establishment. Since the passing of the Emancipation Bill last Year, you wd be astonished to see the Apathy that has seized upon a whole Host of our former Acquaintances, the warmest and staunchest Friends of Church and King, Gentlemen who 3 years ago wd have hazarded their Lives in support of the Church, but who wd not now, I am confident, lift an Arm in its Defence. Of public Distress you will learn enough from the public Prints and in some Districts in this County it is quite appalling. Hence you will be aware that the King's Speech was not received here very courteously. Its general Appellation being Milk and Water.

Politics are now very seldom discussed here. There is a chill thrown over them which never gets dissipated in any Company I mix with, either public or private.

My Mind has not recovered its former Tone and Strength, nor is it probable it ever will. Business increases in quantity and unpleasantness. I begin to feel a want of vigour to combat difficulties.   Rd H.

Atherton   March 1830
I recd yours of the 9th in due time and take the first opportunity of being at the Bank to remit you a Dft for £50. You will please to acknowledge the Rct when it comes to hand and can send me your own Note for it as soon as you have an opportunity of procuring a Stamp for £50 payable on demand which is the usual mode.

My Wife and I went and spent the day last Sunday at Deane Church near Bolton, to hear Lord Lilford's Bro. Horace do Duty at which place he has arrived at the Preferment of being Curate. He is very diligent in his other Parochial Duties & is already become a great Favourite from his easy and familiar manner of calling upon the Parishioners. The Congregation is numerous, but he soon misses Absentees.   RH

Atherton   20th October, 1831
Cottage Property is become very much sunk in value here and is gradually sinking. The Church I apprehend is in the same predicament and yourself and other dignified Clergymen competent to the Task of improving, remodelling, or redeeming it, the Archbishops, Bishops, Deans, Chapter, &c., may save yourselves any trouble in that acc^t as the House of Commons will before long settle the Business for you in their own way,

in less than half the number of Years I told the late Lord Lilford ten Years ago, he w^d not have a Church Living to give after the Catholic Emancipation Bill passed.

You say you don't quite like the aspect of the Times, neither do I. I see nothing in them but a prospect of unmitigated Misery & Distress for Years to come. Ministers have no means of relieving the Country but by robbing and plundering somebody. The Party robbed will not sit down very comfortably under this Inflection & may possibly feel disposed to resist. Hence additional Misery & Distress.

You mention the Loan which I made to you some time ago. I intended writing to you some Weeks since upon that Subject, but Mrs John Guest was then very ill, and supposed dangerous, and had she died I sh^d have informed you of that Circumstance & thought to mention the other business at the same time. She has continued lingering on & I have neglected writing. I wish however, that you could repay it ab^t Christmas. I have some expensive Arrangem^ts to make at that time in placing out my Grandson, Robert Jackson. The Money I believe will be to be paid in the first Week in the new Year. David has paid me no Interest upon this last Loan but that he can settle hereafter.   Rd. Hodgkinson

Crowland   Jany 12th, 1832
The fact is, I let Thomas have some money to clear his acc^ts etc, which he was to return sometime since, but about two months back he & his wife went over to Easton to her grandfather to arrange their future plans, when the old gentleman was seized with an asthma which has confined him ever since & in a short time is likely to place him in the grave.

On Monday his wife wrote to say that Thomas thinks he cannot live more than a fortnight, but even sh^d that be the case some time must elapse, I fear before, much can be done. I have thought it proper thus to state lest I inconvenience you as this was designed to liquidate your account. I hope this will not be the case, as I can ill manage till it come in, ^wh I do hope will not be long.

What think you of Reform? It becomes stale in this neighbourhood, as the Farmers lay to the charge of the Powers that be, much of the change w^d affect their interest. I suppose, however, it must pass in some shape, but, for myself, I fear it w^d produce no great affect. The disfranchisism of the decayed Boros' & the transfer to larger towns is all very well but the £10 suffrage, I fear will make these latter the prize of the factions. Fifteen w^d preserve the balance between numbers & wealth. But administration are too anxious to strengthen their own hands, I fear, to allow it. I wish something could be struck out respecting this. That around here is a sore subject.   J Blundell.

Atherton   21st May, 1832

. . . it is not improbable but you may see David at Crowland in a few days. He set out to London yesterday where he has Business to transact with Lord Kenyon &c.,&c.

A few days ago he paid me two Years' Int. upon your Note. I had not asked him for the first Year's Int. when due, supposing it might have suited you to have remitted the Principal this Spring. If it wd be at all convenient for you to spare that Sum out of your present incoming Rents, I shd very much wish it. I presume that by this time your Son Thomas is settled in some Situation where he can make his Talents available.

                                                    Rd Hodgkinson.

Atherton   17th August, 1832

I have been in constant expectation of receiving a Let. from you ever since your return home. You wd find a Let from me recd after you left home expressing an earnest Wish to have the small Loan of £50 repaid you which had from me some time ago. I also mentd it to you when here and you said you could now pay it in without Inconvenience & also held out an expectation that you cd remit it from Manchester as you passed thro'.

Numerous Reasons, unnecessary to mention, compel me to press for payment of this Sum, which I hope you can effect without any great Inconvenience,

Instances of Mortality among our Friends are daily occurring, of themselves sufficient to warn one at my time of Life to think of setting his house in Order. Miss Crouchley is to be interred today and her brother Joseph is dying daily. At Warrington where much of my Business lies, the Cholera has already carried off above 200 Persons. My Daur Guest has had a very alarming Inflammatory Attack and from several Relapses is not yet out of Danger. Abt a Month ago my Wife and I paid two Visits to your Brother John. His Affliction is that which I dread more than any other. Enough of Melancholy which is too often and for some Year's past has been uppermost in my Mind.

                                                    Rd Hodgkinson.

RH to Blundell's wife
Atherton   11th Dec, 1832
Dear Madam, Some days ago I was at your Aunt Guest's when she
shewed me your Letter to her of the 19th Nov. I have long wondered that
I did not hear from Mr Blundell after his return home from Lancashire
but had not nor could have any conception that the cause was in such a
distressing state of his health as appears from your lett. I now take the first
opportunity of addressing a few Lines to you expressive of every wish for
Mr Blundell's speedy recovery and restoration to the Bosom of his afflicted
family.   Rd. Hodgkinson.

Atherton   15th Jany, 1834
I write to inform you that Mrs John Guest died on Monday last, after a
very protracted Sickness. She has been living in great Poverty a long time
and I have seldom seen her for the last two Years, that I have not given
her something, generally 2/6d. Last Saturday but one I gave her 5/s and
yesterday I called upon the Family & gave them some money towards the
Expence of the Funeral which I shall attend on Friday Forenoon. A few
weeks ago she sent to David to advance her Quars. Rent before he had
received it, which he did, but the Tenant paid him last Monday Morning.

   Your sickness has been long, and attended with distressing
Circumstances to which I am in some degree willing to attribute the non
payment of the Loan of £50 for which during the last two Years I have
made so many pressing Applications & you have as often held out hopes
to me of a speedy Remittance.

   I now make another & more pressing Demand for a Remittance and
you will be aware how I feel upon the Subject when I add I must have
the Acct. settled.   Richard Hodgkinson.

Crowland   February 1834
It is a long time since I wrote to you, so long indeed that I fear you have
construed the silence to wrong causes. Immediately upon leaving Lancr I
went for some time to Yarmouth to be under Tom's Care where I found
great relief. But unfortunately I was seized at Norwich on my return. It
soon passed over and proceeded to my Daughter's at Wisbech where I
experienced a relapse & remained confined for several weeks in a complete state of torpor. When I recovered so as to move so far, I went &
spent a considerable time at Bath, from which I received great benefit.
But partly from torpor and a continued dislike to food, except only what
thus necessity forced for the supply of nature, I became much reduced. In

this way I continued to linger in a weakened state of existence & began to be almost in despair of ever experiencing a complete recovery.

This I state to explain the unfortunate postponement of settling your account which I promised and actually paid with our Agent in Manc^r as I came through. But as I did not mention the address he kept the money for some time and then sent it to Mrs B and so it has passed on the present. Mrs B it seems rec^d a letter on the subject, but feeling it might produce excitement did not mention it, till yours came the other day which produced a full embairesment. [*sic*]

Now, Sir, I am truly sorry to find how the affair has stood, but as it has arisen from such untoward circumstances, I hope I need say no more in apology.

I think I have before mentioned my life Assurances,[8] I will now tell you more. The plan here is general among the Clergy especially among those who have pretty comfortable Preferments. A sacrifice of a few hundreds enables a man to make handsome provision for his family without curtailing his Income to an inconvenience & interfering with education. The education of mine has been heavy, much more so than some thought prudent, But I am quite satisfied the Plan was right, caught only as to the temporary difficulty it has produced. For after my sons were finished I insured very heavily, more considerably than the amount of our private fortune. And as the year is to be advanced at the time of writing, I was obliged to take up a little to empower me to do it. This I long since should have cleared off, had health been spared. But the expence necessarily incurred in travelling thus constantly from place to place, for the present has made this impracticable. I hope now soon to have the power. If therefore you do not absolutely want it, I sh^d wish to allow an extension of the favour, as I fear it at present w^d produce inconvenience. I had a principal tenant who gave up his cropping last Autumn, and the wheat is unharvested. It may soon, however, be made available; but I promised another friend who let me have £100, in this Spring. Possibly he may not want it, and I will in that case let you have it. But as I have a Curate, I sh^d wish to embrace the possibility of going again to Bath.   J Blundell.

Atherton   19th March, 1834
Your last Letter conveyed to me a very distressing Acc^t. of the state of your Health for many Months past and confirmed the Acc^{ts}. I had previously heard of your very serious Affliction and Suffering.

With respect to the little Money you owe me I confess it is a Subject I recur to with regret. I was much disappointed at not receiving it from

Manc^r. as you had promised I sh^d do. I expected it and I wanted it. Many are the Reasons which now urge an immediate Settlement, viz: My advanced Age, your delicate state of Health, the distance we live from each other, and last tho' not least, it w^d be not only unpleasant but unfair both to my Son and to yours to leave this matter at last to have to be settled by them. I cannot think the paymn^t. of so small a Sum as £50 out of your large Income c^d possibly be attended with Inconvenience.

I cannot close this Letter without expressing an ardent Hope that the kind and friendly intercourse which has subsisted between us for more that 40 Years may not be harshly interrupted on acc^t of so paltry a Sum as £50. Richard Hodgkinson.

From Blundell's son, Thomas
Crowland Abbey   March 24th, 1834
My dear Sir, You are aware that my dear Father has for some years past suffered from a paralysis which from time to time has threatened an attack of Apoplexy. You must excuse the brevity of this address, the melancholy theme which swells it being of two poignant a nature for me long to dwell. Up to Tuesday night last, 11 o'Clock, when my dear Father retired to bed, he was as well as usual. At three o'Clock on Wednesday Morning, my Mother awoke & dreadful to say, found my Father speechless! In this state he continued up to yesterday morning, 1/2 past four o'Clock, when Death, which sooner or later overtakes our frail mortality, bathed his fatal Javelin in my dear Father's breast & left me Fatherless!

You can better picture to your Mind, the gloom, the mental anguish, which reigns throughout all the family, than I embody it. His Mortal Remains will be deposited in the Family Vault on Friday next. My Mother, sisters & brother, desire me to convey to you and your Family their best respects, the which accept from, dear Sir, yours very truly,

Thomas Blundell.
The Nature of my Father's attack was 'serious apoplexy.'

Atherton   3rd April, 1834
Dear Madam, My whole Family unite with me in most cordial Sympathy and Condolence with you for the grievous & irreparable Loss you have sustained in the death of your worthy & estimable Husband, and of my old Associate and Friend. The Loss of such a Parent too, must be severely felt by his Sons and his Daughters whose Welfare and Prosperity were his leading Star and the anxiety for whose future Prospects & Settlement in Life he could never lose sight of. Various and long have been our

Discussions for many successive Years on that interesting Subject, but nothing c^d check his Order, nor Disappointment, damp his zeal from fixing a high Standard for the ultimate Settlement of his Children in Life.

Your present Situation is too distressing, and your Case too serious for me to presume to offer any Advice in it. Your own sound Principles and good Sense will point out the best Palliatives, and I trust that you will ere long receive Comfort & Consolation from that Source from whence only they can effectually emanate. Rd. Hodgkinson.

At his death James Blundell's estate was valued at £4,000. He left only £100 to each of his two sons but £600 each to his daughters. The rest went to his 'dear wife' with instructions that she was to divide her estate in a 'fair and equitable disposition bearing in mind . . . the large sums of money expended heretofore on the education of our two sons beyond the money expended on our daughters'.

Notes

1 Mr Selby was the steward at Lilford.
2 Hodgkinson was almost certainly referring to Cowbit.
3 Hodgkinson is not describing here the wide and shallow inlet from the North Sea between Lincolnshire and Norfolk, but rather another definition of a wash, which is land regularly washed by river or tidal waters.
4 The first application of heat in the dressing and finishing of certain kinds of cotton fabrics was said to have been an accidental discovery by a small manufacturer in the neighbourhood of Chowbent. *Pigot and Dean's Directory 1824–25.*
5 James Whitsed was patron of the living of Crowland.
6 This is Whaplode Drove.
7 The Leigh–Bolton railway line opened in 1829, running over land in Atherton owned by Lord Lilford. It gave a new outlet for the town's developing coal industry.
8 Rhino was eighteenth-century slang for money.
9 James Blundell is named in the 1825 list of Proprietors of the Medical, Clerical and General Life Assurance Society.

14

Mary Hodgkinson's Adventure to Lilford, 1812

In the summer of the momentous year of 1812, Hodgkinson took his twenty-one-year-old daughter Mary to visit John Selby, the steward of the Lilford seat in Northamptonshire. On their way home father and daughter visited Crowland where they found the village folk hospitable and kind and the Blundell family almost the source of adoration. Mary, no doubt inspired by her father, kept a detailed and observant journal of her travels through the countryside, towns and villages of nine counties with 'a kind and intelligent Father for companion'.

With Napoleon embarked on his disastrous march into Russia, Mary was astonished to find French prisoners of war walking freely through the town of Ashbourne on their parole of honour and even more surprised to learn that townsfolk abetted the escape of many of them. Mary's impressions of the places they visited range from the mean and dirty town of Mansfield where they stopped to talk to a stocking weaver, to the glories of Chatsworth, seat of the Duke of Devonshire, where rooms 'so far exceeded any idea I had formed of them . . . that I was completely dazzled . . .'

On the day the Hodgkinsons left Lilford, Selby promised to write soon but several weeks went by before he put pen to paper to describe to Mary the terrible events that had stricken his family. The day after the Hodgkinsons left Lilford one of Selby's daughters was taken ill and within a month scarlet fever, measles and whooping cough had carried three of the Selby children to the grave. Selby wrote, 'I never have passed four such weeks of affliction in my life, it being quite out of the reach of any human consolation to reach me . . .'

Journal of a Visit to Lilford,
July 1812

I left home on Tuesday the 28th July, 1812, at 6 o'Clock in the Morning with my Father in a gig for Lilford. The first day we went to Buxton. The neighbourhood of that place is very bleak and having seen only a tree or hedge to be out we travelled thirty miles without seeing any fences except stone walls; they commence at about a mile short of Disley and continued to within 3 miles of Ashburn. That length of road lay entirely over hills, some of them very high, some were cultivated and had tolerable crops on them but others bid defiance to all cultivation both on account of their steepness and the nearness of the rock to the surface.

The Crescent at Buxton is a very handsome building. It was built solely at the expense of the Duke of Devonshire; he has just finished a new Church there which it is said has cost him 30 thousand pounds. It is to be consecrated on Sunday the 9th of August.

We proceeded next to Derby and in our way stopped at Ashburn; by stopping there we escaped one of the most tremendous storms I ever witnessed; the thunder was awful in the extreme, the rain intermixed with hail fell in such torrents that in a very short time the street we were in, though steep, was completely deluged. It continued about an hour. They have no trade at Ashburn except a little lace weaving. Great numbers of French prisoners are sent there on their parole of honour, but as they have liberty to walk a mile out of town and no guard over them, many of them escape, in which they are often assisted by the inhabitants which strongly shew the impropriety of allowing them so much liberty.

Derby is an ancient town, the streets are narrow and the houses mostly old and mean. It contains 3 stone churches, one of which is very handsome with the loftiest tower I ever saw. It is a place of very little trade which accounts for it improving so little. Silk mills are the principal business. The Duke of Devonshire has 2 almshouses there for the support of 12 decayed burgesses of that borough. As their widows they are only allowed 4 shillings a week but at the approaching elections they expect that the burgesses will inform his Grace that it is too little to support them and they think he will increase it. Betwixt there and Leicester we passed through several villages. We inquired the name of one of the largest; they informed us it was Mount Scoril. We thought it an odd name for a place but on examining the map found it was a corruption of Mountsorrel. We got to Leicester by four o'Clock expecting to have time to see most of the town but were disappointed in not meeting with Mr Davis to whom we had a letter of introduction. We expected if we met with him that he could have taking us to see the Stocking weaving and other manufactures of the town, but as he was out we were obliged to give up that. Mrs Davis was very kind and went with me through part of the town. It is a handsome well built place for as the old buildings fall to decay they taken them down and erect good houses in their stead. It contains several Charity schools, a good Infirmary & several churches. The spire of St. Mary's was struck down by lightning about 12 years ago but it is rebuilt in a very pretty stile though I think rather too high.

The next morning we went to Harborough, a stage of 15 miles to breakfast. It was thronging owing to its being a fair for Cows and horses. From there to Kettering the road was very bad which hindered us so much that it was later when we arrived at the latter place than we intended and indeed threw us late all day. While dinner was preparing we went into the Church yard. At Kettering the church is a large good building with a very handsome steeple, indeed there are several churches in that neighbourhood that seem to have been built all at the same time. They have all spires which are very high, the stone is very good that they are all quite perfect though they must be ancient for in modern days they would not have built such good churches in retired situations. Northamptonshire is the County for churches for on entering Thrapston we counted 10 steeples and when going to church on Sunday we could see from one situation in the wood 5 steeples.

We arrived safely at Lilford at 9 o'clock at night, the fourth day from leaving home without having been delayed by the slightest accident; and considering the unsettled state of the weather we had been very little wet.

Lilford is an ancient stone house & stands in a pleasant situation, the Gardens are not extensive but they and all the grounds round it are kept in such neat order that they must please all who see them; a river runs on one side [of] the house with a pretty bridge over it which is a great ornament. On Saturday I went to Mr Selby at Pilton, where I was to remain during my Father's stay at Lilford. On Sunday I went to Lilford to go with the family to church[1] as they have service at Pilton only once a day. The village in which the church stands, that the family attend, is a very plain old building but contains a handsome monument to the memory of Judge Powys, the founder of the family in Northampton. In the afternoon I went to Pilton church.

Lilford hall was built in 1635, a few rooms have been modernized for the family to live in. The rules hung up in the servants hall are:–

Swear not at all
Be not riotous or reprobate
Be not wise in your own conceits
Waste not. Spare not.

The weather was so bad during our stay at Lilford that the last few days there was very a very high flood. Mr Selby had 50 acres of meadow land under water, 15 acres of it was cut. We rode to Aldwinkle on Thursday, the road was flooded knee deep in some places from thence we went to Titchmarsh Lodge to see Mr Coat's family and spent a few hours with them pleasantly. I was surprised at one farm house we went to to see them feeding near a score of pigs with sweet milk.

We left Lilford on Saturday and arrived at Peterboro' to dinner. We went to look at the Cathedral of that place; it is a very handsome building and in a high state of preservation. It is very neat and clean. Mary Queen of Scots was first buried here but afterwards removed to Westminster. Catherine first wife of King Henry the 8th is also buried there. What is very remarkable, both Queens were interred by the same sexton; he lived to the age of 78 years and was one of the few who survived the plague. There was a monument erected to the memory of Mary, part of which still remains, but Catharine has only a plain stone over here with 'Queen Catherine' engraved on a small brass plate. There is the remains of a monument erected by a gentleman of the name of Huntingdon for himself but he lived to see it destroyed by Oliver Cromwell. We were shewn part of a monk's cloak found several years ago in a stone coffin, also a small stone monument erected to the memory of upwards of 400 monks who were murdered in the year 870. It is supposed to be the oldest monument extant.

In the Cathedral are 2 ancient windows of painted glass and a modern one. The road from thence is very flat and generally good land in the neighbourhood of Eye. We passed thro' upwards of 200 acres of corn (mostly wheat) without interruption of a single field of anything else. The principal trade of the villages between Peterboro' & Crowland is basket making. We arrived at Crowland about 6 o'Clock drank tea at the Inn and then walked to Mr Blundell's. Our reception from them was such as we expected, kind & friendly. They used their utmost exertions to make our visit to them agreeable and they succeeded. For the next 3 days we spent with them added very much to the pleasures of our excursion. On Sunday we accompanied them to Church and were introduced to most of

their friends from whom we received great Civilities during our stay.
They are very hospitable kind people and almost adore both Mr & Mrs
Blundell.

The Abbey is a very ancient building and when first built must have
been very noble, it is said to have extended a mile in length but Oliver
Cromwell destroyed the greatest part of it and time fast destroying the
remainder only a small part of one side aisle can be used as a place of worship. The entrance of the town is a bridge which is considered one of the
greatest curiosities of ancient architecture in the Kingdom. It is a century
older than the Abbey. It consists but of one arch and leads into three
streets. It is so steep that it can only be used by foot passengers.

The town is rather larger but contains very few good houses. The
streets are none paved and have all wide drains down the middle which
keeps them always dirty. On Tuesday we went with Mr B to Spalding a
small market town 10 miles from Crowland and had a pleasant ride. The
road for several miles lay on the Banks of the Wash, which is the large
reservoir draining the whole county. Being higher than the surrounding
land the water is lifted into it by windmills of a peculiar construction. It is
many miles in extent and is a source of riches to the town of Crowland
for in winter it is well stocked with fish which finds employment for a
great number of men in catching and taking them to market; in summer it
is dry and is so rich that it keeps hundreds of cattle, besides which many
thousands of geese are kept in it. They pluck them twice a year [see
Blundell letters], in May and September and their feathers are a great article of trade to all parts of the Kingdom.

On Wednesday the 12th of August at 7 o'Clock we took leave of Mrs
Blundell and turned our faces towards home. Mr B went with us to
Stamford 16 miles. We dined together & then parted. Stamford is a large
handsome town it seems prosperous & bustling.

We proceeded to Coulthworth, it is a small shabby village consisting
but one narrow street badly built and worse paved but has the honour to
give birth to Sir Isaac Newton, the cottage is still standing in which he
was born. We soon had seen what was worth seeing so supped early and
retired to rest.

The next morning we went to Grantham to breakfast, after we had
enjoyed our coffee we strolled into the town. We soon found the Church
and were much struck with the size of the chancel and the beauty of the
steeple. While we were admiring it the sexton came and asked if we
should like to see the inside we answered in the affirmative and were
agreeably surprised to find it exceeded the outside for it is built in the

Cathedral stile, in perfect repair and remarkably neat & clean it contains many handsome monuments both stone & marble. The sexton informed us that a few years ago a gentleman of that town left by will the interest for ever to beautify the Church. The persons who have the care of it have done ample justice to the kind intentions of the donor by painting it throughout and purchasing many neat & appropriate ornaments. He also left large sums of money for charitable purposes which have been as well managed but we did not hear the particulars. As there was nothing else worth notice we returned to the Inn and resumed our journey.

We stopped at Newark this was the best paved town we travelled through. It has a very neat town hall and market square on the bank of the river, are the ruins of a castle entirely overgrown with ivy which gives it a very venerable appearance. We drank tea at Kirklington, 7 miles from Mansfield where we meant to sleep and hoped to reach it before dark. We had this day enjoyed the ride more than any proceeding one, the day was very fine, the country pleasant and the roads generally good (but oh sad reverse) we had not left Kirklington above 2 miles before we entered Sherwood forest. The road was deep and heavy sand, none enclosed, not a house or even a tree to be seen. The horse was tired having travelled near 40 miles that day so travelled very slowly, before we had half crossed the forest it was quite dark we were so long in getting to Mansfield that we began to fear we had missed the road and could not see a single person to inquire of (no enviable situation this for 2 persons entire strangers to the country) however by patience and by letting the horse take his own way we at last got safe to the long wished for place.

The next morning we took a walk before breakfast but were soon satisfied for it is a mean town very dirty and noisy for the principal business is blacksmiths. On leaving the town we saw a woman weaving stockings as it was quite new to us both we alighted to take a nearer view of it; it seems to be hard work and must I think injure the chest the woman said she had 8d a pair of weaving coarse cotton stockings & that she could weave 5 stockings a day and take care of her family. This day we made little progress for we were constantly either ascending or descending high hills of limestone, some of them very steep.

We dined at Chesterfield. While dinner was preparing we went to the church for we perceived on entering the town that the spire was very crooked; we enquired of the sexton the reason, for from its curious corkscrew appearance we thought it must have been purposely built so. He said there was no record had ever been found of the time when it was erected or whether it was at first straight. It is composed entirely of wood and lead and was added many years after the church was built. If it was intended for ornament they are much mistaken for instead of that it is a deformity.

Chesterfield is a genteel town of not much trade but a great depot for French prisoners.

They informed us here that our road lay within a mile of Chatsworth, the far famed seat of the Duke of Devonshire, we therefore concluded to devote part of the afternoon to visiting it. We left the gig at Baslow and walked to the house. We soon gained admittance. It is built in the form of a large square with an open area in the centre. The first room we entered was paved with black and white marble with a handsome staircase of the same materials. The walls and ceiling represent the life of Julius Caesar. From thence we ascended the stairs to the state rooms (viz) 2 dining rooms, 2 drawing rooms, music room and picture gallery which is occasionally used as a dancing room. They so far exceeded any idea I had formed of them, in grandeur & elegance that I was completely dazzled. I find it impossible to describe them, all the walls and ceilings are covered with paintings by the most eminent masters representing the actions of several great personages. We were next shewn the ancient state rooms which remain yet as they were first furnished when the house was built. They must then have been very elegant. They contain many valuable paintings and the carving in wood and stone of which there is a great deal is said to be the best in the kingdom. The unfortunate Queen of Scots was confined here some years, she was allowed three rooms only. In one of them is a bed which she used. It is of crimson velvet with silver fringe, it is fast going to decay and is a sad emblem of a fallen greatness. That room is never used but the other two have lately been fitted up for use. The bedrooms are in a stile of elegance equal to the visiting rooms. The walls of all are either covered with paintings or tapestry in a high state of preservation. In the dressing room of the late Duchess are 2 Cabinets of fossils and plants, one filled entirely with productions of Derbyshire, the other are principally foreign. They are very neatly arranged and have a very pretty effect. We were next conducted to the chapel which has been lately finished and is equal if not superior to the other parts of the house. The walls, ceilings represent all the miracles, the Crucifixion and Resurrection of our Saviour. The pulpit and seats are covered with crimson velvet edged with gold. We next went to the garden & water works and returned to the inn highly gratified with our afternoon's excursion. We then went to Stoney Middleton where we slept.

On Saturday we left early and had a delightful ride through Middleton

Dale. You here see nature in reality, rock rising above rock many hundred feet, huge pieces hang seemingly without support as if ready to drop and bury forever the traveller beneath them. We breakfasted at Peak Forest, visited a short time at Chapel in the frith, drank tea at Bullock Smithy[2] and arrived at Ardwick at 8 o'Clock without meeting with any incident worth recording.

Sunday we got home to dinner and found our friends well and in good spirits for they had not had the slightest accident of any kind during our absence. Thus ended the first long journey I ever had, probably the last I ever shall have, at all events a pleasanter I cannot have wherever I may go for I had my kind intelligent Father for my companion, a pleasant season of the year, met with kind friends wherever I expected it & with civility from everyone; had a conveyance the best calculated for seeing the country, not confined to coach houses but at liberty to travel when we pleased did not meet with any accident to cause a moment's delay, and to complete our pleasures found all comfortable at home when we returned to it. We travelled in nine counties, viz; Lancashire, Cheshire, Derbyshire, Leicestershire, Northamptonshire, Cambridgeshire, Lincolnshire, Rutlandshire and Nottinghamshire, but I did not see one that, take for all in all, I preferred to Lancashire, nor a spot in my whole journey that looked as comfortable as my own happy home.

(Footnote) In 2 months after my arrival at home I received a letter from my kind friend Mr Selby informing me that he had lost 2 Children by the Scarlet Fever & Measles, a fine girl in her 5th year and a promising boy in his 3rd year, in a fortnight after he lost an infant son of six months old by the Hooping Cough. What a change from the short time I had left them all well. Truly might he say with young insatiate another could not once suffice. Thrice flew thy shaft & thrice my place destroyed. And that in thrice the moon had filled her horn.

Letter to Miss Hodgkinson from Mr Selby
Lilford   10th Sept, 1812
Dear Miss Hodgkinson, I remember at our parting at Lilford my promise to write your Father on business, but how uncertain are things in this Life; on the following day my poor little girl Maria fell ill of the Scarlet Fever then raging in the Neighbourhood, after a very heavy affliction for over 3 Weeks with that & the Measles, she died tho the Apothecary says of Neither Complaint but the two brought into action a Third. Ann & Eleanor also in a few days taken ill, Ann of the Fever & Eleanor of the

Fever & Measles. Ann is quite recovered, Eleanor is improving tho' rather slowly, she has a very bad cough & is otherwise ill, my poor dear Boy Tom in the midst of this was taken ill & the D^r. said he had the two Complaints together, but it afterwards proved he had in the first instance only the Fever, for after recovering of this attack he was again seized with illness which proved to be Measles and of which he died in six days, under this 2nd affliction if it may be called so tho' I had not recovered from the first I thought I must have sunk, but God who is ever merciful has strengthened and supported me in this our Trial. My poor Wife during this has been tolerable well except of late from Grief, she has very bad pains in her Head but yesterday and today much better. Little David throw out has been very well, passing better Nights than usual, or two Servants have been ill, one very much so of the Measles, the other had a very slight attack of the Fever. I never have passed 4 such weeks of affliction in my life, it being quite out of the reach of any human consolation to help me, but I trust it is for the best as nothing can be done without the knowledge of the Almighty & I pray that I may derive some Christian graces therefrom (viz) Humility, resignation, patience & Christian fortitude. As to my dear Children, they are in Heaven where I hope and trust through Christ's Mercy I may meet them when all tears shall be done away. At present their little playful ways and their last moments are to much before my Eyes. I am lost in Love to them tho' I can say with St. Paul I am not sorrowing without hope. I know you will pardon my dwelling so long on this subject, with the severe Trial I have had. My Wife w^d have wrote but at present it is too much, she has not even wrote to her Sisters. She desires her kind Love to you, to Mrs H., your Father and Brother. Probably ere long I may write your Father or Brother, in the mean time give my very kind respects to all, as I know they will sympathize with us in the affliction. L^d. Lilford &c.,&c., are now at Eastbourne, tho' I suppose Lord L will be leaving in a few days for this place. Lady L & children will remain until near the end of Oct if all is well. I remain, D^r. Miss Hodgkinson, Yours very sincerely,   John Selby.

Notes

1   This church was the Lilford family church at Achurch.
2   Bullock Smithy was at Hazel Grove, near Stockport.

15

The Flavel Letters

Richard Hodgkinson's two-year excursion into Shropshire as a young
teacher was quite brief in the terms of his lifespan but it was an experience
that set his fortunes towards Chowbent and the turn of events which
transformed his life. Echoes of those happy times were heard down the
decades that followed.

This group of letters was the first of Hodgkinson's adult life and began
with a glowing tribute paid to him by Flavel in a note to Joseph
Hodgkinson, the young teacher's father. Could any father want for more
other than to have a son who was 'sober, diligent and ingenious' and a
paragon of Christian virtue?

Hodgkinson maintained his friendship with John Flavel long after he
had left Shropshire and gone to Atherton to seek fame and fortune.
Flavel's rambling letters reflect the ability of a man of perhaps ill–disci-
plined scholarship but they are lightened with humorous passages. Flavel's
family life was tragic. With the exception of his daughter Mary, his other
five children died young, leaving his wife inconsolable.

These letters, together with Hodgkinson's notebooks, give an insight
into the importance placed on education in of the last quarter of the eighteenth century. Boarders, day pupils and free scholars were taught at
grammar schools with much emphasis on the classics, French and the written
word, with an occasional diversion into accountancy and surveying.

In 1786, Flavel moved to the substantial Lacon Childe School at
Cleobury Mortimer in Shropshire, a building that survives to this day.
Flavel was paid a handsome £300 a year and this may have been the basis
of the £13,000 fortune he left to his surviving daughter Mary when he
died. In 1794, twelve years after leaving Shropshire, Hodgkinson visited
his mentor and was deeply moved when the ageing headmaster reflected
on their past companionship and urged him to return to the school.

Flavel spent his last years living with his daughter, Mary, at Pulley and after his death she published a booklet of her father's sermons; convoluted and insubstantial in argument, they are the deeply pious reflections of a Christian country gentleman.

Recruiting teachers for remote country schools was difficult and Flavel delegated the task to Hodgkinson who was asked on several occasions to advertise in the Manchester Mercury and then interview applicants. But even Hodgkinson was not infallible, with one teacher unexpectedly turning up with a wife in tow and another who sought too much solace in drink.

While teaching with Flavel in 1782, Hodgkinson witnessed the unveiling of Rodney's Pillar, erected in tribute to Sir George Brydges Rodney (later Lord Rodney), Admiral of the White. Today the fifty-four-foot monument still commands sweeping views from Shropshire's Breiddon Hills. His essay reflects the self-importance of the organizers, the fun enjoyed by the spectators and the greed of drink sellers with a captive audience on a summer's day. Hodgkinson's description of this fete day is probably unique, for when the monument was renovated some 100 years later no account of the proceedings could be found. Hodgkinson also wrote a brief lyrical description of the Shropshire countryside. Both of these pieces follow the Flavel letters.

The Flavel Correspondence

From John Flavel to Joseph Hodgkinson, Richard's father
Westbury   December 25, 1783
Your Son I take my leave on with great regret; He has behaved himself exceedingly well, and without adulation I tell you, that if I had such a Son, I should really be proud of him. He is sober, diligent, and ingenious; and what completes his Character is, that his chiefest motive seems to be the one Thing needful. Now as the grand Characteristic of a Christian is to do good; and the greatest sphere of action a good man has to move in, consequently the more good is then in his power to do; hence it is that I am inclined to wish that your Son might apply for Holy Orders, as, in my opinion, he is a very fit Person. It is certainly a hurt to this Nation in general, that the greatest part of the young Clergy are thrust into the Church with no other view than a lucrative one; who have no delight or knowledge in the Holy Scriptures or in true Religion: How then can it otherwise be, but that many of the lay People are destroyed (as the prophet complained) for lack of knowledge.   J. Flavel

Westbury   April 20 1784
I congratulate you on your promotion to the School and the favour you
are in with A-n family for without adulation, I think there are but few so
capable as yourself of conducting and managing a School. Now as the care
of a School is a mighty undertaking and such an important Employment
that a Master who has abilities (and who is assisted by Divine Grace)
might be of inestimable service to such of the rising Generation which
providence has committed to his care.

Mr Peace is a very good Classic; but how was I astonished when he
told me he was a married man and brought Mrs P. with him! This he
never disclosed to me till he came to Westbury and had been with one
from Morning till Night leaving his Wife at Geary's all this while! He
should have been more open, as you know it must be quite inconvenient
on several accounts. They were married a few weeks before they came to
W. and as we could get no house, nor proper lodgings in W she seemed
rather discontent, so out of duty we took her with him to Board with us:
but as she seemed still uneasy for want of a House for themselves they saw
the school at Churbury advertised and he wrote to the Trustees who gave
him encouragement to attend their Meeting on Easter Tuesday and he
accordingly went, (first letting me know) where he and two others stood
as Candidates. The Trustees proposed whoever of them exhibited the best
Themes in English and Latin should be the Master; and the preference
was given to Mr Peace: so he leaves me at Whitsuntide and now I am at a
loss for an assistant in that line for which I must immediately apply.

If you think by putting an advert in one of the public papers would be
likely, please put it in (only for one) and charge it to me in your next. I
need not direct you as you know what will do. You might include in the
same advert a writing assistant who is well skilled in figures. Their
Character must be sober and, if a writing assistant should offer, a specimen
of his penmanship will be requisite; which you can enclose to me; but the
chief assistant that I shall be at a loss for, is a Classic Scholar, he should be
tolerably well skilled in Greek and a good Latin Scholar.

Mrs F writes in best respects and will be obliged to you if you'll inform
her of the lowest price of calico wrapping such as we do for lining and
what would be the price of a good cotton counterpane. Vella, Bill & Pall
are all recovered of the Small Pox.

Sir, I need not tell you what to put in the advert but fearing you should
be so busy as not to have the leisure to put it in immediately I'll scribble
one over now. I have the pen in my hand and leave it to you to alter and

correct it before it is invested in the public paper.

Wanted in a school near Shrewsbury (or in a school in Salop) an assistant who is qualified to teach the Classics. He will have the care of about eight or ten classics and also the care of a few English scholars. The Board will be given by the Master. In the same School is also wanted an Usher who is a good penman and also a good accomplant; a species of his writing in the several useful ornamental hand will be expected. As the assistants are to board with the Master they must both be single men who can produce good characters. For further particulars apply to Mr Hodgkinson Junior at Leigh, near Warrington, to whom letters directed (post paid) will be duly answered.

I forgot to insert that if the writing usher understood Land Survey and some of the most needful branches of the mathematics, he would be the more acceptable. I also forgot to mention they should send their lowest terms. J. Flavel.

Westbury May 12, 1784

I shall entirely leave the Choice of the Candidates to you; I confess that the Characters both of Mr Sutcliffe & Mr Bullock seem pleasing; but as you think the latter better calculated for my purpose, I shall acquiesce in which ever you prefer, & also will rest satisfied with whatever Agreement you & he make. You propose £12 for the first Year & every subsequent year to be advanced according to merit: to this I am consenting.

In your next let me know what he will expect to Breakfast on; whether he will be content to breakfast with the Boarders on Milk &c., or whether he will expect a Tea breakfast; to be sure the former wd best suit us because it wd give less trouble & wd be quite as well for him, if not more healthful. J. Flavel.

Westbury Augst 31, 1784

Soon after I received the parcel I intended to have written but then I thought it wd be more prudent to omit it till I could inform you by what channel I should convey the Cash. Accordingly I went to Shrewsbury and asked Mr Staff. Pryse; he replied that he should soon go on Business towards your Country, & having repeatedly had invitations to visit a Friend in Chowbent, he meant to do it, & wd take the Cash for you. But alas! how uncertain are all human Schemes? Before he could visit Lancashire he was suddenly summoned by the King of Terrors to quit his terrestrial Tenem^t. & take a longer journey than that into Lancashire.

Plate 64   When the steam ferry arrived to ply its trade four times each hour between Portsmouth and Gosport in 1840, it reduced John Hodgkinson's wages by half, but after taking his Royal Navy pension, 'and what I earn in the Boat, I can do better than in the waveing [weaving] Buisness', he wrote to his uncle Richard in 1844 (*The Steam Ferry*, 1840, by T.C. Dibdin; City of Portsmouth Leisure Service)

Plate 65   John Christian Curwen, agricultural pioneer and MP (British Museum)

Plate 66 Workington Hall in the last decade of the nineteenth century. This was the home of John Christian Curwen. Here he entertained the young David Hodgkinson, sent by his father to study revolutionary farming methods

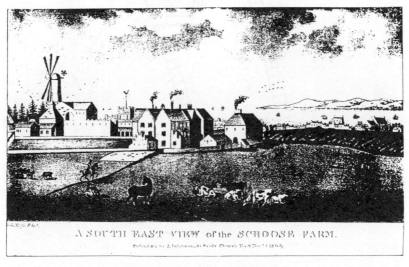

A SOUTH EAST VIEW of the SCHOOSE FARM.

Plate 67 John Christian Curwen's Schoose farm at Workington, even today, retains many of the old eighteenth–century buildings

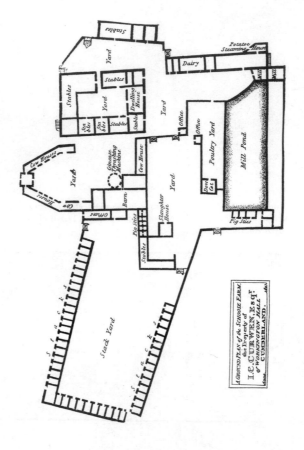

Plate 68   John Christian Curwen's plan of Schoose Farm in 1807

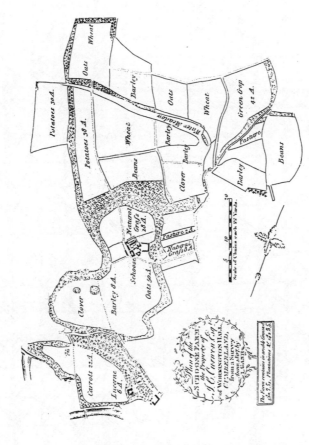

Plate 69 John Christian Curwen's field plan for his crops, showing the use of clover, lucerne and beans alongside grain crops

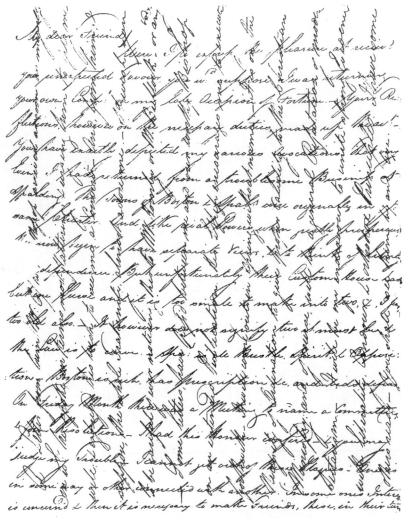

Plate 70   In the days of the stage coach, letters were charged by the sheet, and James Blundell wrote many of his letters to Richard Hodgkinson in this 'cross-hatch' manner to save postage. The letter begins, 'My dear Friend, Where I do express the pleasure of receiving your unexpected favour . . .' (LRO DDX 211/4)

Doctrina Vires promovet insitas,
Rectique Cultus pectora roborant.

CLASSICAL AND COMMERCIAL
EDUCATION,

AT

Leigh, near Manchester.

MR. BLUNDELL respectfully informs the Public,
that he takes TWELVE Young Gentlemen, at

One Guinea Entrance.

*Board, & Education in the Classics, Mathematics,
Geography, Belles Letters, &c.*

25 Guineas per Annum.—Washing not included.

FRENCH, MUSIC, DRAWING, and DANCING, by
approved Masters, at the usual Terms.

As the number is so limited, every attention will be paid to render it
select and respectable.

N.B. The usual notice will be expected.

☞ A GOOD LIBRARY.

R. & W. Dean, Printers.

Plate 71 James Blundell's advertisement for pupils to attend Leigh Grammar School, 1806.
The Latin motto is a quotation from Horace: 'Learning Promotes inate Strengths, correct
ways Strengthen the heart.'

Plate 72   The old Grammar School at Leigh stood alongside the Parish church (Wigan Heritage Services)

Plate 73   Crowland Abbey. 'Oliver Cromwell destroyed the greatest part of it and time fast destroying the remainder, only a small part of one aisle can be used as a place of worship.': Mary Hodgkinson's diary, 1812

Plate 74   Sir Richard Arkwright, made a vastly rich man by the cotton trade, was, said Richard Hodgkinson, 'a barber of the lowest order' and a man whose 'morals were loose and his conduct profligate and debauched.': letter to Blundell in 1816 (Chris Aspin)

Plate 75   Cotton magnate John Horrocks of Preston. 'The reverse of Sir Richard Arkwright, his Character was that of kindness, benevolence and liberality.': Richard Hodgkinson (Harris Museum, Preston)

Plate 76   Mary Hodgkinson in old age. In 1812 she went on a journey to the Lilford family seat in Northamptonshire with 'a kind and intelligent Father for companion'. (Picture: Richard Hodgkinson)

AT A MEETING

OF THE

Cotton Manufacturers,

OF LEIGH, IN THE COUNTY OF LANCASTER,

HELD AT STARKIE'S HALL, ON MONDAY THE SECOND DAY OF JUNE, 1817.

It was Resolved unanimously,

THAT the enormous Quantity of BRITISH COTTON YARN Exported, has tended very much to injure the SALE of BRITISH MANUFACTURED COTTON PIECE GOODS.

THAT when only a small Quantity of British Cotton Yarn was Exported, we were enabled to give our Workmen Wages which maintained them without their having recourse to the Parish.

THAT ever since British Cotton Yarn was Exported in immense Quantities, we have been compelled to lower the Wages of our Workmen; at present our Workmen's Wages are so extremely low, that they cannot maintain themselves, and the Landholders now make good to our Workmen in Poor Leys that Portion of Wages which we have been compelled to deduct.

THAT a Memorial or Petition be forwarded to the Honourable the House of Commons, requesting the Honourable House to take the subject into their most serious consideration.

THAT a Subscription be entered into for defraying the Expences of the said Memorial or Petition, and that the following Gentlemen be appointed a Committee to carry into effect the above Resolutions.

Mr. Schofield,   Mr. Guest,   Mr. Thorp,   Mr. Collier,   Mr. T. Smith,
Mr. Moorhouse,   Mr. Ashton,   Mr. Green,   Mr. A. Smith,   Mr. J. Smith.

J. & J. Haigh, Printers, Manchester.

Plate 77 After the end of the second French War, trade and agriculture in Lancashire were in a parlous way. Cotton manufacturers meeting at Leigh petitioned Parliament. 'The miserable and alarming state of this Country I have not the language to describe', wrote Richard Hodgkinson to James Blundell in 1816, 'The poor in many instances are literally starving.' (Wigan Heritage Services)

Plate 78 Lilford Hall. 'An ancient stone house stands in a pleasant situation . . . the grounds round it are kept in such neat order they must please all who see them.': Mary Hodgkinson, 1812

Plate 79 The triform bridge at Crowland, 'considered one of the greatest curiosities of ancient architecture in the Kingdom': Mary Hodgkinson, 1812

Plate 80   Robert Scarlett, the Elizabethan gravedigger who buried Queen Katherine of Aragon and Mary Queen of Scots (Pitkin Publications, Andover, Hants)

Plate 81   Woolsthorpe Manor, Sir Isaac Newton's birthplace

Plate 82   The Selby grave at Lilford. Within a short time of Richard Hodgkinson and his daughter Mary bidding farewell to John Selby, his family had been devastated by disease and three of his children carried off to the grave

Plate 83 Chatsworth House, view by Cowen, 1828. 'Grandeur and elegance . . . I was completely dazzled.': Mary Hodgkinson, 1812 (Chatsworth Settlement Trustees)

Plate 84   Lacon Childe School at Cleobury Mortimer, Shropshire, where John Flavel was paid a handsome £300 a year as headmaster

Plate 85   In August 1782, Richard Hodgkinson climbed the steep side of Breddyn Hill, Powys, to enjoy a festival of mirth and festivity at the unveiling of Rodney's Pillar, erected to commemorate the gallantry of Admiral Rodney. Hodgkinson complained about the price of drink and said the dregs of barrels were being sold at up to 10d a quart

Plate 86   The old Leigh Workhouse. Richard Hodgkinson's last major task in public office was to introduce in Leigh in 1837 the rigours of the new Poor Law. Hodgkinson complained about the confusion resulting from the 'want of timely instructions' (Wigan Heritage Services)

Plate 87   When Richard Hodgkinson finally retired, he was presented with this silver writing set and a testimonial which read, 'To Mr Richard Hodgkinson from the Rev. James Hornby in memory of the dead and in testimony of cordial esteem for the integrity of principle and fidelity of family attachment.' Hornby was related to the Lilford and Legh families (Picture: Richard Hodgkinson)

V. R.

CORONATION

OF HER GRACIOUS MAJESTY

Queen Victoria,

JUNE 28th, 1838.

King's Head Chowbent, 22nd June 1838.

At a meeting held this Day pursuant to public Notice, to celebrate the Coronation of Her Majesty QUEEN VICTORIA, Richd. Hodgkinson Esq. in the Chair, the following resolutions were unanimously adopted :

RESOLVED,

That there be a procession of the Gentry, Clergy and Inhabitants of Atherton, and the Children of the several Sunday Schools, to meet in the Market Place Chowbent at one o'clock, and that the different Societies in Atherton be invited to form part of the procession.

RESOLVED,

That there be a Subscription entered into for providing Bread and Meat for he aged and indigent.

ESOLVED,

That Mr Thomas Manley, Mr Woodward, Surgeon, Mr Jonan. Hesketh, John Unsworth, Mr Shakeshaft, Mr Hall, Mr Samuel Davis, Mr Thomas e, Mr Nicholas Unsworth and Mr Peter Croston, be appointed to wait on nhabitants of Atherton to solicit subscriptions for the above purpose.

VED,

Mr John Unsworth be Treasurer.

ESOLVED,

That the following Gentlemen be appointed a Committee, to organise the procession and dispose of the Subscriptions for the above purpose, and such other necessary expences as may be incurred in promoting it : T. B. W. Sanderson, Esq. Samuel Newton, Esq. Richd. Hodgkinson, Esq. Mr Selby, Mr Radcliffe, Mr George Hesketh, Mr Norbury, Mr Nicholas Unsworth, Mr George Newton, Mr Wm. Fyldes, Mr Thomas Hope, and Mr Cleworth, with power to add to their numbers.

RESOLVED,

That the Bread and Meat be distributed by Tickets from the Committee, and that each Subscriber be allowed a number of tickets in proportion to his subscription.

RESOLVED.

That it be recommended to the Subscribers to distribute the tickets among the aged and indigent.

RESOLVED,

That the above Resolutions be printed and distributed in the neighbourhood.

RICHARD HODGKINSON, Chairman.

T. WILLIAMS, PRINTER, STAMP-OFFICE, LEIGH.

Plate 88   Poster of Coronation celebrations. 'I will only mention one Circumstance connected with it and which regards myself. I was elected President [of the Coronation festival] which placed me in a Situation in which it is very improbably any Individual will be placed for a Century to come, that is, of being unanimously elected President and presiding at Three successive Coronation Dinners.': Richard Hodgkinson, 1838 (Wigan Heritage Services)

The last letter I wrote in such a hurry in the School, & the Pupils about me, that I suppose it was full of blunders; one mistake I remember, which was an A instead of an O in the Word adopted which I thought, when dry to have altered, but as the bearer was just going to Salop I believe it was sealed in haste & forgot; but a slip of the pen is excusable, especially when in a hurry, it was quite a rough Draught, & should have been directed.   J. Flavel.

Westbury   March 31st 1785
I received your last obliging Letter, and was much Pleased with your live-ly and natural Picture of the generality of the Citizens of London; if a unknown person to you had read it, he must have concluded from the justness of the portraiture, that you was a Cockney.

This hasty letter I send by a Miss Perkins who is just setting off for Manchester. She is a Cousin to my Wife; one that I would recommend to Mr H for a W——. I think she would suit him exactly. She seems a good Girl, genteel and well behaved; she has been with a Milliner in Manchester for some Time and has been over here at the Hursts seeing her Parents. The Gentleman she's with has a mind to turn over the Business to her in 10 or 12 months Time, consequently the old Gentleman's Purse has been besieged, and must undoubtedly surrender on honorable Terms; in the mean Time Mr H should lay close siege or rather attack the Vessel when she is fullrigged and well laden, in full sail, and I make not doubt but should strike to the first broad side, if not, then; yet when she has been more closely fired at fore and after there will then be no fear of success.

But hold, Mr H will think I am rather waggish, then dash out the word aft for fear of a wrong construction.   J Flavel

Cleobury   June 23rd 1787
Mr Bullock informs me that he intends making application for holy Orders, consequently I shall want another Assistant when he leaves me and I have not a Friend that I can so safely rely on to recommend me another as Mr H——.

I need not inform my judicious Friend of the disagreeable hurry of breaking up School. By removing about 40 miles from Westbury, and raising my Terms from £15 to 16 Guins. I lost the greatest part of my Boarders. We have not had since Xmas more than 17 Boarders, about 16 Day Scholars, and 40 Free Scholars; so that I have only had Mr B to assist me; but I do assure you that the burthen has rested mostly on myself; For

Mr B, is not a good Penman, nor much of an Accountant. An Assistant that can write well is a good Accomplishment, as well as a good Classic, would suit me best; but if that can't be had I can dispense with one who is a good Classic only; and then if the School should increase, I can soon procure another Assistant in the Pen Line. Mr B is a good Classic, but I don't think he has exerted himself in pushing them on, nor in increasing the Grammar Rules at Night like Mr H was used to do, and this I told him. This is a secret. I think this is why my Boarders are decreased in number, for I have not one Boarder now that learns Latin or Greek; my own Sons, and one Day Scholar are all in that Line.

Mr B's behaviour and attention is altered very much for the worse, I can assure you since he came to Cleobury, and I shall not regret the parting with him except he alters. I give him £20 per annum Board and Washing and one Pound extra for encouragement (that is 20 Guineas in the whole) thinking that would excite him to push the Pupils on which are under his Care. There is nothing of the fatigue in teaching for an Assistant, comparable to what was at Westbury. I have a very commodious and pleasant House and Garden and a small piece of Land, & £40 per annum to teach the Cleobury youth free, who upon an average are nearly 40. There is £20 pd to anor. man, in a Room for that purpose, to teach them to read; so that not one free Boy comes into my School till he begins to write. J. Flavel.

Cleobury Feb 4th 1788

Mr Bullock informs me that Mr Crowdson by a recent Letter adviseth him to apply for holy Orders speedily, that he might recommend him to Curacy and an Assistant's Place in a School which will soon be vacant. I am constrained, therefore to renew my former Solicitations for your speedy Enquiry for one to succeed him in my School. I could with the sake of my own Children to have a good Classic; for indeed, besides them, at present, I have but one that learns Latin. J Flavel.

Cleobury Dec 25 88

Yours of the 4th Inst gave me great satisfaction, when I found you were entangled in the silken Bands of Hymen. Mrs F unites with me in congratulations and best respects both to you and our unknown Mrs H. That may you and your Bride may enjoy every temporal Blessing consistent with Human Life and finally enter into the blissful Mansion of the celestial abode, in the sincere prayer from your real Friend and obliged hble Servt.

J Flavel

From John Flavel'son.
Cleobury   Jan 22 1790
When your obliging Letter arrived at Cleobury my Father was on a long
Journey into Wales and in his Return visited his Salopean Friends and
likewise those at Westbury and its Vicinity, and not being just returned
and opened School he desired I would answer yours; in the first Place I
will insert the recipe for Blue Ink.

'¹/₂lb of French Verdigrease, 2 oz Cream of Tartar. Bruise the
Verdigrease and put it into and earthen Pot or Pipkin with 3 Pints of
Water; Let simmer an hour or more, then put the Cream into it.

We sincerely sympathize with you in the various Dispensations of
Providence which summon'd all your powers and put your mental and
intellectual Faculties to the Test. The Misfortune which befell your Father
and the loss of the best of Mothers are truly deplorable. We heartily congratulate you on the Birth of a Daughter and wish you and Mrs H. all the
Joy and Comfort in her that can possibly be. ˙   John Flavel Junior.

Cleobury Mortimer   Jan 31st 1791
Dear Sir, Mr Lutener, the young Gentleman you last recommended to
my Father, has lately been ordained, and now serves a Church near
Cleobury, and in all probability will be soon leaving us.

I think Mr Bullock a much better Scholar than Mr L–. Mr L– has lately
taken to stay out late at Night, very often, and sometimes very much disguised in Liquor; this is my Father's chief Objection to him; for an
Assistant here might serve a Church and attend on our School as my
Father keeps two Assist.

Be pleased to send my Father a Line in a Month's Time and give your
Opinion, and where you think the most likely place to have a good
Assistant from. If you should be so fortunate as to hear of one that you
think will do, the Salary will be left to you. If you could hear of one that
can teach the French Language with the Classics so much the better.
                                                                          J Flavel Jnr.

Cleobury Mortimer   Mar 25th 1792
. . . my grateful Thanks for recommending me so steady and sober an
Assistant as Mr Thompson has hitherto turned out; I have inclosed Half a
Guinea as a small Token of gratitude and towards paying the Postage of
letters &c. Excuse Blunders, as he can't stay for me to correct them.
                                                                          J Flavel.

Cleobury Mortimer   May 12th 1795
As my Neighbour Mr Herbert Mercer is just going into Lancashire, I
embrace the Opportunity of sending this hasty Letter by him. I should be
glad to hear from you when you can have a little Relaxation from
Business and inform me how you and your Family are and how the
Lancashire People manage in this Time of scarcity. If in your Travels, or
in the Circle of your Acquaintance you should hear of a Person that
would suit me for an Assistant, either in the Classics or which would be
still better; one that is a good Penman and would teach the Classics and
assist in teaching Accounts, I should esteem it as an additional Favour if
you would then give me a Line of Information. Mrs F unites etc.,

J. Flavel.

PS Please to make our Complements to Mrs H. the unknown.

Rodney's Festival
by Richard Hodgkinson

On the 6th day of August, 1782, a Jubilee was celebrated on Bruddyn Hill
in Montgomeryshire in commemoration of the signal services which this
Nation has received from the Conduct and Valour of Gallant Rodney.[1]

The Ceremony opened by conducting the Lady of the Manor, accompanied by a numerous train of Ladies and Gentlemen, preceded by a noble
Band of Music, to the Pillar where she was addressed in an elegant poetic
Compliment. After they were returned to the Tent which was erected for
their Reception (at the distance of about 300 Yards from the Pillar for the
convenience of being out of the Wind) five most elegant speeches in
prose and verse (two of which were in Latin) were spoken. The Speakers
were the Revd. Mr Rudd, of Hereford, Mr Worthington and two young
Gentlemen from Westminster School. Dinner was provided for 300
Ladies and Gentlemen in a Booth on the Hill erected for that purpose.

The company met together on this occasion was amazingly numerous,
consisting of many of the principal Gentlemen of Montgomeryshire and
the neighbouring Counties, who vied with each other in Songs, Catches
and Glees who sho'd contribute most to the Promotion of mirth & festivity. Several booths were erected for the reception of Company as at Races
&c., but they were so few & the Company so numerous that Wine was
sold at three Shillings per Bottle, Cyder and Perry at 1s.6d. & the very
Dregs of the Barrels at 6d per Quart and some at 10d.

When the speeches were finished (the people still remaining silent after applauding the Orators;) a very pretty song, in three parts, was sung by some famous singers from Hereford, which was followed with three Huzzas to R O D N E Y which were sent forth with such force from the mouths of so numerous an audience that you wou'd have thought them sufficient to burst the Welkin.

RODNEY'S PILLAR, which is about 56 feet high, is erected upon the Bruddyn, the highest Hill in Montgomeryshire, & may be seen at the distance of 30 or 40 Miles. On the day of the Festival the following Inscriptions were upon it, surrounded with Garlands, & Flowers variegated in the most beautiful manner –

On the East Side

GEORGII BRYDGES RODNEY

tante signature nomine marmer
Securum decus & seros sibe sindicet annos

On the North Side

Y Colofnau uchaf a syrthiant, Ar Tyrrau cadarnaf
a ammharant, ond Clod Syr Sior Brydges Rodney a gynnydda beunydd,
ai eriau da ni ddifeiri

The highest Pillars will fall, the strongest Towers
will decay, but the Fame of Sir G. B. Rodney
shall increase continually, and his good name
shall never be obliterated.

About 3 Yards above the last Inscription was printed in large gilt Letters

GOLOFN RODNEY
Rodney's Pillar

On the West Side

Erected in Honour of
Sir George Brydges Rodney, Baronet
Admiral of the White,

by a Subscription of the Gentlemen
of the County.

On the South Side

Summa percunt Columnae
Georgeii Brydges Rodney Baronette
Viget nomen et vigebit.

A Descriptive Account of 'An Evening Excursion'

About a quarter of a Mile from our Village there stands a little Hill raised
by kind Nature's hand and quite unpolished by refining Art. to gain its
summit is my evening's walk. To paint the many beauteous scenes I view
from then, would be a task too hard for my illiterate pen, but few may
prove the agreeableness of this my little Excursion. Beneath me runs a
placid gently Stream, Situated twisted into a thousand serpentine
Meanders; & as if loath to leave the flowery Scene, it measures twice the
length of the green meadow. If to the East I cast my wandering Eye,
Salopia proud Salopia greets my view.

Notes

1   Admiral George Brydes Rodney (1718–1792) won important naval
    engagements against the Spanish, French and Dutch. He served in the
    War of the Austrian Succession, the Seven Years War, but won his
    greatest victories against European supporters of the American War of
    Independence. In 1780 he captured a Spanish Convoy, and a few days
    later defeated the Spanish off Cape St Vincent. In 1782 he defeated a large
    French fleet off Dominica and established British command of the West
    Indian seas.

16

Mary Flavel's Letters to Richard

Richard Hodgkinson was seventy-six years old when the rich fifty-four-year-old spinster, Mary Mabel Flavel, came into his life for the second time. He had first known her as the young daughter of his mentor and friend John Flavel in Shropshire, nearly half a century earlier. Widower Hodgkinson was living at Green Bank with only a housekeeper for company, when a letter arrived in the summer of 1839 from Miss Flavel who was taking the waters at the Lancashire coast resort of Southport. Expressing her father's deep regard for the man he had known as an eager young teacher, she urged a meeting, to which Hodgkinson responded with alacrity.

This touching renewed acquaintanceship added a new interest to Hodgkinson's last years and, apart from their intermittent correspondence the declining Hodgkinson made a remarkable journey to Miss Flavel's home in the hamlet of Pulley, near Shrewsbury, and into the wilds of Wales. These travels began on 13 July 1840, and Hodgkinson, in the company of his granddaughter, Elizabeth, kept the usual, carefully documented, details of his travels. Spurning the relatively new railroad, he and Elizabeth travelled to Liverpool by coach and across the River Mersey by packet boat (fare twopence), and on to Noctorum and his son-in-law's farm for an overnight stay. Following a day of rest after the long coach journey to Shrewsbury through Cheshire and Shropshire, the indefatigable traveller began a series of visits which took him to the scenes of his youth at Ironbridge and Pontesbury. Then, with the vigour of a man half his years, he, Elizabeth and Mary Flavel set off on their adventurous journey through the Cambrian mountains to Devil's Bridge and Aberystwyth, and back to Pulley via Machynlleth and Welshpool. With barely time for rest, the seventy-six-year-old clambered back into a coach at Shrewsbury and, with drunken passengers clinging to the outside, travelled through a rainstorm homeward.

Mary Flavel's letters have a delightful charm and, as befits a woman of substantial private means, they contain many amusing and poignant anecdotes of her travels and social life. An astute manager of her own business affairs, she had inherited as the sole surviving child a fortune of at least £12,500 on her father's death in 1813. She thoroughly enjoyed ill health, regaling Hodgkinson with her various ailments, but this sturdy, independent woman creaked on until March 1867, when she died at the age of 85. Mary Flavel's will reveals some of her foibles, charities and interests. A staunch member of the Established Church she left £1,000 to a charity to convert Jews to Christianity, and a further £1,000 to persuade Roman Catholics to turn to the church of Henry VIII.

From her four-page will it is easy to draw the conclusion that she had a certain amount of distrust in men and she carefully detailed bequests to women friends and relatives to ensure their husbands could not get their hands on their legacies. In her estate of something less than £40,000, Mary left an annuity of £50 and a generous £300 to her 'old and faithfull' maidservant, Sarah Jones, to buy a cottage and furniture.

Mary Flavel's journey through life is remembered in a charming memorial stained-glass window by the renowned William Morris at Meole Brace Church, not far from her home. An engraved brass strip under the window reads: 'To the Glory of God and in the Memory of Mary Flavel of Pulley, who died March 11, 1868, aged 85'. The church at which Miss Flavel had worshipped for many years was pulled down in the mid-1860s and a new one completed in the year of her death.

Mary Flavel's Correspondence

Southport   August, 28th 1839
Dear Sir, I could not leave this Place without writing to enquire into the Health of yourself & Family, well knowing you were highly respected by my Father & Mother. I shall be here a few Days longer & in all probability return again, should much like to hear from you before Monday. My Address is as follows: Miss Flavel, at Miss Pulleyne's Lodgings, Lord Street, Southport.   Mary Flavel.

Green Bank Lodge, Atherton, Manchester   31st August, 1839.
Dear Madam, I was very much pleased & much surprised at receiving yours of the 28th inst. at a late hour last night. The Time you mention of leaving Southport viz: Monday, is too near to admit of any comfortable

Arrangement of my coming to you or your coming to me, except you follow up the hint in your Letter of returning to Southport. Sho^d. this be the case, if you will drop me a Line as soon as you return I would come to Southport and we could then make further Arrangements.

I am now out of all Business & live retired in a very good House and respectable Situation with only one Servant Maid. I lost my Wife three years ago.

If you come from Southport the cheapest, the safest and most convenient Conveyance for you would be by a Boat from Liverpool to Manchester which passes Scarisbrick Bridge daily and carries many Passengers to and from Southport. This wou'd set you down at Leigh about two o'Clock in the Afternoon where you wou'd find easy direction to my house, but if I knew the day of your coming I wou'd meet you at the Boat myself. Richd. Hodgkinson.

Southport, Miss Pullein's [*sic*] September, 2nd 1839
I go very little from Home, a little Country Village 2¹/₂ miles from Salop. My Relatives & Friends have died & left me, and I feel alone in the World, have always had bad Health, very bilious and nervous with indigestion, my mode of living has been very plain & simple for twenty Years, rising early I take a Walk, then breakfast upon weak Tea with bread & butter, sometimes dine upon cold Meat & dry potatoes, at other times Oatmeal in various Shapes and often no Dinner but Tea early, my Beverage is Water from Necessity not choice, there is no Meal I enjoy except my Tea, therefore I go very little into large Parties but keep at Home leading a hum drum Country Life.

I merely mention these circumstances that you may not put yourself out of your way on my account, I mean to go to the nearest Inn to your House & take Tea with you occasionally.

It was my intention to see Lytham & Blackpool this Week but the Weather is very boisterous & rainy, should take a Car.

This is a healthy spot, there were some hundreds of Lancashire People on the Shore last Week, I should suppose from Bolton, Wigan, Preston, Manchester, some Anniversary; all the Machines, Donkeys &c. were in requisition & a pleasant moving Scene was passing before my wondering Eyes on Shore.

Methinks you will, 'ere this, be tired of my monotonous Letter, I mean to take the Packet here as you directed & with many thanks for your kind attention. Mary Flavel.

Atherton   September 5th, 1839
. . . you may choose your own day for coming, only the sooner the better. When you arrive at Leigh it will be far better for you to get a
Messenger to take you immediately to my son David Hodgkinson who
lives within a Qua^r. of an hour's Walk of the place you will get out of the
Packet. You will there meet with every kind attention till I can come to
you.   R^d. Hodgkinson.

Pulley   November 5th, 1839
I remained one Week longer at S'port. I pursued my Course Northwards
meaning to visit the Cities of Edinburgh & Glasgow. I spent a few Days at
Preston, took Boat from thence to Kendal & reached Bowness where I
slept, next Morning Sailed up Windermere Lake before Breakfast to
Ambleside at which Place I was accosted by Col. Colston, who with his
Lady knew Salop, directing me to some good lodgings which they had
left at Keswick whence I remained a Week looking at the Lakes,
Mountain Scenery, Museum, &c. &c. till I became tired, the Weather still
continuing wet and uncomfortable.

I then wished I had taken your good wholesome advice & bent my
way Homewards from S'port, but I must be staring ab^t. and took an open
Car. to see Borrowdale, Newlands, Buttermere & Cummock Water, my
last Excursion amongst these Waterfalls & Mountain Crags where I caught
a bad Cough. The next day I paid my Bills & the first week in Oct. came
back by Coach to Kendal & per Boat from thence to Preston. Not meeting with any other conveyance I ventured by Rail-Way to Liverpool,
finding myself not well enough to proceed, Cough troublesome, I took
quiet Lodgings, Gile St. Pembroke Place. Mrs Davies, West Derby Road,
a Maiden Lady living with a nephew, a very young Clergyman, shewed
me some attention, took me to several Places, the Museum, Lyceum & to
hear Service on Board an old Man of War vessel.

Well now having been a fortnight in Liverpool I thought it high time,
cough better, enough of Lpool, to see where Pulley was, so paid my Bills
and as I was crossing the Mersey to Woodside, saw Col. Colston, his
Lady, with her Maid & Lap Dog, Carriage &c. no children, in the Vessel,
and going to their Friends in Salop, on their way to London. At
Woodside I staid a few Nights, then by Coach to Lion Hotel, Salop, from
thence I took a Chaise with some Provision to Pulley same Night, to my
damp House with good Fires the House habitable and what will surprise
you, found the Apples & Pears hanging upon my trees, none stolen.

My old Wkman & old Betty I think a good Match, sh^d. like to hear a dialogue between them. Mary Flavel.

Green Bank, Chowbent, Leigh, Lancs. 18th November, 1839
I have to apologise for not answering so valuable a Letter sooner, but
Contingencies have successively occurred since, that have laid a heavy
Embargo on my time.

Lord Lilford whose Estates & property I managed for 45 Years, tho' I
retired from his Service more than 3 Years ago, still insists on my taking
the head of the Dinner Tables at all his Court & Rent days as they occur.
Three of these have taken place since I recd your Letter which of course
have so far encroached on my time.

The Season of the Year is unpropitious but favourable Circumstances
may, perhaps, occur after a while. If my own Health continues as good as
it is now is until next Spring it is probable I may see Pulley and then
Elizabeth may have a chance of coming with me. Shd such an Occurrence
take place your Visit to me and my Visit to you will form a singular Era in
our Lives. Rd Hodgkinson.

Pulley March 30th, 1840
The dreary Winter having passed, & Spring commenced, it reminds me of
your promise of visiting Shropshire, & bringing Miss Guest along with
you to Pulley. We can then make up our mind, perhaps, concerning a
Summer trip.

I should like to know exactly the time you can come, that I may be at
Home, Pulley looks best about July. The Weather is congenial, the Fruits
are at that time plentiful, the Country is more luxuriant and a good time
to see the Country. I have a Journey to take this Spring on business &
should be back in time to receive my Visitors. I think from what I saw of
Lancashire you enjoy quite as much of warm temperature or more than
we do in Shropshire. I expected the reverse of this as you are in a more
Northerly Latitude. Mary Flavel.

Chowbent, near Leigh 13th April, 1840
Eliz. Guest . . . expressed herself quite ready to accept the Invitation. But
here a demur arose viz: whether her old Grandfather tho' equally willing
to accept the Invitation wd be equally able to undertake such a journey.
She brot her Aunt, Mrs Robt, home with her & I had her and the
Bedford & Platfold Families to spend the Afternoon with me on the 10th
inst.

The Result of the deliberations of this Family Conclave, taking your

Let^r. for the Text, was that Eliz^th. with her warmest Thanks accepts your kind Invitation & hopes she may be able to fulfil it to the Letter & I on my part promised to do the same if my Health continues as good as it is & no untoward Circumstances intervene before the time you mention, to prevent it of which you shall have timely Notice.

On Monday in Easter Week I am going to spend a few days with a very respectable Gentleman, Geo. Anthony Legh Keck Esq. who married 40 years ago a Sister of the late Lady Lilford, the Lady to whom I went to be Agent at Atherton in 1792, and in whose Service with that of her husband, the late Lord Lilford and of her Son, the present Lord Lilford, I continued till I voluntary resigned in 1836. Mr Keck's Family Estate & Seat is in Leicestershire for which County he was Member upwards of twenty Years. I am going to visit him at a fine Estate called the Bank,¹ which he has ab^t. 20 Miles from hence and about 9 from Ormskirk, in which he has a splendid Mansion in the enlargem^t & improvement of which he has expended, I conceive, not less that ten thousand pounds within the last ten years.   R^d. Hodgkinson.

Pulley   June 12th, 1840
The Farmers in the Neighbourhood seem in good Spirits, the Crops look remarkably well and all kinds of Provision sells well. I consider this side of Shrewsbury to be the finest Part of the County for all kinds of Agriculture. I think the Salopians have for the most Part given up the Idea of bringing the Rail-Road Project to bear, indeed I must needs say I am of opinion it would be of little advantage here. It is not much of a Manufacturing District and would Spoil the Face of the Country.

I am going to Salop in a few Days to get some one to tune my Piano, it is one of old Date, the Keys are got rusty for want of use.

My House wanted some little alteration and I have had the Bricklayers ab^t a Fortnight putting me up a new Kitchen Grate etc, & some other little alterations.   Mary Flavel.

Green Bank   16th June, 1840
Dear Miss Flavel, Yours of the 12th inst I rec^d at 8 o'Clock on the Evening of the 14th and took it with me to Bedford yesterday.

In your Lett^r of the 30th March you write 'Pulley looks best abt July, the Weather then is congenial, the Fruits are at that time plentiful and a good time for seeing the Country' This is exactly the time I sh^d have fixed as most convenient to myself. From 24th of June to ab^t the 10th July several Matters take place every Year which I must necessarily attend to viz:

1st. Within 2 or 3 days of the last day in June, Lord Lilford always sends me in his own handwriting an Order upon his Bankers, Jones Loyd & Co, Manchester, for the paymt of the Annuity which he has so liberally settled upon me for Life, together with the House in which I had the pleasure of receiving you last Year. I always wish to be at home when his Lordship's Letter comes that I may acknowledge the Rect without delay.

2nd. On the first Thursday in July, there will be a large Meeting of our Turnpike Road commissioners of which I am Chairman, not only by right of Seniority, being the oldest commissioner, but also by the unanimous election of all the Commissioners, of course I must attend this Meeting.

3rd. My Dividends from the funds are paid into the hands of my Banker in Warrington in the first Week in July, and usually entered in my Bank Book abt the 9th. When this is done I shall have nothing else to wait for. My Rents & Int of Money are at present so well paid up that there needs no delay on that Acct so that on someday from the 10th to the 13th both inclusive I hope to get to Shrewsbury, it wd most probably have been the 12th but I perceive that day is Sunday which circumstance will possibly hasten me a way a day or two sooner, but this will be the subject of some later Letter nearer the time.   Rd Hodgkinson.

Green Bank   8th July, 1840
Dear Miss Flavel, The weather here for the last ten days has been very stormy and wet and many Acres of Meadow Grass cut and uncut within sight of my House are now lying under Water. It is now quite time that you should be informed of our Plans, and this unsettled state of the Weather has induced us to defer our setting out to you till next Monday, the 13th inst.   Rd. Hodgkinson.

Green Bank   29th July, 1840
Dear Miss Flavel, I feel confident you will be glad to hear that we have arrived at home safe and well, and what is not a little extraordinary, that we have traversed such a large Extent of Country without a single Misfortune, untoward Accident or unnecessary delay. We had but an uncomfortable prospect before us on leaving the Lion Yard with such an enormous weight of Luggage and such a set of drunken outside Passengers, but it so happened that we did not suffer the least Inconvenience from either. We had not got more than three Miles out of Shrewsbury when the Rain set in very heavily, and continued so all the way to Wrexham. It abated a little to Chester and there quite ceased and

the Evening was very fine all the rest of the way. We arrived at
Birkenhead ab^t. half past nine. We had a Carr out immediately and in little more than half an hour were set down in safety at Noctorum. We
found all well there except Mr Jackson who had suffered some injury the
day before by the upsetting of a Cart Load of Hay, but we hope nothing
serious. From Friends from Liverpool calling upon us, and Neighbours
coming to enquire after Mr Jackson, the House was full of Company all
day and was not cleared out till near Bed-time. Soon after nine o'Clock in
the Morning Mr Jackson sent us in his Carr to Birkenhead. We crossed
the River immediately, took a Coach to the Railway Station and leaving
Liverpool in the eleven o'Clock Train arrived at Plat-fold as the Family
were at Dinner.   Rd. Hodgkinson.

Chowbent, near Leigh   24th December, 1840
Miss Flavel, You will recollect that the Morning we were at the Devil's
Bridge was so very wet that we were necessarily confined to the House.
That I might afford to yourself & Eliz^th. Guest some little Amusement I
read to you an Extract for my Journal of a Visit to Cleobury Mortimer in
1794, containing an Acc^t. of my last Interview with your very worthy and
pious Father to whose Example, Instructions and kind Attentions to one
so young as I then was, has given a Complexion and Character to my
general and moral Conduct thro' a long Life. You were pleased to say you
sh^d. like a Copy of it. That copy I now inclose, and beg your kind acceptance of it.

I am myself glad I undertook the Journey, it revived in my Mind the
Recollections of kindnesses received from many worthy Friends who
have now been long mouldering in the Grave, and of many a youthful
pleasure and enjoyment received more than half a century ago. I am the
more satisfied that I undertook the Journey then, as it is very probable I
shall never venture to take another so long. I am now a very few months
short of 78 years old, a time of Life too late to travel for pleasure.

On Wednesday the 23rd. of Sept. Mrs Jackson's eldest Daur. Jane was
married to a respectable Tradesman in Warrington by the name of
Edelsten. Immediately after the Ceremony the new married Couple set
out to the Musical Festival at Birmingham. They had a House ready fitted
up furnished against their Return. These young Relations of mine make
quite a Convenience of me and I had to go to the Wedding to give the
intended Bride away and as they were pleased to say, to sanction the
Ceremony.   Rd. Hodgkinson.

Pulley   January 1st, 1841
I received the Extract from your Journal of a visit to Cleobury Mortimer
in 1794, for which I return you my best thanks and pleased I am to see by
the hand writing your Nerves continue good, and you seem to enjoy
excellent health & spirits.

The beginning of October being very fine I set off with my Servant in
a Phaelanton[2] toward Hereford thro' Church Stretton and the pretty
town of Ludlow where I staid a short time after paying my respects to
some genteel elderly Female and proceeded to Hereford. The Place was
very full of Company. I staid a few Nights at a good Hotel & recollecting
I had a Friend at Stoke, Edith, Miss Attwood, late of Cleobury Mortimer,
whose Sister (the eldest Daughter of the Revd Mr Attwood) at whose
house my Mother put me to Board, taught me the rudiments of the
French Language.

I took a ride to the beautiful Seat of the Foleys where Miss A occasionally resides when she is not with her Bachelor Brother in ye neighbourhood.

Miss Attwood has been in Italy & ascended Mount Vesuvius. The
Foley's are much attached to her. She is related or there is a family connection. However she instructed some of them in early Life & they have
liberally settled an Annuity I suppose upon her some Years since. Having
digressed I must return to my Journey. From the Attwoods, Malvern was
the next attraction, there I stayed a few Days. The Weather being fine
from thence to Worcester for a Day. Not liking that City I traced my
Steps back to Hereford & took Coach to Caermarthen, 80 miles. Next
Day I parted to Tenby in Pembrokshire, a romantic Place. I had the best
Room at the first Hotel. I soon became acquainted with a very kind old
Lady, Widow of one Dr Stokes, of Chesterfield. It was with difficulty we
parted. She had her Carriage & two Servants between 80 & 90. A very
shrewd ingenious Lady. At that age she contrives to manage her own
Affairs, drives out when the Weather permits.

From Tenby I ported thro some miserable Places, to Cardigan,
Aberayvon, Aberystwith & so on to Pool, Home. A very pleasant
Journey. Found all straight and I am looking better the old Gossips say for
this Ramble.   Mary Flavel.

Chowbent near Leigh, Lancashire   6th June
Dear Miss Flavel, I now write to enquire how you have weathered the
'Winter Campaign' and in what Health and Spirits you find yourself in for
'Summer Campaign' which I suppose you will soon be commencing, if it

is not already begun. But I have another reason for writing now, which alas is a melancholy one. It is to inform you that Elizabeth Guest has lost her Father. After being confined to the House all Winter he died on the 26th May and was interred in the Family Vault at Leigh on the 1st June on which day I completed my seventy eighth Year. Mr Guest has left a Family of eight Children, 5 Sons & 3 Dauts.

What serious Circumstances have occurred in Mr Jones' Family. I some time ago observed an Acct of the death of a Mr Jones in a Newspaper. I thought it must allude to him, and I was about to write to you to make the Enquiry, but upon Reflection I thought I might seem to be obtruding myself upon your Notice thro' a medium which whether true or false was in no way interesting to me. I hope your £2000 did not find its way again into their Bank.

You will be glad to hear that I am enjoying good Health, that is I live without pain, internal or external, in possession of all my Faculties, Seeing, Hearing and the full Use of all my Limbs. You will perhaps observe some change in my Writing but I write with Ease and my hand is free from Trembling. But with all these Comforts I am much changed from what I was with you twelve Months ago. I am daily more wedded to Retirmt and more anxious to withdraw from the Public. I have already given up my Situation as Chairman of the Board of Guardians of the Leigh Poor Law Union, and a few Trusts connected with the Church and the Poor and at our next Turnpike Meeting I purpose to resign my Trust as a Commissioner, having been a Commissioner 43 Years and the oldest Commissioner for several Years past.   Rd Hodgkinson.

Pulley   June 16th, 1841
Death! has made solemn & strange alterations in both your & my Family Connexions of late! Mrs Guest has been prepared to expect the melancholy Event and her young Family concerns will arouse and stimulate to action.

I heard whilst at Cleobury the News of Jones's Bank having stopped payment, fortunately I had ye £2000 out before, I hope Mr Teece & you think I did right. You were both blaming me: but I am unfortunate notwithstanding; having 23 five Pound Notes.   Mary Flavel.

Green Bank, near Chowbent, Atherton.   24th December, 1841.
I owe a very Debt of Gratitude and Thankfulness to the Almighty for the uninterrupted good Health I enjoy. I scarcely perceive any decay in my Hearing, my Eyesight or the steadiness of my Hand. I have perfect use of

all my Limbs, without any pain from Gout or Rheumatism &c.,&c. and I can walk any number of Miles up to ten without fatigue or Inconvenience. Still I feel symptoms of Old Age creeping on almost imperceptibly.

The Poor here are in a wretched state, chiefly for want of Employm^t., and of course shop-keepers and small Tradespeople are little better off. We are just now raising a general Subscription in Atherton where I reside to be expended in Blanketts, Food and Fuel. Similar subscriptions are going on all over our Union of eight Townships and in all this part of Lancashire. I am principal Trustee in a Charity which will at this time come very seasonably. I shall from it have to distribute upwards of 2400yds. of Calico, Linen and Flannel in Leigh Church on Christmas Day immediately after Morning Service to ab^t. 150 Families, and on the following day at the same place I shall have to distribute from another Source twenty Shillings a piece to forty poor persons. Early in the following Week we shall distribute the proceeds of the general Subscription, to which I am both a Subscriber and Assistant Manager,

If you see Mr Teece soon you may if you think proper read to him the part of the Letter which relates to the Poor and the Steps we are taking to alleviate the Distress. He will thus see from an authoritative source the State this part of the County is in.   R^d. Hodgkinson.

(Footnote) The day after Christmas day (St. Stephen's) will also be distributed in Leigh Church five Shillings apiece to one hundred and forty eight poor persons. The Fund from whence the Money for this Charity arises was lately left by will by Mrs Prescott, a Maiden Lady a particular Friend of mine when living. This is only the second Year that the Annuity has been payable.

Pulley   December 31st, 1841
I am in a very good State of Health at present and as you very justly observe 'owe a very heavy debt of thankfulness to the Almighty'. An incident of the uncertainty of life occurred at Bewdley. A Maiden Lady & myself were invited to dine at a Gentleman's House. It was the 8th of November and his Birthday. He had a Daughter who kept his House. The Dinner was served up in very good Style & we all, his Guests, drank his health with many happy Returns, but alas! how little we thought of Death! on the 8th of Nov. On the 26th of the same Month he was taken ill & on the 4th of Dec. he died after an illness of 11 days only. In ye midst of Life we are in Death.   Mary Flavel.

Green Bank, Atherton, Manchester   4th. January, 1843
Miss Flavel, One year has now dropped into the Abyss of Eternity and a
new Year has commenced its Career since our last Correspondence . . . I
shd. have written a Week ago but on the day after Christmas Day,
Elizabeth Guest's brother Joshua, a fine Youth of seventeen Years of Age,
died at Birkenhead, where he was living in Lodgings, having been bound
Apprentice only about two Months before to an eminent Merchant in
Liverpool. Soon after he went in to his Lodgings he felt somewhat indisposed and Elizabeth went to him intending to stop a Week or two as a
Companion for him during what was expected to be only a short temporary Confinement, but when she came to him she was so alarmed that she
sent for her Mother who went immediately and continued with him till
his Death which happened on the fifth day after she got there. His dying
so far from home and among Strangers added very much to the Distress of
his Family, but his Mother stayed till she had made complete
Arrangements for bringing the Corpse to Leigh which was effected on
Thursday the 28th Dec. and the Corpse interred at 4 o'Clock in the
Afternoon of that day in the Family Vault where his father had been
interred only abt. 18 Months before. You will feel I am sure for poor
Elizabeth who is much distressed and of course at present not very well.

I am (Thanks to the Almighty) in my usual State of good Health, suffering no Pain externally or internally, but becoming gradually, almost
imperceptibly, somewhat weaker from sheer old Age alone.

The greatest change I find in my self is an increasing Reluctance to go
from home and especially to sleep from home, but still no Time hangs
heavy on my hands you know, I have a good Dwelling House where I
am always glad to see Friends, and an extensive Library to which I
become more attached every day.

With respect to your worldly Affairs, has your visible property escaped
the pilfering Thief and the bolder Midnight Burglar, and in Money
Matters, have you been so fortunate as to have avoided all the
Temptations of joint Stock Banks, or the more dangerous Insinuation of
the wily Speculator.

You will have read more than enough in the Public Papers of the distressed and dangerous State in which the Manufacturing Districts have
been during the whole Year. Want of Employment has been more general than ever before, but I hope the Tide is now beginning to turn. A
Neighbour of mine, an extensive Silk Manufacturer, who has employed
very few Weavers since Augst. has this Week, I am told, let out Work to

upwards of 500 Weavers. All the Family at Bedford except Mrs Guest and Elizabeth are in good health as are also my Son and his Family at Platfold.

R^d. Hodgkinson.

Pulley   January 9, 1843
I wrote to Miss Elizabeth Guest when at Barmouth, a hasty Letter, & was much disappointed I had no answer. My Letter was sent in August and much out of health was I at the time. Remained there abt 6 Weeks, & returned by way of Festiniog, Menai Bridge & Carnarvon, Bangor, Corwen & Oswestry. It may be I may be spared to see you yet, 'ere I die, wishing to make some little Arrangement and to talk Things over. Life is very uncertain. I was very low last Week. Was at the Sacrament yesterday. I feel rather better, was cheered by your letter, very few friends have I now, Death has made sad ravages!! Thank you my Friend for your hints ab^t. Joint Stock Banks, I shall profit by that. There is one which of late Jones's Occupied and I have been induced there to leave some Cash, another is begging to have a Sum to sett up with a Cotton Manufacturer in Liverpool, a Mr Johnstone whom I see, he formerly was a Clerk in Beck's Bank.   Mary Flavel.

Greenbank, Atherton, Manchester   8th January, 1844
I am now paying that heavy Tax who all must pay who live to extreme old Age, that is seeing all our valued Friends, Neighbours and Acquaintances daily dropping into the Grave and leaving us old Folk isolated and almost Strangers in our own Land. I have experienced much of this. Take one Instance. About the Year 1800 I was elected a Commissioner of our Turnpike Road. Additional Commissioners have been elected from Time to Time as others have died off and since I was elected, upwards of four hundred of these Gentlemen, with every one of whom I was extremely well and intimately acquainted, have paid the Debt of Nature. After reading the above you will not be so much surprised at what I am now going to write as you otherwise might of been.

Few Men in my Rank of Life have been more engaged in Public Life than I have been, or had more Acquaintances and Connections with Men of all Ranks and all Degrees from the Peer of the Realm to the Pauper in the Workhouse and strange to say at 81 Years of Age I do not know six Families in Existence with whom I have had so long a Friendship and Association as with your Family. It commenced at 9 o'Clock on the second Saturday Night in January 1782 when I first entered your Father's House at Westbury, and I am happy to say it is still in Continuance, a

period of sixty two Years which is several Years alone twice the Average
of human Life. It is only very lately that this circumstance struck me in
this Point of View but the more I tax my Recollection of my very few
surviving Friends, the more I am convinced of the Truth of the above
Assertion.

Mr Jackson's eldest Dau^t was married ab^t 3 years ago to a Mr Eddleston,
an extensive Pin Manufacturer at Warrington. Last Spring he took and
entered upon some powered Mills at Stroud in Gloucestershire where he
is carrying on the Patent Pin Manufacture at a great Extent. His
Connections extend to all the large Towns in England & Wales and are as
numerous in London as to require his Attendance there one whole Week
in every Month. He does a large Business in Scotland and has some
Connections in Belgium and France. He employs 200 Work People, and
his present prospects are very good.

The Field of Politics is too wide and too confused & complex for me to
enter upon. The great absorbing Subject here now is the Anti-Corn Law
League, that great Monster which has its Origin and Foundation in
Manchester from whence by its Emissaries and Funds spreads its Influence
into every Corner of the Land. Its supporters have already collected and
expended fifty thousand Pounds and are now going in for collecting one
hundred thousand Pounds, one half of which Sum, it is said, is already
secured. How its promoters can proceed farther without getting into an
abyss of Treason and Rebellion I confess I cannot see.   Rd. Hodgkinson.

Pulley,   January 22nd, 1844
I am at present just recovering from an epidemical Disease or the
Influenza of which every Body complains of late, a violent cough, it
leaves me very weak, but am now walking round the House, fields &c. I
went in Autumn to Towyn, a poor Place but comfortable, I also hoped to
see my Friends in Lancashire, but was hurried Home, by a Letter, informing me my House was broken into. The Thieves got in by forcing a
Kitchen Door open with a Crow-Bar. They took nothing of consequence, best part of a Ham, a few Bottles of Wine, some small articles in
hard Ware, tea & sugar &c. I have had much trouble & expence in making every Place secure since the Robbery.   Mary Flavel.

Atherton lodge, Chowbent, Manchester   January 9, 1845
Dear Miss Flavel, The end of the old Year and the beginning of a new
one reminds me that the annual Debt of a letter to you (who are become
nearly my only Epistolary Correspondent excepting my own family) is

now payable and as I thro' Life have carefully avoided being in debt, I am now going to discharge this of yours.

With respect to myself I am as well as a Man of upwards of eighty years of Age can reasonably expect to be. I have full Use of all my Limbs, my Eyesight and Hearing, my Mental Faculties scarcely impaired other than might be expected. Against all these Blessings there is one general Drawback which necessarily attends Old Age viz: a Debility of the whole Frame. Its Effect upon me is to prevent me from undertaking any long or continued Exertion in walking for instance and I find it prudent to take some one with me, and this is inconvenient.

Our Manufactures are in a flourishing State at present, but the Hand loom Weavers, a very numerous Class, are very depressed. They cannot compete with Machinery and their Case is hopeless.

All Trades are turning out for an advance of Wages which causes great Confusion and Disturbance and something serious must result. Each Class want the repeal of something or other. The Tax upon raw Cotton, Tea, Coffee, Sugar, &c.,&c. Others go for the Repeal of the Malt Tax, the Window Tax & in short, they would not leave a single Tax for Revenue, the consequences will be a property Tax or Income Tax or both.

Large Subscriptions are raising to be expended in making extensive Parks, Pleasure Grounds, Play Grounds, Baths &c., for the public. All Mechanics Institutes are converted into Lecturing Rooms, Ball Rooms, Music Rooms, all on a most expensive Scale. It seems the whole Population was let loose for a general Holy Day. All Trades form themselves into Union Clubs and then make Strike, as it is called, that is suspend Work altogether demanding a Pay Increase of Wages. As Trade is now going well they have generally succeeded, but not often to the full Extent of their demands, yet sufficiently to prevent them from going to Extremes. It is a most Dangerous State of Society for this Country, depending so much on Trade and Labour of the population, and gives occasion for the worst of Fears. Rd. Hodgkinson

Pulley January 24, 1845
Why you are surely a wonderful Man! Writing as you do! Here am I, and others much younger, using Spectacles & Sticks, Bath Chairs &c. I visited a Lady this Week, she has just had a Bath Chair because she cannot go a very short distance to Church. Miss (or as we assume the matronly Name of Mrs Hodson who has been here since Nov) is quite astonished at hearing of my Friend's strong mental energetic powers of Mind & Body. We have been tolerably well excepting troublesome Colds.

The elderly Lady is ab^t. leaving, she is a Spinster, has lived in Ludlow, has but a small Income, & being here in winter has enlivened y^e. Scene a little. She goes to a little independent Meetings, sometimes ye Clergy don't like this!

I made a mistake, thought I had got to ye last side. The old Lass is talking often, sometimes I wonder I keep my Head on my Shoulders when I am reckoning or wish to be quiet she must be on the Gab. Now this is one of the miseries of human Life. She must also dinn me with some Book I dislike & when I want her to listen, then she has a Head ache!! Miss Guest will smile, Farewell. Mary Flavel.

Dear Miss Flavel   January 7, 1846
I am pretty much in the same State I was a year ago, but very much feebler. Time has laid a much heavier hand on me of late than heretofore. My extreme debility confines me much at home and prevents me taking outdoor Air and Exercise, sufficient to contribute materially to Health.

My Eye Sight has till lately kept very good, but within the last two Months has materially given way. I do not now attempt to write at all by Candle Light and to read but little, which deprives me of much Enjoym^t. and Amusement these long Winter Nights. Rd. Hodgkinson.

Notes

1   This is now the seat of Lord Lilford.
2   A phaelanton was a four-wheeled horse-drawn carriage without a top.

17

Richard's Retirement

Richard Hodgkinson enjoyed a cordial if formal relationship with his employers during his stewardship of Atherton and Bewsey, no doubt based on his integrity and devotion to the running of the estates for the ultimate benefit of the Lilfords. In this miscellaneous collection of letters leading up to and beyond Hodgkinson's retirement, the 3rd Lord Lilford, now an absentee landlord, sent his sympathy on the death of Hodgkinson's wife and expressed sentiments of appreciation for his agent's devoted service. A promise by Lilford in January 1837 to make a retirement settlement on his steward went unhonoured for months and Hodgkinson wrote a sharp reminder. More than a year later, Lilford met his obligation and granted Hodgkinson a liberal annuity of £100 and the free tenancy for life of the large house at Greenbank.

As Hodgkinson reduced his commitments, he introduced his successor, John Selby,[1] from the Lilford estates in Leicestershire, to the routines of running the Lancashire properties. Despite his advancing years, Hodgkinson's mind and hand stayed clear, and even into his eighties he attended to his own business interests and busied himself with the demands of public and private trusts. One of Hodgkinson's last major public offices was as to assist with the introduction in Leigh in 1837 of the hated Poor Law. Hodgkinson complained at the haste with which the Board of Guardians was expected to reorganize the local relief of the poor by forming the Leigh Union. In a lightly crossed-out paragraph in a letter to Lilford, Hodgkinson wrote: 'How 8 Townships extending over a space of Ground nearly 8 Miles in Diameter and containing a population of more than 24,000 Souls, can be brought in one short Fortnight to act consistently upon any uniform Plan, I am at a loss to know.'

A memorable moment in the twilight of Hodgkinson's life came in June 1838, when he was appointed president of the festival to commemorate the Coronation of Queen Victoria. This 'placed me in a Situation in which it is very improbable any Individual will be placed for a Century to come, that is, of being unanimously elected President and presiding at Three successive Coronation Dinners'. George IV was crowned in 1820, William IV in 1830 and Victoria in 1838.

By 1835, Hodgkinson was preparing the way for John Selby, his successor, to take over the Lilford estate at Bewsey, Warrington. Two years later, Selby also took over the Atherton estate.

The Lilford Letters

Hodgkinson,   June 5th, 1835
I congratulate you upon the arrival of your Seventy-second anniversary, 'The Hoary head is a crown of Man, if it be found in the way of Righteousness' & such I wish to be the way in which you have lived and will die.   Lilford.

Atherton   lst July, 1835
My Lord, My Books are now made up to the 24th of June and ready for inspection & the time is arrived for the surrendering up of my Trust in the Bewsey Property. Ever since I entered upon the Service I felt an undeviating devotedness to the Interest of my Employers accompanied with an earnest desire to meet their Wishes in the managem^t of the Estates. Hence I feel peculiar satisfaction in falling in with the Arrangements made for my giving up the Bewsey Trust, and also at the strong expressions by yr Lords^h in yr Let^r of the 18th June in stating your Satisfaction at the fair, candid, & manly manner in which I had introduced Mr Selby to the Tenants in his new capacity.

I have finished all that cou'd be done and indeed all that wanted doing at present with respect to Repairs at Bewsey. I have in a former Let^r stated that I had discharged all Bills up to this time. I have many Weeks ago furnished Mr Selby with a Copy of the Survey of all the Bewsey Property, which with the Plans I gave him will afford him great facility in making himself acquainted with the locality of all or any particular Farm.

Y^r Lordship will excuse me mentioning a Circumstance or two connected with my Agency which are not perhaps of common occurrence.

lst The Management of yr Lordship's Lancashire Property requires eight Rent days & Court days in the year. The days on which each of these is holden are specially fixed and named. Of these days I have never changed one nor have I been absent one single Court-day or Rent day during the whole of my 43 years Service.

2nd. Of all the Sums, I may say immense Sums of Money which have passed thro' my hands, arising from a great Variety of Sources, such as Sales of Land and Timber of Coals, of Bricks & from Rents of various Denominations, and in Receipts and Payments varying in amts from 1/-s to £20,000, I have never had one single Mistake, Misreckoning or Miscalculation either with Tenant, Tradesman or Banker, since I entered the Service.

3rd. Again, I have been Steward one year longer than Mr Atherton, the Father of your very excellent Mother, was in existence from his Birth to his Tomb.   R. Hodgkinson.

Atherton   28th July, 1836
My Lord, The Time is now arrived which I have for some Weeks antici-pated, when I should have to communicate to your Lordship the melan-choly, to me very melancholy, Event of my Wife's Death. She expired at 5 o'Clock yesterday Evening.

Her Health has been declining for some Months but for the last five Weeks she has been confined to her Room and for the last Month to her Bed. How she has subsisted for the last Month is truly astonishing. During all that time she has scarcely taken any thing but cold Water and that chiefly by tea spoonfuls. She asked for nothing else, & if any Wine, ever so little, was put into it she rejected it. Of any solid Food, she has not, I can safely say, taken half an Ounce a day and what she has attempted to take was thrown up again instantly. She took nothing that was nourishing, no kind of Gruel, Soups or Jelly, and even Beef-tea her Stomach rejected. She said she never felt any Sensation of Hunger and did not suffer any acute Pain. She passed her Nights quietly, seldom disturbing her Nurse who slept with her until within the last Week when she has been rather more restless in the Night. Three days before her Death a Change for the worse took place, and her Decline was rapid. During the last 45 Hours she was wholly unconscious and seemed to suffer much Pain.

Last Week we called in Dr Holme of Manchester. He saved her Life abt 15 years ago in a very dangerous Bowel Complaint. He gave us no Encouragement, he said, she might continue for some time, but it was more likely that she would be taken off suddenly.

I have thus lost an affectionate, a willing and efficient Help-mate and one whom Habit prima 48 years Union sanctified by Affection has ren-dered necessary to my Being, that is my well-being. What other changes, after this great Change in my Circumstances, may await me I cannot at Present foresee.   Rd Hodgkinson.

London   August lst, 1836

Hodgkinson, The Melancholy intelligence which your Letter of the 28th ult., this morning recd. announces, was not wholly unexpected by me in as much as I had long been aware of the declining state of your Wife's health.

I am much aware however, that however long such an event might reasonably have been contemplated, the loss of one whom habit & affection has so long endeared to you must be especially severe. To a mind like yours it would be fruitless to admit to the only solid sources of much consolation as under such circumstances it is capable of ensuing, but it is also a comfort to know that others feel and sympathise in our loss.   Lilford.

Atherton   5th Feby, 1837

My Lord, I recd. yours of the 29th late in the Evening of the 31st Jany. At Noon of that day was received the first Communication from the Poor Law Commissioners respecting the Leigh Union. On my way home from Atherton to Dinner, I met Mr Buchanan, Clerk to the Magistrates, coming to me with the package he had just received from the Commissioners. He said, I might take it home with me and he wd call for it on his return from Leigh. It is dated 26th Jany 1837 and orders and declares the following Townships viz:

1st. Westleigh	5. Bedford
2nd Tildesley	6. Pennington
3. Lowton	7. Culcheth
4. Atherton	8. Astley

'Shall on the 15th of Feby be and thenceforth shall remain united for the Administration of the Laws for the Relief of the Poor by the name of the LEIGH UNION.

'That a Board of Guardians of the Poor of the said Union shall be chosen.

'That the Number of Guardians shall be 18, 3 for each of the Townships of Atherton and Tildesley and 2 for each of the other Townships.'

It then goes on to state the Qualification of Guardian and of the Voters.

That the first Election of Guardians shall be on the 15th of Feb next.

The first Meeting of the Guardians shall be held at the principal Inn in Leigh on the 18th day of Feb. next and commence at 11 o'Clock in the

Forenoon. At this Meeting they shall determine upon some fixed day of the Week and some fixed hour bet. 10 o'Clock in the Forenoon and 4 o'Clock in the Afternoon and also in some convenient place for holding their future Meetings. At this Meeting they must elect out of their Number a Chairman and Vice chairman, and at this Meeting or as soon after as conveniently may be, proceed to the Election of their Clerk and to the Exercise of the Functions assigned to them by a certain Act entitled 'An Act for the Registration of Births, Deaths and Marriages'.

The above contains all that is to be done under the present Order. The Guardians now appointed will not be allow'd to exercise any Functions in the administration of the new Poor Law Act previous to the lst of March. I have thot it best to state all the Provisions in the Order in succession. I have now to observe that Culcheth & Lowton are parts of the Parish of Winwick, why they are put into the Leigh Union we have no means of knowing. It is the general Wish and has been the general Expectation that Leigh Parish wd form a Board of itself. This wish the Inhabitants had no opportunity of expressing as no Commissioner has been among us.

We have already arrive at that state of Confusion which I anticipated in a late letr to yr Lordship & from the same Cause viz: want of timely Instructions.

[Following paragraph is crossed out]

How 8 Townships extending over a space of Ground nearly 8 Miles in Diameter and containing a population of more than 24,000 Souls, can be brought in one short Fortnight to act consistently upon any uniform Plan, I am at a loss to know.

On the other Side I have given the Quantity of Land in Statute Acres, in each of the six Townships in Leigh parish and also the population in 1801 and 1831.

Parish of Leigh Lancashire

	1801	1834	Statute Acres
Astley	1545	1832	1777
Atherton	3249	4181	2327
Bedford	1985	3087	1904
Penington	1759	3165	1320
Tildesley	3009	5038	2961
Westleigh	1429	2780	1680

	12976	20083	11969
Culcheth	1833	2503	
Lowton	1402	2374	
	3235	4877	
	16211	24960	

I will answer the various Queries in your's of the 29th ult at short Intervals, as Information, Time and opportunity occur. Rd. Hodgkinson.

Lilford   March 23, 1837

Hodgkinson, I had been expecting to hear from you for some time past of the progress of the arrangements in the formation of the Leigh Union but your Letter of the 20th just received explains the reasons of your silence.

In referring to your letter of the 25th Feby. I find that you wish for an answer as to the letting of the Workhouse in Atherton. I should of course have no objection to let it on the present terms of Rent for any period which might be decided. Tho' I agree with you in thinking that the purpose of the Act cannot be fully carried into effect without the erection of a General Work House for the whole Union, such as has already been done there & in the neighbouring Unions.

Our union comprises 37 Parishes within a radius of eight miles, with a population of abt. 12,500. It is estimated that the average number of Paupers in the House will be from 250 to 300. Of course from the much greater amount of population in Atherton it must be calculated to hold a much larger number.

I have desired Mr Selby to write & see you on the subject of the future management of the Atherton Property.   Lilford

Atherton   3rd May, 1837

My Lord, The 24th of June is very near at hand and since the fixing upon the two general principles of our Arrangement viz: that on the 24th I sh. retire from the Trust and Mr Selby immediately enter upon it, nothing further has been said or done in it. The commencing Business here will be found a much more serious and complex affair that it was at Bewsey. There, with a few Months previous Residence, Mr Selby became acquainted with the property and personally known to many of the

Tenants. The Farms are large of course, the Tenants not numerous. All necessary Repairs were completed and all Bills & Debts discharged. These Things I am endeavouring to do now and hope to accomplish. Things will be found very different here. The Tenants are very numerous, their Holdings diminutively small, so that with a good deal of Assistance from me which I shall willingly afford, it may take Mr Selby the whole of the Summer accurately to trace out, to say nothing of the daily Occurrences which require constant attention.

In y^r Let^r. of the lst Jany. 1837 In which yr Lordship finally accepted by Resignation, you write:

I think that when Men fully understand & appreciate each others' Motives there cannot be much difficulty upon minor Terms of Agreement and I trust that the way is now cleared towards that arrangem^t (which I feel must be a final one) in which I may look for a repetition of the sound Judgm^t and cordial Co-operation in enabling me to make that Arrangem^t solid & satisfactory.

The Loss of the Services of an old & faithful Servant however bro^t about is always painful. How much more so must it be to me to whom they have been transmitted as almost an hereditary Gift sanctioned by long habit & early Association.

I shall not pursue this Subject further at this time, other Opportunities will arise to good length into this and other Matters of Detail.

Since the said Let^r of the 1st Jany y^r Lordship has not alluded to any of the Subjects mentioned in the above Quotations. I am therefore unacquainted with yr Lordship's views and Intentions respecting them or any of them or upon the 'minor Terms of Agreement or other Matters of Detail.'

Learning from Mr Selby that the House in which I live was not likely to be wanted very soon, and knowing that my being upon or near the Spot, for some time at least, until Mr Selby was thoroughly initiated in his new Undertaking would be beneficial to your Lordship and useful to Mr Selby. I have not looked out for another Residence nor formed any Plan for my future Destination or place of Abode.

We make but slow progress in our new Poor Law Business. When Mr Tower was with us for two hours abt two Months ago, he told he me shd come again in 3 Weeks giving us a few days Notice of his coming and wd then examine all our Workhouses, see how far they coul'd be made available and direct our future operations. Neither he nor any other Commissioner has been with us since. We received Directions for forming Districts for Registrations which we have done, and have fixed Thursday in next Week for electing Registrars. The new Poor Law is unpopular here, but much more so in Bolton, Salford, Bury, Oldham & Rochdale and worse still in some parts of Yorkshire.   Rd. Hodgkinson.

Atherton   7th Aug, 1837
This is the fifth Summer since I have made an excursion either of pleasure or to any watering place. I have never yet seen Mr Jackson's new Farm, and I purpose making my first journey thither. It is near Birkenhead on the Cheshire side of the River opposite to Liverpool. I have not at any time been in that part of Cheshire, all will of course be new to me.

Early in the Summer I had contemplated asking your Lordship to indulge me with the Gig & Horse for 2 journies of a Week each, one to the East of Mancr. to visit that part of the Country lying between Stockport and Bury, comprizing Staley Bridge, Dukenfield, Gorton, Hyde, Ashton, Middleton, Oldham &c., & where I am informed that Factories vast in magnitude and immense in number, with all the Appendages of Weaving, Bleaching, Printing, Dying &c., &c., have risen in a short time with almost magic Rapidity.

The other to Blackburn, Clitheroe, Huntroyd, Whalley and then past the Roman Catholic Establishment at Stoney Hurst, to Preston to spend a day or two with the Miss Rawstornes, to which I have been pressingly and repeatedly invited. But I have given up this Scheme some time ago, not being very partial to long Journies in a Gig, and having no agreeable Companion to accompany me or a proper person to drive me.

                                                    Rd Hodgkinson.

Noctorum, Birkenhead, Cheshire   August 22nd, 1837
My Lord, I arrived at Mr Jackson's in the Evening of Tuesday last, and found all well.

The Assizes were on at Liverpool and on Thursday I crossed the River to Liverpool and went into Court Abt. 10 o'Clock and remained there till five, hearing a Trial between Mr Froggatt to whom my Son has been Steward near 20 years, and Mr Trafford of Trafford near Manchester, a Catholic Gentleman of very large property, and who was High Sheriff 3 years ago.

The Dispute is abt. the Boundary Line between Mr Trafford's Property of the Moss called Astley Moss and Mr Froggatt's. Mr Trafford tracing in a Line which wd include upwards of 200 large Acres of what Mr Froggatt claims. The Line traced by Mr Trafford has all along been disputed by Mr Froggatt who claims by Authority of an Award made by Commissioners under an Act of Parliament for inclosing the Waste Lands in Astley passed somewhere ab^t. the year 1760. By this Award Mr Froggatt's Grandfather, being the largest Land Owner in Astley, had many and large Allotments of Chatt Moss (within Astley) given to him as Land Owner, and if I remember right (I have read the Award, but I now only speak from Memory) somewhere ab^t. 400 Acres were allotted to him as Lord of the Manor. Some Months ago Mr Froggatt sold to a Company as much of his Share of Chatt Moss as came to £12,000. He then proceeded to mark out his Boundary Line which excludes a very large portion of what Mr Trafford claimed by his Boundary Line, but Mr Trafford sent a Set of Men to fill up the Ditch as fast as Mr Froggatt's Men cut it. The part of which Mr Trafford claimed being included in what Mr Froggatt had sold he cd no longer delay taking active Measures and he accordingly commenced legal Proceedings against Mr Trafford which have been carried on up to the present Time. Thus Mr Froggatt became the Plaintiff. There were plenty of Surveyors & Plans, plenty of Attornies & Counsel, and Hosts of Witnesses, many of whom on both Sides were never called. A little bit after 5 o'Clock the Judge finished summing up, the Jury requested to retire and in little more than an Hour returned with a Verdict for the Plaintiff.

It may afford yr Lords^h. some Entertainment to know how Farms are letting here. Mr Jackson's Farm wch. belongs to Mr Wilson Patten is situate ab^t. 3 Miles South West of Birkenhead Ferry, where he has made a Contract with the Owner of a Steam Vessel there to convey himself and all or any part of his Family to Liverpool when and as often as they have occasion to go and also his produce of every Description for £10 a year. The Farm is a parish of itself, has no poor and no Inhabitants but Mr Jackson's Family & Servants. Mr Patten has built for him 2 Small Cottages for 2 Labourers and they serve also as a Gate House and the Entrance upon the Farm.   Rd. Hodgkinson.

London   June 15th, 1838
Hodgkinson, I enclose herewith a Cheque upon Messrs Jones & Lloyds of Manchester for £100, the first paym^t. of the retiring Pension which became due on the 24th inst. & I also wish to state in answer to the inquiry which has been made upon the subject that so long as you continue to occupy the House. . . I hope you will consider that you do so Rent Free.   Lilford.

Green Bank, Atherton   4th July 1838
Your Lordship's Letter of the 25th June with its Inclosure was necessarily
highly gratifying to me and calls for my deep Gratitude and Thanks which
I most sincerely tender. The liberal Amount of the Annuity, the object yr
Lordship professed to have in view in granting it & the handsome Mode
of Remittance, will conspire to enhance its Nature. Your very unexpected but very kind offer for me to continue to reside at Green Bank free of
Rent, is doubly gratifying, it regards both Convenience, respectability and
which I accept with due deference and thanks.

Your Lordshp judged rightly in saying you knew I shd be glad to hear
that Lady Lilford, yourself and Family were all well. I have long felt &
shall continue to feel a deep Interest in the Welfare of your Lordship's
Family & all your Connections.

I owe a heavy Debt of pious Gratitude to divine Providence for the
excellent Health I continue to enjoy. I live without pain either internal or
external, in Bed or abroad, and in all Weathers.

I have felt some slight Changes (particularly with respect to Memory)
since this year commenced & tho' scarcely perceptible they serve to
remind me that I retired from the Agency just in time.

We have got the Coronation Festival over very comfortably and very
creditably at Chowbent, tho we came very late into the Field owing to
Mr Selby's absence. He will of course give your Lordship the Particulars. I
will only mention one Circumstance connected with it and which regards
myself.

At the first Meeting on the 21st June, I was elected President which
placed me in a Situation in which it is very improbably any Individual will
be placed for a Century to come, that is, of being unanimously elected
President and presiding at Three successive Coronation Dinners.

I presented the Check at the Bank yesterday, the Clerk made an
Observation on its being dated London. I believe the Law's Rule regard-
ing Checks is that they be dated at the place where the Bank is that they
are drawn upon or at some place within ten Miles distance of it. The
Amount however was immediately paid.   Richard Hodgkinson.

Atherton Lodge, near Chowbent, Manchester   30th Sept, 1843
My Lord, I write now to acknowledge the Receipt of a very fine Side of
Venison in most excellent Condition and to return my sincere Thanks for
the same. At present I have another Object in view, which is humbly to
request Lady Lilford to be so kind as to favour me with the Name and

Birth Day of your last born Child as she was so good to do of the preceding eight some time ago. I shall be happy to hear a good Acc^t of the Health of her Ladyship & your Lordship and of all the Family. I have now passed my eightieth year and your Lordship will be pleased to hear that I am enjoying very good Health and am free of any bodily Pain or Infirmity, but I feel a general Debility of the whole Frame, the Consequence of mere Old Age which has induced me to give up Travelling from home except for a single day at once and sleeping at home at Night. Hence I have been obliged to decline Mr Keck's kind Invitations to visit him at Bank Hall both the last Autumn and this. I can walk comfortably to Leigh to Platfold and to my Daughter Guest's at Bedford, but from Timidity, I very seldom get into a Carriage of any sort. My Establishment is very small consisting only of myself and one Female Servant. I continue to rise early as usual from 5 to 6 o'Clock. This makes a long Day and induces my Friends and Neighbours to think that I must pass many dull and lonely hours, but this is a Mistake, I have no Time hanging heavy on my hands. Tho' I may be past the Managem^t of any general heavy Business it does not follow that I am to be wholly useless to Society. I have some little Business of my own to attend to, and I have also several Trusts both public and private which require my Attention. And as to hours of Amusement, I have many Resources and I have a pretty extensive Library and am fond of Reading, which I can vary now and then by whiling away an hour or two in my almost forgotten Latin and Greek.

I remain, your Lordship's most humble and obedient Servant,

Rd Hodgkinson.

Note

1   Selby was Lord Lilford's godson.

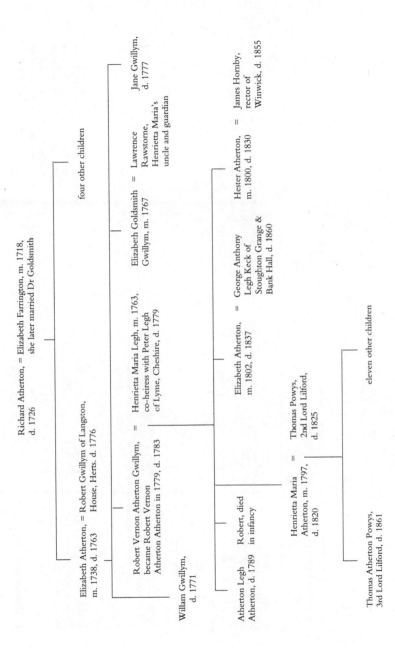

Richard Atherton, = Elizabeth Farrington, m. 1718,
d. 1726   she later married Dr Goldsmith

four other children

Elizabeth Atherton, = Robert Gwillym of Langston,
m. 1738, d. 1763   House, Herts. d. 1776

Robert Vernon Atherton Gwillym, = Henrietta Maria Legh, m. 1763,   Elizabeth Goldsmith = Lawrence   Jane Gwillym,
became Robert Vernon   co-heiress with Peter Legh   Gwillym, m. 1767   Rawstorne,   d. 1777
Atherton in 1779, d. 1783   of Lyme, Cheshire, d. 1779   Henrietta Maria's
                                                        uncle and guardian

Willam Gwillym,
d. 1771

Atherton Legh   Robert, died   Elizabeth Atherton, = George Anthony   Hester Atherton, = James Hornby,
Atherton, d. 1789   in infancy   m. 1802, d. 1837   Legh Keck of   m. 1800, d. 1830   rector of
                                               Stoughton Grange &   Winwick, d. 1855
                                                 Bank Hall, d. 1860

Henrietta Maria = Thomas Powys,
Atherton, m. 1797,   2nd Lord Lilford,
d. 1820   d. 1825

eleven other children

Thomas Atherton Powys,
3rd Lord Lilford, d. 1861

The family tree of the Athertons, Gwillyms and Lilfords

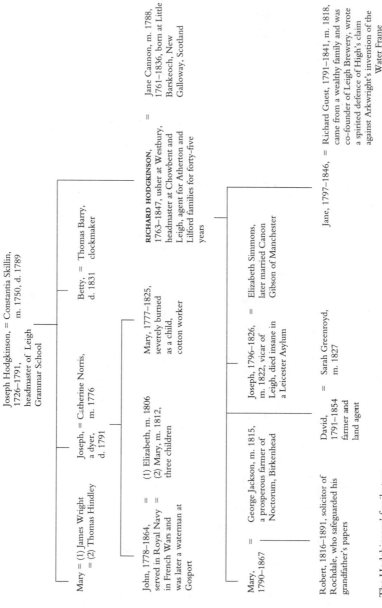

Joseph Hodgkinson, = Constantia Skillin,
1726–1791,   m. 1750, d. 1789
headmaster of Leigh
Grammar School

Mary = (1) James Wright   Joseph, = Catherine Norris,   Betty, = Thomas Barry,
     = (2) Thomas Hindley   a dyer,   m. 1776   d. 1831   clockmaker
                      d. 1791

John, 1778–1864,   =   (1) Elizabeth, m. 1806   Mary, 1777–1825,   RICHARD HODGKINSON,   =   Jane Cannon, m. 1788,
served in Royal Navy   = (2) Mary, m. 1812,   severely burned   1763–1847, usher at Westbury,   1761–1836, born at Little
in French Wars and   three children   as a child,   headmaster at Chowbent and   Barskeoch, New
was later a waterman at   cotton worker   Leigh, agent for Atherton and   Galloway, Scotland
Gosport   Lilford families for forty-five
                                              years

Mary,   =   George Jackson, m. 1815,   Joseph, 1796–1826,   =   Elizabeth Simmons,
1790–1867   a prosperous farmer of   m. 1822, vicar of   later married Canon
              Noctorum, Birkenhead   Leigh, died insane in   Gibson of Manchester
                                 a Leicester Asylum

Robert, 1816–1891, solicitor of   David,   =   Sarah Greenroyd,   Jane, 1797–1846,   =   Richard Guest, 1791–1841, m. 1818,
Rochdale, who safeguarded his   1791–1854   m. 1827   came from a wealthy family and was
grandfather's papers   farmer and   co-founder of Leigh Brewery, wrote
                      land agent   a spirited defence of High's claim
                                                against Arkwright's invention of the
                                                  Water Frame

The Hodgkinsons' family tree

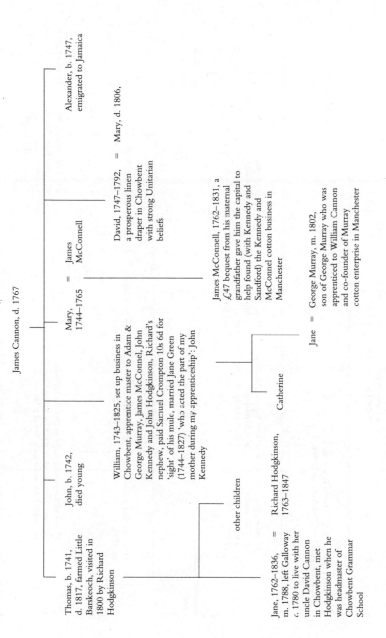

James Cannon, d. 1767

Thomas, b. 1741, d. 1817, farmed Little Barskeoch, visited in 1800 by Richard Hodgkinson

John, b. 1742, died young

William, 1743–1825, set up business in Chowbent, apprentice master to Adam & George Murray, James McConnel, John Kennedy and John Hodgkinson, Richard's nephew, paid Samuel Crompton 10s 6d for 'sight' of his mule, married Jane Green (1744–1827) 'who acted the part of my mother during my apprenticeship': John Kennedy

Mary, 1744–1765 = James McConnell

David, 1747–1792, a prosperous linen draper in Chowbent with strong Unitarian beliefs = Mary, d. 1806,

Alexander, b. 1747, emigrated to Jamaica

other children

Jane, 1762–1836, m. 1788, left Galloway c. 1780 to live with her uncle David Cannon in Chowbent, met Hodgkinson when he was headmaster of Chowbent Grammar School = Richard Hodgkinson, 1763–1847

Catherine

Jane = George Murray, m. 1802, son of George Murray who was apprenticed to William Cannon and co-founder of Murray cotton enterprise in Manchester

James McConnell, 1762–1831, a £47 bequest from his maternal grandfather gave him the capital to help found (with Kennedy and Sandford) the Kennedy and McConnel cotton business in Manchester

The Scottish connection – the Cannon family tree

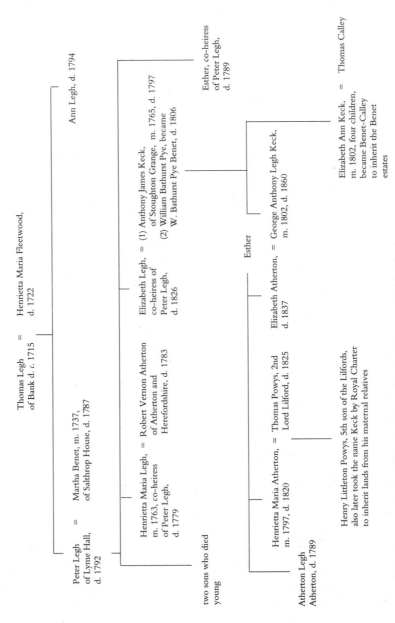

A tangled web – the family tree of the Legh, Benet, Keck, Atherton and Lilford families

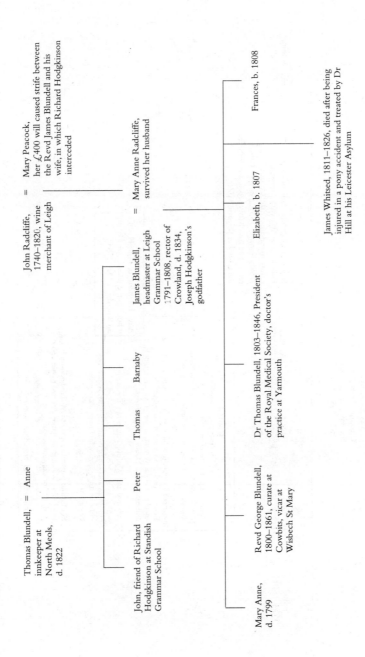

Thomas Blundell, innkeeper at North Meols, d. 1822 = Anne

John Radcliffe, 1740–1820, wine merchant of Leigh = Mary Peacock, her £400 will caused strife between the Revd James Blundell and his wife, in which Richard Hodgkinson interceded

John, friend of Richard Hodgkinson at Standish Grammar School

Peter

Thomas

Barnaby

James Blundell, headmaster at Leigh Grammar School 1791–1808, rector of Crowland, d. 1834, Joseph Hodgkinson's godfather = Mary Anne Radcliffe, survived her husband

Mary Anne, d. 1799

Revd George Blundell, 1800–1861, curate at Cowbits, vicar at Wisbech St Mary

Dr Thomas Blundell, 1803–1846, President of the Royal Medical Society, doctor's practice at Yarmouth

Elizabeth, b. 1807

Frances, b. 1808

James Whitsed, 1811–1826, died after being injured in a pony accident and treated by Dr Hill at his Leicester Asylum

The Blundell family tree

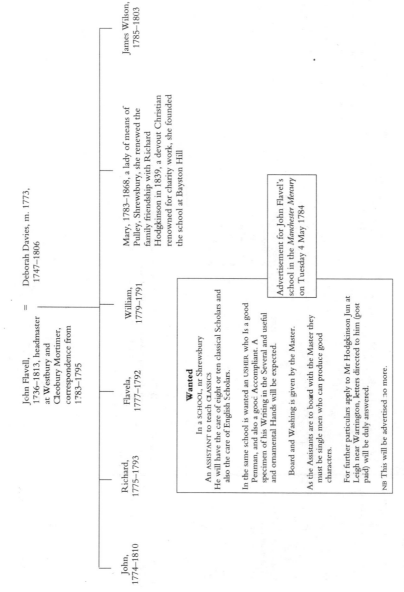

John Flavell,
1736–1813, headmaster
at Westbury and
Cleobury Mortimer,
correspondence from
1783–1795

=

Deborah Davies,
1747–1806, m. 1773,

John,
1774–1810

Richard,
1775–1793

Flavela,
1777–1792

William,
1779–1791

Mary, 1783–1868, a lady of means of
Pulley, Shrewsbury, she renewed the
family friendship with Richard
Hodgkinson in 1839, a devout Christian
renowned for charity work, she founded
the school at Bayston Hill

James Wilson,
1785–1803

Wanted

In a SCHOOL, nr Shrewsbury
An ASSISTANT to teach CLASSICS
He will have the care of eight or ten classical Scholars and
also the care of English Scholars.

In the same school is wanted an USHER who Is a good
Penman, and also a good Accompliant. A
specimen of his Writing in the Several and useful
and ornamental Hands will be expected.

Board and Washing is given by the Master.

As the Assistants are to board with the Master they
must be single men who can produce good
characters.

For further particulars apply to Mr Hodgkinson Jun at
Leigh near Warrington, letters directed to him (post
paid) will be duly answered.

NB This will be advertised no more.

Advertisement for John Flavell's
school in the *Manchester Mercury*
on Tuesday 4 May 1784

The Flavel family tree and advertisement for a teacher

Index

Richard Hodgkinson was not always consistent in spelling names. In this index we have generally used the current forms.